Compaq Visual Fortran

Related Titles from Digital Press

Michael Etzel and Karen Dickinson, *Digital Visual Fortran Programmer's Guide*, ISBN 1-55558-218-4, 756pp

Tony Redmond, *Microsoft® Exchange Server for Windows® 2000: Planning, Design, and Implementation*, ISBN 1-55558-224-9, 1072pp

Matthew Cheek, Scott Fafrak, Steven Hancock, Martin Moore, and Gregory Yates, *Tru64™ UNIX System Administrator's Guide*, ISBN 1-55558-255-9, 488pp

Steven M. Hancock, *Tru64™ UNIX File System Administration Handbook*, ISBN 1-55558-227-3, 534pp

For more information or to order these and other Digital Press titles, please visit our website at www.bh.com/digitalpress!

At www.bh.com/digitalpress you can:

- Join the Digital Press Email Service and have news about our books delivered right to your desktop

- Read the latest news on titles

- Sample chapters on featured titles for free

- Question our expert authors and editors

- Download free software to accompany select texts

Compaq Visual Fortran

A Guide to Creating Windows® Applications

Norman Lawrence

Digital Press
An imprint of Butterworth-Heinemann

Boston • Oxford • Auckland • Johannesburg • Melbourne • New Delhi

Digital Press™ is an imprint of Elsevier.

 This book is printed on acid-free paper.

Library of Congress Cataloging-in-Publication Data

Lawrence, Norman, 1948-
   Compaq Visual Fortran: a guide to creating Windows applications/Norman
Lawrence
         p.   cm.
   Includes bibliographical references and index.
   ISBN 1-55558-249-4 (pbk.)
   1.   FORTRAN (Computer program language) I. Title.

   QA.76.73.F25 L375 2001
   005.13'3—dc21

                              2001052790

British Library Cataloguing-Publication Data

A catalogue record for this book is available from the British Library.

The publisher offers special discounts on bulk orders of this book.
For information, please contact:
Manager of Special Sales
Elsevier Science
200 Wheeler Road
Burlington, MA 01803
Tel: 781-313-4700
Fax: 781-313-4802

For information on all Butterworth-Heinemann publications available, contact
our World Wide Web homepage at http://www.bh.com

10 9 8 7 6 5 4 3 2
Printed in the United States of America.

To Albert, Lizzie, and Maria, and the memories of times filled with warm summer days and snow at Christmas.

Contents

          4.1   Resource Editor   55
          4.2   Using Resource Editor   55
          4.3   Using HTML files as Help files   64
          4.4   Using icons and bitmaps   66
          4.5   Adding version information   72
          4.6   Using callback routines   76
          4.7   What is next?   82

5   Graphics   83

          5.1   Coordinate systems   83
          5.2   Fill masks   99
          5.3   What is next?   105

6   Creating Win32 API Applications   107

          6.1   Win32 basics   107
          6.2   Getting started   108
          6.3   WinMain, the main entry point   112
          6.4   Working with menus   120
          6.5   Windows with style   135
          6.6   What is next?   139

7   Dialog Boxes and Controls   141

          7.1   Creating a modal dialog box   142
          7.2   Modeless dialog boxes   147
          7.3   Currency exchange example   149
          7.4   Common controls   156
          7.5   What is next?   167

8   Common Dialog Boxes   169

          8.1   Using common dialog boxes   169
          8.2   Opening and saving files   170
          8.3   Selecting colors   173
          8.4   Choosing fonts   176
          8.5   Page setup and printing   179
          8.6   Finding and replacing text   185
          8.7   What is next?   191

Preface

Welcome to *Compaq Visual Fortran, A Guide to Creating Windows® Applications*. My computing experiences originated during the early 1970s when, as an undergraduate engineering student, I was introduced to FORTRAN IV complete with the joys of card readers, syntax errors, and an express four to six hour response time between job submission and output. Soon afterward, I was attracted by the immediacy of BASIC, and that language served my computing needs until the late 1980s, when I was involved in some research in which the client wanted software to be written in Fortran for use on the client's mainframe. I then saw Fortran in a new light; the power of portability meant that I could develop a program on a PC and send it to others to compile on their workstation or mainframe. The reverse was also true; I could use on my PC a vast range of software that had been developed for mainframes during a 30-year period.

Around 1994, I started to use Microsoft Visual BASIC 3.0 to provide a Windows graphical user interface (GUI) for my DOS-based Fortran programs. It was a revolutionary way of developing graphical user interfaces. However, my graphics requirements stretched Visual BASIC to the limit, and I often used the Windows Application Programming Interface to get some extra features. With the switch to a 32-bit operating system signaled by Windows 95 and Windows NT 3.5, Microsoft introduced the Fortran PowerStation Version 4.0 compiler, in which one could compile DOS Consol Window Projects, QuickWin Projects, and Windows Projects where the Win32 APIs were called directly. This program and its successors, Digital Visual Fortran 5.0 and 6.0 and now Compaq Visual Fortran 6.6, endowed programmers with the capability to create full-fledged Windows applications using only Fortran. The mixed language capabilities also meant that code segments written in Fortran and C could be compiled and linked into one single executable program.

Until now, one major drawback was the absence of a Fortran-specific book with information on how to develop graphical user interfaces in Fortran. Fortran programmers either had to read books written in C to learn about the Windows API or else buy proprietary software that provided interfaces to the API as a set of subroutines that could be called from Fortran. This book is aimed at Compaq Visual Fortran (CVF) users who want to develop applications with Windows-style graphical user interfaces by using the Win32 API interface definitions supplied with Visual Fortran. It illustrates, through numerous ready-to-run examples, how to develop QuickWin programs, explore the possibilities offered by the Win32 API, and create professional quality graphics using OpenGL. When creating the examples in this book, I worked with the belief that "if it can be done in C, it can also be done in Visual Fortran."

This is not a book on Fortran programming, so you will need to be comfortable with programming in FORTRAN 77 or, preferably, Fortran 90/95. You should also have some familiarity with the online Programmer's Guide that comes with Visual Fortran. To gain maximum advantage from using this book, you will need access to a standard version of CVF 6.6. Because most of the examples were originally created in CVF 6.1, users of previous versions of CVF should be able to use the techniques outlined. However, be aware that differences exist in the interface definitions and the symbolic constants between the previous editions of Visual Fortran and CVF 6.6. For example, the symbolic constant NULL_POINT is used in some applications, but users of CVF 6.1 will have to provide their own equivalent to NULL_POINT. In some places where NULL is used, CVF 6.1 users may need to substitute %Val(0).

Writing this book required me to make judgments on both the content covered and the amount of detail to be included. I have heard from readers of other computing books that they do not like to have details of the Win32 API functions reproduced in the text of a book because they already have access to that information online in Visual Studio. Therefore, I have tried to reach a balance in the material provided in this book by providing step-by-step information at the introductory level to topics and, as the topics progress, to include only the more salient points. I am interested in getting feedback through the publishers as to what readers would like to see included in any subsequent edition.

The source code for all the programs in this book can be downloaded from the companion Web site—the URL, http://www.bh.com/companions/1555582494/, takes you directly to the downloadable material. You

can also access it by going to www.digitalpressbooks.com (or www.bh.com/
digitalpress). Find your way to *Compaq Visual Fortran* (by using the Search
feature, or going to the page on Software Development by using the naviga-
tion buttons in the lower right of the screen). Once you reach the full page
devoted to this book, click on the hot link "Provides downloadable supple-
mentary materials from author" in the box at the right edge of the screen to
go to the material.

Acknowledgments

On the shoulders of giants

Programming graphical user interfaces in any language can be very challenging, and my own understanding has been greatly enhanced over a number of years by various books, user groups, and individuals. In particular, I would like to acknowledge the following sources of information used during the creation of this book.

Appleman, D., 1996, *Visual BASIC, Programmer's Guide to the Win32 API*, Ziff-Davis Press.

Cluts, N., 1998, *Programming the Windows 95 User Interface*, Microsoft Press.

Etzel, M., and Dickinson, K., 1999, *Digital Visual Fortran Programmer's Guide*, Digital Press.

Jerke, N., and Brierly, E., 1996, *Visual BASIC 4 API How-To, the Definitive Guide to Using the Win32 API with Visual BASIC 4*, Waite Group Press.

Neider, J., Davis, T., and Woo, M., 1993, *OpenGl Programming Guide, The Official Guide to Learning OpenGL, Release 1*, Addison-Wesley.

Petzold, C., 1998, *Programming Windows* (5th ed.), Microsoft Press.

Simon, R., 1997, *Windows NT, Win32 API Superbible*, Waite Group Press.

Wright, R., and Sweet, M., 1996, *OpenGL Superbible, The Complete Guide to OpenGL Programming for Windows NT and Windows 95*, Waite Group Press.

I want to acknowledge Leo Treggiari, who showed me how to do C style pointers in Fortran; Steve Lionel, who convinced Digital Press that there was a need for this book and showed me how to use the OpenGL auxiliary library with Fortran Windows Application Projects; John Ready, who introduced me to OpenGL Utility Toolkit (GLUT) and showed me how to tessellate polygons; Bill Conrad, who gave me advice on QuickWin Projects; Guus Nijhuis, who showed me how to use text and mouse selection in OpenGL; Jakub Zlamal, who showed me how to work with toolbars; Adam Kris, who showed me how to put bitmaps and icons in buttons; and Bill Buchholz, who helped me figure out how to save and print OpenGL screens.

Information in this book relating to Win32 API and OpenGL functions is based on the information contained in the Platform SDK online documentation as provided by Microsoft with Visual Studio 6.0.

Information relating to the creation of Help files is based on the online Help documentation for the Win32 Help Compiler Workshop as provided by Microsoft with Visual Studio 6.0.

My thanks

I thank Digital Press and Compaq Computer Corporation for their many contributions to the creation of this book. In particular, I thank Compaq for supplying various beta versions, and Christian Staudinger for providing a release version of Visual Fortran 6.6.

Reviewing draft manuscripts of a book is a big task, and I would like to thank the CVF team for the thoroughness of their comments on all the draft chapters and especially Bill Conrad, Leo Treggiari, Lorri Menard, John Ready, and Steve Lionel. Thanks to Bill Buchholz, John Termine, Jean Vezina, Matt Allen, Ozgur Deli, and Tim Hatamian for their various comments on the draft manuscript.

My thanks to Pam Chester for providing me with the opportunity to write this book and for all her positive and encouraging comments during the entire period of writing it, even when progress was way behind my overly optimistic schedule.

My deepest thanks to Mike Etzel, a very special person, for his incredible help, wisdom, and support during the entire period of writing this book.

I would like to thank my wife Cathy for her unfailing support during both the writing of this book and our 26 years of married life together. A very special thanks to my children, Colin, Chris, and Maree, who patiently watched Dad's show and tell sessions for every program and then would ask simple questions like, "What happens if?" Their lateral thinking and bug-discovering skills are incredible. A big thanks to my brother Al and sister Susan for always being around whenever I needed them.

Getting Started

1.1 A look at Developer Studio

Compaq Visual Fortran (Visual Fortran) uses the same development environment as Microsoft Visual C++. This development environment is shown in Figure 1.1, and it is known as the Microsoft Developer Studio. In Figure 1.1, the left pane has tabs to select a FileView, a ResourceView, and a ClassView. The FileView shows each project and the project files associated with the Workspace. The ResourceView appears if the Workspace uses Resources such as dialogs and icons. The ClassView appears only if Visual C++ is installed. ClassView is not used by Visual Fortran.

The FileView pane shown in Figure 1.1 contains the files associated with the Workspace for the project Plots. The Source Files folder indicates that there are six files in this project workspace: Callbacks.f90, Globals.f90, Main.f90, Menu.f90, Plot.f90, and Resource.rc. The Resource Files folder contains one bitmap and three icons, while the External Dependencies folder lists the files global.mod and resource.fd. Double-click on any of the file icons in the FileView pane to open that file with the Developer Studio text editor in the right-hand pane.

In the right-hand pane of Figure 1.1, the file Main.f90 has been opened in the default text editor. This editor uses green to identify comments in the code, blue for Fortran standard code, and black for other text. There are actually 12 different "colorable items" (including comments and Fortran keywords), and the default color of each item can be changed in Developer Studio by using the Tools menu, selecting the Options menu item, and then choosing the tab labeled Format (Tools -> Options -> Format).

The bottom of Figure 1.1 shows the output pane, which shows text displayed from building the project. Currently it is displaying information about compiler and link errors. The output pane has multiple tabs. The

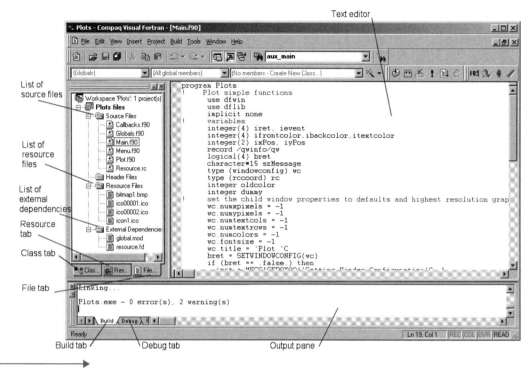

Figure 1.1   *Developer Studio window.*

output pane Build tab is selected after you open a Workspace and compile one or more project files or build the project.

Windows in the Visual Development Studio can be set to have either docking or floating properties. Docking windows do not have a title bar, and they are docked (attached) along an edge of the visual development environment window. Floating windows have a title bar and can be moved by dragging the title bar. By holding down the Ctrl key and pressing the Tab key, you can cycle through each floating window in turn. The docking or floating properties of a window are set by selecting Options from the Tools menu. Click the Workspace tab in the docking view list and click the check box for each window to be displayed with a docking view (see Figure 1.2). Unchecked boxes indicate floating windows.

1.2   Visual Fortran project types

Projects are contained in a workspace and consist of the source files required for an application, along with the specifications for building the project. A project type must be chosen every time you create a new project. The

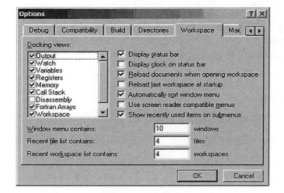

Figure 1.2
Setting the docking properties for windows in the Developer Studio.

project type determines some of the options that Developer Studio will set by default for the project and what needs to be generated. It determines, for instance, the options that the compiler uses to compile the source files, the static libraries that the linker uses to build the project, the default locations for output files, and defined constants.

The following seven project types are available with Visual Fortran:

- *Fortran Console Applications*—These are single-window applications without graphics (character-cell applications), used for a traditional Fortran program. Standard Fortran I/O statements are used to write to the window.

- *Fortran Standard Graphics Applications*—Standard Graphics Applications have a single maximized window covering the entire screen. Standard Graphic Applications do not have programmable menus, but they can use QuickWin graphic routines to draw to the window. Standard Fortran I/O statements are used to write to the window.

- *Fortran QuickWin Applications*—QuickWin Applications can have a range of graphics capabilities and receive user input through menu selections, dialog boxes, and mouse button actions. QuickWin Applications can have multiple windows. Standard Fortran I/O statements are used to write to the window.

- *Fortran Windows Applications*—These are single- or multiple-window projects with a full graphical interface, which can include menus, dialog boxes, and graphical routines and can use any of the available Win32 API routines. In Fortran Windows Applications, the programmer directly calls any Win32 routines that are required. Win32 routines are used to write to the window.

- *Fortran COM Server*—Uses the component object model (COM) to implement a COM server. COM supports client/server interaction between a user of an object, the client, and the server. Clients may be written in Visual Fortran using the Fortran Module Wizard or in other languages, such as Visual C++ and Visual BASIC.

- *Fortran Static Library*—These are library routines that encapsulate some specific functionality. They are linked into .exe files.

- *Fortran Dynamic-Link Library*—These are library routines that encapsulate some specific functionality. They are linked into .DLL files and are used by an .exe file during execution.

1.3   Developing graphical user interfaces

The focus of this book is on using Visual Fortran Version 6.6 to create Fortran applications that have a Windows-based graphical user interface (GUI). The traditional character-cell console applications, including those written in Fortran, are procedural in nature. That is, execution begins with the first line of executable code and then sequentially follows a defined pathway through the application, calling functions and subroutines as required until it reaches the end of the program. Windows-based GUI programs are event-driven in nature. The order in which the code executes depends on which events have been chosen. An event occurs every time the user makes a selection from a range of choices. It could be to open or close a file, to enter data, or to copy the contents of the screen to the clipboard.

GUI applications should always present the user with a valid set of options, respond according to the selections made by the user, and ensure that the user has responded correctly to any input information that the program requested. This may mean that some options are disabled, or it may entail checking that a text box has valid input before proceeding with the next operation.

1.3.1   Graphical user interface etiquette

It is reasonable to assume that most, if not all, of the people who use your applications will have previously used Windows-based applications such as word processors and spreadsheets. This being the case, your application users will have certain expectations of your GUI because applications in the Windows environment share a common "feel" in their user interfaces. Referring to Figure 1.3, users will expect File and Help to be the first and

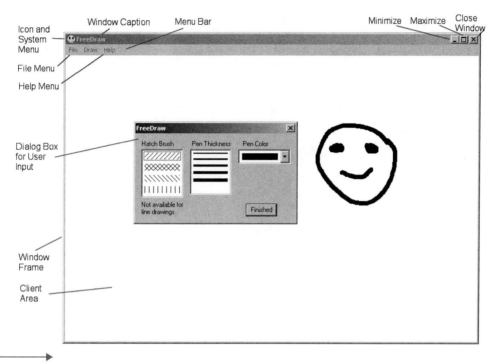

Figure 1.3   *Typical Windows graphical interface.*

last items, respectively, across the menu bar. The last item in the File menu should be Exit. Normally, the main window should not have controls such as radio buttons, edit boxes, and slider bars. In most cases, such controls should be reserved for dialog boxes. The user will often expect certain key combinations to do certain things—for example, Ctrl+X to cut selected text or objects, Ctrl+C to copy selected text or objects, and Ctrl+V to insert text or objects at the caret position.

Windows applications should be able to provide information whenever the user has performed an incorrect action or when a system resource is not available, such as no disk in the floppy drive. Error checking should always be included in any programming code. It is good programming practice to check the return value of every function called to determine the success of the action requested and for the program to take the appropriate action.

Note: In the interest of holding the reader's attention by keeping the example code as short and simple as possible, the examples contained in this book do not model this principle.

1.4   Do I need to know C?

Understanding C is not a prerequisite for creating Fortran programs with graphical interfaces. However, some knowledge of C can be useful when you wish to exploit more advanced features of the Windows operating system. Also, when you do not know how to program a particular Win32 feature, you can look up code examples given in C and determine the methodology; then it is usually a reasonably simple process to write your own Fortran code. If you are not familiar with C, it may be helpful for you to think of C as a type of pseudo-code that can be translated into Fortran. Appendix A provides an overview of C for Fortran programmers.

1.5   Additional resources

Visual Fortran comes complete with a very comprehensive set of sample programs, which illustrate a range of ideas for developing applications using QuickWin, Win32, OpenGL, dynamic-link libraries, and many other possibilities. It is a good idea to work through the sample code, compiling it and thereby seeing the wide range of programming possibilities that exist with CVF. Look through the program code and try to spot useful techniques that you can incorporate into your own code.

This book on creating Windows interfaces is not a substitute for the official documentation of the Windows API. The Windows API information is available as part of the online help documentation that comes with the Visual Fortran CD-ROM, as shown in Figure 1.4. The online documentation may seem a little daunting at first, but it is well worth investing time in learning how to navigate around the information. It contains a lot of guidance not only about programming in Fortran but also about programming in the Windows environment.

Select Online Documentation from the Visual Fortran menu group. Referring to Figure 1.4, click the Contents tab and open the book entitled Compaq Visual Fortran 6.6, to reveal four books: *Visual Fortran, Developer Studio, Platform SDK,* and *SDK Documentation*. The *Platform SDK* book covers just about every possible topic for programming Win32 applications. In particular, the reference section lists alphabetically all the Win32 API routines. The chapter on Graphics and Multimedia Services contains some great information under the headings GDI (Graphical Device Interface) and OpenGL. When using Developer Studio, it is useful to have the online documentation opened at the index section to aid in confirming the

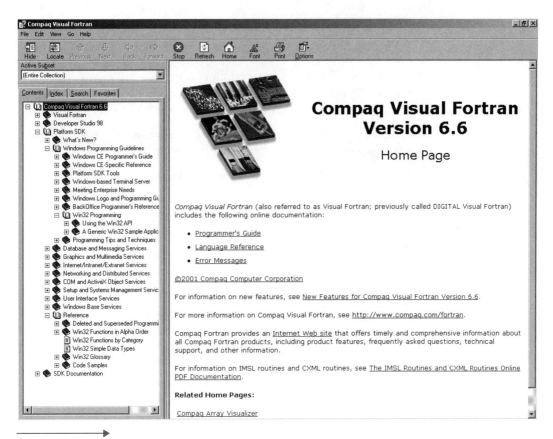

Figure 1.4   *Online Help documentation.*

syntax of any of the Win32 APIs or their associated data structures that are
being used.

The books listed below are those I have personally found to be very use-
ful. This is not an exhaustive list, merely a reflection of my own book collection. Indeed, some of the books are available in more recent editions.
Note that with the obvious exception of the first two books and the *DVF
Programmers Guide*, all the other books are aimed at C programmers. The
OpenGL Programming Guide, often referred to as the "red book," and the
OpenGL Reference Manual, usually referred to as the "blue book," are the
official publications of the OpenGL Architecture Review Board. If you can
afford only one OpenGL book, I would suggest that you get the *OpenGL
Superbible*. The red and blue books are not aimed at any specific hardware
platform, whereas the *OpenGL Superbible* is specifically aimed for Windows-based applications on PC platforms.

Programming Windows by Petzold is regarded as a classic for anyone wanting to write Windows applications. *Programming the Windows 95 User Interface* by Nancy Cluts is a great companion to Petzold's book because it covers the use of most of the common controls—ListViews, TreeViews, Toolbars, and many more. It can also be perused on the Internet in the book section of the MSDN library. The complete list of titles follows.

- Chapman, S., 1998, *Fortran 90/95 for Scientists and Engineers,* WCB/McGraw-Hill.

- Cluts, N. W., 1998, *Programming the Windows 95 User Interface,* Microsoft Press.

- Ellis, T. M. R., Philips, I. R., and Lahey, T. M., 1995, *Fortran 90 Programming,* Addison-Wesley.

- Etzel, M., and Dickinson, K., 1999, *Digital Visual Fortran Programmer's Guide,* Digital Press.

- Neider, J., Davis, T., and Woo, M., 1993, *Open GL Programming Guide, The Official Guide to Learning OpenGL, release 1,* Addison-Wesley.

- Petzold, C., 1998, *Programming Windows* (5th ed.), Microsoft Press.

- Shreiner, D., 1999, *OpenGL Reference Manual: The Official Reference Document to OpenGL, Version 1.1,* Addison-Wesley.

- Simon, J. R., 1997, *Windows NT Win32 API Superbible,* Waite Group Press.

- Wright, R. S., Jr., and Sweet, M., 1996, *OpenGL Superbible, The Complete Guide to OpenGL Programming for Windows NT and Windows 95,* Waite Group Press.

1.6   Useful Web sites

If you have access to the Internet, another good source of information is the Microsoft Developer Network (MSDN) library. There are a number of interesting items that can be searched in the book and partial book sections. A very large selection of code examples can also be browsed in the MSDN library. The Web addresses are as follows:

- http://www.compaq.com/fortran
- http://www.compaq.com/math
- http://microsoft.com

- http://msdn.microsoft.com

- http://www.opengl.org

- http://developer.intel.com

1.7   User groups

User groups are among the greatest resources that a software developer can access. They are peopled by unpaid, unsung heroes, who have "been there, done that," and are happy to pass along the benefits of their experience. The Compaq Fortran users group is an obvious choice because you are in contact with an audience using the same product. However, some questions are often better addressed to other user groups. When asking for help about Fortran-related matters, it is important to be specific about the problem and to state the platform and compiler version that you are using. Often it is a good idea to include a small representative code fragment. Questions relating to Windows and OpenGL should state that you are using Compaq Visual Fortran and want to do "___," and can anyone provide you with an example in C to do "___"? Sometimes you can be very lucky, and a CVF programmer will post Fortran code for you, but most times you will have to do your own translation from C to Fortran. Some of the user groups that I have found helpful include:

- comp.graphics.algorithms

- comp.graphics.api.opengl

- comp.lang.fortran

- comp.os.ms-windows.programmer.win32

- http://www.Compaq.com/fortran—select user message board

1.8   Layout of this book

This book is divided into three parts: QuickWin Applications, Win32 API Applications, and OpenGL Graphics. Each of these three parts is arranged to progress the reader from beginner-level topics to advanced-level techniques in multiple chapters. Where appropriate, the QuickWin part also shows some Win32 API tricks. Experienced programmers may wish to skip the introductory chapter in each of these three parts and move directly into the subsequent chapters.

2

QuickWin Basics

2.1 Before we start

In the next four chapters, we will be looking at how to create graphical user interfaces (GUIs) for Fortran programs using QuickWin. In subsequent chapters, we will learn how to develop GUIs using the Win32 application programming interface (API). QuickWin is essentially a wrapper around a subset of the Win32 API commands to conveniently insulate Fortran programmers from having to develop software in a Win32 environment. Therefore, many of the Win32 API functions described in later chapters can also be used for QuickWin applications. However, some caution must be exercised, because Win32 functions from the graphical device interface (GDI) library cannot be used to draw on a QuickWin window. (QuickWin keeps a window buffer, and the altered window would be destroyed on redraw.)

Most QuickWin programs will need to access functions contained in the DFWIN and DFLIB modules; this is achieved by including USE DFWIN and USE DFLIB statements in your programs. If your application uses dialog boxes and their associated controls, you must also include a USE DFLOGM statement in the application. If you are in doubt about which USE statements to include in your program for a particular function, look up the function name in the online help documentation, and it will give you information about which module is required.

2.1.1 "Hello World!" example

Now it is time to start doing some programming. It is a tradition among programmers that the first program to be written should be an example of writing "Hello World!" to an output device such as the computer screen. Since this is our first program, each of the steps required to build and compile a QuickWin program will be described. Reference should also be made to Figure 2.1.

- Click on File from the Visual Studio menu and select New from the options.

- In the New dialog box, pick Projects tab.

- In the Project name field, type the name of the project as *HelloQW.*

- In the Location field, enter the working directory of your choice.

- Select Fortran Standard Graphics or QuickWin Application from the listed project types.

- The Create new workspace button should be checked, and the platform section should indicate Win32.

- Click on the OK button.

A new dialog box offering a choice between QuickWin and Standard Graphics will appear. Check the option labeled QuickWin (multiple windows) and press the Finish button. A dialog box headed New Project Information will appear to provide you with information about the type of application to be created and the project directory that it will be created in. Click OK to complete the process.

Select New from the File menu again. In the dialog box, pick the Files tab. Select Fortran Free Format Source File. The *Add to project* box should be checked and the *HelloQW* name should be displayed. Type *main* in the file name field and click OK.

Figure 2.1
Creating a new QuickWin project.

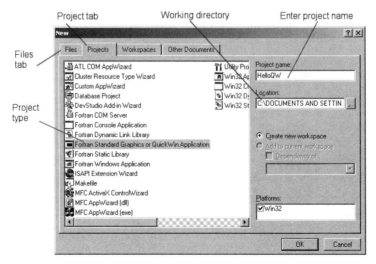

With QuickWin you can write to the screen using Fortran statements just as though you were writing to a file, so the minimum code that needs to be used for writing "Hello World!" to the screen would look something like this:

```
! minimum_hello
    write(*,*) 'Hello World!'
end
```

For our purposes, we will exercise a little more control over the output. The screen can be given a unit number just like other output devices by using the *file* = 'USER' option. The unit is a child window with a scrollable text window having a default of 30 rows by 80 columns. A title can be assigned to each child window using *title* = 'mytitle'. Up to 40 child windows can be opened under QuickWin. The usage is illustrated in the source code Main.f90 below. Enter the following in your main.f90 file:

```
! Listing for Main.f90
program hello
! A hello program using quickwin
    implicit none
    character(15)  string_out
    character(40) string_title
    string_out = 'Hello World!'
    string_title =  'Simple Hello World Using QuickWin'
    open(unit = 4, file = 'user', title = string_title)
    write(4,'(10x,A15)') string_out
end
```

In the Build menu, click the option Execute HelloQW.exe. A warning message is displayed stating that the file does not exist and asks if you want to build it. Select Yes and, after successfully compiling and linking, the HelloQW application is displayed, as shown in Figure 2.2. The QuickWin main window comes with a title bar; minimize, maximize, and close buttons; and six menu items, File, Edit, View, State, Window, and Help. The message "Hello World!" is displayed in a child window.

The message box displays the information that the exit code is 0, which indicates that the program has successfully completed its task. Choose the No option in the message box, so that you can explore the features provided by QuickWin.

- File menu with options to Print or Save the screen (as a bitmap) or to Exit the program.

- Edit menu with options to Select, Copy, and Paste screen items.

- View menu with options for Full Screen or Size to Fit.

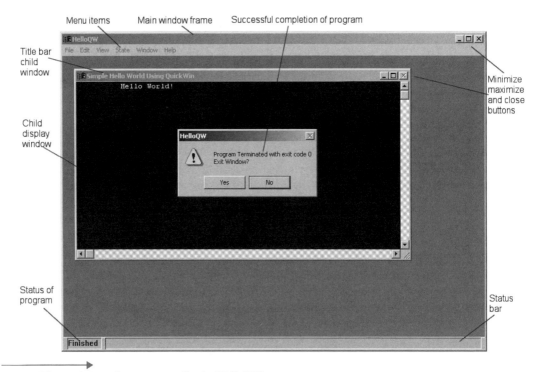

Figure 2.2   *Output screen for the HelloQW program.*

- State menu to permit a Pause in program operation.

- Windows menu with options for arranging and selecting child windows. The status bar may be removed or displayed.

- Help menu with options for displaying the contents of a QuickWin help file for the program, help on using Help, and an About box for the program.

Select Exit from the File menu when you have finished viewing the QuickWin menu.

2.2   Text windows and fonts

The "Hello World!" program illustrates how easy it can be to use existing Fortran programs within a QuickWin graphical environment. However, most programmers want to develop software that goes beyond the bare-bones output afforded by the Fortran WRITE statement. QuickWin provides Fortran programmers with a rich set of possibilities for controlling the font type, size, position, and color of screen text. Two types of display windows are provided by QuickWin for outputting text:

- Text window—Text is positioned using rows and columns
- Graphical window—Text and lines are placed using x and y coordinates

Essentially, these display windows are clipping regions that initially completely overlap. A clipping region is an area on the screen that can be written to or drawn on, but anything outside of the clip area will not be drawn. These two regions, or windows, are both initially the same size as the display screen, but, as will be described later, their size can be redefined using the SETTEXTWINDOW and SETVIEWPORT functions.

The graphical window provides much greater flexibility for text output, because the coordinate system can be made to represent anything from screen pixels to a user-defined Cartesian coordinate system. The two types of windows will be discussed in this chapter from the point of view of placing text at a desired location on the screen. The use of graphical windows is examined more fully in Chapter 4.

2.2.1   Changing display properties with SETWINDOWCONFIG

The QuickWin function SETWINDOWCONFIG is used as follows to alter the display properties of child windows:

```
bret = SETWINDOWCONFIG (wc)
```

where *bret* is a logical variable that is set to .true. if the function has been successful, and .false. if it is unsuccessful. If the return value of *bret* is .false., you should repeat the call to this function so that it can set the best available defaults. The variable *wc* is a derived type with a windowconfig structure, and it is used to set the display properties. The online documentation states that the windowconfig type has the following parameters:

```
TYPE windowconfig
   INTEGER(2) numxpixels
   INTEGER(2) numypixels
   INTEGER(2) numtextcols
   INTEGER(2) numtextrows
   INTEGER(2) numcolors
   INTEGER(4) fontsize
   CHARACTER(80) title
   CHARACTER(32) extendfontname
```

```
    INTEGER(4) extendfontsize
    INTEGER(4) extendfontattributes
END TYPE windowconfig
```

A value of −1 for each of the members of the windowconfig type will result in the highest possible pixel resolution available from the graphics driver, a scrollable text window of 30 lines by 80 columns, and a font size of 8 × 16 (8 pixels wide by 16 pixels high). The number of colors depends on the video driver used. Setting the values for parameters in the windowconfig type is straightforward with the exception of setting a font. Details of the variables to be used for setting the font, style, and pitch are included with the online information for SETWINDOWCONFIG. We will now examine the process of setting a font in more detail.

Once a variable *wc* based on the windowconfig derived type has been declared, the default font size may be set to a width of 12 pixels and a height of 16 pixels using:

```
wc%fontsize = #000C0010
```

The # sign in front of the value given for *wc%fontsize* indicates that the value is a hexadecimal number. The variable *wc%fontsize* is interpreted in two 16-bit parts. The hexadecimal number 000C represents the number 12, and hexadecimal number 0010 is the number 16. Hexadecimal numbers are often used to represent binary numbers, because they represent a compact way of expressing large binary numbers in 4-bit groups. Table 2.1 shows the correspondence between binary, hexadecimal, and integer numbers for a 4-bit group. Any 4-bit group can be represented in hexadecimal notation by a minimum value of 0 and a maximum value of F. If a 16-bit binary number is divided into four 4-bit groups, then each binary group can be represented in hexadecimal notation by a minimum value of 0 and a maximum value of F leading to a minimum hexadecimal value of 0000 and a maximum hexadecimal value of FFFF. A 32-bit number would be composed of eight 4-bit groups ranging from hexadecimal 00000000 to FFFFFFFF.

If you are like me and would prefer not to have to use hexadecimal notation, an easier method is to define the height and width as 16-bit integers and use the Win32 function MakeLong to create a single 32-bit integer. For example:

```
iWidthFont = 12
iHeightFont = 16
wc%fontsize = MakeLong (iHeightFont,iWidthFont)
```

Table 2.1 *Hexadecimal Notations*

Binary Value	Hexadecimal Value	Integer Value
0000	0	0
0001	1	1
0010	2	2
0011	3	3
0100	4	4
0101	5	5
0110	6	6
0111	7	7
1000	8	8
1001	9	9
1010	A	10
1011	B	11
1100	C	12
1101	D	13
1110	E	14
1111	F	15

Note that the low-order 16-bit integer comes first with the MakeLong function.

Additional font features such as changing to bold or italic or using a different font type are set using the *extendfont* fields. These parameters remain unused until the *fontsize* parameter is set equal to QWIN$EXTEND-FONT. When *fontsize* has been set equal to QWIN$EXTENDFONT, then *extendfontsize* is used to set *fontsize*. Font styles, families, and pitch are set using *extendfontattributes*. Multiple attributes can be included using the OR function or the inclusive OR function (IOR). The *extendfontname* should be a name of a font in the font family specified under *extendfontattributes*.

The following code fragment illustrates how to set values in the fields of a windowconfig structure to specify font height, width, style, and family.

The online documentation for SETWINDOWCONFIG provides a table of the symbolic constants that are available for use to set font style, pitch, family, and character sets.

```
!  set font height and size
   iHeightFont = 66
   iWidthFont = 30
   wc%fontsize = QWIN$EXTENDFONT
   wc%extendfontname = 'Algerian'C
   wc%extendfontsize = makelong(iHeightFont, iWidthFont)
   wc%extendfontattributes = ior(QWIN$EXTENDFONT_ITALIC, &
                 ior(QWIN$EXTENDFONT_FF_DECORATIVE, &
                 ior(QWIN$EXTENDFONT_VARIABLE_PITCH, &
                 QWIN$EXTENDFONT_BOLD)))
```

2.2.2 Specifying the text window with SETTEXTWINDOW

Normally the text window and the graphics window occupy all of the child window, and you can write text to either as desired using OUTTEXT, WRITE, or PRINT for the text window, and OUTGTEXT for the graphics window. Sometimes it is convenient for the text window to occupy a specific part of the screen. This is easily done using the SETTEXTWINDOW function, which specifies a window in row and column coordinates, relative to the default graphic window, where text output to the screen using OUTTEXT, WRITE, or PRINT will be displayed. Text is output from the top of the window down. The syntax is:

```
Integer(2) irowtop, icolleft
Integer(2) irowbottom, icolright
CALL SETTEXTWINDOW (irowtop, icolleft, irowbottom, &
                icolright)
```

Text location may be set to a specified position relative to the current text window using the routine SETTEXTPOSITION and then written to the screen using the routine OUTTEXT. An example of usage is as follows:

```
type (rccoord) rc
call SETTEXTPOSITION (irowPos, icolPos, rc)
call OUTTEXT (szMessage)
```

Subsequent text output with the OUTTEXT function (as well as standard console I/O statements, such as PRINT and WRITE) begins at the point (*irowPos, icolPos*).

The derived type rccord contains two fields, *row* and *col*, and after the call to OUTTEXT in the preceding example, the variable *rc* will contain the row and column position of text previously displayed.

2.2.3   Specifying the window size with SETWSIZEQQ

All QuickWin applications call an INITIALSETTINGS function before the creation of a QuickWin window. When an application does not provide a user-defined INITIALSETTINGS function, QuickWin will call a pre-defined INITIALSETTINGS function and use default values to define the window frame and menu. In Chapter 3, we will learn how to write our own user-defined INITIALSETTINGS function so that we can define menus and set the size of a window. However, for the moment we will set the size of a visible window using the QuickWin function SETWSIZEQQ, which has the following syntax:

```
iret = SETWSIZEQQ(unit,winfo)
```

The return value *iret* is an integer(4), and *unit* is an integer(4) specifying a window unit number. The symbolic constant QWIN$FRAMEWIN-DOW can be used as the unit value when setting the size of the main window. The variable *winfo* is a derived type named QWINFO, which has the following structure:

- TYPE: Set size of window using one of the following predefined symbolic constants:

  - QWIN$MIN—Minimizes the window.
  - QWIN$MAX—Maximizes the window.
  - QWIN$RESTORE—Restores the minimized window to its previous size.
  - QWIN$SET—Sets the window's position and size according to the other values in QWINFO.

- X: Window upper left *x* coordinate. Units of pixels when the window is the main window and columns when it is a child window.

- Y: Window upper left *y* coordinate. Units of pixels when the window is the main window and rows when it is a child window.

- H: Window height in pixels or rows.

- W: Window width in pixels or columns.

The height and width specified for a frame window reflect the actual size in pixels of the frame window including any borders, menus, and status bar at the bottom.

When SETWSIZEQQ is called from INITIALSETTINGS, only QWIN$SET will work and the return integer(4) value is –1. When called from somewhere other than INITIALSETTINGS, the return value will be zero if successful and nonzero if unsuccessful. An example of usage in which *qw* is a type QWINFO structure is as follows:

```
qw%type =QWIN$MAX
iret = SETWSIZEQQ(QWIN$FRAMEWINDOW,qw)
```

2.2.4   Simulating menu selection with CLICKMENUQQ

A very useful feature in QuickWin applications is the command CLICK-MENUQQ, which can be used to simulate the effect of clicking or selecting a menu command. The QuickWin application will respond as though the user had selected a menu item. The CLICKMENUQQ function can be used with the following four submenu commands:

- Status (QWIN$STATUS)

- Tile (QWIN$TILE)

- Cascade (QWIN$CASCADE)

- Arrange Icons (QWIN$ARRANGE)

The return value is an integer(4), which is zero if successful; otherwise, it is nonzero. The symbolic constants to be used with CLICKMENUQQ are contained inside the brackets. This command provides a convenient way to maximize a child window within a program by simulating a click on the Tile option in the Window menu as follows:

```
iret = CLICKMENUQQ(QWIN$TILE)
```

In addition to using the four symbolic constants directly, all the predefined menu routines such as WINTILE, WINSTATUS, and so on can be used if you specify them by address using the Fortran loc function. An alternative way of writing the previous line of code is:

```
iret = CLICKMENUQQ(loc(WINTILE))
```

A full list of the predefined menu routines is contained in the online documentation for APPENDMENUQQ.

Note: Although the function CLICKMENUQQ can be used to call the predefined routines during the operation of a program, often it may be more meaningful to use them within the context of a menu item (e.g., WINABOUT and WINHELP).

2.2.5   Specifying text color in QuickWin

Colors can be specified either as an explicit combination of red, green, and blue values, or as an index into a color "palette." Until quite recently, the video display capacity of most computers was limited to the use of a color palette that displayed a maximum of 256 colors at a time. The colors used in a palette may be selected into the palette from a range of colors considerably greater than 256, but the user is restricted to 256 colors in a palette at any one time. With a palette-based color system, the colors in a palette are referred to using an index between 0 and 255. In QuickWin, the functions SETCOLOR, SETBKCOLOR, and SETTEXTCOLOR set the current color, background, and text color to a palette index. The colors in the palette can be changed using the function REMAPPALETTERGB to set a given index value to a new RGB color. The online documentation contains examples of the use of these functions. Currently, all entry-level desktop computers and most laptops can support true color video display in which any color is defined as a combination of shades of red, green, and blue. Each of the colors, red, green, and blue, can be defined as a shade using a number between 0 and 255. This gives a possible 16.7 million colors (256 * 256 * 256) that can be displayed.

The display screen foreground, background, and text colors are set to RGB values using the QuickWin functions SETCOLORRGB, SETBKCOLORRGB, and SETTEXTCOLORRGB. Each of these three functions can have either an integer or a hexadecimal value as an argument. It is often much easier to obtain the red, green, blue (RGB) color integer value using the Win32 macro RGB, as follows:

```
ibackcolor = rgb(255,255,255)        ! white
iret = SETBKCOLORRGB(ibackcolor)
! or it can be used directly as the arguement
iret = SETTEXTCOLORRGB(rgb(0,0,255)) !  blue
```

One point to note when using hexadecimal values to set the color is that of the two bytes defining the color, the most significant byte represents blue. Thus, the following line sets the RGB color as blue:

```
iret = SETTEXTCOLORRGB(#FF0000) !  blue
```

The following line sets green:

```
iret = SETTEXTCOLORRGB(#FF00) !  green
```

2.2.6 Using units and handles

Many Win32 API functions can be used directly in QuickWin applications. A simple example is the Win32 API function SetWindowText, which we will use in the Fonts1 example to set the title at the top of a window. In QuickWin, logical devices such as the console window or input files are identified as Fortran unit numbers. In the Win32 API, logical devices such as windows and controls are specified as "handles." Unit numbers of Quick-Win windows can be converted to Win32 handles with the GETH-WNDQQ QuickWin function:

```
hWnd = GETHWNDQQ (unit)
```

where hWnd is an integer(4) handle to the logical unit, and unit is an integer(4) value. If unit is set to QWIN$FRAMEWINDOW, the handle of the frame window is returned. A value of −1 for hWnd indicates an unsuccessful attempt to get a handle.

2.3   Fonts1 example

The following program, Fonts1, illustrates how to use the SETWINDOW-CONFIG function to set the title and font attributes of a child window. Also included are techniques for controlling the color and position of text within a text window. The Win32 API function SetWindowText is used to change the text in the title bar of the main and child windows. This is how the title at the head of the frame window is changed:

```
szString = "Fonts1 - large fonts and colorful text"C
bret = SetWindowText(hWnd, szString)
```

In this example, hWnd is a handle to the window in which the title `"Fonts1 - large fonts and colorful text"C` is to be placed. Note that *szString* is a null-terminated string (often called a "C string") that contains the text for the new title. The code listing follows; its output is shown in Figure 2.3.

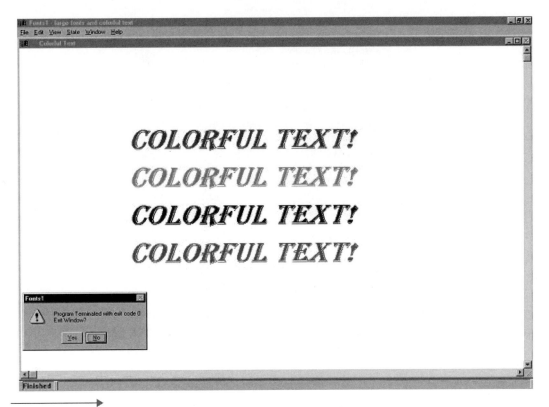

Figure 2.3   *Output screen for Fonts1 program.*

```
! Listing for main.f90
program Fonts1
! using fonts in quickwin Textwindows
      use dfwin
      use dflib
      implicit none
!     variables
      integer(4) iret,ideg,icount
      integer(4) ibackcolor
      integer(4) itextcolor,iTextLength
      integer(2) iHeightFont, iWidthFont
      integer(2) irowPos, icolPos
      record /qwinfo/qw
      logical(4) bret
      character(15) szMessage
      type (windowconfig) wc
      type (rccoord) rc
!     set the child window properties to defaults and
!     highest resolution graphics mode.
      wc%numxpixels = -1
```

```fortran
        wc%numypixels = -1
        wc%numtextcols = -1
        wc%numtextrows = -1
        wc%numcolors = -1
        wc%fontsize = QWIN$EXTENDFONT
        wc%title = '       Colorful Text'C
        wc%extendfontname = 'Algerian'C
!       set font height and size
        iHeightFont = 66
        iWidthFont = 30
        wc%extendfontsize = makelong(iHeightFont,iWidthFont)
!       set font attributes to bold, italic, and decorative
!       font
        wc%extendfontattributes = ior(QWIN$EXTENDFONT_ITALIC,&
                      ior(QWIN$EXTENDFONT_FF_DECORATIVE,&
                      ior(QWIN$EXTENDFONT_VARIABLE_PITCH,&
                         QWIN$EXTENDFONT_BOLD )))
        bret = SETWINDOWCONFIG(wc)
        if (bret == .false.) then
           iret = MESSAGEBOXQQ('Setting QW font using best &
           default'C, 'Error'C,MB$ICONEXCLAMATION .OR.MB$OK)
           bret = SETWINDOWCONFIG(wc) ! reset with best default
        end if
!       enter a new title for the main window
        iret = SetWindowText(GetHwndQQ(QWIN$FRAMEWINDOW)," &
                 Fonts1 - large fonts and colorful text "C)
!       maximize the size of the main window
        qw%type =QWIN$MAX
        iret = SETWSIZEQQ(QWIN$FRAMEWINDOW,qw)
!       maximize child window by simulating a click on the
!       Tile option in Windows menu
        iret = CLICKMENUQQ(QWIN$TILE)
!       set colors for screen
        ibackcolor = rgb(255,255,255)  ! white
        iret = SETBKCOLORRGB(ibackcolor)
!       enter the text message
        szMessage = 'Colorful Text!'C
        iTextLength = len_trim (szMessage )
!       get number of text columns and half to centre the text
        bret = GETWINDOWCONFIG(wc)
        icolPos  = (wc%numtextcols-iTextLength)/2
        irowPos =  (wc%numtextrows/2)-2
!       clear screen and set the text position using
!       rows and columns
        call CLEARSCREEN($GCLEARSCREEN)
        call SETTEXTPOSITION (irowPos, icolPos, rc)
!       write text to screen.
        do icount = 1, 4
           select case (icount)
```

```
            case(1)
                    itextcolor = rgb(255,0,0)        !red
            case(2)
                    itextcolor = rgb(0,255,0)        !green
            case(3)
                    itextcolor = rgb(0,0,255)        !blue
            case(4)
                    itextcolor = rgb(255,0,255)      !magenta
        end select
        iret = SETTEXTCOLORRGB(itextcolor)
        call SETTEXTPOSITION (irowPos+icount, icolPos, rc)
        call OUTTEXT (szMessage)
    end do
end
```

2.4   Graphics windows and fonts

The default graphics window is a single viewport that initially occupies all of the child window. It is possible to redefine the size and number of viewports that are available within the confines of a child window. This will be discussed in Chapter 4 in connection with drawing graphical objects. Our present purpose is to show the capability of the QuickWin function OUTGTEXT for displaying text, and so we will simply write to the default single graphical window.

Before using the OUTGTEXT function to write to a graphics window, the fonts must be initialized using the function INITIALIZEFONTS and a font selected using SETFONT. The function INITIALIZEFONTS must also be called for any subsequent child windows that are opened and the font type set. The syntax is as follows:

```
Use DFLIB
integer(2) inumOfFonts, iret
inumOfFonts = initializefonts()
iret = SETFONT ('t''Arial''h18w10i')
```

The return value from the INITIALIZEFONTS function is the number of fonts that is available, and the return from the SETFONT function is the index number of the font selected. In the preceding code example, *iret* will be less than or equal to *inumOfFonts* if SETFONT function has been successful; otherwise, it will be –1. The SETFONT argument is a character string that describes the font characteristics. In the example, the *t* indicates that what follows is a font name, the *h* is the pixel height of the font, and *w* is the pixel width of the font. The full range of available options is tabled in the SETFONT online information.

Text can be located anywhere in the graphics window by calling the routine MOVETO and displayed at any angle with SETGTEXTROTATION:

```
Use DFLIB
integer (2) ixPos, iyPos
integer(4) ideg
TYPE (xycoord) xypos
CALL MOVETO (ixPos, iyPos, xypos)
CALL SETGTEXTROTATION(ideg)
CALL OUTGTEXT('Radial Text!'C)
```

2.4.1   Fonts2 example

The Fonts2 example illustrates how to set the font attributes and position text in any orientation within a graphics window. The application displays the blue-colored text "Radial Text" in an angular orientation between 0 and 360 degrees. The output is shown in Figure 2.4.

```
! using fonts in quickwin Graphics Window
program fonts2
        use dfwin
        use dflib
        implicit none
!       variables
        integer(4) iret,ideg
        integer(4) ifrontcolor,ibackcolor,itextcolor
        integer(4) hdc,iWidthDisplay,iHeightDisplay
        integer(2) inumfonts
        integer(2) ixPos, iyPos
        integer(2) ixCentre,iyCentre
        integer(2) ixold,iyold,iradius
        real(4) angleStep
        real(4) const1,const2
        RECORD /qwinfo/qw
        LOGICAL(4) bret
        TYPE (windowconfig) wc
        TYPE (xycoord) xypos
!       set the child window properties to defaults
!       and highest resolution graphics mode.
        wc%numxpixels = -1
        wc%numypixels = -1
        wc%numtextcols = -1
        wc%numtextrows = -1
        wc%numcolors = -1
        wc%fontsize =  -1
        wc%title = '      Radial Text'C
        bret = SETWINDOWCONFIG(wc)
!       maximize the size of the main window
```

```
                    qw%type =QWIN$MAX
                    iret = SETWSIZEQQ(QWIN$FRAMEWINDOW,qw)
          !         maximize child window by simulating a click
          !         on the Tile option in Windows menu
                    iret = CLICKMENUQQ(QWIN$TILE)
          !         set colors for text and screen
                    itextcolor = rgb(255,0,0)         ! red
                    ibackcolor = rgb(255,255,255)     ! white
                    ifrontcolor = rgb(0,0,255)        ! blue
                    iret = SETCOLORRGB(ifrontcolor)
                    iret = SETBKCOLORRGB(ibackcolor)
                    iret = SETTEXTCOLORRGB(itextcolor)
                    CALL CLEARSCREEN($GCLEARSCREEN)
          !         now to demonstrate the use of graphics functions
          !         for writing text intiialize fonts
                    iret = INITIALIZEFONTS ( )
                    IF (iret < 0) then
                        iret = MESSAGEBOXQQ('Initializing Fonts'C, &
                              'Error'C,MB$ICONEXCLAMATION .OR.MB$OK )
                    end if
```

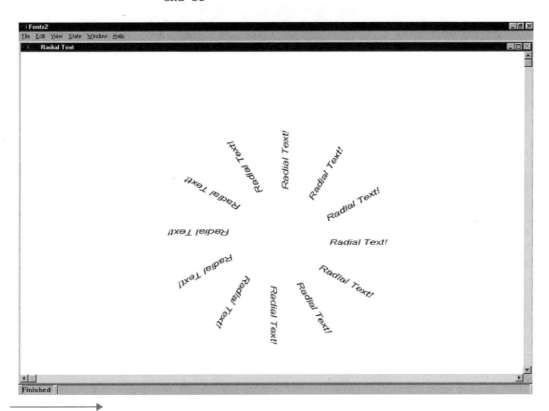

Figure 2.4   *Output screen for the Fonts2 program.*

```
!       then select italic Arial font and size
        iret = SETFONT ('t''Arial''h18w10i')
        if(iret < 0) then
           iret = MESSAGEBOXQQ('Setting Fonts'C, &
                'Error'C,MB$ICONEXCLAMATION .OR.MB$OK )
        end if
!       get device capabilities
        hdc = GetDC (Null)
        iWidthDisplay = GetDeviceCaps (hdc , HORZRES)
        iHeightDisplay = GetDeviceCaps (hdc , VERTRES)
        iret = ReleaseDC (Null,hdc)
!       set angle increments and circle radius
        angleStep = 12.0
        iradius = 100
!       find centre of circle, and trig values
        ixCentre  = iWidthDisplay/2
        iyCentre  = iHeightDisplay/2
        Const1 = Cos(2*3.14156/angleStep)
        Const2 = Sin(2*3.14156/angleStep)
!       set starting position at zero degrees
        ixOld = iradius + ixCentre
        iyOld = iyCentre
        ixPos = ixOld
        iyPos = iyOld
!       now draw the text
        do ideg = 3600, int(3600/angleStep), &
                       -int(3600/angleStep)
           CALL MOVETO (ixPos, iyPos, xypos)
           CALL SETGTEXTROTATION(ideg)
           CALL OUTGTEXT('Radial Text!'C)
           ixPos  = ixCentre+ ((ixOld-ixCentre)*Const1- &
                            (iyOld-iyCentre)*Const2)
           iyPos  = iyCentre+ ((ixOld-ixCentre)*Const2+ &
                            (iyOld-iyCentre)*Const1)
           ixOld = ixPos
           iyOld = iyPos
        end do
  end
```

2.5   What is next?

In the next chapter, we will look at the techniques required to construct our own user interfaces and provide program support for menu items, mouse selection, and the display of an instruction list. We will develop a standard menu (Menu2) that can be easily customized for specific applications. This menu will be further developed in Chapter 4.

3

User Interfaces

3.1   Interface basics

The three programs in Chapter 2 are sequential in operation. Once started, each program continues until it has finished execution of all its instructions. Such a program cannot be used again without exiting from the QuickWin interface and running the program again. By contrast, most Windows programs are event driven. That is, they present the user with a number of valid alternative actions and wait for the user to make a selection. QuickWin programs can also provide this level of choice to the user. This is achieved using a primary and secondary thread. Transparent to the user, QuickWin programs can cycle forever in a loop in the primary thread, while waiting in the secondary thread to respond to events such as the selection of a menu item or a mouse click.

The simplest method for setting up an infinite loop is to use a do-while statement, as shown below:

```
do while (.true.)
   ! Wait forever in this loop to permit event-driven
   ! action.
   Call Sleepqq(500)
end do
```

The user must exit from the program through an exit option in the application's menu. The subroutine SLEEPQQ will remove resource hogging by the do-while loop.

Rather than let the program cycle endlessly in a loop doing nothing, it is also possible to make the program wait in the loop until it receives user input (e.g., the click of a mouse or input from the keyboard). In either case, the additional code contained in the do-while loop will be blocking in nature. The program in the primary thread will have stopped cycling and will be endlessly waiting for input from either the mouse or keyboard before completing each cycle. It is customary to have only one blocking function in this loop; otherwise, the program response may seem erratic to the user. For the same reason, it is also good practice to avoid having a blocking function in both threads. The Menu1 program, which is described later in this chapter, will be used to demonstrate some of these effects.

Keyboard input may be obtained through either the GETCHARQQ function or the INCHARQQ function. In the GETCHARQQ function, when the Ctrl key and a letter are pressed together, the value returned will be 1 for A, 2 for B, and so forth. Use of GETCHARQQ is illustrated in the following code fragment:

```
      do while (.true.)
!        Wait forever in this loop to obtain keyboard input.
      key = GETCHARQQ()
      select case (ichar(key))
         case(2)
            user code goes here      ! Ctrl+B selected
         case(24)
            user code goes here      ! Ctrl+X selected
      end select
      end do
```

The INCHARQQ function can be used in a similar fashion. Consult the online documentation for more information and an example of its usage.

Applications can use the WAITONMOUSEEVENT function to get input from a mouse. The syntax for WAITONMOUSEEVENT is:

```
iret = waitonmouseevent(mouseevents, keystate, x, y)
```

where:

- mouseevents—The function will wait until a specified mouse event has occurred. The mouse event can be any one of the following actions. The corresponding symbolic constants are inside the parentheses.

  - Left mouse button down (MOUSE$LBUTTONDOWN)
  - Left mouse button up (MOUSE$LBUTTONUP)
  - Left mouse button double-click (MOUSE$LBUTTONDBL-CLK)
  - Right mouse button down (MOUSE$RBUTTONDOWN)
  - Right mouse button up (MOUSE$RBUTTONUP)

- Right mouse button double-click (MOUSE$RBUTTONDBL-
  CLK)
- Mouse moved (MOUSE$MOVE)

- keystate—Value returned to indicate the state of the mouse when the
  event occurred. This value can be used to test for the occurrence of
  any combinations of the following events. These events can be combined with an inclusive OR.

  - Left mouse button down during event (MOUSE$KS_
    LBUTTON)
  - Right mouse button down during event (MOUSE$KS_
    RBUTTON)
  - Shift key held down during event (MOUSE$KS_SHIFT)
  - Ctrl key held down during event (MOUSE$KS_CONTROL)

- x,y—The x and y coordinates of the mouse when the event occurred.

In the following code fragment, the do-while loop is blocked at the
WAITONMOUSEEVENT function waiting for the right mouse button to
be down. When this occurs, a value is returned through the integer variable
keystate, which can be tested to determine the state of the Ctrl and Shift
keys in addition to the state of the left and right mouse buttons. Integer values are returned for the x and y coordinates of the cursor position. In the
following code fragment, when the right mouse button is clicked, a message
box will display the coordinates of the mouse cursor:

```
do while (.TRUE.)
   bret = waitonmouseevent(MOUSE$RBUTTONDOWN, &
                           keystate,ixPos, iyPos)
   if (keystate == MOUSE$KS_RBUTTON ) then
      write(szCursorPos,"(' cursor X = ',I4,&
         ' Y = ',I4),' 'C")ixPos ,iyPos
      iret = MESSAGEBOXQQ(szCursorPos, &
         'Mouse Action'C,MB$ICONEXCLAMATION .OR.MB$OK )
   end if
end do
```

3.1.1   Callback routines

Let us say that we want to create in the standard QuickWin menu our
own menu item called *beep*, which does nothing other than beep when it
is selected. The code to actually create the beep must be linked to the item
beep in the menu list. In QuickWin, this is achieved using functions such
as INSERTMENUQQ, MODIFYMENUQQ, or APPENDMENUQQ.

The use of these functions will be discussed in detail shortly. However, if, for example, we want to use APPENDMENUQQ, the code to add the menu item beep into top Menu3 and to link that menu item beep with the subroutine UserBeep would be:

```
external UserBeep
...
bret = appendmenuqq(3, $MENUENABLED , 'Beep'C, UserBeep)
```

In the foregoing context, the routine UserBeep is usually referred to as a *callback routine*. This is because Windows calls back to these routines from outside the code space of the program. In the C language, such a routine must be defined as being a CALLBACK function. Note that the callback subroutine UserBeep must be declared as External. In this example, the callback routine UserBeep is very simple:

```
subroutine UserBeep(checked)
use dflib
implicit none
logical checked
   call beepqq(1200,800)
end subroutine UserBeep
```

The UserBeep argument *checked* is a logical variable sent automatically from the menu item to indicate the checked state of the menu item. Your code can ignore or act on this information as necessary. As discussed later, callback routines are also used by other event-based functions, including:

- Dialog boxes and their associated control items

- Mouse actions when used for event-based situations

3.1.2 Modifying QuickWin menus

All QuickWin multiple document interface (MDI) applications create a default application containing a frame window (i.e., child window, horizontal and vertical scroll bars, a status bar, and a menu bar). The status bar is placed at the bottom of the window and reports the current status of the window program (e.g., running or input pending). The default menu bar contains six menus: File, Edit, View, State, Windows, and Help. However, you do not have to use the default QuickWin menus. The default menu can be extensively modified using the QuickWin routines: APPENDMENUQQ, DELETEMENUQQ, INSERTMENUQQ, MODIFYMENUSTRINGQQ, MODIFYMENUROUTINEQQ, and

MODIFYMENUFLAGSQQ. These routines will now be examined in more detail.

3.1.3   Adding menu items with APPENDMENUQQ

Additions to an existing QuickWin MDI menu can be made using the command APPENDMENUQQ, which inserts a menu item into a menu and registers its callback routine. The syntax is as follows:

```
bret = appendmenuqq(1,$MENUENABLED,'User &
E&xit'C,UserExit)
```

The menu to which the item is to be appended is identified as 1, which indicates that it is the leftmost of the menus on the menu bar. The symbolic constant $MENUENABLED is the flag used to set the menu state to enabled. A choice of alternative flags can be found in the APPENDMENU command in the online help. QuickWin menu items have keyboard access such that keys are by default the Alt key plus the first letter of the menu item name. This can be changed using the ampersand symbol (&) before the letter you want underlined. For example, to set menu item User Exit with the *x* underlined, the text should be "User E&xit." Quick access keys allow program users to activate the menu item with the quick access key combination Alt+X as an alternative to selecting the item with the mouse. The final argument, UserExit, is the name of a subroutine to be called when this menu item is selected. All callback routines have a single logical parameter, which can be used to determine whether the menu item is checked or not. Predefined QuickWin routines include WINEXIT, WINSAVE, and WINABOUT. A complete list of the QuickWin predefined routines can be found in the APPENDMENUQQ routine in the online help. The function returns a logical value true if successful and false if unsuccessful.

3.1.4   Using escape control sequences

In the following code fragment the null-terminated C string, `'User Exit\tCtrl +X'C`, contains the menu item name User Exit and its associated shortcut key combination Ctrl +X:

```
bret = appendmenuqq(1, $MENUENABLED, &
                    'User  E&xit\tCtrl +X'C, UserExit)
```

The backward slash symbol, \, indicates that the next symbol is a C escape character. In this case, the \t is used to indicate that a tab is to occur

Table 3.1   *Common Escape Sequences*

Sequence	Comment
\n	New line
\t	Move the cursor to the next tab stop
\r	Carriage return
\'	Single quote
\"	Double quote

before writing the next part of the string. A list of some common escape characters is given in Table 3.1.

Any null-terminated C string, such as a message box string, can contain the escape control characters of Table 3.1. For example, the QuickWin standard about box can be redefined using

```
iret = ABOUTBOXQQ ("User menu\rfor\'QuickWin\'\n&
                    Version\t\t1.0"C)
```

to display the following message:

```
User menu

for 'QuickWin'

Version 1.0
```

3.1.5   Deleting menu items with DELETEMENUQQ

Existing menu items can be deleted with the DELETEMENUQQ command. The syntax is straightforward:

```
bret = DELETEMENUQQ(1,3)
```

In this case, the menu that contains the menu item to be deleted is number 1 (i.e., the leftmost menu). The menu item to be deleted is number 3. The top menu item is number 0. The entire menu will be deleted if a value of zero is used to identify the menu item. For example, the instruction DELETEMENUQQ(4,0) would cause the entire menu that is positioned fourth from the left-hand side to be deleted. The DELETEMENUQQ has a return value of true if successful; otherwise, it is false.

3.1.6 Inserting menu items with INSERTMENUQQ and APPENDMENUQQ

The APPENDMENUQQ routine causes a new menu item to be added to the bottom of a menu. To insert a menu item between existing menu items, use the routine INSERTMENUQQ. The syntax is

```
bret = INSERTMENUQQ(2, 6, ior($MENUENABLED ,&
            $MENUCHECKED), 'New Item...'C, CheckTest)
```

INSERTMENUQQ has an additional argument, compared with APPENDMENUQQ, that is used to identify where the menu item is to be positioned. In the preceding example, a menu item called 'New Item...' is to be positioned in a Windows menu that is second from the left and in position 6 of that menu. A top menu entry would be indicated by position zero (i.e., 2,0). The ellipses are used to indicate that the user will be presented with some additional information or set of choices. Also note that in this example the $MENUENABLED flag has been combined with the $MENUCHECKED flag using an inclusive OR (IOR). We could also use a logical OR to join them. The inclusive OR can be used with any valid combination of flags when adding or modifying menu items.

3.1.7 Modifying menu item details

Three routines are available for modifying menu flags, menu strings, and menu callback routines. Their use is illustrated in the following code fragment. A menu item called Old with a callback routine CheckTest is created, and then the menu item name is changed from Old to New and the callback routine is changed from CheckTest to NewTest. Finally, the menu item is checked.

```
Use dflib
logical(4) bret
bret = INSERTMENUQQ(2,6,$MENUENABLED,'Old'C,CheckTest)
bret = MODIFYMENUSTRINGQQ(2,6,'New'C)
bret = MODIFYMENUROUTINEQQ(2,6,'NewTest'C)
bret = MODIFYMENUFLAGSQQ(2,6,$MENUCHECKED)
```

3.2 Menu1 example

Let us now look at a simple example that demonstrates most of the principles just described. The Menu1 program listed below has the following five items in the main menu—File, Edit, NewMenu, State, Window, and Help. The File menu contains two default menu items, Print and Save. The QuickWin–supplied menu item Exit normally contained in the File menu has been deleted and a new menu item called User Exit has been appended and given a new shortcut key (Ctrl+X). The key combination Ctrl+C is reserved in QuickWin as a shortcut key for Exit. This choice of key combination is most probably a relic from earlier programming days when Ctrl+C was used to stop program execution. However, in a Windows environment, users expect Ctrl+C to be used for copying from the clipboard and Ctrl+X to be used when cutting to the clipboard. Note that the function PASSDIR-KEYSQQ is called to allow the GETCHARQQ function to detect the key combination Ctrl+C. The combination can then be redefined as a shortcut for some other task.

The User Exit menu item works by calling the QuickWin routine Exit (as opposed to the Fortran statement EXIT) and suppressing the normal QuickWin program–terminated message by using the function SETEXITQQ(*exitmode*). In this function, the three values for integer variable *exitmode* are QWIN$EXITPROMPT, QWIN$EXITNOPERSIST, and QWIN$EXITPERSIST. The default value for SETEXITQQ is QWIN$EXITPROMPT, which displays an exit prompt. QWIN$EXIT-NOPERSIST terminates the application without displaying a message box, and QWIN$EXITPERSIST leaves the application open without displaying a message box. Users are asked to confirm that they want to exit the program.

The QuickWin–supplied menu View has been deleted and replaced by NewMenu, which has two menu items—Options and Beep plus a list of child window names. Options is permanently grayed; Beep uses the Fortran subroutine BEEPQQ to produce a sound when this menu item is selected or when the Ctrl and B keys have been pressed together. Normally, a list of active child window names is appended to the bottom of the Window menu, but this list can be relocated to a different top-level menu using the function SETWINDOWMENUQQ. In this example, the list of active child window names has been relocated to the bottom of NewMenu.

In the Windows menu, a menu item called Focus Unit 3 has been inserted. Focus Unit 3 does nothing other than cycle between being checked and unchecked and displaying a message in either of the child windows to indicate which unit has focus.

The program Menu1 has two parts, main.f90 and Callbacks.f90. The following is a listing of main.f90:

```
program Menu1
! How to customize the standard QuickWin menu
use dflib
use dfwin
implicit none
external ChangeFocus,UserExit,UserBeep
integer(4) iret,unit
integer(4) ibackcolor,ifrontcolor
character(1) key / 'A' /
logical(4) bret
record /qwinfo/qw
    open(unit = 3, file = 'user', title = ' Child window 1'C)
! set screen colors for window 1
    ibackcolor = rgb(255,255,255)   ! white
    ifrontcolor = rgb(0,0,0)        ! black
    iret = SETCOLORRGB(ifrontcolor)
    iret = SETBKCOLORRGB(ibackcolor)
    iret = SETTEXTCOLORRGB(ifrontcolor)
    call CLEARSCREEN($GCLEARSCREEN)
    write(3,*)'This file is unit 3'
    open(unit = 4, file = 'user',title = 'Child window 2'C)
! set screen colors for window 2
    iret = SETCOLORRGB(ifrontcolor)
    iret = SETBKCOLORRGB(ibackcolor)
    iret = SETTEXTCOLORRGB(ifrontcolor)
    call CLEARSCREEN($GCLEARSCREEN)
    write(4,*)'This file is unit 4'
    iret = FOCUSQQ(3)
! set exit for no message
    iret = SETEXITQQ(QWIN$EXITNOPERSIST)
! maximize the size of the main window
    qw%type =QWIN$MAX
    iret = SETWSIZEQQ(QWIN$FRAMEWINDOW,qw)
! Delete Exit from file menu
    bret = DELETEMENUQQ(1,3)
! Allow Ctrl+C to be passed to GetKey function
    iret = PASSDIRKEYSQQ (PASS_DIR_CNTRLC )
! insert separator bar and user exit menu
    bret = appendmenuqq(1, $MENUSEPARATOR, 'sep'C,  NUL)
    bret = appendmenuqq(1, $MENUENABLED, &
                    'User  E&xit\tCtrl +X'C,UserExit)
! Delete entire third menu (View)
    bret = deletemenuqq(3,0)
! insert new menu at position 3 in the menu bar
    bret = INSERTMENUQQ(3, 0, $MENUENABLED, 'NewMenu'C, Nul)
```

```
      bret = appendmenuqq(3, $MENUGRAYED ,'Options'C, Nul)
      bret = appendmenuqq(3, $MENUENABLED , &
                           'Beep\tCtrl +B'C,UserBeep)
!  names of the child windows will be placed at the bottom
!  of the edit menu instead of the default window menu
      bret = SETWINDOWMENUQQ (3)
!  Delete unwanted menu items in window menu
      bret = DELETEMENUQQ(5,5)
      bret = DELETEMENUQQ(5,4)
      bret = DELETEMENUQQ(5,3)
!  insert separator in window menu
      bret = INSERTMENUQQ(5, 3, $MENUSEPARATOR, 'sep'C, Nul)
!  insert new menu item in window menu
      bret = INSERTMENUQQ(5, 4, ior($MENUENABLED ,&
                 $MENUCHECKED ), 'Focus Unit 3'C, ChangeFocus)
!  insert separator in window menu
      bret = INSERTMENUQQ(5, 5, $MENUSEPARATOR, 'sep'C, Nul)
!  simulate click of title menu to enlarge child window
      iret = CLICKMENUQQ (loc(WINTILE))
      do while (.true.)
!  Wait forever in this loop to permit event-driven action.
         key = GETCHARQQ()
         select case (ichar(key))
            case(2)
             call UserBeep(.true.)  ! Ctrl+B selected
            case(3)
                 iret = inqfocusqq(unit)  !  Ctrl+C selected
             if(unit == 3) then
                 iret = FOCUSQQ(4)
                 iret = SETACTIVEQQ(4)
                 iret = PASSDIRKEYSQQ (PASS_DIR_CNTRLC )
             else
                 iret = FOCUSQQ(3)
                 iret = SETACTIVEQQ(3)
                 iret = PASSDIRKEYSQQ (PASS_DIR_CNTRLC )
             end if
                 iret = MESSAGEBOXQQ('Ctrl+C selected'C, &
                 'GetKey'C, &
                 MB$ICONEXCLAMATION .OR.MB$OK )
            case(24)
             call UserExit(.true.)  ! Ctrl+X selected
         end select
      end do
end
```

A listing of the subroutines in Callbacks.f90 follows. Note the use of the logical argument to test the state of the menu item Focus Unit 3 (which calls subroutine ChangeFocus) and that it is checked or unchecked accordingly. Subroutine ChangeFocus is used to check which window currently has focus and to change the focus according to the checked state of Focus Unit.

```
subroutine ChangeFocus(checked)
use dfwin
use dflib
logical checked, bret
integer(4) iret,unit
    if (checked) then
        bret = MODIFYMENUFLAGSQQ(5,4,$MENUUNCHECKED)
        iret = inqfocusqq(unit)
        iret = SETACTIVEQQ(4)
        iret = FOCUSQQ(4)
            write(4,*)'Uncheck menu item "Focus Unit 3"'
        write(4,*)'unit with previous focus = ',unit
        write(4,*)'focus has been set to = ',4
    else
        bret = MODIFYMENUFLAGSQQ(5,4,$MENUCHECKED)
        iret = inqfocusqq(unit)
        iret = SETACTIVEQQ(3)
        iret = FOCUSQQ(3)
        write(3,*)'Check menu item "Focus Unit 3"'
        write(3,*)'unit with previous focus = ',unit
        write(3,*)'focus has been set to = ',3
    end if
end subroutine ChangeFocus
subroutine UserExit(checked)
use dfwin
use dflib
implicit none
logical checked, bret
integer(4) iret
    iret = messageboxqq('Press OK to Exit'C,'Confirm Exit'C,&
            MB$OKCANCEL)
    if(iret.eq.MB$IDOK) then
        call exit()
    endif
end subroutine UserExit
subroutine UserBeep(checked)
use dflib
implicit none
logical checked
    call beepqq(1200,800)
end subroutine UserBeep
```

Note: When working with multiple child windows, it is important to remember that QuickWin applications always display the frame window but not the child window. To display each child window, you must call SETWINDOWCONFIG or execute a write text or draw graphics statement to every child window. This is why, in the program Menu1, both windows are written to immediately after they are created.

Observant readers will note that in Figure 3.1, Child window 2 has the focus, while the status bar displays the statement "Input pending in Child window 1." Which is correct? In a sense, both are correct. QuickWin supports both a primary and a secondary thread; one for the process and one for callback routines. In our example, the function GETCHARQQ in the do-while loop of the main program acts as a blocking function, and the program will wait in that thread until it receives input from the keyboard.

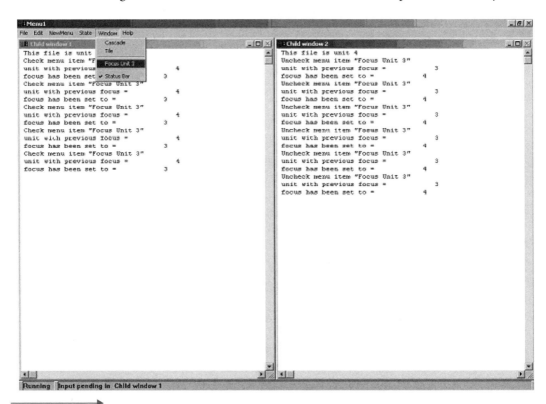

Figure 3.1   *Menu1 shows that the menu item Focus Unit 3 has been used to set the focus to Child window 2.*

Upon receiving keyboard input, the program completes the cycle and returns to wait for more keyboard input. The GETCHARQQ expects input from the file unit that was last opened, unless the unit focus was reset. In our example, unit 4 was the last file opened, but the focus was changed to unit 3 using `iret = FOCUSQQ (3)` before the program goes into the do-while loop. Thus, until the focus is reset for that thread, GETCHARQQ will always expect input from unit 3. Meanwhile, in the thread supporting the callback routines, the focus can be changed between each window at will by clicking on the other window with the mouse, by selecting the Focus Unit 3 menu item, or by selecting the appropriate window from the list of window names at the bottom of New Menu.

This behavior can cause some difficulties, because if the hot keys (Ctrl+X and Ctrl+B) are assigned to unit 3, they will respond while unit 3 has the focus. The status bar correctly reflects that the program is looking for keyboard input (GETCHARQQ) from unit 3. If the focus is changed to unit 4, keyboard input is no longer possible until focus is returned to unit 3. It is necessary to reset the unit focus with the thread supporting the GETCHARQQ routine. In this example, this is demonstrated by using the hot-key combination Ctrl+C to reset the focus between unit 3 and unit 4 for purposes of keyboard input. The status bar reflects this change.

Note that the status will always reflect where it expects to get the next piece of information. For example, if QuickWin has two blocking calls pending, it will display a message in the status bar that corresponds to the blocking call first encountered. This can be illustrated by including READ statements in the callback routine ChangeFocus, as shown below. Then, when you have changed the focus using the Focus Unit 3 menu item, the status bar will reflect which unit number the information (from READ(*,*) x) is expected to come from.

```
integer(4) x
   if (checked) then
      ...
      write(4,*)'focus has been set to = ',4
      write(4,*)' input an integer value'
      read(4,*)x
   else
      ...
      write(3,*)'unit with previous focus = ',unit
      write(3,*)'focus has been set to = ',3
      write(3,*)' input an integer value'
      read(3,*)x
   end if
```

Note that the preceding code has a blocking routine in both the primary and secondary threads. This is bad practice and should always be avoided.

3.3   Using a mouse

QuickWin provides two functions for detecting mouse actions: WAITONMOUSEEVENT and REGISTERMOUSEEVENT. WAITONMOUSEEVENT blocks the sequential flow of a program. We have already examined the use of WAITONMOUSEEVENT in connection with a do-while loop. The important point to remember is that the mouse action must happen in the window that had focus when the WAITONMOUSEEVENT was called. The function returns information to indicate whether the Shift or Ctrl key had been depressed when it detected the set mouse event. The mouse coordinates are also returned.

REGISTERMOUSEEVENT is always used in nonblocking situations, in which asynchronous mouse input is required. In other words, the program does not need to wait for a mouse event to occur before proceeding; it can receive input from the mouse at any time. For example, such an occasion would occur in a drawing program when the user wanted to identify a zoom area. It would not make sense for the program to have a blocking routine in the primary thread to detect this action. It would be much better for the program to asynchronously receive mouse input from the secondary callback thread. This type of input is often referred to as event-based input. The syntax for REGISTERMOUSEEVENT is:

```
iret = registermouseevent(Unit, Mouseevents , Callback)
```

The range of mouse events and keystates previously described for the WAITONMOUSEEVENT function also apply to REGISTERMOUSEEVENT. The user must supply the name of a callback routine that responds to the desired mouse action.

The default cursor displayed may be changed using the SETMOUSECURSOR function for one of the predefined alternative types. A list of options is contained in the online documentation. In this simple example of usage, the Win32 function LoadCursor returns a handle to the newly loaded cursor, which in our case is a cross. The QuickWin function SETMOUSECURSOR is used to set the cursor to the new shape. The old cursor can be reinstated at a later stage.

```
integer(4)  cursor, oldcursor
cursor = LoadCursor(0, IDC_CROSS)
oldcursor = SetMouseCursor(cursor)
```

3.3.1   Changing QuickWin standard messages with SETMESSAGEQQ

The SETMESSAGEQQ function can be used to change QuickWin standard messages. The online documentation lists the full range of standard messages. Here we will use the function to change the message displayed in the status bar. The subroutine SETMESSAGEQQ can be used to change the MOUSEINPUTPENDING state message displayed by the status bar, as follows:

```
USE DFLIB
Call SETMESSAGEQQ('Waiting for mouse input from user in', &
                  QWIN$MSG_MOUSEINPUTPEND)
```

The QWIN$MSG_MOUSEINPUTPEND is the message ID for the status bar mouse message. It is not necessary to specify the window name because QuickWin automatically supplies the identity of where it is expecting the mouse input to come from.

Note: Unlike other QuickWin message functions, SETMESSAGEQQ uses regular Fortran strings rather than null-terminated C strings.

3.3.2   Select example

In the program Select, the mouse is used to create a selection box and then color fill the selected area. Select has three parts—globals.f90, main.f90, and Callbacks.f90. The key features of each file are described before the relevant code listing. The module Global in Globals.f90 contains all the global variables needed to keep track of the mouse cursor position.

```
module Global
!  global variables
real(4)  Xnode1,Xnode2,Ynode1,Ynode2,OldX,OldY
integer(2) SelectBoxflag,Click
integer(4)  cursor, oldcursor
end module Global
```

The following listing for main.f90 demonstrates how to register mouse callback routines and use the WAITONMOUSEEVENT function. The File menu is retained, but it contains only the menu item Exit, while all other menus are deleted and the menu Options is inserted. The default About dialog box message is redefined. An Instructions menu item is included under the Options menu. The message in the status bar is rede-

fined. The program detects when the right mouse button is clicked and will
display different messages according to the state of the Ctrl and Shift keys.
The cursor changes to a cross when the left mouse button has been
depressed and dragged to form a selection box. The old cursor is reinstated
when the mouse button is released. In an effort to reduce the length of code
listed and to promote clarity, some of the code that we have used in previous examples has been omitted. This is signified by use of ellipses (…).

```
program select
! select a rectangular area to be color filled
use dfwin
use dflib
use Global
implicit none
external SelectPoint1,SelectBox, ColorFill
external SelectNotice,Instructions
! variables
integer(4) iret,keystate
integer(4) ifrontcolor,ibackcolor,itextcolor
integer(4) ixPos,iyPos
logical(4) bret
character(15) szMessage
character(50) szCursorPos
type (windowconfig) wc
type (rccoord) rc
type (xycoord) pos
record /qwinfo/qw
!  set the child window properties to defaults
!  and highest resolution graphics mode.
...
!  delete save and print from file menu
   bret = DELETEMENUQQ(1,2)
   bret = DELETEMENUQQ(1,1)
!  Delete remaining menus
   bret = deletemenuqq(6,0)
   bret = deletemenuqq(5,0)
   bret = deletemenuqq(4,0)
   bret = deletemenuqq(3,0)
   bret = deletemenuqq(2,0)
!  insert new menu at position 2 in the menu bar
   bret = INSERTMENUQQ(2, 0, $MENUENABLED, 'Options'C, Nul)
   bret = appendmenuqq(2,$MENUENABLED,'Instructions'C, &
          Instructions)
   bret = appendmenuqq(2,$MENUENABLED,'About'C, WINABOUT)
   iret = ABOUTBOXQQ ('Selection Box \n Version 1.0'C)
   Call SETMESSAGEQQ('Waiting for mouse input from user in', &
                 QWIN$MSG_MOUSEINPUTPEND)
```

```
    ! set colors for text and screen
    ...
       SelectBoxflag = 1
    ! register the mouse events.  Each time the mouse is moved,
    ! or the left mouse button is used in the select
    ! application window, the routines SelectPoint1, SelectBox
    ! or SelectionFinished will be called. Otherwise Select
    ! Notice called when shift or control pressed with right
    ! mouse button
       iret = registermouseevent(0,MOUSE$LBUTTONDOWN &
                                 ,SelectPoint1)
       iret = registermouseevent(0,MOUSE$KS_SHIFT.or. &
           MOUSE$RBUTTONDOWN.or.MOUSE$KS_CONTROL,SelectNotice)
       iret = registermouseevent(0,MOUSE$MOVE,SelectBox)
       iret = registermouseevent(0,MOUSE$LBUTTONUP,ColorFill)
       do while (.TRUE.)
    ! wait forever for right hand mouse button
    ! to be pushed.
          bret = waitonmouseevent(MOUSE$RBUTTONDOWN, &
                                  keystate,ixPos, iyPos)
          if (keystate == MOUSE$KS_RBUTTON ) then
             write(szCursorPos,"(' cursor X = ',I4,&
                   '  Y = ',I4),' 'C")ixPos ,iyPos
             iret = MESSAGEBOXQQ(szCursorPos, &
                  'Mouse Action'C,MB$ICONEXCLAMATION .OR.MB$OK )
          end if
       end do
    end
```

3.3.3   Creating a selection box with RECTANGLE_W

In the example Select, the QuickWin graphics routine RECTANGLE_W is used to create the outline box shape, and when the mouse button is released, RECTANGLE_W is also used to create the final color-filled box. The underscore W designation indicates that this function uses window coordinates (real(8)) rather than viewport integer values. This example can also be used with the QuickWin routine RECTANGLE, which uses integer coordinates, instead of RECTANGLE_W. Just remove the underscore W from all the RECTANGLE_W routines and redefine the global variables *Xnode1*, *Xnode2*, *Ynode1*, *Ynode2*, *OldX*, and *OldY* from real(8) to integer(4) types. The usage for RECTANGLE_W is straightforward:

```
iret = Rectangle_w($GBORDER,X1, Y1,X2,Y2)
```

The coordinates X1, Y1 and X2, Y2 are at diagonally opposite corners of a rectangle. The symbolic constant $GBORDER indicates that the rectan-

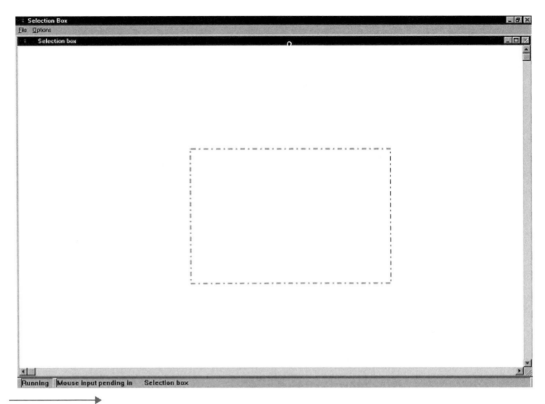

Figure 3.2 *Selection box before being filled.*

gle is to be drawn as a border using the current color and line style. Alternatively, the symbolic constant $GFILLINTERIOR may be used to produce a rectangle that is filled using the current color and fill mask. We shall examine the effects that can be created through changes to the fill mask in Chapter 4. For the moment, we will use the default setting, which produces a solid fill.

The linestyle is defined by a two-byte mask using the QuickWin subroutine SETLINESTYLE(mask). A solid line is defined by a mask value of hexadecimal FFFF, a line of dots would be hexadecimal AAAA, and a dash dot is hexadecimal ECEC. The selection box effect is created using the function SETWRITEMODE and toggling its argument between the symbolic constants $GXOR and $GPSET. (See Figure 3.2.)

This is a listing of routines to be found in Callbacks.f90:

```
subroutine Instructions
use dflib
implicit none
```

```
integer(4) iret
   iret = MESSAGEBOXQQ(&
          'Create a selection box for color filling by \n&
          holding down the left hand mouse button  \n&
          and moving mouse.  Release the mouse \n&
          button to fill the box \n\n&
          Hold Shift or Control button down and click\n&
          right mouse button to display choice \n\n&
          Click right mouse button to get cursor &
          coordinates'C,'Instructions'C, &
          MB$ICONEXCLAMATION .OR.MB$OK )
end subroutine Instructions
subroutine SelectNotice(unit,me,iKeyState,x,y)
use dfwin
use dflib
use Global
implicit none
! variables
integer(2) unit,iKeyState,me
integer(4) iret ,x,y
type (xycoord) viewxy
type (wxycoord) windxy
   if ((MOUSE$KS_CONTROL.AND.iKeyState) == &
      MOUSE$KS_CONTROL) then
      iret = MESSAGEBOXQQ('Control Plus Right Mouse Button &
          Pressed'C, 'Mouse Actions'C,MB$ICONEXCLAMATION&
          .OR.MB$OK )
   end if
   if ((MOUSE$KS_SHIFT.AND.iKeyState) == MOUSE$KS_SHIFT) then
      iret = MESSAGEBOXQQ('Shift Plus Right Mouse Button &
             Pressed'C, 'Mouse Actions'C,MB$ICONEXCLAMATION &
             .OR.MB$OK )
   end if
   return
end subroutine SelectNotice
subroutine SelectPoint1(unit,me,iKeyState,x,y)
use dfwin
use dflib
use Global
implicit none
! variables
integer(2) unit,iKeyState, me
integer(4) iret, x,y
type (xycoord) viewxy
type (wxycoord) windxy
   cursor = LoadCursor(0, IDC_CROSS)
   oldcursor = SetMouseCursor(cursor)
   if (SelectBoxflag == 1) then
      if ((MOUSE$KS_LBUTTON.AND.iKeyState)== &
```

```
                         MOUSE$KS_LBUTTON) then
              call GETVIEWCOORD (X,Y, viewxy)
              call GETWINDOWCOORD(viewxy%xcoord, &
                                 viewxy%ycoord, windxy)
              Xnode1 = windxy%wx
              Ynode1 = windxy%wy
              Xnode2 = Xnode1
              Ynode2 = Ynode1
              Click = 1
              iret = SETWRITEMODE($GPSET)
              iret = Rectangle_w($GBORDER,Xnode1,Ynode1,&
                                 Xnode2,Ynode2)
          end if
      end if
end subroutine  SelectPoint1
subroutine SelectBox(unit,me,iKeyState,x,y)
use dfwin
use dflib
use Global
implicit none
! variables
integer(2) unit,iKeyState, me
integer(4) iret,x,y,style
type (xycoord) viewxy
type (wxycoord) windxy
    if (SelectBoxflag.AND.Click ==1) then
        iret = SETCOLOR(15)
            style = #ECEC
        call SETLINESTYLE(style)
        OldX = Xnode2
        OldY = Ynode2
        iret = SETWRITEMODE($GXOR)
        iret = Rectangle_w($GBORDER,Xnode1,Ynode1,OldX,OldY)
        call GETVIEWCOORD (X,Y, viewxy)
        call GETWINDOWCOORD(viewxy%xcoord, &
                           viewxy%ycoord, windxy)
        Xnode2 = windxy%wx
        Ynode2 = windxy%wy
        iret = Rectangle_w($GBORDER,Xnode1, &
                           Ynode1,Xnode2,Ynode2)
        style = #FFFF
        call SETLINESTYLE(style)
    endif
end subroutine SelectBox
subroutine ColorFill(unit,me,iKeyState,x,y)
use dfwin
use dflib
use Global
implicit none
```

```
! variables
integer(2) unit,iKeyState,me
integer(4) iret,x,y,oldmode
type (xycoord) viewxy
type (wxycoord) windxy
   if (SelectBoxflag.AND.Click ==1) then
       call GETVIEWCOORD (X,Y, viewxy)
       call GETWINDOWCOORD(viewxy%xcoord, &
                             viewxy%ycoord, windxy)
          Xnode2 = windxy%wx
       oldmode = SETWRITEMODE($GPSET)
       iret = Rectangle_w($GBORDER,Xnode1, &
                          Ynode1,Xnode2,Ynode2)
       Click = 0
       OldX = Xnode2
       OldY = Ynode2
       SelectBoxflag = 1
       call CLEARSCREEN($GCLEARSCREEN)
       iret = SETCOLORRGB(rgb(0,255,255)) ! set fill color
       oldmode = SETWRITEMODE($GPSET)
       iret = Rectangle_w($GFILLINTERIOR,Xnode1, &
                          Ynode1,Xnode2,Ynode2)
       iret = SETCOLORRGB(rgb(255,255,255))  ! white
       cursor= SetMouseCursor(oldcursor)
   end if
end subroutine ColorFill
```

3.4   Using INITIALSETTINGS to create user menus

The initial appearance of an application's default frame window and menus can be set by an application through a user-defined INITIALSETTINGS function. When there is no user-defined INITIALSETTINGS function present in an application, QuickWin will call a predefined INITIALSET-TINGS routine to control the default frame window and menu appearance. If an INITIALSETTINGS function is present in an application, then QuickWin will call the function automatically and set the initial menus and the size and position of the frame window according to the defined user settings. The QuickWin routine SETWSIZEQQ can be used in the INITIALSETTINGS function to define the frame window size and position before the window is first drawn. This is illustrated in the listing below for Menu.f90 for menu program Menu2.

```
logical(4) function InitialSettings()
!  This routine is called automatically when the program
!  begins. It sets up the menu structure for the program,
!  and connects "callback" routines with each menu item.
```

```
      use dflib
      implicit none
!  variables
      logical(4)  bret
      integer(2) iret
      record /qwinfo/qw
!  define the external subroutines called by menu items
      external    Browse, Notes, Calculate,Instructions
!  maximize the size of the main window
      qw%type =QWIN$MAX
      iret = SETWSIZEQQ(QWIN$FRAMEWINDOW,qw)
!  menu items
      bret = appendmenuqq(1, $MENUENABLED, 'File'C, NUL)
      bret = appendmenuqq(1, $MENUENABLED, 'Print'C,WINPRINT)
      bret = appendmenuqq(1, $MENUENABLED, 'Save'C, WINSAVE)
      bret = appendmenuqq(1, $MENUSEPARATOR,'sep'C, NUL)
     bret = appendmenuqq(1, $MENUENABLED, 'Explorer'C, Browse)
      bret = appendmenuqq(1, $MENUENABLED, 'NotePad'C,  Notes)
      bret = appendmenuqq(1, $MENUENABLED, 'Calculator'C, &
           calculate)
      bret = appendmenuqq(1, $MENUSEPARATOR,'sep'C, NUL)
      bret = appendmenuqq(1, $MENUENABLED, 'E&xit'C, WINEXIT)
      bret = appendmenuqq(2, $MENUENABLED, 'Help'C,  NUL)
      bret = appendmenuqq(2, $MENUENABLED, 'Instructions'C,&
           Instructions)
      bret = appendmenuqq(2, $MENUENABLED, 'About'C, WINABOUT)
!  Set function logical value.  This will be true if the
!  appendmenuqq is successful
      InitialSettings = bret
      return
end
```

The program file for Main.f90 listed below is similar to previous programs, and some code has been removed to improve clarity.

```
program menu2
!  User created menu
      use dfwin
      use dflib
      implicit none
!  variables
      integer(4) iret, ievent
      integer(4) ifrontcolor,ibackcolor,itextcolor
      logical(4) bret
      character(15) szMessage
      type (windowconfig) wc
      type (rccoord) rc
      record /qwinfo/qw
```

```
          open(unit = 4, file = 'user', title = 'child window')
...
!   customize status bar and about box messages
    iret = ABOUTBOXQQ ("User menu\rfor \'QuickWin\'\n&
                       Version\t\t1.0"C)
    call SETMESSAGEQQ('  Use mouse to select a menu item &
                      for ',QWIN$MSG_MOUSEINPUTPEND)
    do while (.TRUE.)
!     Wait forever to allow event-driven action.
    end do
end
```

The QuickWin function RUNQQ is used to start another program and to wait for that program to finish. (See Figure 3.3.) The syntax for running Explorer is

```
iret = RUNQQ('Explorer.exe',' 'C)
```

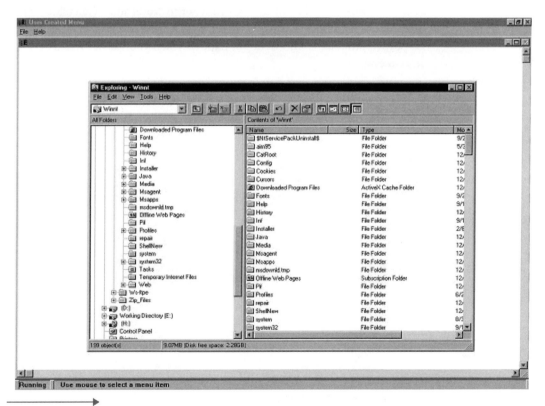

Figure 3.3   *Explorer has been opened within a QuickWin program.*

The second set of quotes may be used to pass any command-line instructions required by the program. In the preceding example, no additional instructions are passed.

The Win32 API function WinExec is a useful alternative to RUNQQ, and in the following code fragment, given that the filename menu.f90 exists, NotePad will open the file menu.f90 as a maximized window.

```
Character(20) FileName
FileName = 'menu'
iret = WinExec('NotePad.exe '//TRIM(FileName)//&
               '.f90'C,SW_MAXIMIZE)
```

Note that the Win32 function CreateProcess could be used in place of the function WinExec. However, WinExec is much simpler to use. Why not just use RUNQQ instead of WinExec to run NotePad.exe? If you use RUNQQ to run programs such as NotePad or Calc from inside your application, all will go well until the user moves the NotePad or Calculator window. The screen does not refresh, and a trail of windows is left behind to mark the path taken. This does not happen when you use WinExec or CreateProcess.

```
subroutine Browse
   use dflib
   implicit none
   integer(2) iret
   iret = RUNQQ('Explorer.exe',' 'C)
end Subroutine Browse
subroutine Notes
   use dflib
   use dfwin
   implicit none
   integer(2) iret
   Character(20) FileName
   FileName = 'menu'
   iret = WinExec('NotePad.exe '//TRIM(FileName)//&
                  '.f90'C,SW_MAXIMIZE)
end Subroutine Notes
subroutine Calculate
   use dflib
   use dfwin
   implicit none
   integer(2) iret
   iret = WinExec('Calc.exe'C,SW_SHOW)
end Subroutine Calculate
subroutine Instructions
   use dflib
   implicit none
```

```
        integer(2) iret
        character(200) szAbout
        szAbout = ' Demonstration of \"user created\" &
                menus.\n Options have been provided,\n &
                in the File menu section for opening \n &
                Windows Explorer, Notepad, and\n &
                Calculator. \n 'C
        iret = MESSAGEBOXQQ(szAbout,'Instructions'C, &
                MB$ICONEXCLAMATION .OR.MB$OK )
end subroutine Instructions
```

3.5   What is next?

In Chapter 4, we will look at how to use the Resource Editor to create dialog boxes with a variety of controls. We will also learn how to use Fill Masks to create interesting fill patterns.

4

Using Resources

4.1   Resource Editor

The Resource Editor is very powerful and easy to use. In this chapter, we will use dialog boxes for simple applications, and in Chapter 5 we will develope more complex dialog boxes for applications to illustrate the use of callback routines and the range of controls that is available to QuickWin Users.

We will use the Resource Editor in this chapter to:

- Create a dialog box that displays information stored in a string table resource.

- Use an HTML file to provide program help capabilities.

- Create an About dialog box that uses icons and bitmaps.

- Show how to store version information in a resource file and display this information in an About box.

Dialog boxes may be "modal" or "modeless." The modal dialog box style is the most commonly used; currently, it is the only type available for QuickWin applications. With a modal dialog box, the user cannot switch between the dialog box and another window or control in the same program. The user must explicitly close the dialog box before any other action can be initiated within the program. As will be demonstrated in the following section, dialog boxes are easy to create and incorporate into a program by using the Developer Studio Resource Editor.

4.2   Using Resource Editor

Use of the Resource Editor is best demonstrated through a simple application that uses a dialog box to provide the program user with instructions.

First, create a new QuickWin multiple window application called Instructions. Then copy the three files—Main.f90, Menu.f90, and Callbacks.f90—from the Menu2 example in Chapter 3 into the project folder. It is a good idea to have your own standard template version of Menu2, which you can use for pasting into a new QuickWin application as a generic starting point. In the Project menu, click Add to Project and then choose Files. Select all three files (i.e., Main.f90, Menu.f90, and Callbacks.f90) from the Insert Files Into Project dialog box. It is also useful at this point to compile the program and check that it executes properly before creating a dialog box.

The Resource Editor stores information about the resources used by a program in a script file. We add a resource script file to the project just like any other file. Select the New option in the File menu. You will be presented with a tabbed dialog box. Click on the Files tab, select Resource Script, type in a suitable name in the File name space, and click the OK button.

In the File name space, you can use the name of the program or you can use a name that is perhaps more meaningful, such as Resource. Assuming you used the name Resource, Developer Studio will create and add a resource file named Resource.rc to the project. Developer Studio also creates a C language header file called Resource.h and a Fortran include file named Resource.fd. The Resource.fd file must be included with any Fortran program code that uses the resources defined in the resource script file.

Note: The default filename Resource that Developer Studio provides for the Fortran include file and the C header file can be changed. If your project has resources displayed in the ResourceView pane, select the option Resource Includes… in the View menu, and change the name in the *Symbol header file* edit box from Resource.h to, say, Newname.h. The Fortran header file will be given the same name with the extension .fd.

Now click on the Insert menu item in Visual Studio and select Resource. You will be presented with an Insert Resource dialog box similar to that shown in Figure 4.1. The + signs, which indicate that additional choices are available at the Cursor and Dialog options, are present only when Visual C++ has also been installed. On a CVF-only installation, there are no + signs in the list box. Resource types Accelerator, Cursor, Menu, and Toolbar are usable only with Win32 API window applications, and their use is covered in later chapters. All the other choices may be used with QuickWin

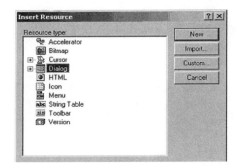

Figure 4.1
Selecting a resource item to insert into the project.

programs, and their use is demonstrated in this chapter. Select Dialog and then click the New button. As shown in Figure 4.2, Developer Studio automatically creates a standard dialog box that is complete with two buttons, one labeled Cancel and the other labeled OK. The dialog box has also been given a default name, IDD_Dialog1, and a default caption, Dialog. We will use this dialog box to create an Instruction box.

Note the Control Toolbar to the right of the dialog box window. If it does not appear with the dialog box, select Customize, Toolbars (tab dialog) from the Tools menu, and check the Controls check box. To add controls to a dialog box, just move the mouse over the desired control in the control toolbox, hold down the left mouse button, and drag the control over to the dialog box. Place the dialog control where you want it to be on the dialog and release the mouse button. Controls can be cut, pasted, deleted, or resized as required. Most of the controls in the toolbar are available for use with Win32 API applications, but only the controls named in Figure 4.3 can be used in QuickWin applications.

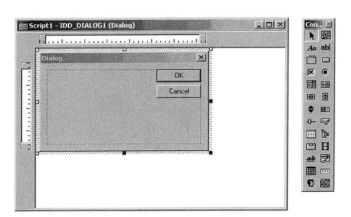

Figure 4.2
Using the Resource Editor to construct a dialog box interface.

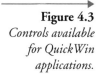

Figure 4.3
Controls available for QuickWin applications.

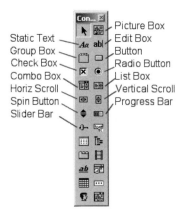

When dialog boxes are being used, Developer Studio inserts a menu called Layout between the Build and Tools menus. The Layout menu provides a number of useful options to help in aligning controls within dialog boxes (see Figure 4.4). In particular, the Guide Settings provide the user with a choice of three Layout guides—None, Rulers and guides, or Grid. The grid spacing is set in dialog units (DLUs). For this example, set the Guide Settings to Rulers and guides. The Tab Order option is used to redefine the tab key progression order in a dialog box. The Test option permits the opportunity of seeing how the dialog box will look and behave in the application without actually having to recompile the program. Try it now and see what happens. Use the dialog box OK button to exit from the test dialog box.

4.2.1   Using character string tables

We will use the dialog box we just created to build an Instruction dialog box, which will use an Edit box control to display text information about the program. Eventually we will invoke this dialog box from our program, modifying code to do this. Our first step will be to set the properties of the

Figure 4.4
Options in Layout menu.

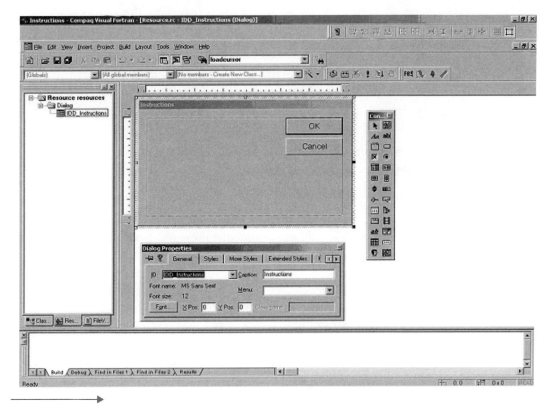

Figure 4.5   *Setting the dialog box properties.*

dialog box. Double-click on the dialog box to open the Dialog Properties
box, and, referring to Figure 4.5:

- Change the dialog box ID name to IDD_Instructions and change its
  caption to Instructions.

- Set the font size to 12.

- Click the Styles tab and uncheck the System Menu option.

- Click the More Styles tab and check the Center option.

The next step is to invoke the dialog box. The program Menu2 already
used a message box to display instructions. All we need to do is to modify
the subroutine Instructions so that it will initialize and display our instruction dialog box.

Each dialog box has an associated variable of the derived type DIALOG,
which is used to hold information about that particular dialog box. The
dialog-derived type is defined in the DFLOGM.F90; hence, USE

DFLOGM must be part of any code working with dialog boxes. We also need to include the resource information file Resource.fd. Every dialog box needs to be initialized with DLGINIT before being displayed with DLG-MODAL. The usage is as follows:

```
type (dialog) dlg
bret = DLGINIT(IDD_Instructions,dlg)
iret = DlgModal(dlg)
```

When the dialog box is no longer needed, the memory space used by the dialog box must be deallocated by calling DLGUNINIT:

```
call DlgUninit(dlg)
```

Replace the subroutine Instructions in the file callback.f90 with the following code. Compile and execute the program. Then click on Instructions in the Options menu and the screen should be similar to that shown in Figure 4.6.

```
subroutine Instructions
use dflib
use dflogm
implicit none
include 'resource.fd   '
type (dialog) dlg
integer(4) iret
logical(4) bret
   bret = DLGINIT(IDD_Instructions,dlg)
   iret = DlgModal(dlg)
   call DlgUninit(dlg)
end subroutine Instructions
```

Our next step is to create a dialog box that provides the user with instructions on how to operate the program. The steps are straightforward.

- Place an edit box on the dialog box.

- Double-click on the edit box to bring up its property box. Click on the Styles tab, and check each of the following four options: Multi-line, Vertical Scroll, Border, and Read Only.

- Uncheck the AutoHScroll option.

- Delete the Cancel button by selecting the button with the mouse and pressing the Delete key.

- Resize and center the OK button at the bottom of the dialog box. Resize the dialog box and the edit box so that they look similar to the example shown in Figure 4.7.

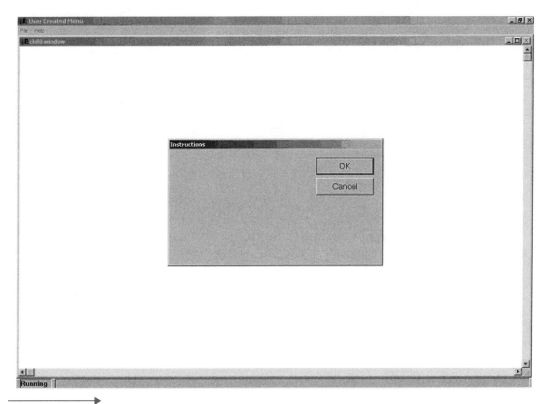

Figure 4.6   *Basic dialog box for instructions.*

Previously in Menu2, we stored our instructions in a character string, but a more elegant way is to store our instructions as a string in the resource script file and to load the string into a character string using the Win32 API function LoadString. The syntax for using LoadString is:

```
iret   = LoadString(handle to module with resource, &
             stringID, pointer to buffer with resource, &
             size of buffer)
```

Figure 4.7
*Edit box resized
and positioned on
dialog box.*

The Win32 API function GetModuleHandle is used to get the handle of the module containing the string resource. A NULL argument used with GetModuleHandle means that it returns a handle to the current application. The interface definitions for the LoadString and GetModuleHandle functions are contained in User32.mod and Kernel32.mod, respectively. We can either declare the two individual modules separately in our program or include a USE DFWIN statement to achieve the same result. Character strings can be displayed in edit boxes using the Dialog routine DLGSET as follows:

```
bret = DlgSet(dlg, Edit box identity, Character string
variable)
```

This versatile function and its inverse DLGGET can be used with a range of controls, and a complete description of their usage is given in the online *Programmers Guide*. We shall be looking at both of these functions in more detail in Chapter 5.

The subroutine Instructions in the file callback.f90 should be replaced with the following code:

```
subroutine Instructions
use dflib
use dflogm
use user32
use kernel32
implicit none
include 'resource.fd    '
type (dialog) dlg
logical(4) bret
integer(4) iret
integer Maxinput
character(512)    szbuffer
   Maxinput = 512
   iret  = LoadString(GetModuleHandle(NULL), &
           IDS_String1, szbuffer, MAXINPUT)
   bret = DLGINIT(IDD_Instructions,dlg)
   bret = DlgSet(dlg,IDC_Edit1, szbuffer )
   iret = DlgModal(dlg)
   call DlgUninit(dlg)
end subroutine Instructions
```

Finally, we need to create a string resource file. Select Resource from the Insert menu, choose String Table and click New. Double-click on the empty table, and a string property box will appear with the ID name IDS_String1.

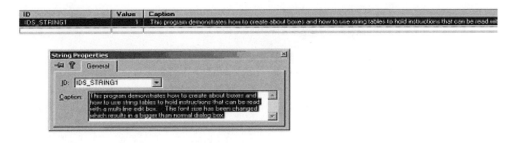

Figure 4.8 *Inserting a String into the string table.*

Enter the following string into the caption box, as shown in Figure 4.8:

```
This program demonstrates how to create dialog boxes and
how to use string tables to hold instructions that can be
read with a multi-line edit box. The font size has been
changed which results in a bigger than normal dialog box.
```

Compile and execute the program. Select Instructions from the Options menu. An instruction dialog box similar to the one shown in Figure 4.9 will be displayed.

What is the advantage in using this string table approach as compared with defining character strings as variables in our source code? Using character string resources makes life a lot easier when you want to translate your program into other languages. All the text used in your program can be kept in one file, the resource script. If the text in the resource script is translated into another language, all that is needed to create a foreign-language version of your program is to relink the program. This is much easier than translating by going through the source code of your program. However, if you are developing code for teaching purposes, the use of string tables rather than the traditional character string variables can make the code appear more

Figure 4.9
*The Instructions
dialog box as
displayed.*

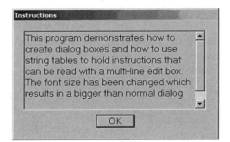

complicated. Hence, in the interest of clarity, in most examples we will use character string variables.

4.3   Using HTML files as Help files

Many commercial programs have help and tutorial files that are in the HyperText Markup Language (HTML) format and are read using a Web browser such as Netscape or Internet Explorer. Provided you have the ability to create files in HTML format, it is very straightforward to incorporate them into a QuickWin (or Win32) program. Here are the steps to follow:

- First, create a new QuickWin multiple-window application called Help. Then copy the three files, Main.f90, Menu.f90, and Callbacks.f90, from the Menu2 example in Chapter 3 into the project folder.

- In the Project menu, click Add to Project, and then choose Files. Select all three files (i.e., Main.f90, Menu.f90, and Callbacks.f90) from the Insert Files Into Project dialog box.

- Add a resource script file. Select the New option from the File menu. Click on the Files tab, select Resource Script, type in a suitable name in the File name space and click the OK button.

- Create an HTML file. Many word processors have the capability to save in HTML format. The process is straightforward. Enter text and diagrams as in a normal word processing application, and then use the SaveAs option to save the information in HTML format—it is that easy. Depending on the word processor, you should also be able to enter hyperlinks so that a user can jump to particular parts of the text. The file Help.htm, which accompanies the QuickWin application Help, was created using Microsoft Word 97, but you can use any program that can generate Web pages in HTML format.

- Copy the HTML file into your project workspace.

- Click Insert and select Resource. Choose HTML as the resource type and click Import.

- In the dialog box, set the file type to HTML, and select the appropriate HTML file. For this example, the file name is Help.htm.

- The default Developer Studio name for this resource is IDR_HTML1. If desired, this name can be changed in the Resources properties box, as shown in Figure 4.10.

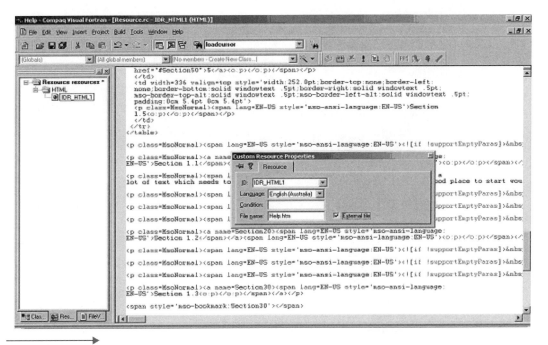

Figure 4.10   *HTML text format of the Help file as it appears to the program developer.*

We need a small amount of code to launch a Web browser and read our HTML file.

In the file menu.f90, add the following lines of code:

```
external help
bret = appendmenuqq(2, $MENUENABLED, 'help...'C, help )
```

In the file callbacks.f90, insert the following subroutine:

```
subroutine Help
   use dflib
   use dfwin
   implicit none
   integer(4) iret
   iret = WinExec('Explorer.exe  help.htm'C,SW_MAXIMIZE)
end Subroutine Help
```

Compile and execute the program. You should obtain a screen similar to that shown in Figure 4.11 when you select the Help item from the Options menu. HTML Help files are easier to create than a Windows Help file, but large HTML files can be much slower than an equivalent Windows Help file. HTML files do not support pop-up help boxes, but they are portable

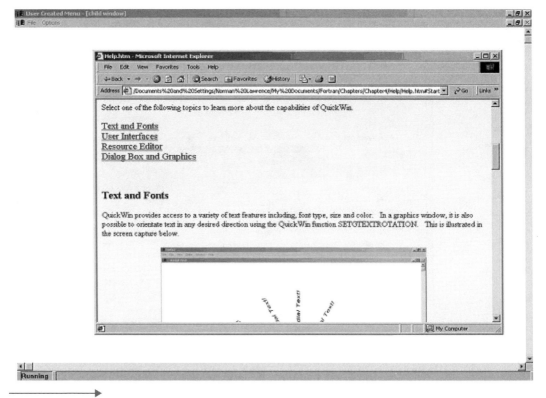

Figure 4.11   *Help file as displayed to the user.*

across most operating systems. Later on in Chapter 14, we will look at how to create the traditional Windows Help files using Rich Text File (RTF) format and the Help compiler that comes with CVF.

4.4   Using icons and bitmaps

We are going to build an About box application, which will use static text controls to display text information about the program and picture boxes to display an icon, a bitmap, and a line. As we shall discover shortly, with the Resource Editor it is easy to create or import icons and bitmaps for our application.

- First, create a new QuickWin multiple-window application called About. Then copy the three files—Main.f90, Menu.f90, and Callbacks.f90—from the Menu2 example in Chapter 3 into the Project folder.

- In the Project menu, click Add to Project and then choose Files. Select all three files (i.e., Main.f90, Menu.f90, and Callbacks.f90) from the Insert Files Into Project dialog box.

- Add a resource script file. Select the New option in the File menu. Click on the Files tab, select Resource Script, type in a suitable name in the File name space, and click the OK button.

- Click on the Insert menu item, and select Resource. Click on Dialog, and select New.

- Double-click on the dialog box to open the Dialog Properties box. Change the ID name from IDD_Dialog1 to IDD_About and the caption from Dialog to About. Click on the tab More Styles and check the Center option.

We need to modify the menu item About so that it calls a subroutine to initiate the dialog box. In the line of code in the file menu.f90 that declares the external callback subroutines, insert the name About, and in the line of code referring to the menu item About, change the callback routine from WinAbout to About, as shown in the following code fragment:

```
external    Browse, Notes, Calculate, About
bret = appendmenuqq(2, $MENUENABLED, 'About...'C, About)
```

Finally, we need to add the subroutine About to initiate the dialog box to the file callbacks.f90.

```
subroutine About
use dflib
use dflogm
use dfwin
implicit none
include 'resource.fd    '
type (dialog) dlg
logical(4) bret
integer(4) iret
!   initialize dialog box
   bret = DLGINIT(IDD_About,dlg)
   iret = DlgModal(dlg)
   call DlgUninit(dlg)
end subroutine About
```

Compile and execute the program. Click on About in the Options menu and the screen should be similar to that shown in Figure 4.12.

For our About dialog box, we will place three picture box controls—one at the top left-hand corner, one in the middle, and the third at the bottom

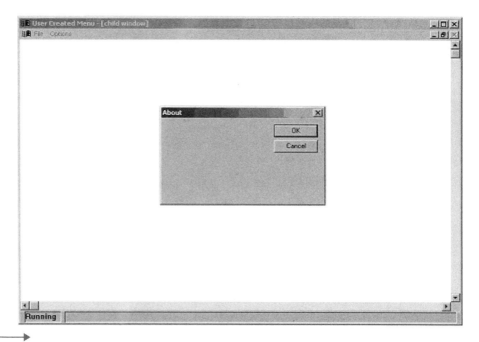

Figure 4.12 *Basic About dialog box.*

right-hand corner of the dialog box, as shown in Figure 4.13. To put picture box controls on the dialog box, hold down the left mouse button over the picture box control in the toolbox and drag it onto the dialog box. By default, the picture boxes are created as being of type Frame, and we need to reset this property according to our needs. First, click on the picture box at the top left-hand corner of the dialog box. The control should become highlighted, and a set of eight resizing rectangles appears, one at each corner and one in the middle of each side. Sometimes the dialog box is highlighted

Figure 4.13
Adding controls to the About dialog box.

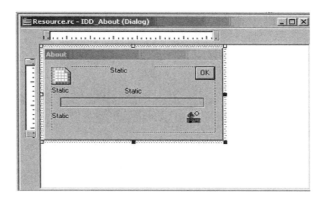

Figure 4.14
*Picture properties
box.*

instead of the control. If this occurs, try placing the mouse cursor on the
black line forming the side of the box and click the left mouse button.

The control can now be resized as required. Either click the right mouse
button and select Properties from the pop-up menu, or double-click the
left mouse button. You should be presented with a properties box like the
one shown in Figure 4.14. Select Icon from the Type combo box. For the
picture box in the middle of the dialog box, select Frame, and set the color
to Black. Click the Styles tab and check the Sunken option. Then resize
this picture box so that it is almost as wide as the dialog box, and reduce its
height until it becomes a line. For the picture box at the bottom right-
hand corner, set its Type to Bitmap. Finally, place four static text controls
on the dialog box, as shown in Figure 4.13. We will not need the Cancel
button; delete the Cancel button by selecting the button with the mouse
and pressing the Delete key. The OK button should be resized, as shown in
Figure 4.13.

Click on to the top static text control and change the text from static to
"About Version 1.0." Select the option Center in Dialog from the Layout
menu. Click Horizontal to have the control automatically centered in the
dialog box. Change the text in the static control immediately below to read
"Copyright 2001" and center the control. The static control immediately to
the left of the copyright message should be modified to "Smiley Soft."
Finally, type the following text into the forth static control: "This program
is purely for demonstration purposes. It illustrates how to use dialog controls in QuickWin." The static text control should be resized so that the text
can fit into three lines. In the dialog box properties, click on the Styles tab
and uncheck the System menu option. Select the Test option in the Layout
menu. Your dialog box should look like the one shown in Figure 4.15.

4.4.1   Creating icons

Our next task is to use the Resource Editor to create an icon and a bitmap
to insert into the appropriate picture boxes. First, we will create an icon.

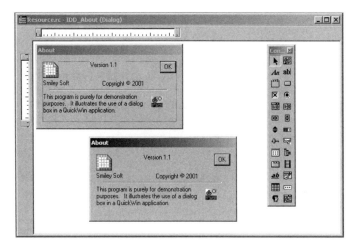

Figure 4.15
The About box
nearing
completion.

From the Insert menu click on Resource. Choose Icon and click on New. We are going to create an icon using the Icon Editor. The screen should now look something like that shown in Figure 4.16. The icon is to be created in a 32-by-32 square using the brushes and color palette on the right. To create a smiley face, you will need to create a black outline circle and yellow fill this circle. Circles are drawn using the ellipse shape. Draw

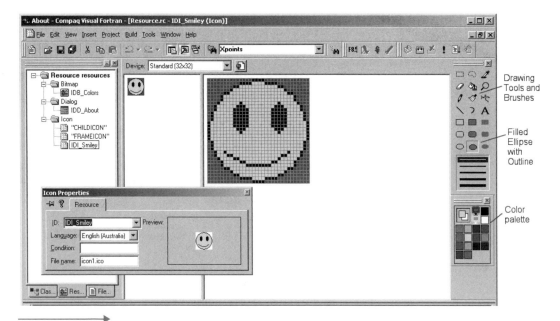

Figure 4.16   *Creating an icon.*

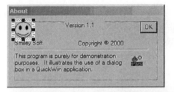

Figure 4.17
Select the smiley icon for display in this picture box.

eyes and a mouth. Move the cursor off the icon and double-click the left mouse button. The property box for the icon should appear and display the icon as IDI_ICON1. Change the icon name to something more meaningful, like IDI_Smiley (see Figure 4.16). If you already have a suitable icon, you should choose Import from the Insert menu to load your icon into the resource file.

Now we need to associate the smiley icon with the appropriate picture box in our About dialog box. In the Resources window, open the dialog (if it is not already open) and double-click on the icon with the name IDD_About next to it. The About dialog box should appear. Open up the properties box of the picture box in the top left corner by double-clicking the left mouse button when the cursor is over the picture box (see Figure 4.17). In the Image combo box, choose the icon IDI_Smiley. Again, it is probably useful at this stage to use the Test option in the Layout menu, just to see what the dialog box will look like.

4.4.2 Creating bitmaps

The process for creating a bitmap is similar to that used for creating an icon.

- Select Resource in the Insert menu.

- Choose Bitmap and click the New button.

- Draw the bitmap. The bitmap created for this example (see Figure 4.18) is named IDB_Colors.

- Open the properties box for the picture control box in the bottom right-hand corner of the dialog box. From the Image combobox, select IDB_Colors or any other bitmap you want to use.

Figure 4.18
Creating bitmap
IDB_Colors.

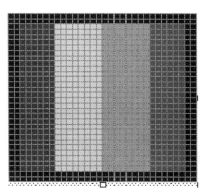

Tip: When working with bitmaps and icons in their respective editors, the Image menu appears in Developer Studio. This menu provides a number of useful image editing options, including rotation of the image, color adjustment, and grid settings.

The final version of the About dialog box is shown in Figure 4.19.

The default icon that appears at the top of the main window frame and child window can be easily changed. Create two icons in the Resource file and name them "Childicon" and "Framicon." It is important to include the quotes in the name. When you compile the program, QuickWin will use these two icons to replace the default icons. In addition, QuickWin uses the first icon with an IDI_ identity in the Resource file as the icon to display with the program's EXE file. Look at the icons in the Resource file for About2 and the About2.exe file in the debug directory to see how simple it is.

4.5   Adding version information

It is very simple to include version information with a QuickWin program. First, select Resource from the Insert menu, choose Version, and click New.

Figure 4.19
The finished About
dialog box.

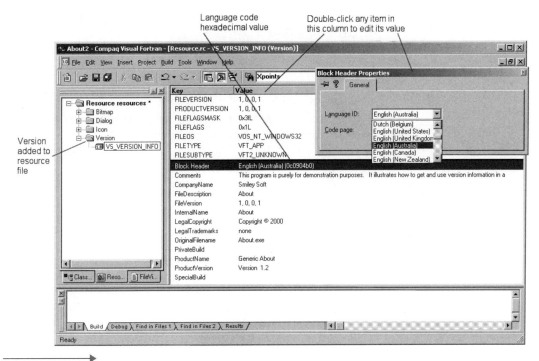

Figure 4.20   *Editing the block header properties in version information and setting the language to English (Australia).*

You will be presented with a version information table containing multiple rows and two column headings—Key and Value—as shown in Figure 4.20. By double-clicking any item in the Value column, you can edit its value to reflect the appropriate program specification. A program user will be able to read this version information later by right-clicking on the program exe file, choosing Properties, and selecting the Version tab.

The question that follows from our ability to enter and store version information in a QuickWin program is: Can we display that information in an about box? The answer is yes, but it involves using some Win32 API functions. All Fortran Win32 generic programs created automatically by the Developer Studio Wizard have an About dialog box that provides version information. All we need to do is use that code in our QuickWin applications. The function used by the Wizard is VersionQueryValue, which is a Fortran wrapper around the Win32 API function VerQueryValue. The VersionQueryValue is used as follows:

```
bRet  = VersionQueryValue(lpstrVffInfo,LOC(szGetName), &
        LOC(lpVersion),LOC(uVersionLen))
```

Chapter 4

where:

- lpstrVffInfo is the address of the buffer for the version resource. It is a pointer to the buffer containing the version-information resource returned by the GetFileVersionInfo function.

- szGetName is the address of the value to retrieve. It is a pointer to a zero-terminated string specifying which version-information value to retrieve. The string must consist of names separated by backslashes (\), and it can have one of three possible forms (check information on Win32 API function VerQueryValue). We will use the following form:

```
\StringFileInfo\lang-codepage\string-name
```

lang-codepage is a hexadecimal value that depends on the language being used. For example, with English (Australia) we would use

```
szGetName = "\\StringFileInfo\\0c0904b0\\"C
```

Note: The double backwards slashes are used in the text string so they will not be interpreted as escape characters.

The language code hexadecimal value is given in the Version Information on the block header row, as shown in Figure 4.21.

The string name must be one of the 12 names contained in the left-hand column underneath the block header in the version information (see Figure 4.20). These 12 names are CompanyName, FileDescription, FileVersion, InternalName, LegalCopyright, OriginalFilename, ProductName, ProductVersion, Comments, Legal-Trademarks, PrivateBuild, and SpecialBuild.

Figure 4.21
About dialog box as it appears to the developer, showing version information string names in static control text boxes.

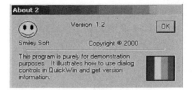

Figure 4.22
About dialog box as it appears to the user.

The get file name string to retrieve the Company Name resource data would become:

```
szGetName = "\\StringFileInfo\\0c0904b0\\CompanyName"C
```

- lpVersion is the address of the buffer for the version value pointer.
- uVersionLen is the address of the buffer length in characters that will contain the requested version-information value.

Before using VersionQueryValue, it is necessary to first call the GetFile-VersionInfoSize function and then the GetFileVersionInfo function. Some Win32 routines are also used to allocate and deallocate memory. The revised version of the subroutine About is listed next. You will need to modify the About dialog box by adding an extra static text box, renaming these four static controls IDC_Version1 to IDC_Version4, and replacing the text in each control with the version string that you want to obtain. In this example, the four strings are: CompanyName, ProductVersion, LegalCopyright, and Comments. Refer to Figure 4.21 for their location in the About dialog box and Figure 4.22 for how the box appears to the user.

```
subroutine About
use dflib
use dflogm
use dfwin
implicit none
include 'resource.fd   '
! Variables
type (dialog) dlg
logical(4) bret
integer(4) iret
integer    dwVerHnd
integer    dwVerInfoSize
integer    uVersionLen
integer    i, length
integer(4) lpstrVffInfo
integer(4) hMem
character(256) szFullPath
character(256) szResult
```

```
character(256) szGetName
character(256) lpversion
!  initialize dialog box
   bret = DLGINIT(IDD_About,dlg)
!  Get version information from the application
   iret = GetModuleFileName (null, szFullPath, &
                               len(szFullPath))
   dwVerInfoSize = GetFileVersionInfoSize(szFullPath, &
                                     LOC(dwVerHnd))
   if (dwVerInfoSize /= 0) then
!     If we were able to get the information, process it:
      hMem = GlobalAlloc(GMEM_MOVEABLE, INT(dwVerInfoSize))
      lpstrVffInfo  = GlobalLock(hMem)
      iret = GetFileVersionInfo (szFullPath, dwVerHnd, &
            dwVerInfoSize, lpstrVffInfo)
!     Cycle through the dialog items that we want to
!     insert version information into:
      do i = IDC_Version1, IDC_Version4
          iret = DlgGetChar(Dlg, i,szResult)
          length = len(trim(adjustL(szResult)))
          szResult(length+1:length+3) = "\\"C
          szGetName = "\\StringFileInfo\\0c0904b0\\"C
          iret =lstrcat(szGetName,szResult)
          bRet  =  VersionQueryValue(lpstrVffInfo,&
            LOC(szGetName),LOC(lpVersion),LOC(uVersionLen))
          if ( bRet /= 0 ) then
!             Replace dialog item text with version info
              iret = lstrcpy(szResult,lpVersion)
              iret = DlgSet(Dlg, i,szResult)
          end if
      end do
      iret = GlobalUnlock(hMem)
      iret = GlobalFree(hMem)
   end if
   iret = DlgModal(dlg)
   call DlgUninit(dlg)
end subroutine About
```

4.6   Using callback routines

So far in this chapter, we have created dialog boxes that required no user
input beyond clicking the OK button when the box was no longer required.
Often, we want to incorporate controls into our dialog boxes to provide the
user with options or to request information from the user. In such cases, we
need to write subroutines (usually referred to as *callback routines*) that will
act according to the input instructions provided by the user. This is

achieved using the function DLGSETSUB during the initializing process of the dialog box, as follows:

```
type (dialog) dlg
bret = DLGINIT(IDD_DIALOG1,dlg)
bret = DlgSetSub(dlg,IDC_SLIDER1,ShowColor)
iret = DlgModal(dlg)
```

In this code, ShowColor is the callback subroutine for a slider control named IDC_Slider1 that is attached to a dialog box called IDD_DIA-LOG1. Any changes to the position of the slider control can be detected in the subroutine ShowColor and the appropriate action taken.

Initial values of controls can be set using DLGSET. The use of this versatile function is illustrated in the following code fragment, which is used to set the min and max range of the control slider to 0 and 255, respectively. The slider starting position is set to 125, and the tick frequency of the scale is set as 35.

```
bret = DlgSet(dlg,IDC_SLIDER1, 255, DLG_RANGEMAX)
bret = DlgSet(dlg,IDC_SLIDER1, 0, DLG_RANGEMIN)
bret = DlgSet(dlg,IDC_SLIDER1, 125, DLG_POSITION )
bret = DlgSet(dlg,IDC_SLIDER1, 35, DLG_TICKFREQ)
```

The symbolic constants DLG_RANGEMAX, DLG_RANGEMIN, DLG_POSITION, and DLG_TICKFREQ are control indexes. The names are specific to a particular type of control. A full list is given in the online guide under control indexes and in the link to available indexes for each dialog control at the bottom of the control indexes page. It is not always necessary to specify a control index. For example, the code to set the initial value of an edit box with the name IDC_EDIT1 to 125 would be:

```
bret = DlgSet(dlg,IDC_EDIT1, "125")
```

4.6.1   Colors example

The Colors program is a simple dialog box application that has three slider controls to set the red, green, and blue values between 0 and 255. A rectangle on the screen is filled with a color that corresponds to the RGB value set by the slider controls. Edit boxes are used to display the current values for red, green, and blue. A screen capture from the program is shown in Figure 4.23. Two separate callback responses are available for the first edit box. One acts when the value in the first edit box is changed and adjusts the slider position and color accordingly. The other acts when the edit box gains focus and does nothing more exciting than produce a beep sound. Check it

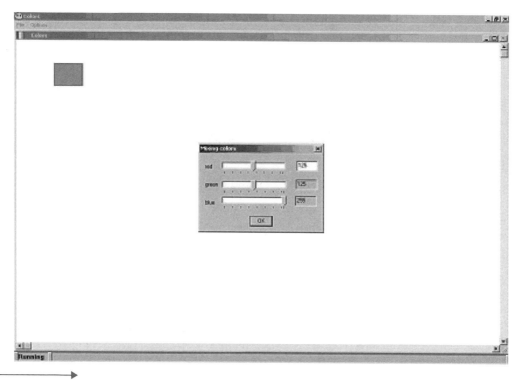

Figure 4.23   *Colors program shows dialog box with slider controls for setting color values.*

out by tabbing around the controls in the dialog box or clicking on the edit box. The remaining two edit boxes are read only. This is a useful property if you only want to provide information to the user.

We start by creating a QuickWin project named Colors and then:

- Copy the three Fortran free format files, named main.f90, menu.f90, and callbacks.f90, from the Menu2 example in Chapter 3 to the project.

- Add a resource script file named Colors to the project.

- Insert a dialog box into the project.

- Using the Resource Editor, position three slider controls and three edit boxes, as shown in Figure 4.24. Delete the Cancel button and center the OK button at the bottom of the box.

- In the property box for each of the edit boxes, click on the Styles tab, and check Number and Border. Check the Read-only option for edit controls 2 and 3.

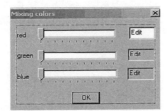

Figure 4.24
Colors dialog box.

- Click on the Styles tab in the property box for each of the slider controls. In the combo boxes, ensure that the option for Orientation is set to horizontal and that for Point it is set to bottom/right. Check the Tick marks, Auto ticks, and Enable selection options.

Copy the appropriate code from Menu2, or a similar program, and paste it into the files main.f90 and menu.f90. Edit the menu file so that the option file provides a menu item named Colors with a callback routine mixcolors as follows.

```
external mixcolors
bret = appendmenuqq(2,$MENUENABLED,'Colors...'C,
mixcolors )
```

In the file callbacks.f90, add the following subroutine to initialize the dialog box and set the control properties:

```
subroutine mixcolors
use dflib
use dflogm
use dfwin
implicit none
include 'resource.fd   '
type (dialog) dlg
logical(4) bret
integer(4) iret,oldcolor
integer(2)  x1, y1, x2, y2
external ShowColor
   bret = DLGINIT(IDD_DIALOG1,dlg)
   bret = DlgSet(dlg,IDC_EDIT1, "125")
   bret = DlgSet(dlg,IDC_EDIT2, "125")
   bret = DlgSet(dlg,IDC_EDIT3, "255")
   x1 = 80; y1 = 50
   x2 = 140; y2 = 100
   oldcolor = rgb(125,125,255)
   iret = SETCOLORRGB(oldcolor)
   iret = RECTANGLE( $GFILLINTERIOR , x1, y1, x2, y2 )
!  Set maximum values for slider range
   bret = DlgSet(dlg,IDC_SLIDER1, 255, DLG_RANGEMAX)
```

```
      bret = DlgSet(dlg,IDC_SLIDER2, 255, DLG_RANGEMAX)
      bret = DlgSet(dlg,IDC_SLIDER3, 255, DLG_RANGEMAX)
!   Set minimum values for slider range
      bret = DlgSet(dlg,IDC_SLIDER1, 0, DLG_RANGEMIN)
      bret = DlgSet(dlg,IDC_SLIDER2, 0, DLG_RANGEMIN)
      bret = DlgSet(dlg,IDC_SLIDER3, 0, DLG_RANGEMIN)
!   Set intervals between the scale ticks
      bret = DlgSet(dlg,IDC_SLIDER1, 35, DLG_TICKFREQ)
      bret = DlgSet(dlg,IDC_SLIDER2, 35, DLG_TICKFREQ)
      bret = DlgSet(dlg,IDC_SLIDER3, 35, DLG_TICKFREQ)
!   Set initial starting values for sliders
      bret = DlgSet(dlg,IDC_SLIDER1, 125, DLG_POSITION )
      bret = DlgSet(dlg,IDC_SLIDER2, 125, DLG_POSITION )
      bret = DlgSet(dlg,IDC_SLIDER3, 255, DLG_POSITION )
!   define the callback subroutine for each control
      bret = DlgSetSub(dlg,IDC_SLIDER1,ShowColor)
      bret = DlgSetSub(dlg,IDC_SLIDER2,ShowColor)
      bret = DlgSetSub(dlg,IDC_SLIDER3,ShowColor)
      bret = DlgSetSub(dlg,IDC_EDIT1,ShowColor,DLG_CHANGE)
      bret = DlgSetSub(dlg,IDC_EDIT1,ShowColor,DLG_GAINFOCUS)
      iret = DlgModal(dlg)
      call DlgUninit(dlg)
end subroutine mixcolors
```

All callback routines have the same interface as that contained in the subroutine ShowColor:

```
subroutine  ShowColor(dlg,control_name, callbacktype)
```

The argument *dlg* is a variable of derived-type DIALOG. The control that caused the callback can be identified by comparing the variable *control_name* with known control IDs using a Select case construct. The argument *callbacktype* is useful when you want to distinguish between two or more triggering events (e.g., a click and a double-click) or whenever a change in the control value occurs. The type of callback can be tested against symbolic integer constants such as DLG_SELCHANGE, DLG_CLICKED, DLG_CHANGE, or DLG_DBLCLICK. Have a look at the section title "Available Indexes for Each Dialog Control" in the online *Programmer's Guide*. Thus, in a callback routine it would be possible to have more than one callback response for a control. A typical usage would be:

```
Case(IDC_EDIT1)
If (callbacktype == DLG_CHANGE) then
    ! insert code to act on value change
end if
if(callbacktype == DLG_GAINFOCUS) then
    call beep(200,200)
end if
```

Some controls have a default Index name. For example, the default for an edit box is DLG_CHANGE. So when using DLGSETSUB to connect the control with its callback routine and the control's two callback responses, we would need to explicitly declare both control indexes:

```
bret = DlgSetSub(dlg,IDC_EDIT1,ShowColor,DLG_CHANGE )
bret = DlgSetSub(dlg,IDC_EDIT1,ShowColor,DLG_GAINFOCUS )
```

In this code fragment from the program Colors, two different callback responses for the edit box would be invoked, depending on whether a change occurred to the contents of the edit box or the edit box had gained focus. For the latter case, the system would beep when the edit box received the focus. Users can demonstrate these two different callback responses in the program Colors by either clicking on the top edit box or by entering data into the top edit box. The following subroutine should also be entered into callbacks.f90:

```
subroutine  ShowColor(dlg,control_name, callbacktype)
use dflib
use dflogm
use dfwin
implicit none
include 'resource.fd    '
type (dialog) dlg
logical(4) bret
integer(4) control_name,newcolor
integer(4) iposition1,iposition2,iposition3
integer(4) callbacktype,iret
character(8) text
integer(2) x1, y1, x2, y2
   x1 = 80; y1 = 50
   x2 = 140; y2 = 100
   select case(control_name)
     case(IDC_SLIDER1)
     bret = dlgget(dlg, IDC_SLIDER1, iposition1,&
                DLG_POSITION )
     bret = dlgget(dlg, IDC_SLIDER2, iposition2,&
                DLG_POSITION )
     bret = dlgget(dlg, IDC_SLIDER3, iposition3,&
                DLG_POSITION )
     newcolor = rgb(iposition1,iposition2,iposition3)
     iret = SETCOLORRGB(newcolor)
     iret = RECTANGLE( $GFILLINTERIOR , x1, y1, x2, y2 )
     write(text,'(I4)') iposition1
     bret = DLGSET (dlg,IDC_EDIT1, text)
     write(text,'(I4)') iposition2
     bret = DLGSET (dlg,IDC_EDIT2, text)
     write(text,'(I4)') iposition3
```

```
      bret = DLGSET (dlg,IDC_EDIT3, text)
   case(IDC_SLIDER2)
   . . . ! code omitted, similar to IDC_SLIDER1
   case(IDC_SLIDER3)
   . . . ! code similar to similar to IDC_SLIDER1
   case(IDC_EDIT1)
   if(callbacktype ==DLG_CHANGE) then
      bret = dlgget(dlg, IDC_EDIT1,text)
      if(text == " ") then
         text = "0"
         bret = dlgset(dlg, IDC_EDIT1,text)
      end if
      read(text,*)iposition1
      if(iposition1 <= 255) then
      bret = DlgSet(dlg,IDC_SLIDER1,iposition1,&
                     DLG_POSITION )
      else
      iposition1 = 255
      bret = DlgSet(dlg,IDC_SLIDER1,iposition1,&
                     DLG_POSITION )
      write(text,'(I4)') iposition1
      bret = DlgSet(dlg,IDC_EDIT1, text)
      end if
      bret = dlgget(dlg, IDC_SLIDER1, iposition1)
      bret = dlgget(dlg, IDC_SLIDER2, iposition2)
      bret = dlgget(dlg, IDC_SLIDER3, iposition3)
      newcolor = rgb(iposition1,iposition2,iposition3)
      iret = SETCOLORRGB(newcolor)
      iret = RECTANGLE( $GFILLINTERIOR , x1, y1, x2, y2 )
      end if
      if(callbacktype ==DLG_GAINFOCUS) then
         call beep(200,200)
      end if
   end select
end subroutine  ShowColor
```

4.7   What is next?

In Chapter 5, we will look at graphic coordinate systems and learn how to develop our own fill patterns for graphic shapes. We will also create dialog boxes that increase the selection choices available to the user.

5

Graphics

5.1 Coordinate systems

QuickWin graphics lets you use one of three alternative coordinate systems to describe how to place graphical entities such as lines, geometric shapes, and graphical text on the screen. The three coordinate systems are usually referred to as:

1. Physical coordinates, which refer to pixels on the computer screen

2. Viewport coordinates, which represent the pixels within the current viewport

3. Window coordinates, which are used to define objects or events that occur in a World coordinate space system. Window coordinates are floating-point numbers. The units for a Window coordinate system depend on what is being drawn. For example, a drawing of a house may use meters or feet, whereas a graph showing the variation of air temperature over a 24-hour period would have temperature on one axis and time on the other axis.

The relationship between the three coordinate systems is illustrated in Figure 5.1. The use of each of the three coordinate systems will be illustrated through sample applications.

5.1.1 Physical (device) coordinates

A physical coordinate system refers to the pixel (picture elements) dimensions in the x and y directions of the screen. The display screen of a computer has an integer-based coordinate axis system with an origin (0,0) located at the top left-hand corner of the screen. Maximum display capabilities depend on the monitor type and screen size. Until recently, most monitors had display capabilities of 640 pixels in the horizontal direction and

Figure 5.1
*QuickWin
coordinate
systems.*

World coordinate space

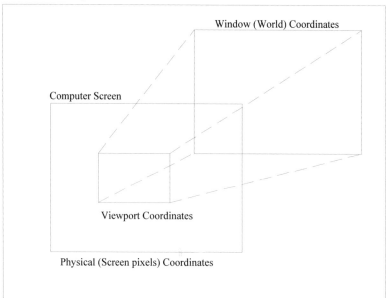

480 in the vertical direction. Monitor physical sizes are increasing, and the more common screen pixel dimensions are currently 800 by 600 or 1,024 by 768. Since display screen origins start at (0,0), a screen with a resolution of 800 by 600 would have a maximum addressable x pixel at 799 and y pixel coordinate of 599.

In some applications, it is useful to have the origin (0,0) translated to another location, perhaps to the center of the screen. Supposing in the screen display resolution of Figure 5.2 that we wanted to have our x-axis range from –400 to +399 and our y-axis to range from –300 to +299. We can do this quite easily by remapping any given pair of coordinates into an equivalent pixel location. Any given value of x and y in our new coordinate system with the origin (0,0) at the center of the screen would be mapped into screen pixel coordinates as follows:

xpixel = x + 400 and *ypixel* = y + 300

Hence (0,0) in our new system is the screen pixel equivalent of (400, 300) and (–400,–300) is the pixel equivalent of (0,0).

QuickWin has a function, SETVIEWORG, that does this for us. Here is how we use the SETVIEWORG function to set our origin in the center:

```
Type (xycoord) oldorigin
Call SetViewOrg( int2(400), int2(300), oldorigin)
```

Figure 5.2
*Screen physical
coordinates.*

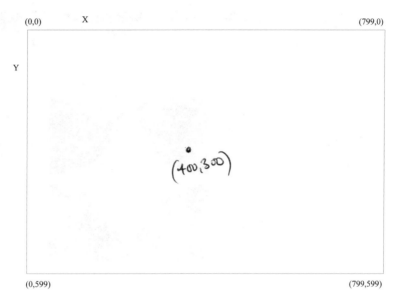

After the call to SETVIEWORG, we can use our new coordinates of −400 to 399 in x and −300 to 299 in y with any of the graphical drawing functions, such as MOVETO, LINETO, RECTANGLE, and so on.

Another useful feature of QuickWin is the function SETCLIPRGN, which defines a rectangle on the screen called a *clipping region*. All graphical drawing is limited to this clipping region. The SETCLIPRGN function does not change the screen physical coordinate system. It masks any graphics output to the screen that has coordinates outside the rectangle defined by the clipping region. The effects are demonstrated by the program Clips. Figure 5.3 is a screen shot from the program Clips that shows the effect of a clipping region on four circles.

In Clips, the origin has been set to be in the center of an 800-by-600 screen by the following line of code in main.f90:

```
call SETVIEWORG(INT2(400), INT2(300), xy)
```

This creates an axis that ranges from −400 to + 399 in x and −300 to +299 in y and a zero that is in the center of the screen. The subroutine draw in the Callbacks.f90 file is used to draw four circles of 260-pixel diameter with centers located at $x = −140$ and $y = −140$, $x = 140$ and $y = −140$, $x = −140$ and $y = 140$, and $x = 140$ and $y = 140$. The circles are filled using blue as the fill color. The clipping region is defined in pixels in relation to the screen coordinate system with (0,0) starting at the top left-hand corner. Thus the viewport coordinates $x = −140$ and $y = −140$ are converted into

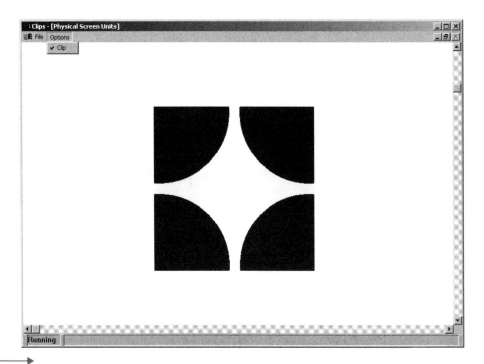

Figure 5.3   *Clips program showing effect of SETCLIPRGN on four circles.*

clipping region coordinates by adding the *x* and *y* offsets (i.e., *x* = −140 + 400 = 260 and *y* = −140 + 300 = 160). This is the code used in subroutine Draw:

```
subroutine Draw
use dflib
implicit none
integer(2) status, x1, y1, x2, y2
integer(4) oldcolor, iret
type ( xycoord ) xy
   call CLEARSCREEN($GCLEARSCREEN)
   oldcolor = SETCOLORRGB(#FF0000) !blue
   x1 = 10;   y1 = 10; x2 = 270; y2 = 270
   status = ELLIPSE($GFILLINTERIOR, x1, y1, x2, y2)
   x1 = -10;   y1 = -10; x2 = -270; y2 = -270
   status = ELLIPSE($GFILLINTERIOR, x1, y1, x2, y2)
   x1 = 10;   y1 = -10; x2 = 270; y2 = -270
   status = ELLIPSE($GFILLINTERIOR, x1, y1, x2, y2)
   x1 = -10;   y1 = 10; x2 = -270; y2 = 270
   status = ELLIPSE($GFILLINTERIOR, x1, y1, x2, y2)
end subroutine Draw
```

The subroutine Clip, which is also in the Callbacks.f90 file, tests the checked state of the menu item Clip.

- If the menu item is unchecked, it will be checked, and the clipping region is set to cover a rectangular area with an upper left origin at $x = 240$ and $y = 160$. The lower right corner of the clipping region is at $x = 540$ and $y = 440$. A call is then made to subroutine Draw.

- If the menu item is checked, it will be unchecked and the clipping region set to cover a rectangular with an upper left origin at $x = 0$ and $y = 0$. The bottom right corner of the clipping region is at $x = 799$ and $y = 599$. A call is then made to subroutine Draw.

```
subroutine Clip(checked)
use dfwin
use dflib
external Draw
logical checked, bret
integer(4) iret,unit
   iret = FOCUSQQ (4)
   if (checked) then
       bret = MODIFYMENUFLAGSQQ(2,1,$MENUUNCHECKED)
       call SETCLIPRGN( INT2(0),INT2(0),INT2(799),&
                    INT2(599))
   else
       bret = MODIFYMENUFLAGSQQ(2,1,$MENUCHECKED)
       call SETCLIPRGN( INT2(240),INT2(160),INT2(540),&
                    INT2(440))
   end if
     call draw
end subroutine Clip
```

Remember: Functions used for drawing lines, ellipses, and so on use the redefined coordinate system based on the call to SETVIEWORG, but the clipping region is always based on screen pixels (0,0) at the top left corner of the screen. This must be factored into the SETCLIPRGN coordinates by the offset value used in SETVIEWORG.

Note: In this example, the origin has been set to correspond to the center of an 800 × 600 screen. This is very restrictive if your screen resolution is different. A more elegant way would be to test for the current display resolution using the Win32 API function GetDeviceCaps. We will use this function in later chapters, and you may wish to modify the Clips program to test for the display resolution. In this way, the program will always have an axis origin that is in the center of the screen.

5.1.2   Viewport coordinates

A viewport is a graphical area of the screen that you can draw in using graphical functions such as LINETO and write to using the OUTGTEXT function. By default, the viewport coordinates have a one-to-one correspondence with the physical screen coordinates; therefore, the viewport occupies the entire screen's available display space. However, the viewport dimensions can be redefined so that the viewport occupies only a part of the available screen space. The location of the viewport on the screen is defined in physical screen coordinates (i.e., pixels) using the following command:

```
CALL SETVIEWPORT (x1, y1, x2, y2)
```

The variables $x1$, $y1$ are integers (2) for the upper-left corner of the viewport and $x2$, $y2$ are integers (2) for the lower-right corner of the viewport. All graphical functions will be drawn in the viewport area, which will have an origin of (0,0) at its top left corner, with an x pixel dimension of ($x2 - x1$) and a y pixel dimension of ($y2 - y1$). In one sense, the SETVIEWPORT has the same effect as SETVIEWORG and SETCLIPRGN. That is, it specifies a limited area of the screen just like SETCLIPRGN, and it sets the viewport origin to be at the upper-left corner of the region. It is also special because, as illustrated in Figure 5.1, the Window (World) coordinate system is mapped into viewport space. All the standard graphics functions, such as LINETO, RECTANGLE, ELLIPSE, ARC, and so on are integer based and work in either viewport or physical coordinates.

Straight lines are normally drawn solid, but the subroutine SETLINE-STYLE can be called to change the way a line is drawn. Calls to SETLINE-STYLE affect only the drawing of straight lines, as in LINETO, POLYGON, and RECTANGLE. They have no effect on the drawing of curved lines, as in ARC, ELLIPSE, or PIE.

```
integer(2) mask
CALL SETLINESTYLE (mask)
```

A hexadecimal mask value is passed as the argument for the SETLINE-STYLE function, which produces lines that cover a certain percentage of the pixels in that line according to the mask value. The hexadecimal mask value FFFF represents a solid line, while a hexadecimal mask value 0000 would result in no line being drawn. All other mask values represent line styles that fall somewhere in between these two extremes of solid line and no line. The mask value is mapped to the line style that most closely corresponds to the percentage and configuration of bits set in the mask. Some typical line styles and their equivalent mask values are given in Table 5.1.

Table 5.1   *Line Styles and Mask Values*

Lines Style	Mask Value
Solid	#FFFF
Dash	#EEEE
Dash Dot	#ECEC
Dash Dot Dot	#ECCC
Dot Dot Dot	#AAAA

The current logical write mode is used when drawing lines with the LINETO, POLYGON, and RECTANGLE functions. The appearance of lines drawn on the display depends on the symbolic constant used by the SETWRITEMODE function:

```
integer(2) mode
result = SETWRITEMODE (mode)
```

Mode is one of the symbolic constants defined in Table 5.2.

Alternatively, a binary raster operation constant such as R2_MASKPEN can be used. These constants and their effects are described in the online documentation for the Win32 API function SetROP2

Table 5.2   *Symbolic Constants for the Function SETWRITEMODE*

Symbolic Constant	Effect
$GPSET	Causes lines to be drawn in the current graphics color (default).
$GAND	Causes lines to be drawn in the color that is the logical AND of the current graphics color and the current background color.
$GOR	Causes lines to be drawn in the color that is the logical OR of the current graphics color and the current background color.
$GPRESET	Causes lines to be drawn in the color that is the logical NOT of the current graphics color.
$GXOR	Causes lines to be drawn in the color that is the logical exclusive OR (XOR) of the current graphics color and the current background color.

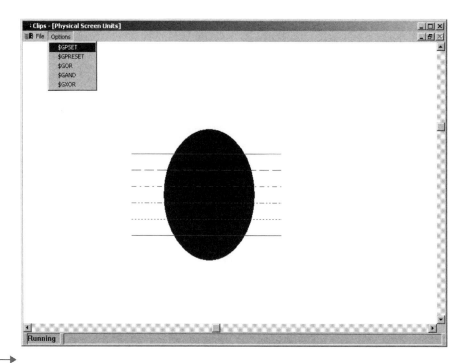

Figure 5.4   *Lines program showing the effects created using SETWRITEMODE and SETLINE-
STYLE functions.*

The effects of SETLINESTYLE and SETWRITEMODE are demonstrated by the program Lines. The program sets a viewport to the screen
pixel coordinates of $x = 300$ and $y = 200$ for the top left corner and $x = 600$
and $y = 500$ for the bottom right corner. A solid filled ellipse is drawn with
the viewport coordinates of top left corner coordinates $x = 80$ and $y = 30$.
The bottom right coordinates are $x = 250$ and $y = 270$. Lines are drawn in a
variety of line styles horizontally across the viewport. The ellipse is filled in
blue, and the lines are drawn in red. In the Options menu are menu items
corresponding to the SETWRITEMODE symbolic constants given in
Table 5.2. The effects created are illustrated in the screen capture of Figure
5.4.

This is the code used in the Lines program to draw the ellipse and lines:

```
subroutine Draw
use dflib
implicit none
integer(2) x1, y1, x2, y2
integer(2) iy, icount
integer(4) oldcolor, iret
integer(2), dimension(5) :: style
```

```
type ( xycoord ) xy
   style(1) = #FFFF
   style(2) = #EEEE
   style(3) = #ECEC
   style(4) = #ECCC
   style(5) = #AAAA
   icount = 1
   x1 = 80;   y1 = 30; x2 = 250; y2 = 270
   call CLEARSCREEN($GCLEARSCREEN)
   oldcolor = SETCOLORRGB(#FF0000) !blue
   iret = ELLIPSE($GFILLINTERIOR, x1, y1, x2, y2)
   oldcolor = SETCOLORRGB(#0000FF) !Red
   do iy = 75, 225, 30
      call SETLINESTYLE(style(icount))
      call MoveTo(20,iy,xy)
      iret = LineTo(300,iy)
   if(icount <5) then
      icount = icount+1
   else
        icount = 1
   end if
   end do
end subroutine Draw
```

5.1.3   Window coordinates

Using window coordinates allows graphics applications to be based on a coordinate system that is not limited to integer values or to number values based on the screen resolution. With window coordinates, the viewport is independent of the actual screen resolution, and floating-point values can be used to represent the dimensions of real-world objects. Furthermore, the window coordinates of a viewport can be changed to create the effect of zooming in or panning across an object. Window coordinates use the current viewport as their boundaries. Any graphics that are drawn to window coordinates beyond the boundaries of the window are clipped. By default, the current viewport is the same size as the entire screen. If you wish to use only a part of the screen, it is necessary to create the desired viewport area first with a call to SETVIEWPORT. The viewport is mapped to world coordinates using the SETWINDOW function, as follows:

```
logical(2) invert
real(8) wx1, wy1, wx2, wy2
result = SETWINDOW (invert, wx1, wy1, wx2, wy2)
```

The first argument is the *invert* flag, which, if it has a value .true., causes the lowest *y* value to be in the lower-left corner rather than the normal top-left corner. The minimum and maximum values of x and y that follow ($wx1$, $wy1$, $wx2$, $wy2$) are double-precision floating-point coordinates. All graphics routines that use Windows coordinates must be the double-precision coordinate type. Double-precision graphics functions are indicated by an underscore followed by a W, such as SETPIXEL_W, LINETO_W, and RECTANGLE_W.

Plots example

The Plots program illustrates the principles of working with window coordinates through a simple plotting program. It also presents a user with a selection of choices in a single dialog box. Referring to Figure 5.5, the program Plots contains a dialog that has:

- A group box named Plot Style that conveniently separates a set of plot choices

- A combo box containing a selection of plot functions

- Two edit boxes paired with spin buttons to set integer values for a and x

- A plot button to permit a variety of plots to be explored before finishing the session

The graphics capability of Plot can be determined from the screen capture shown in Figure 5.5. The option to draw points instead of lines provides an opportunity to show the use of subroutine GETVIEW-COORD_W. If we want to place a character x at a given set of coordinates x and y, one way would be to move to the given coordinates and write the letter x at that spot. A disadvantage of this approach is that the character x will be positioned in such a way that its lower left-hand edge is at the given coordinates. This does not look right, because what we really want is for the middle of the x to be located at the desired position. Another approach is to set the color of pixels around the given location to provide the desired symbol. In our application, we define a point, but it would be just as easy to define an x or any other symbol. The idea is straightforward; the challenge is that we need to mix our coordinate system, because the SETPIXELS routine works in pixel coordinates and our plotting window is in real-world floating-point coordinates. This is where GETVIEWCOORD_W is useful, because it translates physical (floating-point) window coordinates into viewport (pixel) coordinates. The inverse of this command, GETWIN-DOWCOORD, is useful when you want to translate screen pixel coordinates (perhaps from a mouse) into floating-point window coordinates. In the program the method used is to call a subroutine point with a pair of

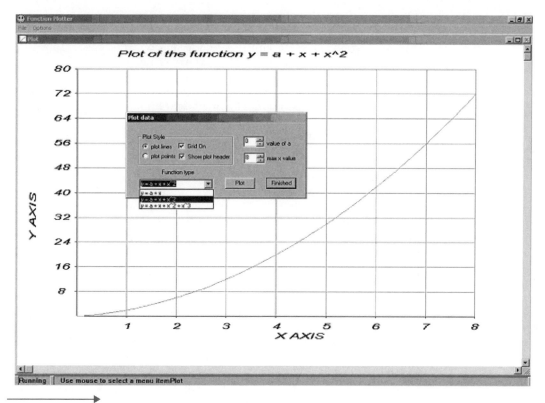

Figure 5.5 *Screen capture from the Plot program.*

floating-point x and y coordinates and to have returned a set of pixel coordinates (*xposition* and *yposition*)—and their corresponding color—that define a point (or any other desired symbol). The arrays of pixel locations and colors are passed to the SETPIXELS subroutine for drawing. The subroutine point is part of the file plot.f90:

```
subroutine point(x,y,xposition,yposition,color)
use dfwin
use dflib
implicit none
real(8) x, y
integer(2) xposition(9), yposition(9), xtemp,ytemp
integer(2) Icount,Iadd
integer(2) color(9)
type(xycoord) t
call GETVIEWCOORD_W(x,y,t)
   xtemp = t%xcoord
   ytemp = t%ycoord
   Iadd=-1
```

```
        do Icount = 1,3
           xposition(Icount) = xtemp+Iadd
           yposition(Icount) = ytemp-1
           xposition(Icount+3) = xtemp+Iadd
           yposition(Icount+3) = ytemp
           xposition(Icount+6) = xtemp+Iadd
           yposition(Icount+6) = ytemp+1
           color(Icount) = 13
           color(Icount+3) = 13
           color(Icount+6) = 13
           Iadd = Iadd+1
        end do
     end subroutine point
```

The plotting routine is straightforward. The window is defined in window coordinates using double-precision floating-point variables. The starting point for zero, y, is set at the bottom right-hand corner by setting the logical variable *invert* to TRUE in the function SETWINDOW. The syntax is:

```
iret = SETWINDOW(invert, xwmin, ywmin, xwmax, ywmax)
```

The graphical command MOVETO is used to move to a position without drawing a line, and the command LINETO draws a line between the present position and the final destination. The MOVETO also has a variable structure that retains the initial coordinates. All coordinate values need to be specified as real(8) variables, and all corresponding graphical routines end with W. The following code fragment illustrates the use of MOVETO_W and LINETO_W to create a line for the x axis and place tick marks on it.

```
!  draw X axis
call MOVETO_W(xmin, ymin, wxy)
iret = LineTo_W(xmax, ymin)
call MOVETO_W(xmin, ymin, wxy)
do i = xstep,xmax, xstep
     call MOVETO_W(dfloat(i), ymin, wxy)
     iret = LineTo_W(dfloat(i), ymin+tickY)
     iret = LineTo_W(dfloat(i), ymin-tickY)
end do
```

Text is positioned on the graph using the routines that we met in Chapter 2. The commands have been coded into the subroutine writeText shown; they allow the text to be oriented in any direction from a given x and y location.

```
subroutine writeText(ideg,xpos,ypos,text)
use dflib
implicit none
character(70) text
integer(4) ideg
real(8) xpos, ypos
type (wxycoord) wxy
   call SETGTEXTROTATION(ideg)
   call MOVETO_W(xpos, ypos, wxy)
   call OUTGTEXT(text)
end subroutine writeText
```

The dialog box is created as follows:

1.   Add a resource script file named Resource to a QuickWin project named Plots.

2.   Insert a dialog box into the project.

3.   Using Resource Editor, position two radio buttons, two check boxes, two edit boxes, two spin buttons, a group box, a static text control, and a combo drop-down box, as shown in Figure 5.6. Set the captions of each control to what is shown in Figure 5.6.

4.   Change the name of the cancel button to IDC_Plot and the caption to Plot data. Change the caption on the OK button to Finished. Position the buttons according to Figure 5.6.

Next, the properties are set:

1.   In the property boxes of the radio buttons, enter the ID names IDC_RADIO_Lines and IDC_RADIO_Points.

2.   In the property boxes of the check boxes, enter the ID names IDC_CHECK_GridOn and IDC_CHECK_Header.

3.   In the property box for each of the edit boxes, click on the Styles tab, and check the Number and Border options. Enter the ID names IDC_EDIT_a and IDC_EDIT_xmax.

Figure 5.6
Adding controls to the dialog box.

Figure 5.7
Setting the tab order for controls.

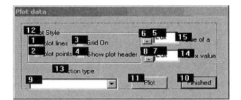

4.   In the property box for each of the spin buttons, click on the Styles tab, and check the Auto buddy and Set buddy integer options. Set the Alignment combo box to Right. Enter the ID names IDC_SPIN_a and IDC_SPIN_xmax.

Spin controls are usually associated with a "buddy" edit box or possibly a static control. We have already set the Auto buddy style in the properties box. By default, a spin control is associated with the control that immediately precedes it in the tab order; therefore, we need to reset the tab order. Select Tab Order in the Layout menu and set the tab order so each edit box precedes its buddy spin control in the tab order, as shown in Figure 5.7.

The coding in the subroutine graphtype to initialize the dialog box is straightforward. It shows how to set spin button values, put choices into a combo box, and set radio buttons. Some of the initial code is the same as used in the preceding example and has been omitted from the following listing, which goes into callbacks.f90:

```
subroutine graphtype
use global
...
external SetPlotData
!   set plot defaults
    xvalue = 12
    avalue = 0
    a = dfloat(avalue)
    xmax = dfloat(xvalue)
!   initialize dialog box
    bret = DLGINIT(IDD_PlotData,dlg)
!   set range and values of spin buttons
    bret = DlgSet(dlg,IDC_EDIT_a, '0')
    bret = DlgSet(dlg,IDC_SPIN_xmax, 25, DLG_RANGEMAX)
    bret = DlgSet(dlg,IDC_SPIN_xmax, 5, DLG_RANGEMIN)
    iret = dlgset(dlg,IDC_SPIN_xmax, xvalue )
    bret = DlgSet(dlg,IDC_SPIN_a, 100, DLG_RANGEMAX)
    bret = DlgSet(dlg,IDC_SPIN_a, 0, DLG_RANGEMIN)
    iret = dlgset(dlg,IDC_SPIN_a, avalue )
!   Set plot type choices in combo box
```

```
          bret = DlgSet(dlg,IDC_COMBO1, 3, DLG_NUMITEMS)
          bret = DlgSet(dlg,IDC_COMBO1, "y = a + x", 1)
          bret = DlgSet(dlg,IDC_COMBO1, "y = a + x + x^2", 2)
          bret = DlgSet(dlg,IDC_COMBO1, "y = a + x + x^2 + x^3", 3)
          bret = DLGSET (dlg,IDC_COMBO1,"y = a + x")
          PlotType = 1
!     Set plot styles in check boxes and radio button
          bret = DlgSet(dlg,IDC_CHECK_GridOn, .true.)
          bret = DlgSet(dlg,IDC_CHECK_Header, .true.)
          bret = DlgSet(dlg,IDC_RADIO_Lines, .true.)
          ShowTitle = .true.
          Lines = .true.
          ShowGrid = .true.
!     define the callback subroutine for each control
          bret = DlgSetSub(dlg,IDC_COMBO1,SetPlotData)
          bret = DlgSetSub(dlg,IDC_CHECK_GridOn,SetPlotData)
          bret = DlgSetSub(dlg,IDC_CHECK_Header,SetPlotData)
          bret = DlgSetSub(dlg,IDC_RADIO_Lines,SetPlotData)
          bret = DlgSetSub(dlg,IDC_RADIO_Points,SetPlotData)
          bret = DlgSetSub(dlg,IDC_EDIT_xmax,SetPlotData)
          bret = DlgSetSub(dlg,IDC_SPIN_xmax,SetPlotData)
          bret = DlgSetSub(dlg,IDC_SPIN_a,SetPlotData)
          bret = DlgSetSub(dlg,IDOK,SetPlotData)
          bret = DlgSetSub(dlg,IDC_Plot,SetPlotData)
          iret = DlgModal(dlg)
          call DlgUninit(dlg)
          call Drawit
end subroutine graphtype
```

The subroutine SetPlotData contains the callback routines for the controls. The global logical variables are set according to states of the radio buttons and check buttons. The plot type depends on the selection made in the combo box, and the plot x range and the value for a on the y axis are set according to the spin buttons. The plot button (IDC_Plot) is used to call the plotting subroutine Drawit, and the finished button (IDOK) is called when the user wants to end the plotting session.

```
subroutine  SetPlotData(dlg,control_name, callbacktype)
use dflib
use dflogm
use dfwin
use global
implicit none
include 'resource.fd   '
type (dialog) dlg
logical bret
integer control_name,oldcolor
```

```
integer iposition1,iposition2,iposition3
integer callbacktype,hdc,iret,xvalue,avalue
integer local_callbacktype
character(40) string
logical retlog
logical checked_state
   local_callbacktype = callbacktype
   select case(control_name)
      case(IDC_COMBO1)
      bret = DLGGET (dlg,IDC_COMBO1,string)
      if (string == 'y = a + x')then
         PlotType = 1
      else if (string == "y = a + x + x^2")then
         PlotType = 2
      else
         PlotType = 3
      end if
      case(IDOK)
       bret = DlgGet(dlg,IDC_CHECK_GridOn, checked_state )
         if (checked_state == .true.) then
           ShowGrid = .true.
         else
           ShowGrid = .false.
         end if
        bret = DlgGet(dlg,IDC_CHECK_Header, checked_state )
         if (checked_state == .true.) then
           ShowTitle = .true.
         else
           ShowTitle  = .false.
         end if
         bret = DlgGet(dlg,IDC_RADIO_Lines, checked_state )
         if (checked_state == .true.) then
           Lines = .true.
         else
           Lines  = .false.
         end if
         iret = dlggetint(dlg,  IDC_SPIN_a,avalue)
         a = dfloat(avalue)
         iret = dlggetint(dlg,  IDC_SPIN_xmax,xvalue)
         xmax = dfloat(xvalue)
         call DLGEXIT (dlg)
      case(IDC_Plot)
        call Drawit
      case(IDC_CHECK_GridOn)
         bret = DlgGet(dlg,IDC_CHECK_GridOn, checked_state )
         if (checked_state == .true.) then
           ShowGrid = .true.
         else
```

```
                    ShowGrid = .false.
                  end if
              case(IDC_CHECK_Header)
                bret = DlgGet(dlg,IDC_CHECK_Header, checked_state )
                if (checked_state == .true.) then
                  ShowTitle = .true.
                else
                  ShowTitle  = .false.
                end if
              case(IDC_RADIO_Lines)
                bret = DlgGet(dlg,IDC_RADIO_Lines, checked_state )
                if (checked_state == .true.) then
                  Lines = .true.
                else
                  Lines  = .false.
                end if
              case(IDC_RADIO_Points)
                bret = DlgGet(dlg,IDC_RADIO_Points, checked_state )
                if (checked_state == .true.) then
                  Lines = .false.
                else
                  Lines  = .true.
                end if
              case(IDC_SPIN_xmax)
              iret = dlggetint(dlg, IDC_SPIN_xmax,xvalue)
              xmax = dfloat(xvalue)
              case(IDC_SPIN_a)
              iret = dlggetint(dlg, IDC_SPIN_a,avalue)
              a = dfloat(avalue)
          end select
      end subroutine SetPlotData
```

5.2   Fill masks

During a fill operation of a shape such as a rectangle, a mask area 8 bits by 8 bits is replicated over the entire fill area. Pixels in the mask that are set to a value of 1 are set to the current graphics color, and bits with a value of 0 are set to a background color of black. If no fill mask is set or if the mask has all ones, the current color is used to produce a solid fill. The fill mask is used to control fill patterns for the graphic routines FLOODFILLRGB, PIE, ELLIPSE, POLYGON, and RECTANGLE as well as their double-precision counterparts. The current fill mask is changed using the function SET-FILLMASK(mask), where mask is an array of eight one-byte integers that correspond to the desired bit pattern, as illustrated in Table 5.3.

PIE_W

Table 5.3   *Mask Bit Fill Pattern Thick Vertical Lines*

Bit Pattern Bit 7654 3210	Value in Mask
0000 1111	mask(1) #0F
0000 1111	mask(2) #0F
0000 1111	mask(3) #0F
0000 1111	mask(4) #0F
0000 1111	mask(5) #0F
0000 1111	mask(6) #0F
0000 1111	mask(7) #0F
0000 1111	mask(8) #0F

The mask given in Table 5.3 is used in the following code to produce a rectangle filled with thick red vertical stripes on a black background. Note that the current fill mask is saved using GETFILLMASK and then it is subsequently restored.

```
use dflib
integer(1) mask(8), oldmask(8)
integer(4) iret, maskcolor
integer(2) xmin, ymin,xmax,ymax
data mask   /#0F,#0F,#0F,#0F,#0F,#0F,#0F,#0F/
xmin = 20; xmax = 150
ymin = 20; ymax = 100
call GETFILLMASK( oldmask)
call SETFILLMASK( mask)
maskcolor = rgb(255,0,0)
iret = SETCOLORRGB(maskcolor) ! set fill color
iret = Rectangle_w($GFILLINTERIOR ,xmin, ymin,xmax,ymax)
call SETFILLMASK( oldmask)
```

5.2.1   Draw example

Our Draw program, shown in Figure 5.8, presents the user with a dialog box containing two list boxes offering a choice of objects to be drawn and a selection of fill patterns that can be used. The user can also determine the fill color to be used. The Draw button is used to draw an object according to the current selection settings, and the Finish button closes the dialog box.

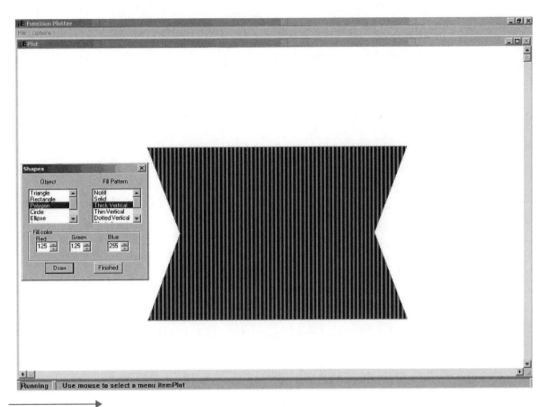

Figure 5.8   *Draw screen showing a polygon filled with a thick vertical line pattern.*

Caution: The number of pixels in the *x* direction divided by the number of pixels in the *y* direction is referred to as the *screen aspect ratio*. The aspect of PC screens works out at 4/3 (e.g., 800/600). QuickWin graphics routines, such as rectangle and ellipse, are based on an aspect ratio of 4/3. At this ratio, a rectangle with all sides having the same dimension will be drawn as a square. When you define your own window coordinate system, it is useful to define it in such a way that the aspect ratio of 4/3 is maintained so you can use the standard graphics routines. Otherwise, you will either have to accept a square that does not look square and circles that do not look circular or do your own scaling so that they are drawn properly.

Note in the list of global variables contained in Globals.f90, that user-defined symbolic constants (FS_Slanted is a fill style with slanted lines) are used to define our fill patterns:

```
module global
integer(2)  DrawType
integer(2)  FillType
integer(4)  Linecolor
integer(4)  Fillcolor
integer(4)  Redvalue
integer(4)  Greenvalue
integer(4)  Bluevalue
integer(1)  FS_Solid (8)
integer(1)  FS_ThickVertical(8)
integer(1)  FS_ThinVertical(8)
integer(1)  FS_DottedVertical(8)
integer(1)  FS_Slanted (8)
integer(1)  FS_CrissCross (8)
integer(1)  FS_ThickHorizontal (8)
data FS_Solid /#FF,#FF,#FF,#FF,#FF,#FF,#FF,#FF/
data FS_ThickVertical  /#0F,#0F,#0F,#0F,#0F,#0F,#0F,#0F/
data FS_ThinVertical  /#18,#18,#18,#18,#18,#18,#18,#18/
data FS_DottedVertical  &
              /#18,#00,#00,#18,#18,#00,#00,#18/
data FS_Slanted  /#93,#C9,#64,#B2,#59,#2C,#96,#4B/
data FS_CrissCross  /#6f,#00,#00,#6f,#00,#00,#6f,#00/
data FS_ThickHorizontal  &
              /#ff,#00,#00,#00,#00,#00,#ff,#00/
end module Global
```

The subroutine Shapes used in Callbacks.f90 illustrates how to fill a list box and set its callback subroutine. The initializing of edit boxes and spin buttons has been covered previously; therefore, the relevant code has been omitted from the listing.

```
subroutine Shapes
use global
... ! information has been omitted
!   initialize dialog box
    bret = DLGINIT(IDD_Shapes,dlg)
!   Set choice of objects to draw in list box
    bret = DlgSet(dlg,IDC_LIST1, 7, DLG_NUMITEMS)
    bret = DlgSet(dlg,IDC_LIST1, "Triangle", 1)
...
    bret = DlgSet(dlg,IDC_LIST1, "Pie", 7)
    bret = DLGSET (dlg,IDC_LIST1,"Line")
!   Set choice of draw styles in list box
```

```
      bret = DlgSet(dlg,IDC_LIST2, 8, DLG_NUMITEMS)
      bret = DlgSet(dlg,IDC_LIST2, "Nofill", 1)
...
      bret = DlgSet(dlg,IDC_LIST2, "Thick Horizontal", 8)
      if(DrawType == 6 )then
         bret = DLGSET (dlg,IDC_LIST2,.false., DLG_ENABLE)
      else
         bret = DLGSET (dlg,IDC_LIST2,.true., DLG_ENABLE)
      endif
      bret = DlgSet(dlg,IDC_SPIN_Red , 255, DLG_RANGEMAX)
...  ! information has been omitted
!  define the callback subroutine for each control
      bret = DlgSetSub(dlg,IDC_LIST1,SetPlotData)
      bret = DlgSetSub(dlg,IDC_LIST2,SetPlotData)
...  ! information has been omitted
      bret = DlgSetSub(dlg,IDOK,SetPlotData)
      iret = DlgModal(dlg)
      call DlgUninit(dlg)
      call Drawit
end subroutine Shapes
```

In the callback subroutine SetPlotData, when a change occurs to List1, the function DLGGET is called to get the string selected. The selected string is compared against the string names in the list box, and a global integer variable, *DrawType*, is set according to the position of the geometrical shape in the list. Since arcs cannot be filled, List2 is invalidated each time an arc is selected. The process is repeated for List2 and the global integer variable, *FillType*, is set according to the user selection. When the Draw button is pressed, the contents of the three edit boxes are read and checked for validity in the range 0 to 255. Any out-of-range values are set to 255, and the subroutine Drawit is called. The listing is as follows:

```
subroutine  SetPlotData(dlg,control_name, callbacktype)
use dflib
use dflogm
use dfwin
use global
implicit none
include 'resource.fd   '
type (dialog) dlg
logical bret
integer control_name,oldcolor
integer iposition1,iposition2,iposition3
integer callbacktype,iret
integer local_callbacktype
character(40) string
```

```
logical retlog
logical checked_state
   local_callbacktype = callbacktype
   select case(control_name)
      case(IDC_LIST1)  !  get object type
      bret = DLGGET (dlg,IDC_LIST1,string)
      if (string == 'Triangle')then
         DrawType = 1
         bret = DLGSET (dlg,IDC_LIST2,.true., DLG_ENABLE)
      else if (string == 'Rectangle')then
         DrawType = 2
          bret = DLGSET (dlg,IDC_LIST2,.true., DLG_ENABLE)
...
      else if (string == 'Pie')then
         DrawType = 7
          bret = DLGSET (dlg,IDC_LIST2,.true., DLG_ENABLE)
      end if
case(IDC_LIST2)  ! get fill style
      bret = DLGGET (dlg,IDC_LIST2,string)
                FillType = 1
      if (string == 'Nofill')then
         FillType = 0
      else if (string == 'Solid')then
         call SETFILLMASK(FS_Solid)
         bret = DLGSET (dlg,IDC_LIST2,.true., DLG_ENABLE)
...
      else if (string == 'Thick Horizontal')then
         call SETFILLMASK(FS_ThickHorizontal)
         bret = DLGSET (dlg,IDC_LIST2,.true., DLG_ENABLE)
      end if
      case(IDC_Draw)
      bret = DlgGet( dlg,IDC_Red, string )
        if(string == '  ') then
          string = '0'
          bret = DlgSet( dlg,IDC_Red, string )
        end if
        READ (string, '(I4)') Redvalue
        if(Redvalue > 255) then
           Redvalue = 255
           iret = dlgset(dlg,IDC_SPIN_Red , Redvalue )
        end if
      bret = DlgGet( dlg,IDC_Blue, string )
        if(string == '  ') then
          string = '0'
          bret = DlgSet( dlg,IDC_Blue, string )
        end if
        READ (string, '(I4)') Bluevalue
```

```
              if(Bluevalue > 255) then
                 Bluevalue = 255
                 iret = dlgset(dlg,IDC_SPIN_Blue, Bluevalue )
              end if
           bret = DlgGet( dlg,IDC_Green, string )
             if(string == '    ') then
               string = '0'
               bret = DlgSet( dlg,IDC_Green, string )
             end if
             READ (string, '(I4)') Greenvalue
             if(Greenvalue > 255) then
                Greenvalue = 255
                iret = dlgset(dlg,IDC_SPIN_Green, Greenvalue)
             end if
             Fillcolor = rgb(Redvalue,Greenvalue,Bluevalue)
              call drawit
           case(IDOK)
             call DLGEXIT(dlg)
         return
       end select
     end subroutine SetPlotData
```

5.3   What is next?

We have finished with QuickWin, and in the chapters ahead, we will look at developing Win32 applications. In the next chapter, we will come to grips with the generic Win32 application created by the Wizard and see how to develop context pop-up menus. Remember that many of the non-graphical Win32 functions we will consider can also be applied to Quick-Win programs.

Creating Win32 API Applications

6.1   **Win32 basics**

In the preceding chapters, we created programs with graphical interfaces using QuickWin. One advantage of using QuickWin is that once you start creating Win32 applications, a lot of the functions used will be familiar. This is to be expected, because QuickWin is a wrapper around a subsection of the Windows 32 application programming interface (Win32 API) functions. While using QuickWin, we were introduced to some very useful Win32 APIs that could be used with QuickWin programs. Even if you want to write nothing but QuickWin applications, you should find much of what is covered in the following chapters to be useful.

Users of CVF should be able to develop Win32 applications with very few limitations, and in Chapters 6 through 14 we will examine a very wide range of those possibilities. The Win32 application programming interface (API) functions provided by the Windows operating system are divided into a number of dynamic-link libraries (DLL), which must be included, by means of a USE statement, in any program segment that wishes to use the features of a particular DLL. The Win32 functions are called from C, but CVF has interface block definitions for almost all APIs to simplify calling Win32 functions from Fortran. The Win32 API functions are described in the Platform SDK online documentation. Information is provided on the calling format, together with a description of the routine's arguments, and the QuickInfo at the bottom of the Win32 routine documentation page lists the library to be used. Some of the more commonly used libraries are listed in Table 6.1. Any DLL library can be included in your program with the relevant USE statement (e.g., USE Kernel32). If you are not certain which of the individual library files to use, you should include the DFWIN module by means of a USE DFWIN statement. The DFWIN module con-

Table 6.1   *Most Commonly Used Windows DLLs*

DLL Name	Description
KERNEL32	Low-level operating functions. Memory management, task management, and resource handling.
USER32	Windows management. Contains message, menu, cursor, and most nondisplay functions.
GDI32	The graphics device interface library. Needed if application requires drawing, display context, metafile, coordinate, and font functions.
COMDLG32	Common dialogs, including printing and file handling.
VERSION	Version control.
COMCTL32	Used when common controls (up and down buttons, toolbars, status bars, etc.) are included in a window.

tains the routine interface definitions for almost all of the Win32 APIs that you might use.

In this chapter we will work with Fortran Windows application projects to create generic single document interface (SDI) applications for displaying and entering text. In subsequent chapters we will create applications with dialog boxes, common controls, common dialog boxes, Win32 graphics, multiple document interfaces (MDI), and Help files. All the Win32 example applications for Chapters 6–14 can be downloaded from the Web site.

6.2   Getting started

A certain amount of programming code is standard in every Windows program, whether we are writing in C or Visual Fortran. As a minimum, a Win32–based program must contain the following two functions:

- WinMain()—Entry point for the application. In this function, a window class is registered, a main window is created and displayed, the message loop is processed, and any messages for this application are sent to the designated function (MainWndProc).

- MainWndProc()—Processes messages for the main window.

Fortunately, we do not need to remember this code when developing applications, because the CVF Wizard in Developer Studio will create a generic Fortran Win32 program. This generic program has a standard window, a menu bar, and an about box. We need to add only the code to produce the additional functionality that we desire from our application. However, if we do decide to start from scratch, CVF also provides an option to create a Windows workspace with a blank project.

Let us now go through the steps of creating a generic Windows application, looking at the code written on our behalf, and then adding some code so that the program will write a "Hello World!" message on the main window.

Select File from the Visual Studio menu, and click on New. In the project name slot type "HelloWin," and set the directory in the slot marked location. You may need to click on the button at the end of the slot to choose a directory. Select Fortran Windows Application from the radio buttons, and then click on the OK button.

A new dialog box appears, offering a choice of window applications. Check the option labeled, Single Document Interface (SDI), and select Finish. The next dialog box gives information about the type of application that will be created and the project directory that it will be created in. Click OK to complete the process.

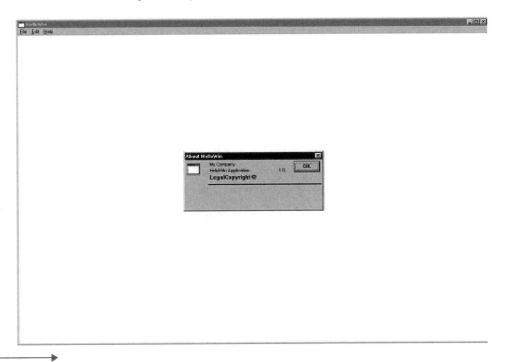

Figure 6.1   *Generic window showing an About box.*

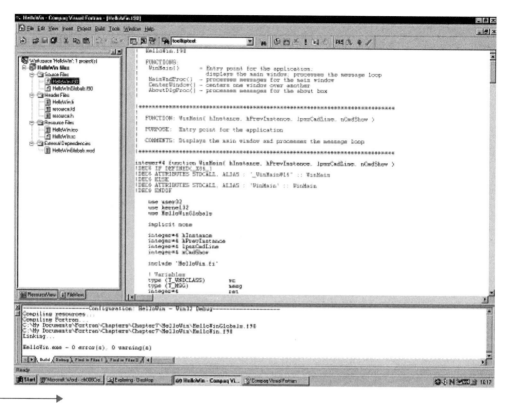

Figure 6.2   *The project workspace created by CVF Wizard in Developer Studio.*

Select Build and then click on Execute HelloWin.exe. A warning message is displayed stating that the file does not exist and asks if you want to build it. Select Yes, and after successfully compiling and linking, the HelloWin About dialog box can be displayed, as shown in Figure 6.1. The window comes with a title bar; minimize, maximize, and close buttons; and three menu items: File, Edit, and Help.

Exit the program. We can now look at the code that was generated for this generic application. Notice in the left-hand pane that the HelloWin file contains four folders. Click on the Source Files folder, and click on HelloWin.f90 file. The view in the right-hand pane should be something like that shown in Figure 6.2.

The comments header of HelloWin.f90 states that it has the following four functions: WinMain, MainWndProc, CenterWindow, and AboutDlgProc. For the moment, we shall concentrate on the first two functions, but the AboutDlgProc is a useful template any time you need to create a dialog box callback procedure. The following is the source code created by the CVF Wizard for the function WinMain.

```
integer*4 function WinMain(hInstance, hPrevInstance, &
                           lpszCmdLine, nCmdShow )
!DEC$ IF DEFINED(_X86_)
!DEC$ ATTRIBUTES STDCALL, ALIAS : '_WinMain@16' :: WinMain
!DEC$ ELSE
!DEC$ ATTRIBUTES STDCALL, ALIAS : 'WinMain' :: WinMain
!DEC$ ENDIF
    use user32
    use kernel32
    use HelloWinGlobals
    implicit none
    integer*4 hInstance
    integer*4 hPrevInstance
    integer*4 lpszCmdLine
    integer*4 nCmdShow
    include 'HelloWin.fi'
    ! Variables
    type (T_WNDCLASS)        wc
    type (T_MSG)             mesg
    integer*4                ret
    logical*4                lret
    integer                  haccel
    character(SIZEOFAPPNAME) lpszClassName
    character(SIZEOFAPPNAME) lpszIconName
    character(SIZEOFAPPNAME) lpszAppName
    character(SIZEOFAPPNAME) lpszMenuName
    character(SIZEOFAPPNAME) lpszAccelName
    ghInstance = hInstance
    ghModule = GetModuleHandle(NULL)
    ghwndMain = NULL
    lpszClassName ="HelloWin"C
    lpszAppName ="HelloWin"C
    lpszIconName ="HelloWin"C
    lpszMenuName ="HelloWin"C
    lpszAccelName ="HelloWin"C
    !  If this is the first instance of the application,
    !  register the window class(es)
    if (hPrevInstance .eq. 0) then
        !  Main window
        wc%lpszClassName = LOC(lpszClassName)
        wc%lpfnWndProc = LOC(MainWndProc)
        wc%style = IOR(CS_VREDRAW , CS_HREDRAW)
        wc%hInstance = hInstance
        wc%hIcon = LoadIcon( hInstance, LOC(lpszIconName))
        wc%hCursor = LoadCursor( NULL, IDC_ARROW )
```

```
            wc%hbrBackground = ( COLOR_WINDOW+1 )
            wc%lpszMenuName = NULL
            wc%cbClsExtra = 0
            wc%cbWndExtra = 0
            if (RegisterClass(wc) == 0) goto 99999
        end if
        ! Load the window's menu and accelerators and create
        ! the window
        ghMenu = LoadMenu(hInstance, LOC(lpszMenuName))
        if (ghMenu == 0) goto 99999
        haccel = LoadAccelerators(hInstance,&
            LOC(lpszAccelName))
        if (haccel == 0) goto 99999
        ghwndMain = CreateWindowEx(  0, lpszClassName, &
        lpszAppName, INT(WS_OVERLAPPEDWINDOW), CW_USEDEFAULT, &
            0, CW_USEDEFAULT, 0, NULL,ghMenu, hInstance, NULL)
        if (ghwndMain == 0) goto 99999
        lret = ShowWindow( ghwndMain, nCmdShow )
        ! Read and process messages
        do while( GetMessage (mesg, NULL, 0, 0) )
          if ( TranslateAccelerator (mesg%hwnd, haccel, mesg) &
            == 0) then
              lret = TranslateMessage( mesg )
              ret  = DispatchMessage( mesg )
          end if
        end do
        WinMain = mesg.wParam
        return
99999 ret = MessageBox(ghwndMain, "Error initializing &
          application HelloWin"C, "Error"C, MB_OK)
        WinMain = 0
end
```

The format and contents of the function WinMain code are standard for all Win32 programs; only the project name varies between applications. Now we shall examine the code of WinMain, listed above, in more detail.

6.3   WinMain, the main entry point

The entry point to a Windows program is the function WinMain, which always appears like this:

```
integer*4 function WinMain( hInstance, hPrevInstance, &
                              lpszCmdLine, nCmdShow )
```

The first parameter to WinMain is called an *instance handle*. In Windows programming, a handle is simply a number used to uniquely identify something. In this case, the handle identifies the current instance of the program. It is required as an argument to some other Windows function calls.

The second parameter to Windows is a relic from the Win16 days and for Win32, it is always NULL (defined as zero).

The third parameter to WinMain is a pointer to the command line used to run the program, excluding the program name. Some Windows applications use this to load a file into memory when the program is started. Look up WinMain in the online documentation if you want more information on this parameter.

The fourth parameter to WinMain indicates how the program should be initially displayed; either normal (default), minimized (nCmdShow = SW_SHOWMINIMIZED), or maximized (nCmdShow = SW_SHOWMAXIMIZED) to fill the window.

6.3.1 Defining and registering a Windows class

Look now at the rest of the code contained in the listing of WinMain. The first task is to fill up a data structure of Fortran type T_WNDCLASS, which in the above code is named wc. This is a Windows structure WND-CLASS, which is coded in Fortran as T_WNDCLASS. Online information is available for all data structures under their Windows structure name. The structure contains the information required to uniquely define a window for our application. The data include the class name, icon name, and menu name, among other things. In our example this is "HelloWin," the name of the program.

***

Note: The prefix lpsz at the beginning of the variable *lpszClassName* indicates that it is a long pointer to a zero- (null) terminated string. The prefix *lpfn* indicates that variable is a long pointer to a function. The terms *long* and *near pointers* are relics of Win16 programming practice and have no meaning in Win32.

***

Some of the fields in the structure to note include:

- `wc%lpfnWndProc = LOC(MainWndProc)`—This is used to set the name of the procedure that will process all messages to any window based on this window's class. Note that in using the Fortran function Loc, we are effectively pointing to the function MainWndProc.

- `wc%style = IOR(CS_VREDRAW, CS_HREDRAW)`—This sets the Class Style identifiers. These bit flags can be combined with the Inclusive OR bitwise operator. In our case, all windows created using this class are to be repainted whenever the horizontal window size (CS_HREDRAW) or the vertical window size (CS_VREDRAW) changes. When the window of HelloWin is resized, the first text string ("Hello from Win 32!") is redrawn to be in the new horizontal center of the window, and the second string ("And Again Hello World from Win 32!") is redrawn to be horizontally and vertically in the center of the window.

- `wc%hIcon = LoadIcon(hInstance, LOC(lpszIconName))`—The load icon function is used to load the class icon, which in our case is called HelloWin. We could also use the ID of an icon instead of its name—for example, if we had an icon in our resource script with the ID IDI_ICON1, the load icon function would become `Load-Icon(hInstance, IDI_ICON1)`. In that case, make sure that you have included the Resource.fd file in the WinMain program.

- `wc%hCursor = LoadCursor(NULL, IDC_ARROW)`—When the load cursor function is used with a null instance, the cursor will be loaded from one of the predefined stock items. We could also create our own cursor in resources and load that. In that case, the function would become `LoadCursor(hInstance, IDC_CURSOR1)`, where IDC_CURSOR1 is the ID of a cursor that has been created in, or imported into, the resource editor. Again the Resource.fd file must be included in the WinMain program.

- `wc%hbrBackground = (COLOR_WINDOW+1)`—Set the background color. The symbolic constant COLOR_WINDOW is defined in dfwinty.f90 as being equal to 5, which gives a gray background. We are setting the background to a value of 6 to obtain a white background.

- `wc%lpszMenuName = NULL`—The Wizard sets this field to NULL and then uses a load menu function later. However, instead of loading the menu separately, you could change this field to read `wc%lpsz-MenuName = LOC(lpszMenuName)`.

- `RegisterClass(wc)`—Note that the RegisterClass function requires only a single parameter, which is the class data structure. In our case, this is wc.

6.3.2 Creating a Windows class

Once the class is registered. the window can be created. In the above source code, the menu and accelerator keys are loaded before the following call to CreateWindowEx.

```
ghwndMain = CreateWindowEx(0, lpszClassName, lpszAppName, &
    INT(WS_OVERLAPPEDWINDOW), CW_USEDEFAULT, 0, &
    CW_USEDEFAULT, 0, NULL, ghMenu, hInstance, NULL)
```

The functions CreateWindow and CreateWindowEx are identical, except that CreateWindowsEx has one extra argument, which is located at the beginning of the argument list. The additional argument is for the extended Windows styles such as WS_EX_CONTEXTHELP or WS_EX_MDI-CHILD. These styles are used, respectively, for creating a window with context help capabilities or a multiple document interface (MDI) child window. In the example of HelloWin, the first argument is set to zero. All the remaining arguments are identical to those of CreateWindow. The next two arguments are zero-terminated C strings containing the class and application name, which in our example will be "HelloWin."

The fourth argument specifies the style of the window being created. The window styles are bit flags, which can be combined with the Inclusive OR bitwise operator. In addition, if the window is a control, then the individual control styles can also be combined with the window styles. In our case, we are using the window style WS_OVERLAPPEDWINDOW, which itself is already a combination of the following styles: WS_OVERLAPPED, WS_CAPTION, WS_SYSMENU, WS_THICKFRAME, WS_MINI-MIZEBOX, and WS_MAXIMIZEBOX.

Arguments five and six specify the horizontal and vertical position of the window, and arguments seven and eight are the width and height of the window. In our case, defaults are to be used.

The next three arguments are the handles to be used by the window being created. These are handle to parent window, handle to menu, and handle to instance.

The final argument is a pointer to a createstruct data structure. This structure is used when creating MDIs. Since we are creating a main window rather than a child window—and in any case we are working only with single document interfaces—this parameter is set to zero.

Once the window has been created, all that remains is for the ShowWindow function to display the window. The global handle to the main window is used, as is the variable *nCmdShow*, whose value is passed as an argument to the WinMain function call. Although the documentation on ShowWindow would indicate that you should use the value of nCmdShow passed in the argument for WinMain, you could also reset the value using `nCmdShow = SW_MAXIMIZE` so that the window opens in its maximized state rather than the normal state.

That's the hard work in creating a Windows graphical interface; the only task left for the program is to wait endlessly in a loop waiting to act on any operating system messages addressed to this particular Windows class.

6.3.3   Message loops

When an input event (keyboard or mouse) occurs, the event is translated into a message that is placed into a program's message queue. Windows maintains a message queue for every program that is currently running under the Windows operating system. Each program retrieves messages from the message queue through the following block of code, which is referred to as a message loop.

```
do while(GetMessage (mesg, NULL, 0, 0))
  if (TranslateAccelerator (mesg%hwnd, haccel, mesg) == 0)
  then
     lret = TranslateMessage(mesg)
     ret  = DispatchMessage(mesg)
  end if
end do
```

The GetMessage call passes a pointer to an MSG (coded in Fortran as T_MSG) structure named mesg. The second argument is the handle of the window. The GetMessage function will retrieve messages belonging to that window and its children. A NULL value has a special meaning in that the GetMessage call retrieves messages for any window that belongs to the calling thread and thread messages posted to the calling thread via PostThread-Message. The third and fourth arguments are filters for setting the range of messages to be returned. When these arguments are set to zero, no filtering is performed and all available messages are returned.

Windows fills in the fields of the message structure with the next message from the message queue. The fields of the MSG structure are:

- hwnd—A handle to the window to which the message is directed.

- message—A number that identifies the message. Each window message has a corresponding symbolic constant that begins with the identifier WM.

- wParam—A 32-bit message parameter, whose meaning and value are message specific.

- lParam—Another 32-bit message parameter, whose meaning and value are message specific.

- time—The time the message was placed.

- pt—The mouse position in screen coordinates at the time the message was placed.

The messages are processed by the procedure named in the WND-CLASS structure, which in our case is MainWndProc. The message loop continually processes three functions in the following order.

- The TranslateAccelerator function processes accelerator keys for menu commands. The function translates a WM_KEYDOWN or WM_SYSKEYDOWN message to a WM_COMMAND or WM_SYSCOMMAND message (if there is an entry for the key in the specified accelerator table) and then sends the WM_COMMAND or WM_SYSCOMMAND message directly to the appropriate window procedure. This function does not return until the window procedure has processed the message.

- The TranslateMessage function translates virtual-key messages into character messages. The character messages are posted to the calling thread's message queue, to be read the next time the thread calls the GetMessage function.

- The DispatchMessage function dispatches messages for processing by the Windows procedure named in the WNDCLASS structure (in our case, MainWndProc).

This neatly leads us into examining MainWndProc, which is the second of the two functions that must be included in every Win32 program.

6.3.4   MainWndProc, the callback entry point

The Windows procedure is where the operating system calls back to our program; it is our application's equivalent of a post office sorting and distribution center. The incoming messages from the operating system are sorted and delivered according to the recipient's postal addresses. In a Windows procedure, postal addresses look like WM_Create, WM_Paint, or IDM_New. Sometimes, just as in the mail system, Windows procedures will give the recipient a pointer to an address for collecting messages that are too large for direct delivery. The name of the Windows procedure is associated with a particular class through a call to RegisterClass. The procedure can have any name that does not cause conflict with an existing name. In our program, the Windows procedure is defined as:

```
integer function MainWndProc (hWnd, mesg, wParam, lParam)
```

Note that the arguments to the function MainWndProc are identical to the first four fields of the MSG structure. The first argument is a handle to the window receiving the message. It is the same handle as that returned from the CreateWindowEx function when the window was created. The second argument contains a message identity number, which corresponds to symbolic constants such as WM_Destroy or WM_Command. The last two arguments, wParam and lParam, are 32-bit message parameters that provide more information about the message. Their content is specific to each message. Sometimes a message parameter may be composed of two 16-bit values or it may be a pointer to a data structure.

Windows messages are processed using a Select Case construction, which dictates how each individual message is processed. In the MainWnd-Proc of HelloWin, the structure looks like this.

```
select case ( mesg )
   case (WM_DESTROY)
      call PostQuitMessage( 0 )
      MainWndProc = 0
      return
   case (WM_COMMAND) ! WM_COMMAND: user command
      select case (IAND(wParam, 16#ffff))
         case (IDM_EXIT)
         ret = SendMessage(hWnd, WM_CLOSE, 0, 0)
         MainWndProc = 0
         return
         ... code omitted here
         case DEFAULT
         ! Default window proc handle all other messages
         MainWndProc = DefWindowProc(hWnd,mesg,wParam,&
                            lParam)
         return
      end select
   ! Let the default window proc handle all other messages
   case default
   MainWndProc = DefWindowProc( hWnd, mesg, wParam, lParam)
end select
```

At the end of both select case constructions in MainWinProc, there is a default case, which calls the function DefWindowProc. This function provides default processing for any window messages that an application does not process to ensure that every message is processed.

Note: When the message is equal to WM_Command, the low word of wParam is tested using `select case (IAND(wParam, 16#ffff))`. An alternative and more readable way to write this piece of code is to use `select case (LOWORD(wParam))`. If you use the LOWORD or HIWORD functions, make sure that dfwin is included as part of the USE statement group.

6.3.5   HelloWin example

Now we shall add some code of our own to create a "Hello Windows" message that will be displayed on the screen. All the code additions are made to MainWndProc. The following variables should be inserted into the function MainWndProc:

```
integer(4) hDC
integer(2)    nDrawX
integer(2)    nDrawY
type (T_PAINTSTRUCT)      ps
type (T_RECT)    rc
character(256)    FileBuf
```

Then add the following code immediately after `select case (mesg)`

```
case (WM_PAINT)
   ! Get pixel dimensions of Client Area
   ret = GetClientRect(hWnd, rc)
   ! Set up a display context to begin painting
   hDC = BeginPaint (hWnd, ps)
   FileBuf = "Hello from Win32!"C
   ret = DrawText(hdc, FileBuf, lstrlen(FileBuf), &
               rc, DT_CENTER)
   FileBuf = "And Again Hello World from Win32!"C
   nDrawY = rc%bottom/2  ! pixels to vertical center
   nDrawX = rc%right/2   ! pixels to horizontal center
   ! Set coordinates of TextOut to be center of text
   ! string
   ret = SetTextAlign(hDC, TA_Center)
   ret = TextOut (hDC, nDrawX, &
               nDrawY,FileBuf,lstrlen(FileBuf))
   ! end painting and release hDC
   ret = EndPaint( hWnd,ps)
```

Figure 6.3   *Screen capture of HelloWin showing effect of TextOut and DrawText.*

Recompile and execute the program. The screen should look similar to that shown in Figure 6.3.

Note: The WM_Paint message is sent to an application when part or all of the window's client area needs to be redrawn or painted. It is, therefore, very important that all routines for placing text and graphics on the screen are contained in the WM_Paint section. Otherwise, when a redraw is required, perhaps because the window has been resized, the information currently displayed on the screen will not be redrawn. Initially, this may seem to be restrictive, especially if you are used to programming in QuickWin, but it also provides great flexibility, since you can force a redraw from anywhere in an application through calling the InvalidateRect function.

6.4   Working with menus

The Resource Editor simplifies the creation of Win32 menus. It is easy to create menus with submenus and even submenus with submenus. In the latter case, however, it is usually best not to go beyond one submenu layer. In this section we shall be creating menus with submenus, finding out how to use accelerator keys, and, finally, how to create a floating pop-up menu.

As a framework for our menu program, we will create a font and make changes to the logical font structure to discover what the effects are on a piece of text. First, we need to look at how to create fonts. Creating a font can be through a call to the CreateFont function, which requires 14 arguments to be passed, or by a call to the CreateFontIndirect function, which passes a pointer to a LOGFONT structure. The LOGFONT structure has 14 fields, which correspond to the 14 arguments used in the CreateFont function. The fields of the LOGFONT structure are defined as follows:

- lfHeight—Specifies the height, in logical units, of the font's character cell or character. The character height value is the character cell height minus the internal leading value. Effectively, the character cell height is like a line-spacing height. A positive value for lfHeight corresponds to the cell height, and a negative value corresponds to the character height. A value of 0 will result in a default height being set.

- lfWidth—Specifies the average width of characters in the font. A value of 0 means that the width will be related to the font height through a suitable aspect ratio,

- lfEscapement—Specifies the angle, in tenths of a degree, between the escapement vector and horizontal axis. The escapement vector is parallel to the base line of a row of text. In normal use, this value should be the same as that of lfOrientation.

- lfOrientation—Specifies an angle in tenths of a degree, measured from the horizontal in a counterclockwise direction. It specifies how the successive characters in a string are placed.

Note: Normally, lfEscapement and lfOrientation must be set to the same value; but in Windows NT, with the graphics mode set to GM_ADVANCED and using TrueType fonts, the values can be specified independently. This means that lfEscapement allows character strings to be written at an angle to the horizontal, but with the baseline of each character still parallel to the horizontal axis. Then, using lfOrientation, each character can be tilted individually.

- lfWeight—A value of 400 (FW_NORMAL) specifies normal font and 700 (FW_BOLD) indicates bold font.

- lfItalic—Specifies an italic font if set to true.

- lfUnderline—Specifies an underlined font if set to true.

- lfStrikeOut—Specifies a strikeout font if set to true.

- lfCharSet—Specifies the character set. A range of options is given in the online information; some values include ANSI_CHARSET (value 0) and DEFAULT_CHARSET(value 1).

- lfOutPrecision—Specifies how closely the output must match the requested font's specification.

- lfClipPrecision—Specifies how to clip characters that are partially outside the clipping region.

- lfQuality—Specifies how carefully the graphics device interface must attempt to match the logical-font attributes to those of an actual physical font.

- fPitchandFamily—Specifies the pitch and family of the font. This value is composed of two parts. The two lowest bits specify the pitch of the font and can be one of the following values: DEFAULT_PITCH, FIXED_PITCH, or VARIABLE_PITCH. The second part specifies the font family, which can be one of the following values: FF_DECORATIVE, FF_DONTCARE, FF_MODERN, FF_ROMAN, FF_SCRIPT, or FF_SWISS. The font families describe the general look of a font. The value for fPitchandFamilyis obtained by using the Boolean OR operator to combine one pitch constant with one family constant.

- lfFaceName—A null-terminated 32-character string that specifies the name of a type face. Suitable typefaces include Times New Roman, Arial, and Courier.

This sets the background information that we need to know as we create the Win32Menu program example.

6.4.1 Drop-down menus

First create a Windows SDI generic program called Win32Menu, and then modify the menu as follows. Click on the Resource View tab in the left-hand pane, and open the Menu Resources folder if it is not already in expanded view. Then click on the menu icon. The Resources Editor will display the default menu created by the Wizard. We shall modify the menu by deleting some of the existing menu items and adding some of our own menu items as follows.

Click on the menu item Edit and then delete it by selecting Delete from the Visual Studio menu item Edit. A warning prompt comes up to inform you that this will delete the pop-up menu item and all the commands that it contains. Click OK. Now click on the File menu and delete everything but the Exit command. These menu items are deleted using either Cut or Delete in the Developer Studio Edit menu. Also delete everything in the Help menu with the exception of About.

We will enter our own menu items shortly, but, for the moment, we will insert the code to create a LOGFONT structure and write a simple text to the screen. The process is similar to that used for our HelloWin program. First, include the USE DFWIN statement; then, insert the following variables in the function MainWndProc:

```
character(256) TextBuf
integer(4) hmenu
integer(4) iret
integer(4) hDC
integer(4) alignText
integer(4) hfont
integer(4) hfontOld
integer(4) sizeFont
integer(4) directionText
integer(4) fontFamily
integer(4) fontWeight
logical(4) fontItalic
logical(4) bret
type (T_PAINTSTRUCT)     ps
type (T_RECT)      rc
type (T_LOGFONT)  lf
```

Then add the following code immediately after the line select case(mesg):

```
case (WM_CREATE)
    alignText = DT_VCENTER.or.DT_SINGLELINE.or.DT_CENTER
    sizeFont = 20
    directionText = 0
    fontWeight = 700
    fontItalic  = .true.
    fontFamily = FF_ROMAN
    lf%lfHeight = sizeFont
    lf%lfWidth = 0
    lf%lfEscapement = directionText
    lf%lfOrientation = directionText
    lf%lfWeight = fontWeight
    lf%lfItalic = fontItalic
    lf%lfUnderline = 0
```

```
                    lf%lfStrikeOut = 0
                    lf%lfCharSet = 0
                    lf%lfOutPrecision = 0
                    lf%lfClipPrecision = 0
                    lf%lfQuality = 0
                    lf%lfPitchAndFamily = fontFamily
                    MainWndProc = 0
                    return
           case (WM_PAINT)
                    ! Get pixel dimensions of Client Area
                    iret = GetClientRect(hWnd, rc)
                    !  Set up a display context to begin painting
                    hDC = BeginPaint (hWnd, ps)
                    lf%lfPitchAndFamily = fontFamily
                    lf%lfEscapement = directionText
                    lf%lfOrientation = directionText
                    lf%lfHeight = sizeFont
                    lf%lfItalic = fontItalic
                    lf%lfWeight = fontWeight
                    hfont = CreateFontIndirect(lf)
                    hfontOld = SelectObject(hDC,hfont)
                    TextBuf = "Hello from Win32!"C
                    iret = DrawText(hdc, TextBuf, &
                                    lstrlen(TextBuf), rc,alignText)
                    hfontOld = DeleteObject(hfont)
                    hfontOld = SelectObject(hDC,GetStockObject&
                                    (SYSTEM_FONT))
                    !  end painting and release hDC
                    iret = EndPaint( hWnd,ps)
                    MainWndProc = 0
                    return
```

If you compile and execute the program, you should have a message displayed on the screen similar to the one shown in Figure 6.4.

Now we will insert our own menu items. Click on the rectangle with the dotted edges in the menu bar, then drag it to a space between the File and Help menu options and release it. Now double-click on the rectangle and the menu item properties dialog should appear. It has the pop-up box ticked so the ID and Prompt are grayed out. Type "&Font Style" into the Caption entry box and press Enter. Our new menu item, Font Style, should appear in the Menu's menu bar situated between File and Help. Then repeat this process and add Text Direction and Text Position as additional top-level menu items (see Figure 6.5).

Click on menu item Font Style. This should cause a drop-down menu box to appear with an empty rectangle. Double-click on the rectangle, and

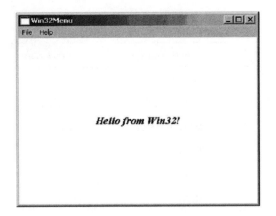

Figure 6.4
*The basic
text message
displayed by the
Win32Menu
application*

the menu item properties box will appear. In the ID section enter
IDM_FontBold, and for the caption enter &Bold\tCtrl+B. Check the
checked section in the properties box. The menu item should look the one
shown in Figure 6.5. Repeat the process for the menu item Italic, using the
IDM_FontItalic for the ID, and the caption is entered as &Bold\tCtrl+I.
Also check this menu item. Our next menu item has two submenu items.

Create a new menu item Size and this time check the pop-up box. Then
click on the menu item Size to bring up the submenu entry box and, as
shown in Figure 6.5, create two submenu entries captioned Font 20 and
Font 50 together with the accelerator keys. This process is repeated for the
menu item Type, which is located on the Font Style menu, and two submenu items, Roman and Swiss, are created. The complete menu additions
are summarized in Table 6.2, including the accelerator keys to be used.

Now we need to incorporate these menu items into the program. Click
on the FileView tab in the Tab view pane. If the Source folder is showing a
+ sign, click on the + sign box to open the folder. Then double-click on the
Menu.f90 Click on the Find option in the Edit menu (or use Ctrl+F), and
type in the find what box IDM_EXIT. This should advance to just below
the line `case(WM_COMMAND)`. Enter the following code between the lines
`select case(IAND(wParam, 16#ffff))` and `case(IDM_EXIT)`, in the
function MainWndProc.

Figure 6.5
*Menu creation
using the Resource
Editor.*

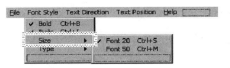

Table 6.2 *Summary of the Menu Items Used in Win32Menu*

Menu Name	Location	Type/Menu ID	Accelerator	Initial Status
Font Style	Top level	Pop-up		
Bold	Font Style	IDM_FontBold	Ctrl+B	Checked
Italic	Font Style	IDM_FontItalic	Ctrl+I	Checked
Size	Font Style	Pop-up		
Type	Font Style	Pop-up		
Font20	Size	IDM_Font20	Ctrl+S	Checked
Font50	Size	IDM_Font20	Ctrl+M	Clear
Roman	Size	IDM_FontRoman	Shift+R	Checked
Swiss	Size	IDM_FontSwiss	Shift+S	Clear
Text Direction	Top level	Pop-up		
Right	Text Direction	IDM_TextRight	Ctrl+R	Checked
Up	Text Direction	IDM_TextUp	Ctrl+U	Clear
Left	Text Direction	IDM_TextLeft	Ctrl+L	Clear
Down	Text Direction	IDM_TextDown	Ctrl+D	Clear
Text Position	Top level	Pop-up		
Left	Text Position	IDM_Left	Alt+L	Clear
Center	Text Position	IDM_Left	Alt+L	Checked
Right	Text Position	IDM_Left	Alt+L	Clear

```
case (IDM_FontBold)
   ! Get a handle to the font style menu.
   ! This is at position 1
   hMenu = GetSubMenu (ghMenu, 1)
   if(fontWeight == 700) then
      fontWeight = 400
   else
      fontWeight = 700
   end if
!    iret = BoldMenuCheck(hMenu,fontWeight)
   iret = InvalidateRect (hwnd, NULL_RECT, .TRUE.)
   MainWndProc = 0
   return
```

```
case (IDM_FontItalic)
   ! Get a handle to the font style menu.
   ! This is at position 1
   hMenu = GetSubMenu (ghMenu, 1)
   if(fontItalic == .true.) then
      fontItalic  = .false.
   else
      fontItalic  = .true.
   end if
!  iret = ItalicMenuCheck(hMenu,fontItalic)
   iret = InvalidateRect (hwnd, NULL_RECT, .TRUE.)
   MainWndProc = 0
   return
case (IDM_Font20)
   sizeFont = 20
   ! Get a handle to the font style menu.
   ! This is at position 1
   hMenu = GetSubMenu (ghMenu, 1)
!   iret = SetFontMenuCheck(hMenu,sizeFont)
   iret = InvalidateRect (hwnd, NULL_RECT, .TRUE.)
   MainWndProc = 0
   return
case (IDM_Font50)
   sizeFont = 50
   ! Get a handle to the font style menu.
   ! This is at position 1
   hMenu = GetSubMenu (ghMenu, 1)
!   iret = SetFontMenuCheck(hMenu,sizeFont)
   iret = InvalidateRect (hwnd, NULL_RECT, .TRUE.)
   MainWndProc = 0
   return
case (IDM_FontRoman)
   fontFamily = FF_ROMAN
   ! Get a handle to the font style menu.
   ! This is at position 1
   hMenu = GetSubMenu (ghMenu, 1)
!   iret = SetFontFamilyMenuCheck(hMenu,fontFamily)
   iret = InvalidateRect (hwnd, NULL_RECT, .TRUE.)
   MainWndProc = 0
   return
case (IDM_FontSwiss)
   fontFamily = FF_SWISS
   !  et a handle to the font style menu.
   ! This is at position 1
   hMenu = GetSubMenu (ghMenu, 1)
!   iret = SetFontFamilyMenuCheck(hMenu,fontFamily)
   iret = InvalidateRect (hwnd, NULL_RECT, .TRUE.)
   MainWndProc = 0
   return
```

```
case (IDM_TextRight)
   directionText = 0
   !  Get a handle to the text direction menu at position 2
   hMenu = GetSubMenu (ghMenu, 2)
!    iret = SetAngleMenuCheck(hMenu,directionText)
   iret = InvalidateRect (hwnd, NULL_RECT, .TRUE.)
   MainWndProc = 0
   return
case (IDM_TextUp)
   directionText = 900
   !  Get a handle to the text direction menu at position 2
   hMenu = GetSubMenu (ghMenu, 2)
!    iret = SetAngleMenuCheck(hMenu,directionText)
   iret = InvalidateRect (hwnd, NULL_RECT, .TRUE.)
   MainWndProc = 0
   return
case (IDM_TextLeft)
   directionText = 1800
   !  Get a handle to the text direction menu at position 2
   hMenu = GetSubMenu (ghMenu, 2)
!    iret = SetAngleMenuCheck(hMenu,directionText)
   iret = InvalidateRect (hwnd, NULL_RECT, .TRUE.)
   MainWndProc = 0
   return
case (IDM_TextDown)
   directionText = 2700
   !  Get a handle to the text direction menu at position 2
   hMenu = GetSubMenu (ghMenu, 2)
!    iret = SetAngleMenuCheck(hMenu,directionText)
   iret = InvalidateRect (hwnd, NULL_RECT, .TRUE.)
   MainWndProc = 0
   return
case (IDM_Left)
   alignText = DT_VCENTER.or.DT_SINGLELINE.or.DT_LEFT
   !  Get a handle to the Format text. This is at position 3
   hMenu = GetSubMenu (ghMenu, 3)
!    iret = SetFormatMenuCheck(hMenu,alignText)
   iret = InvalidateRect (hwnd, NULL_RECT, .TRUE.)
   MainWndProc = 0
   return
case (IDM_Center)
   alignText = DT_VCENTER.or.DT_SINGLELINE.or.DT_CENTER
   !  Get a handle to the Format text. This is at position 3
   hMenu = GetSubMenu (ghMenu, 3)
!    iret = SetFormatMenuCheck(hMenu,alignText)
   iret = InvalidateRect (hwnd, NULL_RECT, .TRUE.)
   MainWndProc = 0
   return
```

```
case (IDM_Right)
   alignText = DT_VCENTER.or.DT_SINGLELINE.or.DT_RIGHT
   !  Get a handle to the Format text at position 3
   hMenu = GetSubMenu (ghMenu, 3)
!   iret = SetFormatMenuCheck(hMenu,alignText)
   iret = InvalidateRect (hwnd, NULL_RECT, .TRUE.)
   MainWndProc = 0
   return
```

Select Execute Menu.exe from the build menu (or use Ctrl plus the function key F5) to recompile and execute the program. The modified Menu program should appear. Click on the Font Style menu and select the menu item Bold. The message "Hello from Win32!" should change from a bold font to a normal font weight. The menu item Bold will still stay checked, because the code has not yet been included to check and uncheck menu items.

If you are cutting and pasting the code from the example Win32Menu code, then note that some lines of code need to be commented out so that the program will compile and run. You can look through the previous listing to see which lines have been commented out, or you can compile the program and comment out any code lines that cause the compiler to flag an error message. The lines of code that need commenting out are those that call functions to change the check state of each menu item. For example, in the Bold menu item the line:

```
iret = BoldMenuCheck(hMenu,fontWeight)
```

is commented out.

Before we add the code to check and uncheck menu items, we shall install the accelerator keys. Menu accelerator keys are special keys that the user can type at any time to select the corresponding menu item. They differ from shortcut keys, which can be used only when the target item is visible (i.e., its menu is open). To add an accelerator key, open the Accelerator Editor, as shown in Figure 6.6.

Double-click on the empty rectangle at the bottom of the list view. A dialog box should appear. Click on the Down Arrow button in the box labeled ID. A list box appears. Scroll down the contents of the list box, and select IDM_TextUp when it appears. Then type U in the edit box marked Key. Make sure that the Ctrl button is checked in the Modifiers group and that Virtual key is checked in the Type group. Figure 6.6 shows the accelerator editor when all the accelerator keys required for Win32Menu have been entered.

Figure 6.6
Adding the accelerator key Ctrl+U to the menu item with the ID IDM_TextUp.

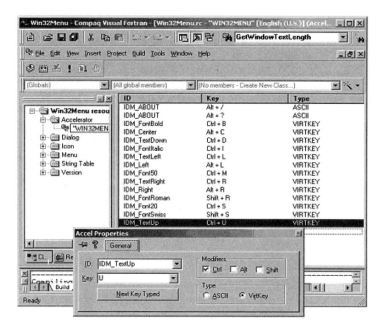

Close the Dialog, recompile and execute the program, and test out the accelerator keys. Even in this simple example, it is much easier to cycle through the menu commands using the accelerator keys than to select each individual menu item with a mouse click.

6.4.2   Checking menu items

The following line of code can be used to check menu item IDM_FontBold:

```
iret = CheckMenuItem (hMenu, IDM_FontBold,&
                      IOR(MF_BYCOMMAND, MF_CHECKED))
```

This line of code will uncheck menu item IDM_FontBold:

```
iret = CheckMenuItem (hMenu, IDM_FontBold,&
                      IOR(MF_BYCOMMAND, MF_UNCHECKED))
```

Normally, these statements would be included as inline code in the appropriate section. For example, for IDM_Bold this would be:

```
case (IDM_FontBold)
hMenu = GetSubMenu (ghMenu, 1)
if(fontWeight == 700) then
   fontWeight = 400
```

```
      iret = CheckMenuItem (hMenu, IDM_FontBold, &
            IOR(MF_BYCOMMAND, MF_UNCHECKED))
   else
      fontWeight = 700
      iret = CheckMenuItem (hMenu, IDM_FontBold, &
            IOR(MF_BYCOMMAND, MF_CHECKED))
   end if
   iret = InvalidateRect (hwnd, NULL_RECT, .TRUE.)
   MainWndProc = 0
   return
```

In our case we are going to extend the program to include a floating menu, which will also need to have its menu items checked. The checked state of menu items in a floating pop-up menu can be set only during each short life of this pop-up menu, and this raises the potential for duplication of code. Our approach will be to create functions to check and uncheck the menu state and then let either the floating menu or the normal menu items call the appropriate function. The process is illustrated through the following code, which sets the checked state in the font size submenu.

```
      integer(4) function SetFontMenuCheck(hMenu,Size)
      use user32
      use Win32MenuGlobals
      implicit none
      include 'Resource.fd'
      integer(4) iret
      integer(4) hMenu, Size
      select Case (Size)
         case (20)
         iret = CheckMenuItem (hMenu,IDM_Font20, &
               IOR(MF_BYCOMMAND, MF_CHECKED))
         iret = CheckMenuItem (hMenu,IDM_Font50, &
               IOR(MF_BYCOMMAND, MF_UNCHECKED))
         SetFontMenuCheck = 1
         return
         case (50)
         iret = CheckMenuItem (hMenu,IDM_Font20, &
               IOR(MF_BYCOMMAND, MF_UNCHECKED))
         iret = CheckMenuItem (hMenu,IDM_Font50, &
               IOR(MF_BYCOMMAND, MF_CHECKED))
         SetFontMenuCheck = 1
         return
         end select
         SetFontMenuCheck = 0
         return
      end
```

Since these are functions, we also need to include the appropriate function interfaces in WinMainProc. This is the interface for the function that sets the checked state in the font size submenu.

```
interface
    integer(4) function SetFontMenuCheck(hMenu,Size)
    integer(4) hMenu
    integer(4) Size
    end function
end interface
```

The function can be called from the application code as follows:

```
case (IDM_Font20)
    sizeFont = 20
    ! Get a handle to the font style menu.
    ! This is at position 1
    hMenu = GetSubMenu (ghMenu, 1)
    iret = SetFontMenuCheck(hMenu,sizeFont)
    iret = InvalidateRect (hwnd, NULL_RECT, .TRUE.)
    MainWndProc = 0
    return
case (IDM_Font50)
    sizeFont = 50
    ! Get a handle to the font style menu.
    ! This is at position 1
    hMenu = GetSubMenu (ghMenu, 1)
    iret = SetFontMenuCheck(hMenu,sizeFont)
    iret = InvalidateRect (hwnd, NULL_RECT, .TRUE.)
    MainWndProc = 0
    return
```

6.4.3 Floating (pop-up) menus

Adding a floating menu to our program so that it pops up when the right-hand mouse button is clicked is easy. All we need to do is create the menu, and through the TrackPopupMenu function, let Windows do the rest. Figure 6.7 shows the menu named "Floating" being created for our Win32Menu example. The top-level menu name has a single entry—PopUp. We could also create a family of similar menus to be used in particular contexts with a program.

Note: The name PopUp has been given purely to indicate its function; there is no other meaning to the name. Indeed, as far as the system is concerned, its name is zero, since it is the first menu in a zero-based menu index.

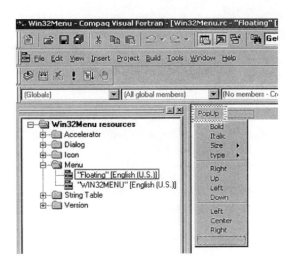

Figure 6.7
A floating menu being created for our Win32Menu application.

Once the menu has been created, we use the function TrackPopUpMenu to activate the floating menu. This is achieved through the WM_R-BUTTONUP message section, where the position of the mouse pointer is obtained and converted to screen coordinates. These coordinates and a handle to the menu are passed to TrackPopUpMenu. Both the main menu and the floating menu have checkmarks against the menu items to indicate the current selection state. To ensure that both menus have the corresponding menu items, checked calls are also made to the various functions for setting the menu checks. The following code needs to be added to the function MainWndProc section of the file Win32Menu.f90. The finished product is shown in Figure 6.8.

In the declaration section of MainWndProc, add the following:

```
use dfwin
integer(4)        hMenuTrackPopup
logical(4)        bret
type (T_POINT)    pt
```

Anywhere between the `select  case  (mesg)` and before the `case (WM_COMMAND)` section of MainWndProc add the following code (a good place would be after the WM_CREATE and WM_PAINT sections):

```
case (WM_RBUTTONDOWN)
    iret = SetCapture(hWnd)
    !  Draw the "floating" popup in the app's client area
    pt%x = INT4(LOWORD(lparam))
    pt%y = INT4(HIWORD(lparam))
    ! get a handle to floating menu
  hMenu = LoadMenu (ghInstance, LOC("Floating"C))
```

```
                    ! get a handle to menu of given index (0)
                 hMenuTrackPopup = GetSubMenu (hMenu, 0)
            !  set check state for menu items
              iret = SetAngleMenuCheck(hMenuTrackPopup,directionText)
              iret = SetFormatMenuCheck(hMenuTrackPopup,alignText)
              iret = SetFontMenuCheck(hMenuTrackPopup,sizeFont)
              iret = SetFontFamilyMenuCheck(hMenuTrackPopup,&
                                  fontFamily)
              iret = BoldMenuCheck(hMenuTrackPopup,fontWeight)
              iret = ItalicMenuCheck(hMenuTrackPopup,fontItalic)
              ! Convert the mouse point to screen coordinates
              bret = ClientToScreen (hwnd, pt)
              !Draw and track the "floating" popup
              bret = TrackPopupMenu (hMenuTrackPopup, 0,&
                                  pt%x, pt%y, 0, hwnd, NULL_RECT)
              !    Finished with menu
              bret = DestroyMenu (hMenu)
              MainWndProc = 0
              return
```

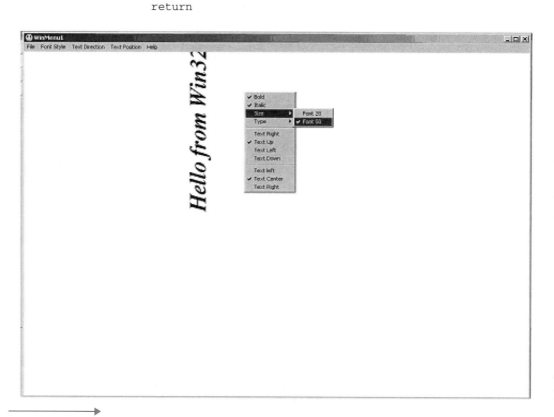

Figure 6.8   *Floating pop-up menu for Win32Menu application. (Note the use of checkmarks to indicate the current selection status.)*

6.5 Windows with style

In a Windows operating system, the name window refers to an area on the screen that can be used for user input and/or the display of information in the form of text and graphics. Controls such as edit boxes, scroll bars, list boxes, buttons, and dialog boxes are all examples of windows, and they can be created using either the CreateWindow or CreateWindowEx functions. The CreateWindowEx function is used to provide an extended choice of styles, in addition to the styles supported by CreateWindow. General Windows styles begin with the letters WS_ (e.g.,WS_BORDER) and the extended Windows styles begin with the letters WS_EX_ (e.g., WS_EX_CONTEXTHELP).

All windows belong to a class, and when a window is assigned to a class such as an edit class or a scroll bar class, it is given a set of attributes that distinguish fundamental aspects of its functionality and appearance from any other window class. Essentially, a window class is a set of attributes that the

Table 6.3   *Styles for the Edit Class*

Style	Action
ES_AUTOHSCROLL	Text will be scrolled to the right by ten characters when the user types a character at the end of the line.
ES_AUTOVSCROLL	Text will be scrolled up one page when the user presses the enter key on the last line.
ES_CENTER	Text will be centered in the edit box.
ES_LEFT	Text will be left-aligned in the edit box.
ES_LOWERCASE	All characters will be converted into lowercase as they are typed into the edit control.
ES_MULTILINE	The edit box will be set as a multiline edit control. The default is single-line edit control.
ES_NUMBER	Allows only numbers to be entered into the edit control. This useful feature limits user input to positive integers.
ES_PASSWORD	Displays an asterisk (*) for each character typed into the edit control windows.
ES_RIGHT.	Text will be right-aligned in the edit box.
ES_UPPERCASE	All characters will be converted into uppercase as they are typed into the edit control.

system uses as a template to create one or more copies of that particular window type. When using either CreateWindow or CreateWindowEx, the class must be either one of the predefined window classes (e.g., a button or an edit box) or it must have a user-defined window structure that has been registered using either the RegisterClass or RegisterClassEx function. A complete description of available Windows classes and styles is contained in the online documentation for CreateWindow or CreateWindowEx.

The characteristics of a window within a class are defined using the style attributes that belong to that class of window, and they help determine its appearance. These attributes include border style, caption, scroll bars, text alignment, and so forth. We are going to investigate some of the available Edit class style attributes listed in Table 6.3. You should already be familiar with the majority of the styles listed in Table 6.3 because they correspond to those given in the edit control property box of Resource Editor.

The first step is to create a Windows SDI generic program called Scribe1 and insert the following program variables into WinMainProc:

```
integer(4)   hInstance,glnWidth,glnLength
integer(4)   hwndEdit,iret
logical :: redraw = .true.
```

Then immediately after the line `select case (mesg)`, insert the following code:

```
case (WM_CREATE)
   hwndEdit = CreateWindow("EDIT"C, "  "C, IOR(WS_VISIBLE ,&
              IOR(WS_CHILD ,IOR(WS_VSCROLL,IOR(ES_LEFT,&
              IOR(WS_BORDER,IOR(ES_Multiline, &
              IOR(ES_NOHIDESEL,IOR(ES_Autovscroll, &
              WS_CLIPSIBLINGS)))))))),0,0, 0,0,hwnd, &
              NULL, ghInstance, NULL)
   ret = SendMessage (hwndEdit, EM_LIMITTEXT, Buffer_Len, 0)
   MainWndProc = 0
   return
case (WM_SIZE)
   glnWidth = iand(lParam, #0000FFFF)  !  low word
   glnLength = ishft(lParam, -16)      !  high word
   ret = MoveWindow(hwndEdit ,0,0, glnWidth,&
              glnLength,redraw)
   MainWndProc = 0
   return
case (WM_SETFOCUS)
   ret = SETFOCUS(hwndEdit )
   MainWndProc = 0
   return
```

Finally, insert the following code after the line `select case (IAND (wParam, 16#ffff))`, which follows after the line `case (WM_COMMAND)`.

```
case(IDM_NEW)
    iret = SetWindowText (hwndEdit, "\0"C)
    MainWndProc = 0
    return
case (IDM_UNDO)
    iret = SendMessage (hwndEdit, WM_UNDO, 0, 0) ;
    MainWndProc = 0
    return
case (IDM_CUT)
    iret = SendMessage (hwndEdit, WM_CUT, 0, 0)
    MainWndProc = 0
    return
case (IDM_COPY)
    iret = SendMessage (hwndEdit, WM_COPY, 0, 0)
    MainWndProc = 0
    return
case (IDM_PASTE)
    iret = SendMessage (hwndEdit, WM_PASTE, 0, 0)
    MainWndProc = 0
    return
case (IDM_Clear)
    iret = SendMessage (hwndEdit, WM_CLEAR, 0, 0)
    MainWndProc = 0
    return
case (IDM_SelectAll)
    iret = SendMessage (hwndEdit, EM_SETSEL, 0, -1)
    MainWndProc = 0
    return
```

Then in the resources menu editor, uncheck the grayed box for all of the Edit menu and add the following menu items: After Paste, add `Delete \ tDel`; insert a separator bar; and add `Select All \tCtrl+A`. The menu should look like that shown in Figure 6.9. The menu ID for Delete should be IDM_Clear, and for Select All it should be IDM_SelectAll.

Figure 6.9
Edit menu of Scribe1.

Figure 6.10
Adding an accelerator key to menu item undo.

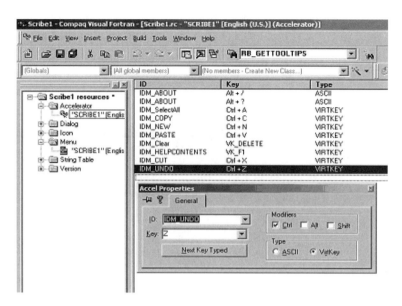

The final task is to insert the accelerator keys. Referring to Figure 6.10, open the Accelerator folder and click on Scribe1. The right-hand pane should look something like Figure 6.10, but it will have only the top three entries. Click on the new (empty) slot at the bottom of the list, and an accelerator property box will appear. Click on the ID combo box, and select the menu item that you want to attach an accelerator key to—say, IDM_Undo. Then make sure that the Ctrl radio button is ticked, and enter the letter Z as the corresponding key. The process is repeated for all the menu items with the exception of IDM_Clear, which we want to associate with the Delete key. In this case, we need to uncheck the Ctrl radio button and ensure that the VirtKey radio button is checked. You could then click on the Key combo box and scroll down until you find VK_Delete, or you could click on the Next Key Typed button and press the Delete key.

Normally the accelerator keys would work without any additional modifications, but because we are working in the edit control, we need to make the following modification to the message loop.

Replace Windows handle from `mesg%hwnd` in the following line:

```
if (TranslateAccelerator (mesg%hwnd, haccel, mesg) == 0)
then
```

to `ghwndMain`, as shown here:

```
if (TranslateAccelerator (ghwndMain, haccel, mesg) == 0)
then
```

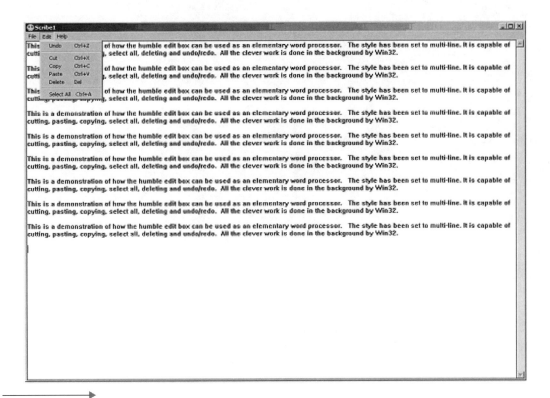

Figure 6.11 *Scribe1 uses an edit box with multiline style capabilities to cut, copy, and paste text.*

Now compile the program and try it. You should be able to paste into the edit box from the clipboard, cut or copy from the edit box to the clipboard, and undo and redo (Undo-Undo) previous edits. See Figure 6.11. Essentially, we have created a basic text editor. We will revisit this example in later chapters and add common dialog boxes so that we can open and save files, select fonts, and print the contents of the edit box.

6.6   What is next?

In the next chapter, we will create modal and modeless dialog boxes and learn how picture boxes can detect mouse selections. We will also create applications that have status bars, toolbars, and tool tips.

7

Dialog Boxes and Controls

In Chapter 4, during our study of QuickWin programming, we learned that Dialog boxes may be "modal" or "modeless." With a modal dialog box, the user cannot switch between the dialog box and another window or control in the program. The user must explicitly close the dialog box before any other action can be initiated within the program. On the other hand, a user can keep a number of modeless dialog boxes open while working in the client area. A toolbox in a drawing application is one example of how it would be useful to have a dialog box open while working in the main client area.

In this chapter, we will be creating Win32-based applications to demonstrate the use of both modal and modeless dialog boxes and illustrate the techniques to be used for receiving and sending messages for a range of controls. The controls will include edit text boxes, static text controls, spin buttons, radio and check buttons, track bars (slider controls), and progress bars. In addition, we will place icon and bitmap images on buttons and static controls. Mouse clicks on the images will be detected and acted upon. We will also be looking at using some of the common controls to create a user interface with a toolbar that has tool tips and a status bar.

Dialog boxes are created according to a DLGTEMPLATE structure. The DLGTEMPLATE structure may be created transparently by using the Resource Editor facilities of Developer Studio, or the fields of the structure can be defined manually. However, it is unusual to define a dialog box template manually, because it is so easy to create dialog boxes using the Resource Editor facilities of Developer Studio. We will be using the Resource Editor to create all our dialog boxes. The actual creation of a modal dialog box, based on the fields of a DLGTEMPLATE structure, is achieved by calling either the DialogBox function or the DialogBoxParam function. Modeless dialog boxes are also based on the fields of a DLGTEMPLATE structure, and either the CreateDialog or the CreateDialogParam function can be used to create them.

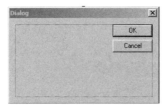

Figure 7.1
Dialog box created in the Resource Editor.

7.1   Creating a modal dialog box

If you have not read Chapter 4, it would be a good idea to go back and read the information about creating dialog boxes using the Resource Editor before starting the examples in this chapter. We will begin by creating a simple dialog box to get a feel for the techniques used. The dialog box will contain one edit box for entering a password and an Enter button. The following are the steps to take when creating the dialog box in Resource Editor:

- First, create a new Win32 SDI project called Password.

- Select Resources from the insert menu.

- Choose Dialog box and click the New button. A standard dialog box like that shown in Figure 7.1 will be created.

- Double-click on the dialog box to display the properties box. In the properties box, set the caption to Enter Password, and leave the default ID as IDD_DIALOG1.

- Delete the Cancel button, then center and resize the OK button at the bottom of the dialog box. Change the caption on the OK button from OK to Enter. Refer to Figure 7.2 for details.

- Add an edit box to the dialog box. In the Styles tab of the property box check the Password style. Reset the tab order (use menu items Layout -> Tab Order) so that the edit box is number 1 and the OK button is number 2.

Figure 7.2
Edit box with the password style set.

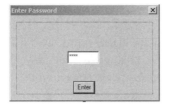

7.1.1   Dialog box procedures

Before we can open the dialog box in our application, we need to write a dialog box procedure and some interfacing code. A dialog procedure is required to initalize any controls placed on a dialog box, to process any messages from the controls, and to close the dialog box when it is no longer required. Dialog procedures are used with both modal or modeless dialog boxes. The generic form of a dialog procedure is as follows:

```
integer(4) function DialogProc(hDlg, uMsg, wParam, &
    lParam)
```

The arguments have the same grouping as a main window callback procedure and are as follows:

- DialogProc—User-supplied name.

- hDlg—Handle to the dialog box.

- uMsg—Specifies the message.

- wParam—Additional message-specific information.

- lParam—Additional message-specific information.

The dialog box procedure should return a nonzero value if it processes the message, and zero if it does not. For a WM_INITDIALOG message, the dialog box procedure should return zero if it calls the SetFocus function to set the focus to one of the controls in the dialog box. Otherwise, it should return nonzero, in which case the system sets the focus to the first control in the dialog box that can be given the focus.

When a control (e.g., a button) in a dialog box is clicked with the mouse, that control sends its parent window (dialog box) a WM_COMMAND message. The low word of wParam is set to the ID of the control. The high word of wParam is a notification code and lParam is the window handle of the control

---

Note: The dialog box procedure is similar to a window procedure. One difference is that it must not call the DefWindowProc function to process unwanted messages. Unwanted messages are processed internally by the dialog box window procedure.

The code used in the dialog procedure for the Password application is as follows:

```fortran
integer(4) function PassWordDlgProc(hDlg, message, &
                                    uParam, lParam)
!DEC$ IF DEFINED(_X86_)
!DEC$ ATTRIBUTES STDCALL, ALIAS : '_PassWordDlgProc@16' &
            :: PassWordDlgProc
!DEC$ ELSE
!DEC$ ATTRIBUTES STDCALL, ALIAS : 'PassWordDlgProc'&
            :: PassWordDlgProc
!DEC$ ENDIF
use dfwin
use PasswordGlobals
implicit none
integer     hDlg         ! window handle of the dialog box
integer     message      ! type of message
integer     uParam       ! message-specific information
integer     lParam
include 'resource.fd'
! Variables
integer(4) iret
integer(4) MaxCharacters
character(10) text
   select case (message)
      case (WM_INITDIALOG) ! message: initialize dialog box
         ! Center the dialog over the application window
         call CenterWindow (hDlg, GetWindow (hDlg,&
                        GW_OWNER))
                        MaxCharacters = 10
         PassWordDlgProc = 1
         return
      case (WM_COMMAND)
         if (LOWORD(uParam) .EQ. IDOK) then ! Close command
            iret = GetDlgItemText(hDlg, IDC_EDIT1, text, &
                           MaxCharacters)
            if(text(1:7) == 'Fortran') then
             iret = MessageBox( hDlg, "Password is Valid"C,&
                      "Checking Password"C, MB_OK )
            else
              iret = beep(200,200)
              iret = MessageBox(hDlg, "Today's Password is &
                      Fortran"C, "Bad Password"C, MB_OK)
            end if
            iret = EndDialog(hDlg, TRUE)  ! Exit the dialog
            PassWordDlgProc = 1
            return
         end if
   end select
```

```
        PassWordDlgProc = 0 ! Didn't process the message
        return
end
```

Note: In the preceding code, the lines beginning with `!DEC$ ATTRIBUTES` are compiler directives and are shown with Fortran continuation signs (&) at the end of each line, indicating that the code continues onto a second line. This is for typographical convenience only. If you type these lines, they must be entered as a single line.

7.1.2   Displaying the dialog box

Applications display a modal dialog box by calling the DialogBoxParam function. This function creates a modal dialog box based on a dialog box template. In our Password example, we used the Resources Editor to create a dialog box template. The Param term at the end of the function name indicates that before displaying the dialog box, the function will pass an application-defined value to the dialog box procedure as the lParam parameter of the WM_INITDIALOG message. An application can use this value to initialize dialog box controls. The function arguments are as follows:

```
DialogBoxParam(hInstance,lpTemplateName, hWndParent, &
               lpDialogFunc, dwInitParam)
```

Here:

- hInstance identifies the instance whose executable file contains the dialog box template.

- lpTemplateName identifies the dialog box template. This parameter is either the pointer to a null-terminated character string that specifies the name of the dialog box template or an integer value that specifies the resource identifier of the dialog box template.

- hWndParent identifies the window that owns the dialog box.

- lpDialogFunc is a pointer to the dialog box procedure.

- dwInitParam specifies the value to pass to the dialog box in the lParam parameter of the WM_INITDIALOG message. Usually this parameter is set to zero, but it could also be used as a pointer to a data structure that is to be used for initializing the dialog controls.

    If the function succeeds, the return value is the value of the *nResult* parameter specified in the call to the EndDialog function used to terminate

Figure 7.3
*The password
dialog box at run
time with a
message box that
indicates an
incorrect password
has been entered.*

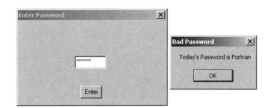

the dialog box. If the function fails, the return value is –1. To get extended error information, call the Win32 function GetLastError.

The DialogBoxParam function uses the CreateWindowEx function to create the dialog box. The function displays the dialog box (regardless of whether the template specifies the WS_VISIBLE style), disables the owner window, and starts its own message loop to retrieve and dispatch messages for the dialog box. When the dialog box procedure calls the EndDialog function, DialogBoxParam destroys the dialog box, ends the message loop, enables the owner window (if previously enabled), and returns the *nResult* parameter specified by the dialog box procedure when it called EndDialog.

The dialog box at run time for our Password application can be seen in Figure 7.3. The dialog box is initiated from within the program by selecting the menu item Password in the Options menu, which calls the following code in WM_COMMAND.

```
case (IDM_Password)
    iret = DialogBoxParam(ghInstance,IDD_DIALOG1,hWnd,&
                          LOC(PassWordDlgProc), 0)
    MainWndProc = 0
    return
```

To ensure that the system can communicate with our dialog callback procedure, the following function interface definition for the PassWordDlg-Proc needs to be placed in the main window callback function MainWnd-Proc.

```
interface
    integer(4) function PassWordDlgProc(hDlg,message,&
                         wParam,lParam)
    !DEC$ IF DEFINED(_X86_)
    !DEC$ ATTRIBUTES STDCALL, ALIAS : '_PassWordProc@16'&
              :: PassWordDlgProc
    !DEC$ ELSE
    !DEC$ ATTRIBUTES STDCALL, ALIAS : 'PassWordDlgProc' &
              :: PassWordDlgProc
```

```
     !DEC$ ENDIF
     integer*4 hwnd
     integer*4 mesg
     integer*4 wParam
     integer*4 lParam
     end function
  end interface
```

Note: In the preceding code, the lines beginning with `!DEC$ ATTRIBUTES` are compiler directives and are shown with Fortran continuation signs (`&`) at the end of each line, indicating that the code continues onto a second line. This is for typographical convenience only. If you type these lines, they must be entered as a single line.

7.2 Modeless dialog boxes

A modeless dialog box allows a user to switch between the dialog box and the parent window. Modeless dialog boxes are preferred when the user would find it more convenient to keep the dialog box displayed while working in the main window. For example, you may wish to use the mouse to select a point on a drawing and then change its coordinates in the dialog box. The functions CreateDialog or CreateDialogParam are used to create modeless dialog boxes. The two methods are essentially the same, except that the CreateDialogParam allows you to pass a parameter across to the dialog box procedure. The parameter can be a data structure, thereby eliminating the need to use global variables. CreateDialogParam has the following form:

```
CreateDialogParam (hInstance, lpTemplateName, &
    hwndParent, lpDialogFunc, dwInitParam)
```

The function arguments are identical to the function arguments for DialogBoxParam. The difference between CreateDialogParam and DialogBoxParam is that CreateDialogParam returns immediately with the window handle of the dialog box. Normally this handle would be stored as a global variable.

Working with modeless dialog boxes is similar to working with modal boxes, but there are several important differences. In the More Styles options of the dialog properties, the visible option should be checked; otherwise, you will need to call the ShowWindow function immediately after the CreateDialogParam call.

Note: Failure to either set the Visible check box or call ShowWindow will mean that the modeless dialog box will not be displayed. It is so easy to forget this point and then try all sorts of different options to make the dialog box appear.

Modeless dialog boxes must be closed using the DestroyWindow function rather than the EndDialog function used for modal dialog boxes. The user closes the dialog box using either a pushbutton or Close from the system menu:

```
if (LoWord(wParam) == IDOK) then      ! OK Selected?
   iret = DestroyWindow (hdlg)         ! Exit the dialog
   ghDlgModless = 0    ! Set global variable to zero
   ConvertDlgProc = 1
   return
end if
```

Note: The difference between the two window handles: the hDlg parameter to DestroyWindow is the parameter to the dialog box procedure; *ghDlg-Modless* is the global variable returned from CreateDialog that you test within the message loop.

7.2.1 **Modeless dialog box messages**

Unlike modal dialog boxes, messages to modeless dialog boxes come through the program's message queue. The message queue must be altered to pass these messages to the dialog box Windows procedure. Here is how to do it. When creating a modeless dialog box, save the dialog box handle, returned from the call as a global variable. For example:

```
ghDlgModeless = CreateDialogParam (...)
 Then modify the message loop as follows:
do while( GetMessage (mesg, NULL, 0, 0))
   if (ghDlgModeless == 0 .or. IsDialogMessage &
      (ghDlgModless, mesg) == 0) then
      if ( TranslateAccelerator (mesg%Hwnd, haccel, mesg)&
         == 0) then
        bret = TranslateMessage(mesg)
        iret  = DispatchMessage(mesg)
      end if
   end if
end do
```

The IsDialogMessage function performs all necessary translating and dispatching of messages; a valid dialog box message must not be passed to the TranslateMessage or DispatchMessage functions. In the above code, the functions TranslateAccelerator, TranslateMessage, or DispatchMessage will be offered the message only if ghDlgModless is zero or if the message is not for the dialog box. If the message is intended for the modeless dialog box, then IsDialogMessage sends it to the dialog box window procedure and returns TRUE (nonzero); otherwise, it returns FALSE (0).

The IsDialogMessage sends WM_GETDLGCODE messages to the dialog box procedure to determine which keys should be processed. When IsDialogMessage processes a message, it checks for keyboard messages and converts them into selection commands for the corresponding dialog box.

7.3   Currency exchange example

This application illustrates the basic principles of creating a modeless dialog box, but the example could also be created as a modal dialog box. The program also demonstrates how to use common dialog controls such as edit boxes, static text boxes, slider bars, progress bars, and radio buttons. We are already familiar with the use of these controls in a QuickWin environment and need only to see how they are used in a Win32 application. However, before reviewing the use of controls in this application, we will examine how to program some new features to familiar controls. The additional features are illustrated in Figure 7.4.

Edit controls send a WM_CTLCOLOREDIT message to the parent window when the control is about to be drawn. By responding to this message, the parent window can use the specified device context handle to set the color of the text and its background in the edit box. When an application processes this message, it must also return the handle of a brush, which the system uses to paint the background of the edit box. The following is an example of how to change the background color of an edit box:

```
case (WM_CTLCOLOREDIT)
   iret = SetBkColor (wParam, rgb(0,255,250))
   ConvertDlgProc = hEditbrush
return
```

Interestingly, when an edit control is set to read only, it uses the WM_CTLCOLORSTATIC message rather than a WM_CTLCOLOR-EDIT message. The following is an example of how to set the text and

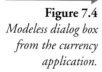

Figure 7.4
*Modeless dialog box
from the currency
application.*

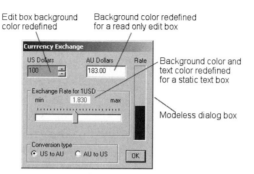

background of a static text control (hrate) and to set the background of an
edit box (hEdit2) that has the read-only property:

```
case (WM_CTLCOLORSTATIC )
   if(lparam ==  hrate) then
      iret = SetTextColor (wParam, rgb(250,0,0))
      iret = SetBkColor (wParam, rgb(255,255,226))
      ConvertDlgProc = hStaticBrush
      return
   end if
   if(lparam == hEdit2) then
      iret = SetBkColor (wParam, rgb(255,255,226))
      ConvertDlgProc = hStaticBrush
      return
   end if
   ConvertDlgProc = 1
   return
```

Note: The system does not destroy the brushes that have been created. It is
the application's responsibility to destroy these brushes when they are no
longer needed.

It is worth looking up the Win32 API index in the WM_CTLCOLOR
section to examine the messages that are available for changing the colors in
dialog boxes, list boxes, and scroll bars.

Spin (up-down) controls are defined in the common controls dynamic-
link library; therefore, we need to include this library by including "use
comctl32" in any program module with this control style. When using
common controls, we also need to define structure based on the type
T_INITCOMMONCONTROLSEX and use that structure to set the
structure size and determine which of the common control class(es) we
want to use. The structure is then used to register class(es) to be used in the

application. The following illustrates how the spin controls are registered for use:

```
type (T_INITCOMMONCONTROLSEX) iccex
iccex%dwSize = sizeof(iccex)
iccex%dwICC = ICC_UPDOWN_CLASS
call initcommoncontrolsex(iccex)
```

Up-down controls are initialized by sending a message to the control. To send a message, we need to have a handle for the control, as follows:

```
hSpin1 = GetDlgItem(hDlg,IDC_SPIN1)
```

The maximum and minimum values of the control are set by sending a UDM_SETRANGE message. The maximum and minimum are compounded into one long (32-bit) value with the MAKELONG macro.

```
iret = SendMessage(hSpin1,UDM_SETRANGE, &
                MAKELONG(MAX_SPIN, MIN_SPIN))
```

The initial starting value for the up-down control is set using the UDM_SETPOS message:

```
iret = SendMessage(hSpin1,UDM_SETPOS,0,MAKELONG(Dollar1,0))
```

Information is placed in an edit box using:

```
iret = SetDlgItemText(hDlg, IDC_EDIT1, &
                trim(adjustl(text))//' 'C)
```

and retrieved text using:

```
Dollar1  = GetDlgItemInt(hDlg, IDC_EDIT1, &
                LOC(result) ,.TRUE.)
```

The progress bar and track bar have messages for setting their range and initial position that correspond to the equivalent up-down button message:

```
iret = SendMessage(hslider1,TBM_SETRANGE,0, &
                MAKELONG(min_slider, max_slider))
iret = SendMessage(hprogress1,PBM_SETRANGE, 0,&
                MAKELONG(min_slider, max_slider))
iret = SendMessage(hprogress1,PBM_SETPOS,slideposition,0)
iret = SendMessage(hslider1,TBM_SETPOS,1,MAKELONG &
                (slideposition ,0))
```

Changes to a track bar position are obtained through the WM_HSCROLL message:

```
case (WM_HSCROLL)
   slideposition = SendMessage(hSlider1,TBM_GETPOS,0,0)
```

Changes to edit box control, Up-Down button controls, and button controls are sent to the WM_COMMAND for testing the low word of wParam against the control's identity number.

```
case (WM_COMMAND)
    if (LoWord(wParam) .EQ. IDC_EDIT1)  then
```

or

```
    if (LoWord(wParam) == IDOK) then     ! OK Selected?
```

Note: Finally, not everyone wants to know exchange rate information between the American and Australian dollar. It would be a very useful exercise for readers to modify this program so that users could, from a list, select the currencies of interest to them.

7.3.1 Image example

In Chapter 4, the About example was used to demonstrate the techniques required for displaying icons and bitmaps in a dialog box. In this section, the Image example will be used to expand these techniques so that we can do the following:

■ Display a metafile in a dialog box.

■ Display icons and bitmaps in buttons.

■ Detect a mouse click on an icon, bitmap, or metafile.

Open a new Win32 SDI project called Images and then create a bitmap named IDB_Finished like that shown in Figure 7.5 and an icon named IDI_Cancel, as shown in Figure 7.6.

Now insert a new dialog box into the project. In the properties box, set the caption to images, and leave the default ID as IDD_DIALOG1. Add on three static controls (picture boxes), and two group boxes. Arrange the above items so that they look like Figure 7.7. Note that in Figure 7.7, the

Figure 7.5
Finished bitmap.

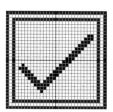

Figure 7.6
Cancel icon.

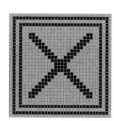

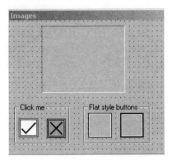

Figure 7.7
*Image dialog box
being created in the
Resource Editor.*

extended style of Tool window has been checked, while System menu in the styles tab has been unchecked. The large single static control type is set to Enhanced Metafile, the style is set to "sunken," and it is given the name IDC_EMFrame.

One of the static controls within the Click me group box is given the name IDC_Bit1; its type is set to bitmap, and its image selected is IDB_Finished. The other static control type is called IDC_Icon1; its type is icon and its image selected is IDI_Cancel.

The OK and Cancel buttons in the "flat-style buttons" group are modified as follows. In the Style tab of the Cancel button, the styles flat and icon are checked, and in the Style tab of the OK button, the styles flat and bitmap are checked.

7.3.2   Dialog procedure for images application

Some of the functionality of this dialog box has a direct parallel with the QuickWin About application, but there are three new features that are worth highlighting as we look at the complete code. These features are placing icon and bitmap images in a button, placing enhanced metafiles in a picture box, and detecting mouse clicks on a picture box. Note that to place an image in a button, we send the button message, BM_SETIMAGE, together with a handle for both the button and the image. We also need to specify whether the image is an icon (IMAGE_ICON) or a bitmap (IMAGE_BITMAP). The enhanced metafile is treated in a similar fashion, except that it is being placed on a static control; therefore, we need to send a static control message, STM_SETIMAGE. Mouse clicks on static controls can be detected in just the same way as mouse clicks on buttons by testing the low word of wParam. The only requirement is that in the Styles tab of the property box of the static control, the notify box must be checked. The code for the Image dialog procedure is as follows:

```
integer(4) function ImageDlgProc(hDlg, message, &
                      wParam, lParam)
! Processes messages for "Image" dialog box
!DEC$ IF DEFINED(_X86_)
!DEC$ ATTRIBUTES STDCALL, ALIAS : '_ImageDlgProc@16'&
          :: ImageDlgProc
!DEC$ ELSE
!DEC$ ATTRIBUTES STDCALL, ALIAS : 'ImageDlgProc' &
          :: ImageDlgProc
!DEC$ ENDIF
use dfwin
use ImagesGlobals
implicit none
integer     hDlg        ! window handle of the dialog box
integer     message     ! type of message
integer     wParam      ! message-specific information
integer     lParam      ! message-specific information
include 'resource.fd'
! Variables
integer(4) iret
integer(4) hButton1,hButton2
integer(4) hIcon1,hBmp1, hEmf
   hIcon1 = LoadIcon(ghInstance, &
      MAKEINTRESOURCE(IDI_Cancel))
   hBmp1 = LoadBitmap(ghInstance, &
      MAKEINTRESOURCE(IDB_Finished))
   hEmf = GetEnhMetaFile("clickme.emf")
   hButton1 = GetDlgItem(hDlg,IDOK)
   hButton2 = GetDlgItem(hDlg,IDCancel)
   select case (message)
      case (WM_INITDIALOG)
         ! Center the dialog over the application window
          call CenterWindow (hDlg, GetWindow (hDlg,&
             GW_OWNER))
         ! message: initialize dialog box
         iret = SendMessage(hButton2, BM_SETIMAGE,&
             IMAGE_ICON, hIcon1)
         iret = SendMessage(hButton1, BM_SETIMAGE, &
             IMAGE_BITMAP, hBmp1)
        iret = SendMessage(GetDlgItem(hdlg, IDC_Emframe), &
              STM_SETIMAGE,IMAGE_ENHMETAFILE,hEmf)
         ImageDlgProc = 1
         return
      case (WM_COMMAND)
         if ((LoWord(wParam) .EQ. IDOK) .OR. &
            (LoWord(wParam) .EQ. IDCANCEL)) then
            iret = EndDialog(hDlg, TRUE) ! Exit the dialog
            iret = DeleteObject(hIcon1)
            iret = DeleteObject(hBmp1)
            iret = DeleteObject(hEMF)
            ImageDlgProc = 1
            return
```

```
                  end if
                  if (LoWord(wParam) .EQ. IDC_EMFrame) then
                     iret = MessageBox (NULL,'Enhanced Metafile'C,  &
                              'Static control with an'C , &
                              IOR(MB_OK ,MB_ICONINFORMATION))
                     ImageDlgProc = 1
                     return
                  end if
                  if(LoWord(wParam) .EQ. IDC_Bit1) then
                     iret = MessageBox (NULL,'Bitmap 'C,  &
                              'Static control with a'C , &
                              IOR(MB_OK ,MB_ICONINFORMATION))
                     ImageDlgProc = 1
                     return
                  end if
                  if(LoWord(wParam) .EQ. IDC_Icon1) then
                     iret = MessageBox (NULL,'Icon 'C,  &
                              'Static control with an'C ,&
                              IOR(MB_OK ,MB_ICONINFORMATION))
                     ImageDlgProc = 1
                     return
                  end if
            end select
            ImageDlgProc = 0 ! Didn't process the message
            return
      end
```

Note: In the preceding code, the lines beginning with !DEC$ ATTRIBUTES are compiler directives and are shown with Fortran continuation signs (&) at the end of each line, indicating that the code continues onto a second line. This is for typographical convenience only. If you type these lines, they must be entered as a single line.

7.3.3 Displaying the dialog box

In our Images application, the dialog box is initiated from within the program by selecting the menu item Image, which calls the following code in WM_COMMAND:

```
      case (IDM_Images)
         iret = DialogBoxParam(ghInstance,IDD_DIALOG1,hWnd,& 
               LOC(ImageDlgProc), 0)
         MainWndProc = 0
         return
```

Figure 7.8
*The dialog box at
run-time
displaying a
message box after
the enhanced
metafile was
clicked.*

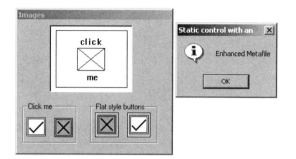

Figure 7.8
*The dialog box at
run-time
displaying a
message box after
the enhanced
metafile was
clicked.*

Click on any one of the three "click me" pictures to display a message identifying which picture type has been clicked. In Figure 7.8, the enhanced metafile has been clicked. The flat-style buttons are the modified OK and Cancel buttons; therefore, clicking onto either button will have the normal effect of closing the dialog box.

7.4   Common controls

7.4.1   Status bars

We encountered the term *common controls* when using Up-Down buttons in the preceding example. The comctl32 dynamic link library provides support for a wide range of controls, including status bars and toolbars. In this chapter, we will focus on status bars, toolbars, and tool tips; in Chapter 11, we will look at some additional common controls. Status bars provide a convenient way to display information about the status of an application. Previously in QuickWin we had no real say in the design of a status bar, but now, using Win32 API calls, we can design our own application-specific status bars with ease (see Figure 7.9).

The status-bar window class must be registered through an application call to InitCommonControlsEx before the status bar can be defined. A sta-

Figure 7.9
*Multiple-part
status bar.*

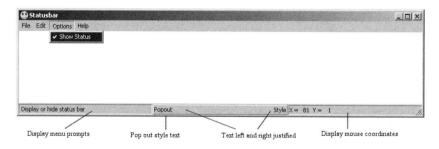

tus bar can be created with the function CreateStatusWindow, which has only four arguments, or it can be created using the CreateWindow or CreateWindowEx functions and specifying the class name as either STATUS-CLASSNAME or the string:

```
"msctls_statusbar32"C
```

Note: The function CreateStatusWindow is used for ASCII (or, more correctly, ANSI) text, while CreateStatusWindowW is the function to use if you need to work with Unicode (or wide characters). All the associated functions, such as SetText, GetText, and so on, end with the letter A for the ANSI version and the letter W for the Unicode (Wide version). Hence, SetTextA and SetTextW refer, respectively, to the ANSI and Unicode versions of the generic function for setting text in a status bar. The status and toolbar examples in this chapter are for ANSI code, but they could also be created for Unicode text.

7.4.2   Multiple-part status bars

A status bar can have up to a maximum of 255 different parts, each displaying a different line of text. The status bar is divided into parts by sending an SB_SETPARTS message, which specifies the number of parts to create and the address of an integer array. This array contains one entry for each part, to specify the client coordinate of the right-hand edge of that part.

Text for any part of a status bar is set by sending the SB_SETTEXTA message and specifying the zero-based index of a part, an address of the string to draw in the part, and the technique for drawing the string (e.g., pop-out style). By default, text is left-aligned within the specified part of a status bar. However, tab characters (\t) embedded in the text will cause the text to be centered or right-aligned. Text to the right of a single tab character is centered, and text to the right of a second tab character is right-aligned.

Here are the code fragments from the example status bar to illustrate the process of creating, sizing, and communicating with a multiple-part status bar. First, the status bar is created in WM_CREATE as follows:

```
case (WM_CREATE)
   ihWndstatus = CreateStatusWindow(IOR(WS_CHILD, &
          WS_VISIBLE), " "C, hWnd , IDC_StatusBar)
   ! set global status bar flag
   gStatusBar = 1
   !  Set number of parts in Status bar
```

```
      iParts = 3
      MainWndProc = 0
      return
```

Next, the status bar is sized to the width of the client area and divided into three parts. The middle section of the status bar has the property of pop-out. This is achieved by combining the section number (starts at 0) with the style SBT_POPOUT:

```
case (WM_SIZE)
   cxClient = loword(lParam)
   cyClient = hiword(lParam)
   iret = GetWindowRect(ihWndStatus,RectStatus)
   iSBheight = Abs(RectStatus%bottom-RectStatus%top)
   iret = GetClientRect(hWnd,rcClient)
   cxWidth = rcClient%right/iParts
   iStep = cxWidth
   do i = 0,iParts-1
      lpParts(i) = cxWidth
      cxWidth = cxWidth + iStep
   end do
   iret = SendMessage(ihWndStatus, SB_SETPARTSA, iParts, &
         loc(lpParts))
   iret = MoveWindow(ihWndStatus ,0,cyClient-iSBheight, &
         cxClient, cyClient, redraw)
   szStatusText ='Popout \t\tStyle'C
   iret = SendMessage(ihWndStatus, SB_SETTEXTA, &
         ior(1,SBT_POPOUT), loc(szStatusText))
   szStatusText =' Ready'C
   iret = SendMessage(ihWndStatus, SB_SETTEXT,0, &
         loc(szStatusText))
   return
```

When menu prompts are filled in the property box for each menu item, they are saved in the string table with a value corresponding to the menu item ID. It is a simple matter of detecting where the mouse is on the menu from the low word of wParam in WM_MENUSELECT and obtaining the corresponding prompt string. The following code provides a ready prompt when the mouse is over a separator bar:

```
case (WM_MENUSELECT )
   value = 0
   szStatusText = "Ready "c
   value = loword(wparam)
   iret=LoadString(ghinstance,value, szStatusText, 80)
   if(value < 200) then
      szStatusText = " Ready"c
   end if
```

```
iret = SendMessage(ihWndStatus, SB_SETTEXTA,0, &
       loc(szStatusText))
MainWndProc = 1
return
```

Mouse *x* and *y* coordinates are taken from the low word and high word of lParam, respectively, and then they are written to the third section of the status bar as follows:

```
case (WM_MOUSEMOVE)
    x = int2(LOWORD(lParam))
    y = int2(HIWORD(lParam))
    write(szStatusText,'("X = ",I4,2X,"Y = ",I4)')x,y
    iret = SendMessage(ihWndStatus, SB_SETTEXTA,2, &
           loc(szStatusText))
    MainWndProc = 1
    return
```

When creating a status bar, the user is required to provide an ID value as a control identifier for the status bar. Windows uses this value to identify any messages that it sends to the parent window. We need to provide a unique number that is not already in use. One method is to open the Resource.h file and place an ID for the status bar after the last control ID. (See Figure 7.10.) In this example, the ID number for the status bar is 1006. You also need to increment the next control value from 1006 to 1007. Then enter the same status bar ID value into the Resource.FD file and recompile the program.

Figure 7.10

Directly setting an ID value for the status bar in Resource.h.

```
// Used by Statusbar.rc
//
#define IDC_VER1              1001
#define IDC_VER2              1002
#define IDC_VER3              1003
#define IDC_VER4              1004
#define IDC_VER5              1005
#define IDC_StatusBar         1006
#define IDM_EXIT              30001
#define IDM_NEW               30002
#define IDM_OPEN              30003
#define IDM_SAVE              30004
#define IDM_SAVEAS            30005
#define IDM_PRINT             30006
#define IDM_PRINTSETUP        30007
#define IDM_UNDO              30008
#define IDM_CUT               30009
#define IDM_COPY              30010
#define IDM_PASTE             30011
#define IDM_HELPCONTENTS      30012
#define IDM_HELPSEARCH        30013
#define IDM_HELPHELP          30014
#define IDM_ABOUT             30015
#define IDM_ShowStatus        30016

// Next default values for new objects
//
#ifdef APSTUDIO_INVOKED
#ifndef APSTUDIO_READONLY_SYMBOLS
#define _APS_NEXT_RESOURCE_VALUE    104
#define _APS_NEXT_COMMAND_VALUE     30023
#define _APS_NEXT_CONTROL_VALUE     1007
#define _APS_NEXT_SYMED_VALUE       101
#endif
#endif
```

The advantage of this approach is that the ID number allocated to the status bar will not conflict with any current or still to be created control ID number defined by the Resource Editor.

7.4.3   Toolbar

Typically, the buttons in a toolbar correspond to items in the application's menu, providing an additional and more direct way for the user to access an application's commands. Figure 7.11 shows a window that has a toolbar positioned below the menu bar. Toolbars can also be positioned at the bottom of the window, a more suitable position for an application displaying an animation sequence.

Toolbar creation is a straightforward process using either the CreateToolbarEx function or the CreateWindowEx function. With the CreateWindowEx function, the window class name is specified as either TOOLBARCLASSNAMEA or as the string `"ToolbarWindow32"`C. This creates a toolbar that initially contains no buttons. Buttons are added to the toolbar by sending either a TB_ADDBUTTONSA or a TB_INSERT-BUTTON message. The TB_AUTOSIZE message should be sent after all of the items and strings have been inserted into the control so that the toolbar will recalculate its size based on its content. The TOOLBARCLASS-NAMEA window class is registered when the common control dynamic-link library (DLL) is loaded through an application call to InitCommon-ControlsEx.

Note: Remember to use the function TOOLBARCLASSNAMEW to get the Unicode version, and to use TB_ADDBUTTONSW.

A toolbar that is created using the function CreateWindowEx must specify the WS_CHILD window style, whereas CreateToolbarEx includes the WS_CHILD style by default. Essentially, both functions are the same.

Figure 7.11
Standard toolbar.

In this example, we will use CreateWindowEx, and in the next example, we will use CreateToolbar. The initial parent window is specified when a toolbar is created, but the parent window can be changed after creation by using the TB_SETPARENT message. The CCS_TOP and CCS_BOTTOM common control styles determine whether the toolbar is positioned along the top or bottom of the client area. By default, a toolbar has the CCS_TOP style.

7.4.4 **Toolbar bitmaps**

A toolbar stores the information that it needs to draw bitmaps in an internal image list. Each image has a zero-based index. The first image added to the internal list has an index of zero, the second image has an index of one, and so on. The message TB_ADDBITMAP is sent to add images to the end of the image list. An image's index in the list is used to associate the image with a toolbar button.

Toolbar bitmap images can be created in the Resource Editor by clicking the sequence Insert, Resource, Toolbar, and New. This will cause a toolbar image with an ID like IDR_Toolbar1 to be displayed with blank button images. You can then draw your own images directly onto the buttons, or you can import bitmap images and paste them onto individual buttons. Another way is to use a single bitmap that contains a standard set of toolbar images. A bitmap of this type ships with the CVF samples. Here is how to import this bitmap into the Resource Editor and use it for creating a toolbar.

In the mixed-language section of the CVF samples, open the RES folder of the Spline example and copy the toolbar.bmp into a suitable working folder. Then in Developer Studio, click the sequence Insert, Resource, Bitmap, and Import. Locate the bitmap named toolbar.bmp and click the Import button. The imported single bitmap will contain a series of button bitmap images similar to those in Figure 7.12.

The bitmap can be converted into a set of button images by clicking on the Image menu in Developer Studio and selecting Toolbar Editor. Accept the default button height of 16 pixels and width of 15 pixels, and you will be presented with a toolbar containing individual buttons with their associ-

Figure 7.12
Toolbar bitmap imported from the CVF Spline example.

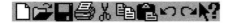

ated bitmaps. Individual button bitmaps can now be copied, pasted, or modified with ease. If you double-click on a button and open up its property box, you will discover that it has an ID something like ID_BUTTON30026. It is a good idea to click on the combo box and choose the ID of the menu item that corresponds to the bitmap—for example, IDM_New or IDM_Open. This is not necessary for this example, but it is necessary in the next example, in which the button tool tip is taken from the prompt string of the corresponding menu item.

Here are the steps required in creating a toolbar complete with buttons and bitmaps:

- Ensure that the common control DLL is loaded.

```
type (T_INITCOMMONCONTROLSEX) iccex
iccex%dwSize = sizeof(iccex)
iccex%dwICC = ICC_BAR_CLASSES
call initcommoncontrolsex(iccex)
```

- Create a toolbar:

```
hwndTB = CreateWindowEx(WS_EX_TOPMOST, TOOLBARCLASSNAMEA, &
        ""C, WS_CHILD, 0, 0, 0, 0, hwnd, Null, &
        ghInstance, NULL)
```

- Load ten bitmap images into the toolbar, using a `type` `T_TBADDBITMAP` variable.

```
type (T_TBADDBITMAP) TBaddBitmap
```

- Send the TB_BUTTONSTRUCTSIZE message:

```
iret=SendMessage(hwndTB, TB_BUTTONSTRUCTSIZE,20, 0)
```

Note: Note that the value of 20 that is sent with the TB_BUTTON-STRUCTSIZE message is related to the size of that structure and has nothing to do with the size of a button.

Now add the bitmap containing button images to the toolbar:

```
TBaddBitmap%hInst = ghInstance
TBaddBitmap%nID   = IDB_BITMAP1
iret=SendMessage(hwndTB, TB_ADDBITMAP,&
            10,LOC(TBaddBitmap))
```

Information concerning ten buttons and five separators is entered in the array TBbutton(15), which is based on the T_TBBUTTON type. Values for `TBbutton(i)%iBitmap` are ignored when buttons have the separator style.

```
do i = 1,15
   TBbutton(i)%iBitmap = tbbitmaps(i)
   TBbutton(i)%idCommand = tbCommands(i)
   TBbutton(i)%fsState = TBSTATE_ENABLED
   TBbutton(i)%fsStyle =  TBSTYLE_BUTTON
   TBbutton(i)%dwData =  0
   TBbutton(i)%iString = 0
end do
```

Now set the separators:

```
TBbutton(1)%fsStyle = TBSTYLE_SEP
TBbutton(3)%fsStyle = TBSTYLE_SEP
TBbutton(7)%fsStyle = TBSTYLE_SEP
TBbutton(11)%fsStyle = TBSTYLE_SEP
TBbutton(14)%fsStyle = TBSTYLE_SEP
```

Finally, the buttons are added to the toolbar:

```
iret=SendMessage(hwndTB, TB_ADDBUTTONSA, 15,LOC(TBbutton))
iret=SendMessage(hwndTB,TB_SETBUTTONSIZE,0,MAKELONG(16,16))
iret=SendMessage(hWndTB,TB_AUTOSIZE,0,0)
iret=ShowWindow(hwndTB, SW_SHOW)
```

7.4.5   Toolbar with tool tips

Toolbars that have been created with the style TBSTYLE_TOOLTIPS provide tool tip support for toolbar buttons. A tool tip control is a small pop-up window that contains a line of text describing a toolbar button. The width of the tool tip window varies according to the length of text being displayed. When the toolbar receives a WM_MOUSEMOVE message, it sends a notification message to the tool tip control. The tool tip control sets a timer. If, after approximately one second, the cursor is still at the same location and it is on a toolbar button, the tool tip control will send a TTN_GETDISPINFOA notification message to the parent window to retrieve the descriptive text for the button. Then the tool tip control creates a pop-up window and displays the text in the window. The tool tip control destroys the pop-up window when the user clicks a mouse button or moves the cursor of the button.

Once the tool tip control has been created for the buttons, it is a straightforward matter to provide additional tool tip support for tools such as edit boxes and combo boxes (see Figure 7.13). These tools are registered with the tool tip control by sending a TTM_ADDTOOLA message.

Figure 7.13
*Tool tip support for
toolbar controls.*

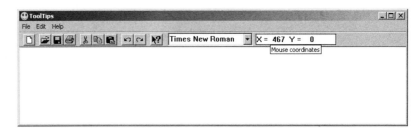

The TTM_ADDTOOLA message includes the address of a
TOOLINFO structure, which is required to provide information needed to
display the text for the tool. The WIN32 TOOLINFO structure (defined
in CVF as type T_TTTOOLINFO) has the following members:

- cbSize—Size of the TOOLINFO structure, in bytes.

- uFlags—Set of bit flags. This member can be a combination of flags;
  see the online information for options.

- hwnd—Handle to the window that contains the tool.

- uId—Application-defined identifier of the tool. If uFlags includes the
  TTF_IDISHWND flag, uId must specify the window handle to the
  tool.

- rect—Tool's bounding rectangle coordinates. The coordinates are relative to the upper-left corner of the client area of the window identified by hwnd. If uFlags includes the TTF_IDISHWND flag, this
  member is ignored.

- hinst—Handle to the instance that contains the string resource for
  the tool. If lpszText specifies the identifier of a string resource, this
  member is used.

- lpszText—Address of the buffer that contains the text for the tool, or
  identifier of the string resource that contains the text.

- lParam—Version 4.70. A 32-bit application-defined value that is
  associated with the tool.

This structure is implemented for a combo and edit box in the Tooltips
program, as follows:

```
type (T_TTTOOLINFO) lpToolInfo
```

The toolbar has already been created with the tool tip style. The toolbar
handle is hwndTB. Next we get a handle to the tool tip control and check
that it has been successfully created.

```
hWndTT = SendMessage(hwndTB, TB_GETTOOLTIPS,0,0)
if(hWndTT /= 0) then
```

Tool tip handle is valid, so we set the tool tip information for the combo box:

```
lpTipText = 'Select Font'C
   lpToolInfo%cbsize = sizeof(lpToolInfo)
   lpToolInfo%uflags = ior(TTF_IDISHWND,ior(TTF_SUBCLASS, &
                           TTF_CENTERTIP))
   lpToolInfo%lpsztext = loc(lpTipText)
   lpToolInfo%hwnd = hwndTB
   lpToolInfo%uId =  ghWndCombo
   lpToolInfo%hwnd = ghInstance
   iret = SendMessage(hwndTT,TTM_ADDTOOLA,0,&
                      loc(lpToolInfo))
```

Now set the information for the edit box:

```
lpTipText = 'Mouse coordinates'C
   lpToolInfo%uId = ghWndEdit
   iret = SendMessage(hwndTT,TTM_ADDTOOLA,0,&
                      loc(lpToolInfo))
else
   iret = MessageBox (hwnd, "Cannot create tooltip"C,&
                "Create TooLTip"C, IOR(MB_SYSTEMMODAL,&
                IOR(MB_OK, MB_ICONHAND)))
end if
```

The tool tip control will now automatically display the tip associated with the combo box and edit box every time the mouse remains over the control.

Implementing the tool tips for the toolbar buttons is somewhat more involved. When the mouse is over a button for a short period of time, the tool tip control will send a TTN_GETDISPINFOA (or, for a Unicode version, TTN_GETDISPINFOW) notification request to the parent window so that it can retrieve the descriptive text for the button. The TTN_GETDISPINFOA request is handled through the parent window's WM_NOTIFY message. The lParam associated with the WM_NOTIFY message is a pointer to an NMTTDISPINFO structure whose first member is an NMHDR structure called hdr, which contains information about the button that sent a TTN_GETDISPINFOA request.

The NMHDR structure has the following information about a notification message:

- hwndFrom—Window handle to the control sending a message

- idFrom—Identifier of the control sending a message

- code—Member notification code

We need to check the notification code in an NMHDR structure to determine whether it is a TTN_GETDISPINFOA request. If it is, then the requested text is placed in an NMTTDISPINFO structure. Until now, we needed only to point to a location and so we used the Fortran `loc` statement; but on this occasion, we need to point to a structure, which requires us to use C-style pointers. Fortunately, CVF provides support for C-style pointers, and here is how we can define the pointer ptext, as pointing to an NMTTDISPINFO structure called lpToolTipText.

```
type (T_NMTTDISPINFO) lpToolTipText
pointer(ptext, lpToolTipText)
```

The following WM_NOTIFY message contains the code used to handle any TTN_GETDISPINFOA requests. If the code member of that structure is equal to TTN_GETDISPINFOA, then we must process the request. If this is a valid TTN_GETDISPINFOA request, ptext is set to lparam, and a string is loaded from the string table into szTipText. Notice that idfrom member of the hdr (NMHDR type) member of lpToolTipText (NMTTDISPINFO type) is used to select the correct string.

```
case(WM_NOTIFY)
   ptext = lparam
   if(lpToolTipText%hdr%code == TTN_GETDISPINFOA) then
      ptext = lparam
      iret  = LoadString(ghinstance, &
                 lpToolTipText%hdr%idfrom, &
                 szTipText, MAXLEN)
      lpToolTipText%lpszText = loc(szTipText)
   end if
           MainWndProc = 0
           return
```

Note: The tool tip and the corresponding menu item can either share the same text or display different text. The system will automatically strip the ampersand (&) accelerator characters from all strings passed to a tool tip control, unless the control has the TTS_NOPREFIX style.

7.5   What is next?

In the next chapter, we will look at common dialog boxes and find out how to select fonts and colors, use a printer, get file names for opening and closing files, and find sample text in a file.

8

Common Dialog Boxes

8.1   Using common dialog boxes

The common dialog box library promotes a standardized user interface that can be used from QuickWin or Win32 applications. This library consists of functions that include standard dialog boxes for opening and saving files, finding and replacing text, choosing fonts, and printing files. The USE commdlg32 statement must be included in any file that uses the common dialog box library. All the dialog boxes are modal with the exception of the find and replace dialog boxes, which are modeless so that when they are displayed, the focus can be with either the control or the application. Common dialog boxes are easy to display, although you need to write the code that is actually used to read, write, and print files; set fonts; change colors; and find or replace text. To use these dialog boxes, you must initialize the fields of a structure and pass a pointer to the structure to a function in the common dialog library. The function creates and displays the common dialog box. After the user makes a selection and closes the dialog box, control is returned to your program where, by examining the field members of the relevant structure, you can obtain information input by the user.

When an error occurs with the initialization or opening of a common control, the error can be obtained by calling the CommDlgExtendedError function, which returns an error value that identifies the cause of the most recent error. The online documentation contains information describing each error. It is obviously convenient for application users to have the application provide them with error information, especially if the user does not have access to the online information. This can be achieved by creating a string table entry in the application resource file to link the error code and the error message. The application can then display the appropriate error message. However, I tend to use the file COMDLGER.F90, which comes with the Chaos example in the QuickWin section. This subroutine can be copied to any program. The only change needed is to the message box line, depending on whether the program is a QuickWin or a Win32 application. One caveat is that COMDLGER.F90 as it is supplied does not detail all the possible errors for the common dialog boxes. I have just used COM-DLGER.F90 as supplied, but you may wish to look up the online information on the CommDlgExtendedError function for additional error messages and add them to COMDLGER.F90.

In the following sections, the application Scribe1 from Chapter 6 is used as the base example to demonstrate each of the following common dialog controls.

- Getting name of file to open or save

- Selecting a color

- Selecting a font

- Page setup and printing a file

- Finding a text

- Replacing a text

8.2   Opening and saving files

In addition to getting the name of a selected file, the Open and Save As common dialog boxes also permit the user to create files and navigate through any file and directory system. As you can see in the OpenScribe2 dialog box example shown in Figure 8.1, the current folder's contents are displayed in a list control. By clicking the rightmost toolbar button, a user can toggle the display between details view and list view. In this example, you can see not only the object's name, but also its size, type, and when it was last modified.

The Open common dialog box and the Save As common dialog box both use the same dialog template and the same structure, OPENFILE-NAME, to initialize them. The only real difference is in the way you display the dialog boxes: To open a file, you use the GetOpenFileName function, and to save a file, you use the GetSaveFileName function.

Applications using open and close dialog boxes must first fill out the OPENFILENAME structure, which includes the items needed to initialize the dialog box. Descriptions of the field members associated with the OPENFILENAME structure can be found in the online documentation. The following code is from OpenScribe2. An OPENFILENAME structure,

Figure 8.1

Open common dialog box from OpenScribe2 shown in a Windows 2000 environment.

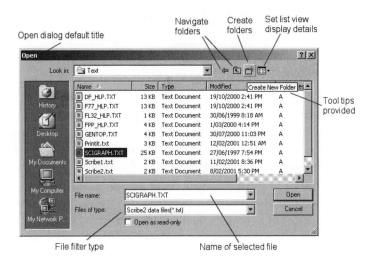

Ofn, is declared in the global variables as a Fortran type T_OPEN-FILENAME. The structure is initialized through a call made in WM_CREATE to the function InitializeOpen and the fields are filled as follows:

```fortran
integer(4) function InitializeOpen()
! initialize open file name structure
use OpenScribe2Globals
use comctl32
implicit none
   szfilter = 'Scribe2 data files(*.txt)' &
            // char(0) // '*.txt' // char(0)
   Ofn%lStructSize = sizeof(Ofn)
   Ofn%hwndowner = ghwndMain
   Ofn%hinstance = gHinstance
   Ofn%lpstrfilter = LOC(szfilter)
   Ofn%LPSTRCUSTOMFILTER = NULL
   Ofn%NMAXCUSTFILTER = 0
   Ofn%NFILTERINDEX = 1
   Ofn%LPSTRFILE = LOC(szFileName)
   Ofn%NMAXFILE = LEN(szFileName)
   Ofn%LPSTRFILETITLE = loc(szTitleName//".txt"C)
   Ofn%NMAXFILETITLE = 25
   Ofn%LPSTRINITIALDIR = NULL
   Ofn%LPSTRTITLE = null
   Ofn%FLAGS = NULL
   Ofn%NFILEOFFSET = NULL
   Ofn%NFILEEXTENSION =NULL
   Ofn%LPSTRDEFEXT = loc("*.txt"C)
   Ofn%LCUSTDATA = NULL
```

```
    Ofn%LPFNHOOK = NULL
    Ofn%LPTEMPLATENAME = NULL
    initializeOpen = 1
    return
end
```

Once the structure has been filled out, calling the function GetOpen-FileName and passing the structure as the sole argument opens the Open common dialog. The function will return a value of .true if no errors have occurred and the file can be opened. The global character string szFileName will contain the selected file name including the full path to the application. If the function returns a value of .false., then the user has either pressed "cancel" or an error has occurred. The subroutine COMDLGER is called to determine the cause of the error message. This subroutine displays a message box with information about the nature of the error, and it returns the error code for the application to process as required. This is the code in OpenScribe2, which responds to the selection of the menu item Open in the File menu.

```
case (IDM_OPEN):
! get open file dialog box
Ofn%Flags = null
bret = GETOPENFILENAME(Ofn)
!   check to see if the OK button has been pressed
if(bret == .false.) then   !   check for error
    call COMDLGER(ierror)
    ! ierror is the returned error value
else
    ...
    call LoadFile(hWndEdit)
end if
MainWndProc = 0
return
```

The Save As dialog box uses the same OPENFILENAME structure as the Open dialog box with one exception. For the Save As dialog box, the flags are set to OFN_OVERWRITEPROMPT, so that the program will prompt the user to confirm whether the user wants to overwrite an existing file. This flag is set to NULL before using the Open dialog box. This is the code from OpenScribe2 for the Save As menu item:

```
case (IDM_SAVEAS)
!   get save file dialog box
Ofn%flags = OFN_OVERWRITEPROMPT
bret = GETSAVEFILENAME(Ofn)
! check to see if the OK button has been pressed
if(bret == .false.) then   !   check for error
```

```
       call COMDLGER(ierror)
       ! ierror is the returned error value
    else
       ...
       call SaveFile(hWndEdit)
    end if
    MainWndProc = 0
    return
```

8.2.1   Unicode considerations

The actual modification to the generic load and save file code of Scribe1 is trivial, since it involves only replacing the fixed file name with the character variable *szFileName*. We can open any text files, not only the one that we created, and this leads to an interesting problem. Until recently, text files were based on single-byte ASCII (or more correctly, ANSI) characters, but with increasing emphasis on international standardization, the double-byte character set Unicode is becoming more popular. For this reason, applications processing text should determine whether a file is ANSI or Unicode and then use the appropriate Win32 functions. In Win32, the letter A (ANSI) or W (wide) is added at the end of a generic function name, as appropriate. For example, the generic function GetWindowText is implemented both as GetWindowTextA and as GetWindowTextW. Windows NT and 2000 provide complete support for Unicode, whereas Windows 98 and ME provide only limited support. If you are not sure whether a function is available in Unicode or ANSI form on a particular operating system, look up the generic function in the online documentation, and the Quick Info section will provide information about the existence of Unicode and ANSI versions. However, our Scribe program is purely a framework to demonstrate possibilities rather than a complete application; therefore, it only uses single-byte (ANSI) characters. Currently, in Visual Fortran, the generic function name can be used for ANSI functions.

8.3   Selecting colors

The Color common dialog box provides users with an easy way to select from a provided choice of colors or to interactively create their own colors. The basic dialog box shown in Figure 8.2 contains a control that can display 48 basic colors plus 16 custom colors. Initially, the color dialog box presents only the left-hand side of the dialog displayed in Figure 8.2, but when the user clicks the Define Custom Colors button, the width of the dialog box expands to include the custom colors control on the right-hand side. With

Figure 8.2
The Color common dialog box as displayed in ColorScribe2.

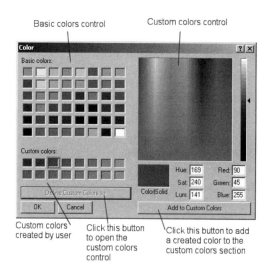

Basic colors control

Custom colors control

Custom colors created by user

Click this button to open the custom colors control

Click this button to add a created color to the custom colors section

this control, the user can create a new color by specifying red, green, and blue (RGB) values; or by specifying hue, saturation, and luminosity (HSL) values. The Color/Solid control displays both the dithered color (a mixture of solids) and the solid color that corresponds to the user's selection. After the user has created a custom color, clicking the Add To Custom Control button will cause the new color to be displayed in a Custom Colors section of the dialog box.

Before displaying a Color common control dialog box, an application must initialize a CHOOSECOLOR structure, which contains information such as the parent of the dialog box, the custom colors that should appear initially, and the use of hooks and templates to customize the dialog box. The following code demonstrates how to fill out the structure and make the subsequent call to ChooseColor, the function that displays and handles the dialog box. Refer to the online help documentation for a description of the field members associated with the CHOOSECOLOR structure. Notice that the custom colors are filled with a variety of colors. The CHOOSE-COLOR structure getcolor, which is declared as a global variable, is initialized in WM_CREATE by calling to the function initializeColors. The field members of getcolor are filled in as follows:

```
integer(4) function initializeColors(hWnd)
! initialize the CHOOSECOLOR structure
use ColorScribe2Globals
use comct132
implicit none
integer iCustomColors(16)
integer(4) hWnd
```

```
integer(2) i
   do i = 1, 8
      iCustomColors(i) = RGB( i*30, i*15, 255)
   end do
   do i = 9, 16
      iCustomColors(i) = RGB(i*15,i*10, 255-(i*15))
   end do
   getcolor%lstructSize = sizeof(getcolor)
   getcolor%hwndOwner= hWnd
   getcolor%hInstance = ghInstance
   getcolor%rgbResult = rgb(0,0,0)
   getcolor%lpCustColors = LOC(iCustomColors)
   getcolor%lCustData = 0
   getcolor%Flags = CC_RGBINIT
   getcolor%lpfnHook = Null
   getcolor%lpTemplateName = Null
   initializeColors = 1
end
```

In ColorScribe2, selection of the Edit menu item Color causes a pointer to the CHOOSECOLOR structure to be passed in a call to the function ChooseColor, after which the Choose Color dialog box is displayed. If the return value from the function is zero, then the subroutine COMDLGER is called to determine whether the Cancel button was pressed or an error had occurred.

```
case (IDM_Color)
iret= ChooseColor(getcolor)
if ( iret .ne. 0) then
   iret = GetClientRect (hWndEdit, rc)
   iret = InvalidateRect (hWndEdit, rc, TRUE)
else
  call COMDLGER(ierror)
end    if
MainWndProc = 0
return
```

The InvalidateRect function causes the edit box to be redrawn, and the new color for the text is set using the function SetTextColor to get-color.rgbResult by means of a WM_CTLCOLOREDIT message. Note that the use of SetTextColor will also require the file dfwina to be used instead of dfwin.

```
case (WM_CTLCOLOREDIT )
   iret = SetTextColor (wParam, getcolor.rgbResult)
   MainWndProc = 0
   return
```

8.4   Choosing fonts

Font selection, along with its associated effects, is only a click of a button away when you use the Font common dialog box. This dialog displays lists of typefaces, styles, and point sizes that correspond to the available fonts, and a dialog box displays sample text rendered in the chosen font, as shown in Figure 8.3. Users can choose special effects such as strikeout, underline, and font color. FontScribe2 is used as the medium for demonstrating the potential of this common dialog box. It must be remembered that FontScribe2 is based on a humble multiline edit box, which means that any font settings will be applied to all the text. If your application needs to provide significant word processing effects, then a Rich Text edit box must be used to take full advantage of this control. Currently CVF does not provide an interface to the Rich Text edit box, so you will need either to wait until this feature is implemented or to provide your own interface definitions.

To use the Font common dialog box, fill out the CHOOSEFONT structure and call the ChooseFont function. The CHOOSEFONT structure contains information such as the attributes of the initial font, the point size, and the types of fonts (screen fonts or printer fonts), as well as hook and template information. In addition to filling out the CHOOSEFONT structure for this common dialog box, we also need to fill out a LOGFONT structure and provide the CHOOSEFONT structure with a pointer to the LOGFONT structure. A description of the fields used in both of these structures can be found in the online documentation.

In the following code from FontScribe2, a LOGFONT structure, lf, has been declared in the global variables as a Fortran type T_LOGFONT, and a CHOOSEFONT structure, chf, has been declared in the global variables as

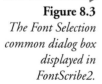

Figure 8.3
The Font Selection common dialog box displayed in FontScribe2.

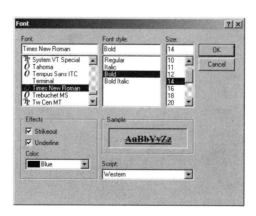

a Fortran type T_CHOOSEFONT. The structures are initialized through a
call made in WM_CREATE to the functions InitializeFont and Initial-
izeChooseFont. The fields in the LOGFONT structure lf are filled in as
follows:

```
integer(4) function InitializeFont()
! intitialize font structure
use FontScribe2Globals
use comctl32
implicit none
   lf%lfHeight = 13
   lf%lfWidth = 0
   lf%lfEscapement = 0
   lf%lfOrientation = 0
   lf%lfWeight = 400
   lf%lfItalic = 0
   lf%lfUnderline = 0
   lf%lfStrikeOut = 0
   lf%lfCharSet = 0
   lf%lfOutPrecision = 0
   lf%lfClipPrecision = 0
   lf%lfQuality = 0
   lf%lfQuality = 0
   lf%lfPitchAndFamily = VARIABLE_PITCH .OR. FF_ROMAN
   lf%lfFaceName  = "Times New Roman"C
   initializeFont = 1
   return
   end
```

The following code demonstrates how to fill in the CHOOSEFONT
structure. In the sample, the flags indicate that the strikeout, underline,
and color effects should be enabled (CF_EFFECTS) and that the fonts
listed should include only the screen fonts supported by the system
(CF_SCREENFONTS).

```
integer(4) function InitializeChooseFont( hWnd )
use dfwina
use FontScribe2Globals
use comctl32
integer hWnd
integer hDC
   hDC = GetDC( hWnd )
   chf%hDC = CreateCompatibleDC( hDC )
   iret = ReleaseDC( hWnd, hDC )
   chf%lStructSize = sizeof(chf)
   chf%hwndOwner = hWnd
   chf%lpLogFont = LOC(lf)
```

```
        chf%Flags = IOR(CF_INITTOLOGFONTSTRUCT,   &
                    ior(CF_SCREENFONTS,   CF_EFFECTS))
        chf%rgbColors = RGB(INT1(0), INT1(0), INT1(0))
        chf%lCustData = 0
        chf%hInstance = NULL
        chf%lpszStyle = NULL
        chf%nFontType = Null
        chf%nSizeMin = 0
        chf%nSizeMax = 0
        chf%lpfnHook = NULL
        chf%lpTemplateName = NULL
        iret = DeleteDC( hDC )
        InitializeChooseFont = 1
    end
```

The font selection dialog box is opened through a call to the Choose-
Font function. The common dialog box automatically sets the font to the
selected specification.

```
case (IDM_FONT)
    iret = ChooseFont( chf )
    if (iret /= 0) then
        iret = DeleteObject(hFont )
        hFont = CreateFontIndirect(lf)
        iret = SendMessage (hwndEdit, WM_SETFONT, &
               hFont, .true.)
        iret = GetClientRect (hWndEdit, rc)
        iret = InvalidateRect (hWndEdit, rc, TRUE)
        !   check for error
        call comdlger(ierror)
    end if
    MainWndProc = 0
    return
```

The text color is set through a call to the rgbcolors part of the
CHOOSEFONT structure. The InvalidateRect function causes the edit
box to be redrawn, after which the new color for the text is set using
the function SetTextColor to chf%rgbColors) by means of a
WM_CTLCOLOREDIT message. The use of SetTextColor will also
require the file dfwina to be used instead of dfwin.

```
case (WM_CTLCOLOREDIT )
    iret = SetTextColor (wParam, chf%rgbColors)
    MainWndProc = 0
    return
```

8.5   Page setup and printing

The common dialog library provides a Print common dialog box, which lets the user configure the printer for a particular print job, and a Page Setup box, which allows the user to set properties such as margins, paper orientation, and paper source. First, we will look at how to use the Print setup dialog box in our applications, and then we will find out how Page Setup is used.

8.5.1   The Print common dialog box

To display a Print dialog box, an application needs only to fill out a PRINTDLG structure and call the function, PrintDlg, with the structure passed as an argument. A sample dialog box is shown in Figure 8.4.

The PRINTDLG structure contains data such as printer device context and initial values for the dialog box controls (such as number of copies and page range). The online documentation provides a full description of the fields in a PRINTDLG structure. The following code shows how to fill in a PRINTDLG structure named pd. The flags PD_USEDEVMODE-COPIES and PD_COLLATE indicate that the application does not support multiple copies or collations of output. If the printer does not support multiple copies, then the number of copies member always returns a value

Figure 8.4
The Printer Selection common dialog box displayed in PrintScribe2.

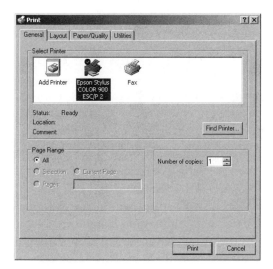

of 1. An application that does not use these styles must handle its own printing and collating of multiple copies.

```
integer(4) function InitializePrintStructure(hWnd)
! intitialize print structure
use PrintScribe2Globals
use comctl32
implicit none
integer(4)hWnd
!  initialize PRINTDLG structure
   pd%lStructSize = sizeof(pd)
   pd%hwndOwner = hWnd
   pd%hDevMode = NULL
   pd%hDevNames = NULL
   pd%hDC       = NULL
   pd%nFromPage = 1
   pd%nToPage = 1
   pd%nMinPage = 1
   pd%nMaxPage = 1
   pd%nCopies = 1
   pd%hInstance = ghInstance
   pd%Flags = IOR(PD_RETURNDC , IOR(PD_ALLPAGES , &
     ior(PD_COLLATE,ior(PD_USEDEVMODECOPIESANDCOLLATE,&
   IOR(PD_NOSELECTION,PD_HIDEPRINTTOFILE)))))
   pd%lpfnSetupHook = NULL
   pd%lpSetupTemplateName = NULL
   pd%lpfnPrintHook = NULL
   pd%lpPrintTemplateName = NULL
   InitializePrintStructure = 1
end
```

8.5.2   The Page Setup common dialog box

The Page Setup common dialog box allows the user to set the paper size, paper source, document orientation, and margins for printing. The sample representation of the page at the top of the dialog box gives the user an idea of what the printed output will look like (see Figure 8.5).

To use the Page Setup common dialog box, an application needs to fill out a PAGESETUPDLG structure and call the PageSetupDlg function. The PAGESETUPDLG structure contains information regarding paper size, paper margins, and minimum margins. A complete description of the fields used in this structure can be found in the online documentation. In PrintScribe2, a call is made from WM_CREATE to the function Initial-izePageStructure to set the fields of a PAGESETUPDLG structure called pageSetUp. Some of the fields such as paper size, margin, and minimum

Figure 8.5
*The Page Setup
common dialog box
displayed in
PrintScribe2.*

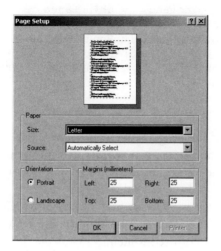

margin are Fortran point and rectangle types. Values for these types should
be specified before setting the fields of the PAGESETUPDLG structure.
This is how it is done in PrintScribe2 with the function InitializePage-
Structure.

```fortran
integer(4) function InitializePageStructure(hWnd)
! intitialize page setup structure
use PrintScribe2Globals
use comctl32
implicit none
integer(4)hWnd
    ! set up page defaults for printer
    rtMinMargin%left = 1000
    rtMinMargin%top = 1000
    rtMinMargin%right = 1000
    rtMinMargin%bottom = 1000
    rtMargins%left = 2500
    rtMargins%top = 2500
    rtMargins%right = 2500
    rtMargins%bottom = 2500
    pageSetUp%lStructSize = sizeof(pageSetUp)
    pageSetUp%hwndOwner = hwnd
    pageSetUp%hDevMode = Null
    pageSetUp%hDevNames = NULL
    pageSetUp%Flags = ior(PSD_DISABLEPRINTER, &
                      ior(PSD_INHUNDREDTHSOFMILLIMETERS, &
                      ior(PSD_MARGINS,ior(PSD_MINMARGINS, &
                      PSD_NONETWORKBUTTON))))
    pageSetUp%ptPaperSize = ptPaperSize
    pageSetUp%rtMinMargin = rtMinMargin
    pageSetUp%rtMargin = rtMargins
```

```
      pageSetUp%hInstance   = ghInstance
      pageSetUp%lCustData = NULL
      pageSetUp%lpfnPageSetupHook   = NULL
      pageSetUp%lpfnPagePaintHook   = NULL
      pageSetUp%lpPageSetupTemplateName   = NULL
      pageSetUp%hPageSetupTemplate   = NULL
      InitializePageStructure = 1
   end
```

Both the Print and Page Setup dialog boxes enable a user to specify paper orientation and size. This provides us with the task of ensuring that the selections made in one box are reflected in the settings displayed in the other box. For our code to make this happen, we need to use another structure that is associated with the printer and called a DEVMODE structure. The structure contains information about the printer and its environment. In our code, we do not need to define any of the fields in a DEVMODE structure, so we will not examine the fields of this structure. However, the interested reader is encouraged to spend a few minutes looking at the online information for the DEVMODE structure.

The Print setup and Page setup information are linked through the field %hDevMode of DEVMODE and PAGESETUPDLG structures. In the code below, before the PageSetupDlg function is called, the field %hDevMode in the PAGESETUPDLG structure is equated with the equivalent field in the PRINTDLG structure, and then the pointer p.dmode is set to the value of pageSetUp%hDevMode. The same idea is applied in reverse when we open the Print setup dialog box. Both dialog boxes will reflect the selection made in the other box. Here is the code for opening these two dialog boxes.

```
      case (IDM_PRINT)
      ! Open up print dialog box
      call PrintFile( hWnd,hwndEdit )
      MainWndProc = 0
      return
      case (IDM_PAGESETUP)
       ! Open up page set up dialog box
      ! Set page dev mode equal to print setup settings
      pageSetUp%hDevMode = pd%hDevMode
      p_dmode = pageSetUp%hDevMode
      bret = PageSetupDlg(pageSetUp)
      if (bret == .false.) then
      !   check for error
      call comdlger(ierror)
      end if
      MainWndProc = 0
      return
```

The other task that we need to address is that of writing the code to get the printer to print pages according to our specifications. Here is the subroutine used in PrintScribe2 to control the printing process. Comments are included to indicate the steps involved.

```
subroutine PrintFile( hWnd,hwndEdit )
use PrintScribe2Globals
use dfwin
use comdlg32
implicit none
integer(4) hWnd,hwndEdit
integer(4) ierror,iret
integer(4) iFileLength
integer(4) itotalLines, itotalPages
integer(4) iPage,iLine,iLineNum
integer(4) cxLeft,cyTop,cyBottom,cxRight
integer(4) iCharsPerLine,iLinesPerPage
integer(4) iCharsPerTextLine
integer(4) cyChar
integer(4) cxCenter,cyFooter
integer(4) metricInch
integer(4) i,j,k
Character(1024) pstrBuffer,currentLine
logical(4) bret
type(T_TEXTMETRIC) :: TEXTMETRIC_Struct
type(T_DEVMODE):: DEVMODE_Struct
pointer(p_dmode,DEVMODE_Struct)
metricInch = 25
pstrBuffer =  "    "C
iFileLength = GetWindowTextLength(hWndEdit)
iret = GetWindowText(hWndEdit, filebuffer, iFilelength+1)
itotalLines = SendMessage(hwndEdit, EM_GETLINECOUNT,0,0)
if (itotalLines == 0) then
return
end if
! Set print dev mode equal to page setup settings
pd%hDevMode = pageSetUp%hDevMode
p_dmode = pd%hDevMode
! Open up print dialog box
iret = PrintDlg(pd)
! If the user clicks the OK button, the return value
! is nonzero
if (iret) then
!  Set margins to device coordinates
cxLeft = pageSetUp%rtMargin%left/100
cxRight = pageSetUp%rtMargin%right/100
cyTop = pageSetUp%rtMargin%top/100
cyBottom = pageSetUp%rtMargin%bottom/100
```

```
cxLeft = GetDeviceCaps(pd%hDC,LOGPIXELSX)*cxLeft /
metricInch
cxRight = GetDeviceCaps(pd%hDC,LOGPIXELSX)*cxRight/
metricInch
cyTop = GetDeviceCaps(pd%hDC,LOGPIXELSY)*cyTop /metricInch
cyBottom = GetDeviceCaps(pd%hDC,LOGPIXELSY)*&
cyBottom /metricInch
!Call the StartDoc function to begin a new print job
iret  = StartDoc(pd%hDC, di)
! Calculate necessary metrics for file
bret = GetTextMetrics(pd%hDC ,TEXTMETRIC_Struct)
cyChar = TEXTMETRIC_Struct%tmHeight + &
            TEXTMETRIC_Struct%tmExternalLeading
iCharsPerLine = (GetDeviceCaps(pd%hDC, HORZRES)- &
            (cxLeft+cxRight))/
TEXTMETRIC_Struct.tmAveCharWidth
iLinesPerPage = (GetDeviceCaps(pd%hDC, VERTRES) - &
                (cyTop+cyBottom))/cyChar
cxCenter = (GetDeviceCaps(pd%hDC, HORZRES))/2
cyFooter =  GetDeviceCaps(pd%hDC, VERTRES) - (cyBottom/2)
iTotalPages = (itotalLines + iLinesPerPage-1) /
iLinesPerPage
! Start the document
di%lpszDocName = Loc(filebuffer)
! Print text
do iPage = 0, iTotalPages
!Prepare the printer driver to accept data by calling
! the StartPage function
iret = StartPage(pd%hDC)
do iLine = 0, iLinesPerPage-1
iLineNum = iLinesPerPage*iPage+iLine
if (iLineNum > iTotalLines) then
exit
end if
iCharsPerTextLine = SendMessage(hwndEdit, EM_GETLINE,&
                    iLineNum,Loc(pstrBuffer) )
! remove any tab stops in line
j=1
currentLine = " "
if( iCharsPerTextLine > 1) then
do i=1, iCharsPerLine
if(pstrBuffer(i:i)== char(9)) then
do k = 1, tabStop
currentLine(j:j) = " "
j = j+1
end do
else
currentLine(j:j) = pstrBuffer(i:i)
j = j+1
```

```
end if
end do
else
currentLine(j:j) = " "
end if
iCharsPerTextLine = j
iret = TextOut(pd%hDC, cxLeft, cyTop+cyChar* &
      iLine, currentLine,iCharsPerTextLine )
end do
if(iPage < iTotalPages)then
write(pstrBuffer,'(I3)')iPage+1
iret = TextOut(pd%hDC, cxCenter, cyFooter,pstrBuffer,3 )
! Finished writing to a page, advance to a new page.
iret = EndPage(pd%hDC)
endif
end do
! End print job
iret = EndDoc(pd%hDC)
iret = DeleteDC(pd%hDC)
if (pd%hDevMode .ne. 0) then
iret = GlobalFree(pd%hDevMode)
end if
if (pd%hDevNames .ne. 0) then
iret = GlobalFree(pd%hDevNames)
end if
else
call comdlger(ierror)
end if
end
```

This code will remove any tab stop controls in the document, adjust the printing margins to reflect the users' choices, and include page numbers in the output. It does not provide any word wrapping when the line of text is too long for the printed page. It will print what it can and discard the rest of the line. With that limitation, it works well and demonstrates a good range of printing techniques.

8.6   Finding and replacing text

The Find dialog box, shown in Figure 8.6, and the Replace dialog box, shown in Figure 8.7, are modeless, which means that the user can switch between the dialog box and the window that created it. With the Find dialog box, the user enters a string of text to be found, and the Replace dialog box is used to search for a specified string then replace it with a specified replace string. As with all modeless dialog boxes, the IsDialogMessage func-

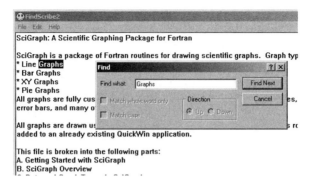

tion should be first in the message loop to ensure that the dialog box sees all messages first.

The Find and Replace dialog boxes use a global FINDREPLACE structure named frText. Look up the online documentation for a complete description of the fields in the FINDREPLACE structures. In FindScribe2, the fields in frText are initially set by calling the function initializeFindText from WM_CREATE. The application may then call the FindText function to display the Find dialog box or the ReplaceText function to display the Replace dialog box. (See Figure 8.7.) Both dialog boxes display an edit box to enter the string to search for and check boxes to provide choices regarding whether to match the case of the string and whether to match the entire string. A listing of the function initializeFindText follows.

```
integer(4) function initializeFindText(hWnd)
! initialize the FINDREPLACE structure
use FindScribe2Globals
use comctl32
implicit none
integer hWnd
   frText%lStructSize = sizeof( frText )
   frText%hwndOwner = hwnd
   frText%hInstance = ghInstance
   frText%lpstrFindWhat = LOC(szFindString)
   frText%wFindWhatLen = len(szFindString)
   frText%lpstrReplaceWith = loc( szReplaceString)
   frText%wReplaceWithLen = len( szReplaceString)
   frText%lCustData = 0
   frText%Flags =  IOR(FR_NOMATCHCASE, IOR(FR_NOUPDOWN, &
                   FR_NOWHOLEWORD))
   frText%lpfnHook = NULL
   frText%lpTemplateName = NULL
   initializeFindText = 1
end
```

Figure 8.7

*The Find and
Replace dialog box
used in
FindScribe2 to
replace the word
"graphs" with
"charts" in this
SciGraph text file.*

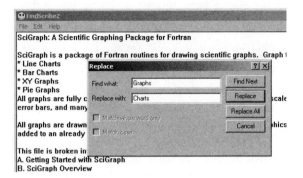

The code used in FindScribe2 to open the Find and Replace boxes follows the pattern used for the previous common dialog boxes. One difference is that the values returned from the call to the functions are used as global handles in the message loop to ensure that keyboard messages, such as tab, are sent to the dialog box. The values for the fields lpstrReplaceWith and wReplaceWithLen in the FINDREPLACE structure are toggled according to whether the Find dialog box or the Replace dialog box is to be used.

```
type (T_FINDREPLACE) fr
pointer (lpFR,   fr)
character(FILE_LEN)  lpszText
pointer(ptext,lpszText)
   select case ( mesg )
         ... code omitted here
      case (IDM_Find)
         ghDlgModeless = FindText(frText)
         if ( ghDlgModeless == .false.) then
            !   check for error
            call comdlger(ierror)
         end if
         MainWndProc = 0
         return
      case (IDM_Replace )
         ghDlgModeless = ReplaceText(frText)
         if ( ghDlgModeless == .false.) then
            !   check for error
            call comdlger(ierror)
         end if
         MainWndProc = 0
         return
```

For an application to process messages from a Find or a Replace dialog box, the application must use the RegisterWindowMessage function to resister the dialog box's unique message. The following piece of code is placed in the WM_CREATE section:

```
FindReplaceMsg = RegisterWindowMessage(FINDMSGSTRINGA)
```

All messages from the Find and Replace dialog boxes are processed in the default messages section by comparing the Windows message with the stored value for the variable *FindReplaceMsgA*. When the Windows message is from a Find or a Replace dialog box, then lParam is a pointer to a FIND-REPLACE structure and the flags of that structure can be tested to determine which button the user has selected. In the following code from FindScribe2, a local FINDREPLACE structure named fr is used as the structure at which the lParam message points, and the flags of fr are tested to find which button has been pressed. However, it is the global FIND-REPLACE structure frText that contains the text input by the user to the displayed dialog box. The following code is used to determine which button has been pressed and then take the appropriate action. The two functions called in the following code, FindNextText and ReplaceThisText, do the actual work of finding and replacing text, and both of them will be examined immediately after this code listing.

```
case default
! Process Find-Replace messages
if (mesg == FindReplaceMsg) then
   lpFR= lParam
   if(Iand(fr%Flags ,FR_FINDNEXT)== FR_FINDNEXT) then
      ptext= frText%lpstrFindWhat
      szFindString = lpszText
      iret= FindNextText(hwndEdit)
      if(iret == 0) then
      iret = MessageBox(Null, "No match found", &
            "Find Text"C, MB_OK )
      endif
      MainWndProc = 0
      return
   end if
   if(Iand(fr%Flags ,FR_REPLACE) == FR_REPLACE) then
      ptext= frText%lpstrFindWhat
      szFindString = lpszText
      ptext=  frText%lpstrReplaceWith
      szReplaceString = lpszText
      iret= ReplaceThisText(hwndEdit)
      if(iret == 0) then
         iret = MessageBox(Null, "Cannot replace text",&
            "Replace Text"C, MB_OK )
      endif
```

```
            MainWndProc = 0
            return
         end if
         if(Iand(fr%Flags ,FR_REPLACEALL) == FR_REPLACEALL) then
            ptext= frText%lpstrFindWhat
            szFindString = lpszText
            ptext=  frText%lpstrReplaceWith
            szReplaceString = lpszText
            iret=1
            do while (iret /=0)
               iret= ReplaceThisText(hwndEdit)
            end do
            MainWndProc = 0
            return
         end if
         if(Iand(fr%Flags ,FR_DIALOGTERM) == FR_DIALOGTERM ) then
            ipos= 0
            iOffset=1
            ghDlgModeless = 0
            MainWndProc = 0
            return
         end if
         MainWndProc = 0
         return
      end if
! Let the default window proc handle all other messages
MainWndProc = DefWindowProc(hWnd, mesg, wParam, lParam)
```

The work of the Find and Replace dialog boxes is now finished, and we need to write the code to make the user's choice happen. Here is the code, used in FindScribe2, to find the next occurrence of a given string in a file. The technique makes use of simple Fortran string-handling concepts and is self-explanatory. The string to be found is contained in the global variable *szFindString*. The code is located in the file FindAndReplace.f90.

```
integer(4) function FindNextText(hwndEdit)
use FindScribe2Globals
integer(4) ilen
integer(4) ilength
integer(4) iret
integer(4) hwndEdit
   iLength = GetWindowTextLength(hWndEdit)
   iret = GetWindowText(hWndEdit, filebuffer, ilength+1)
   do ilen= 1, FILE_LEN
      if(iachar(szFindString(ilen:ilen))<1) exit
   end do
   ilen = ilen - 1
```

```
   if(iOffset==0) then
      iOffset=1
   endif
   ipos=index(filebuffer(iOffSet:ilength), &
         szFindString(1:ilen))
   if(ipos==0)then
      iOffset= ipos
      FindNextText= 0
   else
      iOffset= iOffset+ipos
      iret=SendMessage(hWndEdit,EM_SETSEL,&
            iOffset-2,iOffset+ilen-2)
      iret:SendMessage(hWndEdit,EM_SCROLLCARET,0,0)
      FindNextText= 1
   endif
end function
```

The code to perform the replace is just an extension of the code used to find a specified string. Once the required string has been identified and highlighted by sending the EM_SETSEL, it is a simple matter of sending the EM_REPLACESEL message together with the address of the replace string. The operating system does the rest. The string to be replaced is contained in the global variable *szFindString*, and the string containing the new character sequence is contained in the global variable *szReplaceString*. Here is the code, which is also located in the file FindAndReplace.f90.

```
integer(4) function ReplaceThisText(hwndEdit)
use FindScribe2Globals
integer(4) ilen
integer(4) ilength
integer(4) iret
integer(4) hwndEdit
integer(4) irepLen
   iLength = GetWindowTextLength(hWndEdit)
   iret = GetWindowText(hWndEdit, filebuffer, ilength+1)
   do ilen= 1, FILE_LEN
      if(iachar(szFindString(ilen:ilen))<1) exit
   end do
   ilen = ilen - 1
   do irepLen= 1, FILE_LEN
      if(iachar(szReplaceString(irepLen:irepLen))<1) exit
   end do
   irepLen = irepLen - 1
   if(iOffset==0) then
      iOffset=1
   endif
   ipos=index(filebuffer(iOffSet:ilength) &
         ,szFindString(1:ilen))
```

```
      if(ipos==0)then
         iOffset= ipos
         ReplaceThisText = 0
      else
         iOffset= iOffset+ipos
         iret=SendMessage(hWndEdit,EM_SETSEL,&
               iOffset-2,iOffset+ilen-2)
         iret=SendMessage(hWndEdit,EM_REPLACESEL,0, &
               loc(szReplaceString(1:irepLen)))
         iret=SendMessage(hWndEdit,EM_SCROLLCARET,0,0)
         ReplaceThisText = 1
      endif
end function
```

Note: Scribe1 in Chapter 6 and the various Scribe2 examples described in this chapter are essentially Visual Fortran variations of the POPPAD theme from the book *Programming Windows* by Charles Petzold. I would never have been able to get the Find and Replace example, FindScribe2, working without the benefit of having an example in C by Charles. The Multiple Document Interface version Scribe3, described in Chapter 12, is a natural, logical extension of the basic idea.

8.7   What is next?

In the next chapter, which covers vector graphics, we will learn how to use pens and brushes to create some interesting graphics effects. We will also discover the power of regions and explore the potential of enhanced meta-files as a means for creating, editing, and storing graphical information.

9

Vector Graphics

9.1   Introduction

In this chapter, we concentrate on using vector graphics, and then in Chapter 10 we will explore the use of bitmapped graphics. If you have not already done so, it would be a good idea to read Chapter 5. Chapter 5 covers QuickWin graphics, and many of the ideas discussed there provide useful background knowledge for Win32 graphics. In particular, the discussion on coordinate systems and viewports should be reviewed because it also applies to Win32 graphics and is not repeated here. The correspondence between QuickWin graphics and Win32 graphics is hardly surprising given that QuickWin is a wrapper around a selection of Win32 API functions. QuickWin graphics provide users with access to the power of Win32 graphics while protecting them from its complexities. However, the Win32 graphic system provides programmers with greater power and flexibility compared with QuickWin graphics. Once the concepts and rules to be followed are understood, Win32 graphics are also surprisingly simple to use in an application.

The Win32 API functions used for displaying graphics on video displays and printers are contained in the graphics device interface (GDI) library. In Visual Fortran, use of the GDI functions is restricted to Fortran Windows projects. With the GDI, coordinate systems may be based on world coordinates or display coordinate systems. As is discussed later in this chapter, device contexts permit the GDI to provide graphics capabilities that are independent of the device being used for drawing on. A device context is used to maintain information about the current drawing environment for a particular window or device. Such information includes the window size (page size when printing) to draw on, the color to draw with, the background color, the pen to use for drawing lines, the brush to use for filling areas, and the type of device display (or printer). This information repre-

Table 9.1   *Pen Styles*

Symbolic Constant	Pen will draw a line that is
PS_SOLID	solid.
PS_DASH	dashed.
PS_DOT	dotted.
PS_DASHDOT	composed of alternating dashes and dots.
PS_DASHDOTDOT	composed of alternating dashes and double dots.
PS_NULL	invisible.
PS_INSIDEFRAME	solid.

sents the context (i.e., device context) in which the application will draw the graphics objects.

In the GDI, lines are drawn with a pen, and areas are filled with a brush. All drawing objects such as pens, brushes, bitmaps, and device contexts must have a handle so that the Win32 API functions can uniquely identify them. The function CreatePen is used as follows to create a logical pen with the handle name hPen:

```
hPen  = CreatePen (Style, Width, Color)
```

If the value for the argument Width is 0, lines drawn with the pen will always be a single pixel wide regardless of the current transformation; otherwise, values for Width will be based on logical units. If the value specified by Width is greater than 1, the Style parameter must be PS_NULL, PS_SOLID, or PS_INSIDEFRAME. The pen styles available in Win32 and their corresponding symbolic constants are listed in Table 9.1.

If the pen style PS_INSIDEFRAME is used with any GDI drawing functions that have a bounding rectangle, the dimensions of the figure will be shrunk so that it will fit entirely inside the bounding rectangle, with allowances made for the width of the pen.

Before a pen can be used for drawing lines and curves, it must be selected into a device context by calling the SelectObject function. When a pen is no longer required, it should be deleted using the function Delete-Object. Table 9.2 lists the steps required to select a device context; to create a pen for drawing a line in a specified color, width, and style; to draw a line; and, finally, to release the device context.

Table 9.2   *Using Device Context for Drawing a Line*

Code	Task
`hdc = getDC(hWnd)`	Get a handle to a device context (hdc) to use for drawing to a window with the handle hWnd.
`hPen = CreatePen (Style, Width, Color)`	Create a pen to be used for drawing a line that has the specified parameters of style, width, and color.
`HPenOld = SelectObject(hdc, hPen)`	Select the pen that is to be used for drawing the line in the device context.
`iret = MoveToEx (hdc,x1,y1, OldPoint)`	Move without drawing to the position with the coordinates $x1, y1$. The argument OldPoint is a Win32 API point structure in which the coordinates of the current position are to be stored.
`iret = LineTo (hdc, x2,y2)`	Draw a line, using the pen selected, from the current position to the position specified by the coordinates $x2, y2$.
`iret = SelectObject(hdc, hPenOld)`	Select the old pen back into the device context.
`iret = DeleteObject (hPen)`	Delete pen because it is no longer needed.
`iret = ReleaseDC(hWnd, hdc)`	Release the device context.

When the display cannot use the exact pen color specified, the closest available color will be used. Since the Win32 operating system looks after the details of how to access the display area, the code steps listed in Table 9.2 for drawing a line on a display screen can also be used to draw a line on a printer. All that is necessary is to replace the window device context with the device context of a printer.

9.2 Lines2 example program

The program Lines2 is the Win32 version of the QuickWin program Lines. It demonstrates how to draw a line and set the color, thickness, and style. Line styles (Pen Styles) such as PS_DASH, PS_DASHDOT, and so on can be used only with a line thickness of unity. For a line thickness greater than unity, the pen style must be either PS_SOLID or PS_INSIDEFRAME. When a GDI pen draws a line, it performs a bitwise Boolean operation with pixels that is generically known as ROP2 because it involves a raster operation (ROP) between the pixels of the pen and the pixels of the destination's

display surface. (See Figure 9.1.) The SetROP2 function is used to define
how pen colors are combined with the colors of an existing image.

```
iret = SetRop2(hdc, R2_COPYPEN)
```

The online information on the Win32 function SetROP2 contains a list
of the 16 symbolic raster operation constants (e.g., R2_COPYPEN) that
may be used to specify mix modes (combinations) of source and destination
colors when drawing with the current pen. The mix modes involve the use
of the binary operations AND, OR, and XOR (exclusive OR), and the
unary operation NOT. Note that these raster operations apply only to raster
devices; they cannot be used with vector devices such as plotters.

The background mode of hatched brushes and dashed pens can be
either opaque or transparent. For an opaque background mode, the background area will be set to the background color; when it is transparent, the
background area will be undisturbed. With hatched brushes, the background is the area between the hatched lines, whereas for dashed pens, the
background is the area between the dots or the dashes.

In the following code fragment from the Lines2 program, a pen and
solid brush are created by the WM_CREATE message, and a WM_PAINT
message is used for drawing ten lines and a filled ellipse. Finally, the pens are

Figure 9.1
*Lines2 program
with the lines
drawn using the
ROP2 Setting
R2_Not X or Pen.*

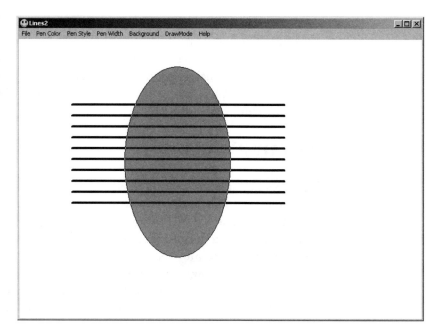

deleted when a WM_DESTROY message is sent. Although not shown in the code below, the user can select menu items to investigate how changing colors, pen width, pen style, ROP2 values, and background mode will determine how the lines are drawn.

```
select case (mesg)
    case (WM_CREATE)
        LineColor = rgb(0,0,0)
        LineStyle = PS_SOLID
        LineWidth = 1
        hPenLine = CreatePen (LineStyle, LineWidth, LineColor)
        hBrush = CreateSolidBrush(rgb(0,255,255))
        DrawMode = R2_COPYPEN
        DrawBkGrd = Opaque
        MainWndProc = 0
        return
    case (WM_PAINT)
        hdc = BeginPaint(hwnd, ps)
        iret = SetBkMode(hdc,DrawBkGrd)
        iret = SelectObject(hdc, hBrush)
        bret = Ellipse(hdc, 200,50,400,400)
        iret = SetROP2(hdc,DrawMode)
        do i = 1, 10
            hPenLine = CreatePen (LineStyle, LineWidth, &
                    LineColor)
            iret = SelectObject(hdc, hPenLine)
            iret = MoveToEx (hdc,100, 100+20*i, NULL_POINT)
            iret = LineTo (hdc, 500,100+20*i)
        end do
        iret = EndPaint (hwnd, ps)
        MainWndProc = 0
        return
    case (WM_DESTROY)
        call PostQuitMessage( 0 )
        iret = DeleteObject(hBrush)
        iret = DeleteObject(hPenLine)
        MainWndProc = 0
        return
```

9.3   DRAW2 example program

Shapes such as rectangles, polygons, ellipses, and the like are filled with the currently selected brush. Areas bounded by lines are filled with the current brush using the function ExtFloodFill. Brushes are GDI objects used for filling areas; they are categorized as solid, pattern, or hatch according to

Table 9.3   *Hatch Patterns*

Symbolic Constant	Use to create a
HS_BDIAGONAL	45-degree downward left-to-right hatch.
HS_CROSS	horizontal and vertical crosshatch.
HS_DIAGCROSS	45-degree crosshatch.
HS_FDIAGONAL	45-degree upward left-to-right hatch.
HS_HORIZONTAL	horizontal hatch.
HS_VERTICAL	vertical hatch.

their ability to fill an area. The GDI will always use a color that the display device can render and that is nearest to the RGB color specified for the brush.

Solid brushes to fill in a given color are created using the following code:

```
hBrush = CreateSolidBrush( color)
```

Patterned brushes are created using:

```
hBrush = CreatePatternBrush( hBmp)
```

Figure 9.2
Ellipse filled using a brush with the HS_BDIAGONAL fill pattern.

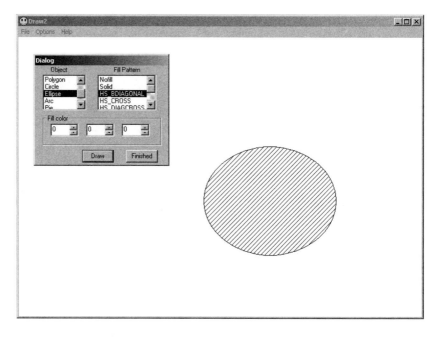

The argument hBmp is a handle to the bitmap that should be used as the fill pattern. Finally, a hatch brush is created using:

```
hBrush = CreateHatchBrush( hatchstyle, color)
```

The parameter hatchstyle should be one of the six symbolic constants listed in Table 9.3. When a brush is no longer required, it should be deleted using the DeleteObject function.

The program Draw2 is the Win32 version of the QuickWin program Draw described in Chapter 5. The user can fill a range of shapes with the hatch brush patterns of Table 9.3. (See Figure 9.2.) The following code fragment from the Draw2 program illustrates the use of the CreateBrushIndirect function, which passes a Logical brush structure as its sole parameter. The Logical brush structure LOGBRUSH contains three members: brush style, brush color, and a brush hatch. In the code excerpt, a logical brush structure, LOGBRUSH, has already been declared as brush, and its members filled in by a WM_CREATE message. All the drawing is done with a WM_PAINT message, as follows:

```
case (WM_PAINT)
   hdc = BeginPaint(ghwndMain, ps)
   hPenLine = CreatePen (PS_SOLID, 1, &
                            rgb(iRed,iGreen,iBlue))
   iret = SelectObject(hdc, hPenLine)
   hBrush = CreateBrushIndirect(brush)
   iret = SelectObject(hdc, hBrush)
   select case(iShape)
      case(0)
         iret = SelectObject(hdc, hPenLine)
         iret = MoveToEx (hdc,475,200, NULL_POINT)
         iret = LineTo (hdc, 600,450)
         iret = LineTo (hdc, 350,450)
         iret = LineTo (hdc, 475,200)
         bret = ExtFloodFill(hdc,475,400, rgb(iRed,&
                   iGreen,iBlue), FLOODFILLBORDER)
      case(1)
         bret = Rectangle(hdc, 350,200,600,450)
      case(2)
         Vertices(1)%x = 400
         Vertices(1)%y = 325
         Vertices(2)%x = 350
         Vertices(2)%y = 200
         Vertices(3)%x = 600
         Vertices(3)%y = 200
         Vertices(4)%x = 550
         Vertices(4)%y = 325
         Vertices(5)%x = 600
```

```
                    Vertices(5)%y = 450
                    Vertices(6)%x = 350
                    Vertices(6)%y = 450
                    bret = Polygon(hdc,Vertices(1),6)
                case(3)
                    bret = Ellipse(hdc,350,200,600,450)
                case(4)
                    bret = Ellipse(hdc,350,200,600,400)
                case(5)
                    bret = Arc(hdc,350,200,600,450,450,450,350,450)
                case(6)
                    bret = Pie(hdc,350,200,600,450,450,450,350,450)
            end select
            iret = EndPaint (ghwndMain, ps)
            DrawDlgProc = 0
            return
```

9.4   Bezier curve example program

The Frenchman Pierre Bezier developed the curve that is today known as a "Bezier curve" for use in the automobile industry. The Bezier curve enables designers to define complex curved shapes by controlling a few simple input parameters. The four vertices of a polygon are all that are required to completely define the shape of a Bezier curve. The curve passes through the first and last vertices of the polygon and the curve is a tangent to the polygon at those points, as can be seen in Figure 9.3. In Win32, one or more Bezier curves can be constructed by calling the PolyBezier function, as follows:

```
            iret = PolyBezier(hDC,apt(0),4)
```

The arguments inside the bracket are, respectively, a handle to the device context, an array of a Point structure variable, and the number of points in the array. For one Bezier curve, four points are required. The first and fourth points are end points, and the second and third points are the control points. For multiple Bezier curves, there should be four points for the first curve and three for each subsequent curve. This is because the end point of one curve is also the beginning point for the next curve. Thus, each succeeding curve needs only the two control points and an end point to be explicitly defined.

The interactive program Bezier is a very useful aid for developing an appreciation of the capabilities of a Bezier curve. Each of the four vertices can be moved to any location within the screen area. By appropriate moving of the vertices, it is possible to generate curves that range from a straight line

Figure 9.3

Sample curve generated by varying the position of the Bezier curve control points.

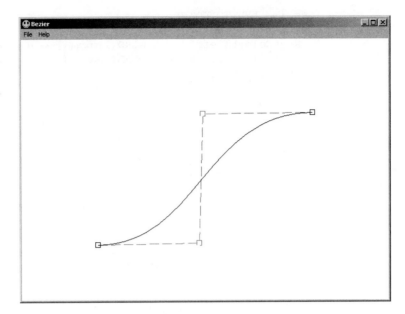

at one extreme to a teardrop shape at the other extreme. Code excerpts from the Bezier program are listed below. Note the use of the PtInRect function to determine which vertex has been chosen. This very helpful function can be used in a variety of selection applications. As an aid to visualization, the control polygon is drawn as a green line using the PD_DASH pen style.

```
case (WM_PAINT)
    hDC = BeginPaint(hWnd, ps)
    iret = SelectObject(hDC,  hPenLine )
    bret = MoveToEx(hDC,apt(0)%x, apt(0)%y, Null)
    bret = LineTo(hDC, apt(1)%x, apt(1)%y)
    bret = LineTo (hDC, apt(2)%x, apt(2)%y)
    bret = LineTo (hDC, apt(3)%x, apt(3)%y)
    bret = Rectangle(hdc,apt(1)%x-5,apt(1)%y-5, &
           apt(1)%x +5, apt(1)%y+5)
    bret = Rectangle(hdc,apt(2)%x-5,apt(2)%y-5,apt(2)%x+5, &
           apt(2)%y+5)
    iret = SelectObject(hDC, hPenBlack)
    iret = PolyBezier(hDC,apt(0),4)
    bret = Rectangle(hdc,apt(0)%x-5,apt(0)%y-5,apt(0)%x+5, &
           apt(0)%y+5)
    bret = Rectangle(hdc,apt(3)%x-5,apt(3)%y-5,apt(3)%x+5, &
           apt(3)%y+5)
    iret = EndPaint(hWnd, ps)
    MainWndProc = 0
    return
```

```
case (WM_LBUTTONDOWN)
case (WM_MOUSEMOVE)
    RectSelect%left   = LOWORD(lParam) - 10
    RectSelect%right  = LOWORD(lParam) + 10
    RectSelect%top    = HIWORD(lParam) - 10
    RectSelect%bottom = HIWORD(lParam) + 10
    if(Loword(WParam) == MK_LBUTTON )   then
        do index = 0,3
            if (PtInRect (RectSelect, apt(index)) .EQV..TRUE.)&
               then
               hDC = GetDC(hWnd)
               ! Erase lines using white pen.
               iret = SelectObject(hDC, hPenWhite )
               bret = MoveToEx(hDC,apt(0)%x, apt(0)%y, Null)
               bret = LineTo(hDC, apt(1)%x, apt(1)%y)
               bret = LineTo (hDC, apt(2)%x, apt(2)%y)
               bret = LineTo (hDC, apt(3)%x, apt(3)%y)
               bret = Rectangle(hdc,apt(1)%x-5,apt(1)%y-5, &
                      apt(1)%x+5, apt(1)%y+5)
               bret = Rectangle(hdc,apt(2)%x-5,apt(2)%y-5, &
                      apt(2)%x+5,apt(2)%y+5)
               iret = PolyBezier(hDC,apt(0),4)
               bret = Rectangle(hdc,apt(0)%x-5,apt(0)%y-5, &
                      apt(0)%x+5,apt(0)%y+5)
               bret = Rectangle(hdc,apt(3)%x-5,apt(3)%y-5, &
                      apt(3)%x+5,apt(3)%y+5)
               ipoint = index
               !  Get the new coordinates for mouse position.
               apt(ipoint)%x = int2(LOWORD(lParam))
               apt(ipoint)%y = int2(HIWORD(lParam))
               !  Draw new lines.
               iret = SelectObject(hDC,  hPenLine )
               bret = MoveToEx(hDC,apt(0)%x, apt(0)%y, Null)
               bret = LineTo(hDC, apt(1)%x, apt(1)%y)
               bret = LineTo (hDC, apt(2)%x, apt(2)%y)
               bret = LineTo (hDC, apt(3)%x, apt(3)%y)
               bret = Rectangle(hdc,apt(1)%x-5,apt(1)%y-5, &
                      apt(1)%x+5,apt(1)%y+5)
               bret = Rectangle(hdc,apt(2)%x-5,apt(2)%y-5, &
                      apt(2)%x+5,apt(2)%y+5)
               iret = SelectObject(hDC, hPenBlack)
               bret = Rectangle(hdc,apt(0)%x-5,apt(0)%y-5, &
                      apt(0)%x+5,apt(0)%y+5)
               bret = Rectangle(hdc,apt(3)%x-5,apt(3)%y-5, &
                      apt(3)%x+5,apt(3)%y+5)
               iret = PolyBezier(hDC,apt(0),4)
               iret = ReleaseDC(hwnd, hDC)
               exit
            end if
```

```
        end do
    end if
    MainWndProc = 0
    return
```

9.5   Coordinate systems

The Win32 Graphics Device Interface (GDI) works with four coordinate systems, which are as follows:

- World coordinates

- Logical (or page) coordinates

- Device (or client) coordinates

- Physical (printer page or screen) coordinates

With the GDI, all drawing takes place on a device context, which has its own coordinate system that is independent of the actual physical device. This coordinate system is referred to as the logical coordinate system (also called page space), and it defines a logical window as compared with device coordinates that define a physical or device window. The use of a logical coordinate system enables the GDI to draw on a variety of devices with differing resolutions, such as printers, plotters, and display screens. It is important to differentiate between logical and device coordinates when using Windows API functions. Logical coordinates are used for most GDI drawing operations and describe the logical window that you are drawing to. Physical or device coordinates are used for most Windows management

Table 9.4   *Win32 Functions for Converting between Coordinate Systems*

Function	Used to convert
DPtoLP	a point in the device coordinate system to the logical coordinate system for a device context.
LPtoDP	a point in the logical coordinate system for a device context to the physical or device coordinate system.
ClientToScreen	client coordinates of a specified point to screen coordinates. The screen coordinates are relative to the upper-left corner of the screen.
ScreenToClient	screen coordinates of a specified point on the screen to client coordinates. The client coordinates are relative to the upper-left corner of the specified window's client area.

functions and describe actual physical pixels or bits on a device. Table 9.4 lists GDI functions that can be used to convert the coordinates of a point between one coordinate system and another.

The eight mapping modes listed in Table 9.5 are used to define or partially define the logical coordinate system for a device context. The default-mapping mode MM_TEXT provides a one-to-one correspondence between logical and physical device coordinates. The MM_ANISO-TROPIC and MM_ISOTROPIC mapping modes enable users to define an arbitrary mapping between logical units and device coordinates. The remaining mapping modes are in real-world coordinates of inches or millimeters, and they are displayed in logical inches or millimeters. When printed, images drawn in these modes will be scaled accurately; otherwise, the actual displayed size will depend on the display in use. The mapping modes listed in Table 9.5 are set using the SetMapMode function, as follows:

```
iret = SetMapMode(hdc,MapMode)
```

The parameter hdc is a handle to the display context, and the parameter MapMode should be one of the symbolic constants listed in Table 9.5.

The SetWindowOrgEx and SetViewportOrgEx functions can be used to set the origins in logical coordinates for the window or viewport of a device

Table 9.5   *Windows Mapping Modes*

Symbolic Constant	In this mapping mode, each logical unit is mapped to
MM_ANISOTROPIC	an arbitrary unit. The axes are arbitrarily scaled—that is, one unit along the *x*-axis is not equal to one unit along the *y*-axis.
MM_HIENGLISH	0.001 inches. Positive *x* is to the right; positive *y* is up.
MM_HI METRIC	0.01 millimeters. Positive *x* is to the right; positive *y* is up.
MM_ISOTROPIC	an arbitrary unit. The axes are equally scaled—that is, one unit along the *x*-axis is equal to one unit along the *y*-axis.
MM_LOENGLISH	0.01 inches. Positive *x* is to the right; positive *y* is up.
MM_LOMETRIC	0.1 millimeters. Positive *x* is to the right; positive *y* is up.
MM_TEXT	one device pixel. Positive *x* is to the right; positive *y* is down.
MM_TWIPS	one-twentieth of a printer's point (1/1440 inch, also called a "twip"). Positive *x* is to the right; positive *y* is up.

context with any of the mapping modes listed in Table 9.5. However, the functions SetWindowExtEx and SetViewportExtEx are used to set the units and orientation of the axes for only the MM_ANISOTROPIC and MM_ISOTROPIC mapping modes. With the isotropic mapping mode, the window extent (SetWindowExtEx) must be set before setting the viewport extents (SetViewportExtEx). None of the examples in this chapter uses the viewport functions; however, the Bitmap2 example in Chapter 10 illustrates the use of a viewport with the MM_ISOTROPIC mapping mode.

9.6   **Transforms example program**

Sometimes, we may want to enlarge the scale of a picture to obtain more detail or reduce it so that more of the picture is visible; on other occasions, we may need to rotate a picture through some angle to get a better view of an object. These manipulations or transformations are basic to computer graphics, and they are accomplished through geometric transformation techniques. Geometric transformations involve using a set of equations to redefine the size, orientation, and shape of objects in two- and three-dimensional space.

Applications using Windows NT or Windows 2000 can call the GDI SetWorldTransform function to scale, rotate, translate, shear, and reflect an object in a two-dimensional plane. The function SetWorldTransform is used to define a two-dimensional (2D) linear transformation between world space and in logical Windows coordinates (also known as page space). These logical coordinates are then mapped to display coordinates according to the viewport settings. The calling syntax for SetWorldTransform is as follows:

```
iret = SetWorldTransform (hdc, TranX)
```

The argument hdc is a handle to a device context and the parameter TranX is an XFORM structure, which contains the following six members: $eM11$, $eM12$, $eM21$, $eM22$, eDX, and eDY. These six members are used to change any coordinates (X, Y) in world space, into the transformed coordinates (X', Y') in logical or page space according to the following equations:

$$X' = X \times eM11 + Y \times eM21 + eDX$$

$$Y' = X \times eM12 + Y \times eM22 + eDY$$

The member eDX specifies the horizontal translation component, and the member eDY specifies the vertical translation component. The various effects of the other members on the transformation are listed in Table 9.6.

Table 9.6 *Two-Dimensional Transformations*

Operation	eM11	eM12	eM21	eM22
Rotation	Cosine	Sine	Negative sine	Cosine
Scaling	Horizontal scaling	zero	zero	Vertical scaling
Shear	zero	Horizontal shear	Vertical shear	zero
Reflection	Horizontal reflection	zero	zero	Vertical reflection

The transformation equations are often expressed in the form of a 3×3 transformation matrix:

$$\begin{bmatrix} eM11 & eM12 & 0 \\ eM21 & eM22 & 0 \\ eDX & eDY & 1 \end{bmatrix}$$

Using this notation, the default world transformation is the identity matrix:

$$\begin{bmatrix} 1 & 0 & 0 \\ 0 & 1 & 0 \\ 0 & 0 & 1 \end{bmatrix}$$

The graphics mode for a given device context must be first set to GM_ADVANCED by calling the SetGraphicsMode function before any calls are made to the SetWorldTransform function. For a device context with the handle hdc, the graphics mode to use world transforms is set as follows:

```
iret = SetGraphicsMode(hdc,GM_ADVANCED)
```

and the call to reset to the default graphics mode is:

```
iret = SetGraphicsMode(hdc,GM_COMPATIBLE)
```

Note that the world transformation must be restored to the default identity transformation by calling SetWorldTransform or ModifyWorldTransform before the graphics mode for the device context is reset to the default GM_COMPATIBLE.

The program Transforms enables users to change the values of a transformation matrix and so to cause a square to be scaled, rotated, sheared, and translated. Unfortunately, the use of this program is restricted to Windows

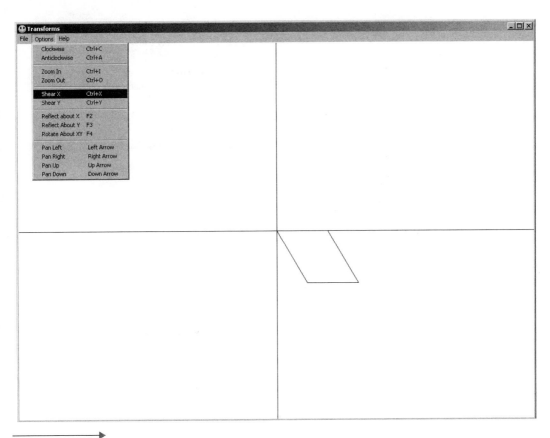

Figure 9.4 *Square drawn using the shear in X transform.*

NT and 2000 platforms, because world transform functions are not supported under Windows 95, 98, and Me. In the application Transforms, all the menu items have corresponding accelerator keys to enable users to view the action of the transforms as a continuous sequence. The following code fragment shows how the WM_PAINT message is used to set the graphics mode to GM_ADVANCED; the viewport origin is moved to the center of the screen and the axis lines are drawn. The world transform is set using the current values in the transformation matrix. The square will be drawn scaled, rotated, sheared, or translated according to the current values in the transformation matrix. The code for the menu item AntiClockwise is also given to illustrate how the four trigonometric values are calculated and put into the transformation matrix. In Figure 9.4, a square is displayed with shear in the X direction. The code is as follows:

```
case (WM_PAINT)
    hdc = BeginPaint(ghwndMain, ps)
```

```
            iret = SetGraphicsMode(hdc,GM_ADVANCED )
            iret = SetViewportOrgEx(hdc, center%x, center%y, &
                                    NULL_POINT)
            iret = SelectObject(hdc, hPenLine)
            iret = MoveToEx (hdc,center%x,0, NULL_POINT)
            iret = LineTo (hdc, -center%x,0)
            iret = MoveToEx (hdc,0,center%y, NULL_POINT)
            iret = LineTo (hdc, 0,-center%y)
            iret = SetWorldTransform (hdc, TranX)
            bret = Rectangle(hdc, 0,0,100,100)
            iret = EndPaint (ghwndMain, ps)
            MainWndProc = 0
            return
        case (IDM_AntiClockwise)
            Angle = Angle-30
            ! Convert degrees to radians
            Theta = Angle/57.2957795
            TranX%eM11 = Cos(Theta)
            TranX%eM22 = Cos(Theta)
            TranX%eM12 = Sin(Theta)
            TranX%eM21 = -Sin(Theta)
            iret = InvalidateRect (Null, NULL_RECT, .TRUE.)
            MainWndProc = 0
            return
```

9.7   Regions

A region is a GDI object that describes a simple or complex area in a device
context. Since region functions always use device coordinates, they are independent of mapping modes or transformations. Regions can be used for
drawing, outlining, filling, and clipping. Furthermore, regions can also be
combined to form larger and more complex regions.

In the following piece of code a rectangular region is created and the
return value is a handle to that region:

```
hRgn = CreateRectRgn(xLeft,yTop,xRight,Ybottom)
```

Since regions are GDI objects just like pens and brushes, all regions
should be deleted using the function DeleteObject once an application has
finished using them.

The program Select2 illustrates how to create regions using the Create-
RectRgn, CreatePolygonRgn, and CreateEllipticRgn functions to form a
shape that represents a Ute (utility wagon). The areas where the wheels
overlap the bodywork are combined to form a new region, which I have
called a wheel cover. The regions are filled using one of four brushes,

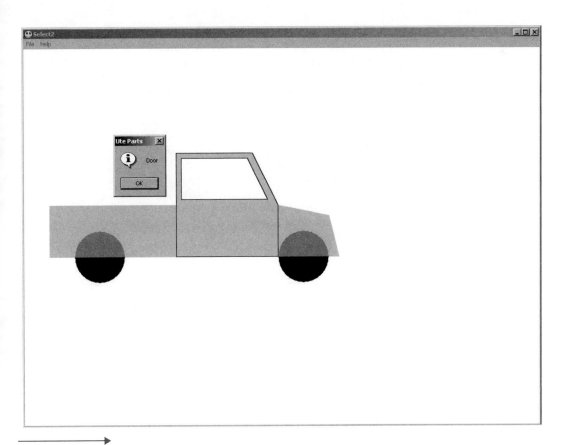

Figure 9.5   *Individual regions can be selected using the function PtInRegion.*

according to whether they represent bodywork, wheels, wheel covers, or a window. The door region is outlined in black. This effect is obtained using the FrameRgn function to create a black frame around the door and window regions. Users may click on any part of the Ute to have that part named. Identification of the different regions is achieved using the function PtInRegion. (See Figure 9.5.) The following code fragment illustrates the techniques:

```
case (WM_PAINT)
    hdc = BeginPaint(hwnd, ps)
    hrgn(1) = CreateRectRgn(50,300,300,400)
    hrgn(2) = CreatePolygonRgn(door(1),6, WINDING)
    hrgn(3) = CreatePolygonRgn(bonnet(1),4, WINDING)
    hrgn(4) = CreateEllipticRgn(100,350,200,450)
    hrgn(5) = CreateEllipticRgn(500,350,600,450)
    hrgn(6) = CreatePolygonRgn(window(1),4, WINDING)
    bret = FillRgn(hdc,hrgn(1),hBrush1)
```

```
      bret = FillRgn(hdc,hrgn(2),hBrush1)
      bret = FillRgn(hdc,hrgn(3),hBrush1)
      bret = FillRgn(hdc,hrgn(4),hBrush2)
      bret = FillRgn(hdc,hrgn(5),hBrush2)
      bret = FillRgn(hdc,hrgn(6),hBrush3)
      hrgn(7) = CreateEllipticRgn(100,350,200,450)
      hrgn(8) = CreateEllipticRgn(500,350,600,450)
      iret = CombineRgn(hrgn(7),hrgn(4),hrgn(1),RGN_AND)
      bret = FillRgn(hdc,hrgn(7),hBrush4)
      iret = CombineRgn(hrgn(8),hrgn(5),hrgn(3),RGN_AND)
      bret = FillRgn(hdc,hrgn(8),hBrush4)
      bret = FrameRgn(hdc,hrgn(2),hBrush2,1,1)
      bret = FrameRgn(hdc,hrgn(6),hBrush2,1,1)
      iret = EndPaint (hwnd, ps)
      MainWndProc = 0
      return
   case (WM_LBUTTONDOWN)
      !  Getthe X and Y coordinates for the current mouse
      !  position.
      x = int2(LOWORD(lParam))
      y = int2(HIWORD(lParam))
      do Index = 8,1,-1
         if(PtInRegion(hrgn(Index), x,y) /= 0) then
            iret = MessageBox (NULL,szMessage(Index), &
            "Ute Parts"C, IOR(MB_OK ,MB_ICONINFORMATION))
            exit
         end if
      end do
      MainWndProc = 0
      return
   case (WM_DESTROY)
      call PostQuitMessage( 0 )
      do index = 1,8
         if(hrgn(index) /= 0) then
            iret = DeleteObject(hrgn(index))
         end if
      end do
      MainWndProc = 0
      return
```

Regions can also be used to define a clipping area. In this case, every time a program calls a graphics or text output function, every pixel is tested to determine whether the output falls within a clipping area. Initially, the clipping region for any window is the window itself, but the clipping region may be set to any position of a window. The SetWindowRgn function allows applications to redefine the clipping region for the entire window. Look up the function in the online documentation and try experimenting to see if you can a create nonrectangular window.

9.8   **Paths**

Paths do not do any actual drawing; they are best thought of as recordings that contain drawing commands to a device context. Paths are started with the BeginPath function. Since device contexts can contain only one path at a time, creating a new path will cause any existing path in the device context to be discarded, and a new recording will made of the subsequent drawing commands. All the normal drawing functions or TextOut can be recorded in the path. Calling the EndPath function indicates the end of the storage session for path information. Paths can be made up of one or more unconnected groups of line segments known as subpaths. Any subpath that is an open figure can be turned into a closed figure by calling the CloseFigure function or by filling the path. Some benefits of using paths are as follows:

- All drawing operations into a path use logical coordinates. Paths can be created in logical or world coordinates.

- Very complex shapes can be easily filled if they are created as a path, from line segments, arcs, Bezier curves, and the like.

- Path can be converted into a region or clipping region, thereby allowing you to take advantage of complex fills or to use complex clipping regions that are based on logical coordinates.

- In addition to drawing commands, text can be drawn into a path. If the text is drawn using a TrueType or vector font, the path will be loaded with the outline of the text. The text can be filled with arbitrary patterns, or a clipping region can be created out of the text.

A list of functions that relate to paths is given in Table 9.7.

Windows NT4 and 2000 provide path support for the full set of GDI drawing functions. Users of Windows 95, 98, and Me can record only the following drawing functions in a path: CloseFigure, ExtTextOut, LineTo, MoveToEx, PolyBezier, PolyBezierTo, Polygon, Polyline, PolylineTo, Poly-Polygon, PolyPolyline, and TextOut.

If the function TextOut is placed inside a path bracket, the system will generate a path for the TrueType text that includes each character plus its character box. Surprisingly the region generated is not the text but the character box minus the text. The region enclosed by the outline of the True-Type text can be obtained by setting the background mode to transparent before placing the TextOut function in the path bracket. This effect can be demonstrated in the application Paths by switching between opaque and transparent backgrounds while in a stroke-and-fill mode.

Table 9.7   *Path Functions*

Function	Use this function to
AbortPath	remove the current path.
BeginPath	create a path.
CloseFigure	change the current path segment to a closed figure
EndPath	finish the creation of a path.
FillPath	close and fill any open figures in the path, using the current brush.
FlattenPath	convert all curves in the path for the specified device context into lines.
GetPath	retrieve information about the path.
PathToRegion	convert a path into a region.
SelectClipPath	combine the path of a device context with its clipping region.
StrokeAndFillPath	draw the segments of the path, closing and filling the figures in the path.
StrokePath	draw the segments of the path.
WidenPath	convert the path into lines, widening the path according to the pen selected into the device.

The program Paths is interactive and provides an insight into the effect of stroke, fill, and stroke and fill on path construction as well as the differences between transparent and opaque backgrounds and Winding and Alternate fill modes. The SetPolyFillMode function, which is used to define how polygons are to be filled, may be set to either ALTERNATE or WINDING. The ALTERNATE mode causes the area between odd-numbered and even-numbered polygon sides on each scan line to be filled, while the WINDING mode causes any region with a nonzero winding value to be filled. The online information provides further details of these filling modes.

In the program Paths, the text "Smiley" is written into a path, and then an ellipse and a rectangle are set over the text before the path is ended. (See Figure 9.6.) Since the rectangle and ellipse functions are not recorded in a path constructed under Windows 95, 98, and Me, two similar subroutines (ellipse95 and rectangle95) have been included for these operating systems. Users of Windows NT4 and 2000 can delete the subroutines ellipse95 and

Figure 9.6
*A path drawn
using the stroke
option.*

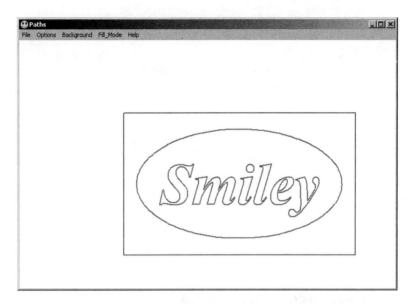

rectangle95, together with lines that call them, and uncomment the lines containing the normal ellipse and rectangle functions. The following code fragment demonstrates how the WM_PAINT message is used to create and draw a path.

```
case (WM_PAINT)
    hdc = BeginPaint(hwnd, ps)
    if(FillType == 2) then
        iret = SetPolyFillMode(hdc,WINDING)
    else
        iret = SetPolyFillMode(hdc,ALTERNATE)
    end if
    if(Background == 2) then
        iret = SetBkMode (hdc, OPAQUE)
    else
        iret = SetBkMode (hdc, TRANSPARENT)
    end if
    iret = SelectObject(hdc, hBrush)
    iret = GetClientRect (hwnd, rect1)
    iret = SelectObject(hdc, hPenPath)
    iret = SetViewportOrgEx (hdc, rect1%right/4, &
                rect1%bottom/4, NULL_POINT)
    hfont = CreateFontIndirect(lf)
    hfontOld = SelectObject(hDC,hfont)
    iret = BeginPath (hdc)
    iret = TextOut (hdc, 90, 90, "Smiley"C, 6)
    ! next two line for win95/98 and me users
    call ellipse95(hdc,45, 50,435, 250)
```

```
            call rectangle95(hdc,20,20,460,280)
            ! next two line for Nt4 and 2000 users
            !  iret = Rectangle(hdc,20,20,460,280)
            !  iret = Ellipse (hdc, 45, 50,435, 250)
            iret = EndPath (hdc)
            select case(PathType)
               case(1)
                  iret = StrokePath (hdc)
               case(2)
                  iret = FillPath(hdc)
               case(3)
                  iret = StrokeAndFillPath(hdc)
               end select
               iret = SelectObject(hDC,hfontOld)
               iret = DeleteObject(hfont)
               iret = EndPaint (hwnd, ps)
               MainWndProc = 0
               return
```

9.9   Enhanced metafiles

Enhanced metafiles are a convenient way of storing (in memory or on disk) for playback on some later occasion pictures created using the Win32 GDI drawing functions. Each record in an enhanced metafile contains a single GDI command. Enhanced metafiles are useful for any situation in which an image needs to be saved. Compared with bitmaps, enhanced metafiles are smaller, device independent, and scalable, but they are slower when rendering, because each of the GDI commands recorded in the metafile must be executed sequentially to create the image. No computation can be done inside an enhanced metafile, since enhanced metafiles are only recording devices. However, all the normal GDI drawing commands, including path, window, viewport, and map mode functions, can be used with an enhanced metafile.

9.10   MetaSketch example program

The program Metasketch is a very simple drawing program, which allows the user to create a series of straight lines in a choice of pen styles, colors, and widths. The user can toggle a drawing grid on or off, and choose to have each point drawn either at the nearest grid point or at the current cursor location. The drawing can be saved as an enhanced metafile. The drawing will be saved with or without a border depending on the checked state of the Border item in the Options menu. (See Figure 9.7.)

Figure 9.7
*Creating a box
using MetaSketch.*

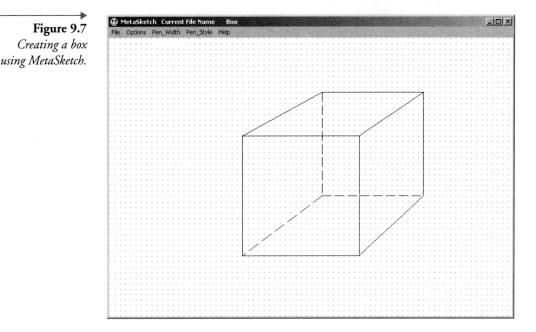

A simple line type has been defined in the global variables. For this application, it is useful to have all the line attributes grouped into one convenient location. Greater flexibility could be achieved by storing the point numbers for the start and end of a line rather than the actual coordinate values. When coordinate values are kept separate from the line information, and if the coordinate value of a point is changed, all the lines will move with the point.

Once the drawing has been created for display on the screen, it is a straightforward process to record the graphical commands used for the screen display in an enhanced metafile. The first step is to create an enhanced metafile in which to store the information by calling the Create-EnhMetaFile function:

```
hdcEMF = CreateEnhMetaFile(hdcRef ,lpFilename, lpRect, &
                           lpDescription)
```

where:

   hdcEMF—Handle to the device context for the enhanced metafile.

   hdcRef— Handle to a reference device context.

   lpFilename—Pointer to the filename for the enhanced metafile to be created. (This parameter is NULL for a memory-based enhanced metafile.)

lpRect—Pointer to a bounding rectangle.

lpDescription—Pointer to an optional description string.

Once an application has finished storing drawing information in an enhanced metafile, it should close the enhanced metafile by calling the function CloseEnhMetaFile, as follows:

```
hemf = CloseEnhMetaFile (hdcEMF)
```

The return value hemf is a handle to an enhanced-metafile device context. An application can use this handle to create copies of the enhanced metafile; to display a picture stored in an enhanced metafile; and to enumerate, edit, or copy individual records in the enhanced metafile. When an enhanced metafile handle is no longer needed, it should be released by calling the DeleteEnhMetaFile function as follows:

```
bret = DeleteEnhMetaFile (hemf)
```

It can be seen from the following code fragments that the commands used for a WM_PAINT message to draw on the display screen are the same commands as those stored in the enhanced metafile by the subroutine SaveEnhMetaFile. The important difference between the two routines is in the use of two different device contexts. Notice that when creating the enhanced metafile, a rectangle corresponding to the client area is drawn. This bounding rectangle ensures that all the objects will always be drawn with the same size in relation to the screen as when they were created.

Note: The use of the style PS_NULL to draw an invisible border ensures that objects will retain their size in relation to the client area that they were created in, even when the border is not visible.

```
case (WM_PAINT)
   hdc = BeginPaint(hwnd, ps)
   if(DrawGrid == .true.) then
      iret =  GetClientRect (hwnd, rect)
      do i = 1, rect%right, GridStep
         do j = 1,rect%bottom, GridStep
            iret = setpixel(hdc,i,j,gridcolor)
         end do
      end do
   end if
   if(gLineCount >=1) then
      do i = 1, gLineCount
```

```fortran
                     hPenLine = CreatePen (gLines(i)%LineStyle, &
                            gLines(i)%LineWidth,gLines(i)%LineColor)
                     iret = SelectObject(hdc, hPenLine)
                     iret = MoveToEx (hdc,gLines(i)%LineStart%x, &
                               gLines(i)%LineStart%y, NULL_POINT)
                     iret = LineTo (hdc, gLines(i)%LineEnd%x, &
                               gLines(i)%LineEnd%y)
                  end do
               end if
               iret = EndPaint (hwnd, ps)
               MainWndProc = 0
               return
      subroutine SaveEnhMetaFile
      use MetaSketchGlobals
      use dfwin
      implicit none
      integer(2) iret,i
      integer(4) hdcEMF,hPenLine
      logical bret
      type (T_RECT) rect1
         hdcEMF = CreateEnhMetaFile(Null,&
                     TRIM(szTitleName)//'.emf'C,&
                     Null, "MetaSketch\0EMF \0\0")
         if (hdcEMF == 0) then
            iret = MessageBox(Null, "Cannot save metafile"C, &
                        "Error"C, MB_OK)
            return
         end if
         iret =  GetClientRect (ghwndMain, rect1)
         if(DrawBorder == .true.) then
            hPenLine  = CreatePen (PS_SOLID, 2, rgb(0,0,0)
         else
            hPenLine  = CreatePen (PS_NULL, 2, rgb(0,0,0))
         end if
         iret = SelectObject(hdcEMF, hPenLine)
         ! put a border around the enhanced metafile
         bret = Rectangle(hdcEMF, 0, 0, rect1%right,rect1%bottom)
         if(gLineCount >=1) then
            do i = 1, gLineCount
               hPenLine  = CreatePen (gLines(i)%LineStyle, &
                      gLines(i)%LineWidth,gLines(i)%LineColor)
               iret = SelectObject(hdcEMF, hPenLine)
               iret = MoveToEx (hdcEMF,gLines(i)%LineStart%x, &
                        gLines(i)%LineStart%y, NULL_POINT)
               iret = LineTo (hdcEMF, gLines(i)%LineEnd%x, &
                           gLines(i)%LineEnd%y)
            end do
         end if
```

```
      hemf = CloseEnhMetaFile (hdcEMF)
      bret = DeleteEnhMetaFile (hemf)
      bret = DeleteObject(hPenLine)
end subroutine SaveEnhMetaFile
```

9.11   MetaView example program

Enhanced metafile pictures are device independent, and they will maintain their shape and proportion irrespective of whether they are displayed on a screen, a printer, or a plotter. The enhanced metafile format is standardized, and pictures stored in this format can be imported into any Win32-based application that can read files with the .emf extension. This is illustrated in Figure 9.8, which shows how the box shape created in MetaSketch (see Figure 9.7) appears when it is imported as a picture into Microsoft Word.

Note that the dashed lines of the box in Figure 9.7 have become more solid in Figure 9.8. Figure 9.7 is a bitmap of a screen capture; therefore, it will just be reproduced as a bitmap (raster) image of the screen. However, Figure 9.8 shows a picture that has been imported as an enhanced metafile and, because it is an enhanced metafile, it contains GDI drawing information. The picture will be drawn properly on a device such as a display screen that has the capability of drawing dashed lines, whereas printers normally draw only solid (vector) lines.

It is quite easy to create an application for replaying (displaying) enhanced metafiles to a screen or printer, as is demonstrated with the program MetaView. A handle to an enhanced metafile is obtained using the GDI function GetEnhMetaFile with the name of the enhanced metafile

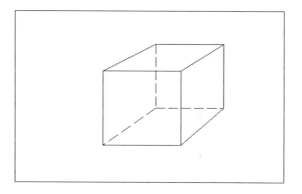

Figure 9.8
The enhanced metafile box created in MetaSketch imports directly into Word.

supplied as the sole parameter to the function, as shown in the following
piece of code from MetaView.

```
case (IDM_OPEN )
   ! get open file dialog box
   bret = GETOPENFILENAME(Ofn)
   !   check to see if the OK button has been pressed
   if(bret == 0) then
      ! check for error
      call COMDLGER(ierror)
   else
      MyName = FullName(1+Ofn%NFILEOFFSET:&
                    Ofn%NFILEEXTENSION-1)
      lpszHeader =" MetaView     &
                    Current File Name        "//MyName
      bret = SetWindowText(ghwndMain,lpszHeader//' 'C)
         hEMF = GetEnhMetaFile(FullName)
         bFileOpen = TRUE
   end if
   iret = InvalidateRect (hwnd, NULL_RECT, .TRUE.)
   MainWndProc = 0
   return
```

When the handle (hEMF) to the enhanced metafile is no longer
required, it is deleted by calling the DeleteEnhMetaFile function. The Play-
EnhMetaFile function is used to display an image stored in an enhanced
metafile, as follows:

```
bret = PlayEnhMetaFile( hDC, hEMF, rect)
```

where:

hdc—Handle to a device context for the output device on which the
picture will appear.

hemf—Handle to an enhanced metafile.

rect—Rectangle structure containing the coordinates of the bounding
rectangle that are to be used for displaying the picture. Coordinates
are specified in logical (page space) units.

Enhanced metafiles are recordings of GDI drawing commands; therefore, applications can cause pictures to be displayed as rotated or sheared
images by setting the world transform in the output device before calling
PlayEnhMetaFile. Similarly, applications that set a clipping region in the
output device before playing an enhanced metafile can cause clipped
enhanced metafile pictures to be displayed. The following piece of code

Figure 9.9
*Displaying the
enhanced metafile
house in
MetaView.*

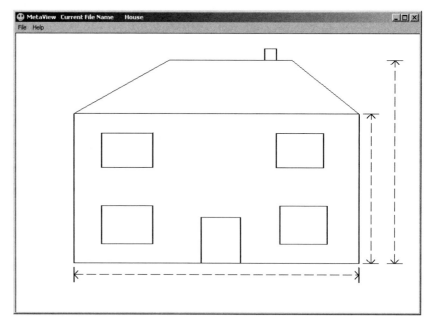

from MetaView shows how easy it is to play an enhanced metafile on a display screen. Figure 9.9 displays an enhanced metafile that was created previously using MetaSketch.

```
case (WM_PAINT)
    hdc = BeginPaint (hwnd, ps)
    if( bFileOpen .ne.0) then
        bret = GetClientRect( hWnd, rect)
        bret = PlayEnhMetaFile( hDC, hEMF, rect)
    endif
    iret = EndPaint (hwnd, ps)
    MainWndProc = 0
    return
```

One great advantage of enhanced metafiles is that it is just as easy to display them on a printer as it is to display them on a screen. In the following code from MetaView it can be seen that, once the device context handle for a printer is obtained, the actual playing of the enhanced metafile is identical to the procedure used for displaying to the screen. In the following code, prndlg is a print dialog structure (PRINTDLG), and di is a document information structure (DOCINFO). The GetDeviceCaps function is used to get information about the horizontal and vertical resolution of the printer to set the bounding rectangle of the enhanced metafile. As noted previously, printers draw dashed and dotted lines as solid lines.

```
case (IDM_PrintMetaFile)
   if(hemf == 0)then
      iret = MessageBox (NULL,'Open Enhanced &
              MetaFile first'C, 'Print MetaFile Error'C ,&
              IOR(MB_OK ,MB_ICONQUESTION))
      return
   end if
   ! initialize PRINTDLG structure
   prndlg%lStructSize = sizeof(prndlg)
   prndlg%hwndOwner = hWnd
   prndlg%Flags = IOR(PD_RETURNDC ,IOR(PD_NOSELECTION, &
              PD_NOPAGENUMS))
   !  Open up print dialog box
   bret = PrintDlg(prndlg)
   If(bret == 0) then
      return
   end if
   hdcPrn = prndlg.hDC
      if(hdcPrn == 0) then
        iret = MessageBox(NULL,'Cannot get a printer DC'C, &
                 MyName//''C ,IOR(MB_OK ,MB_ICONQUESTION))
        return
      end if
   di%cbSize = sizeof(di)
   di%lpszDocName = loc(MyName//''C)
   di%lpszOutput = Null
   di%lpszDatatype = 'emf'
   di%fwType  = 0
   rect%left = 0
   rect%right = GetDeviceCaps (hdcPrn, HORZRES)
   rect%top = 0
   rect%bottom = GetDeviceCaps (hdcPrn, VERTRES)
   iret  = StartDoc(prndlg%hDC, di)
   iret = StartPage(prndlg%hDC)
   bret = PlayEnhMetaFile(hdcprn, hemf, rect)
   if(EndPage(hDCPrn) > 0) then
      iret = EndDoc(hDCprn)
   else
      iret = MessageBox (NULL,'Cannot Print metafile'C, &
                 MyName//''C ,IOR(MB_OK ,MB_ICONQUESTION))
   end if
   bret = DeleteDC(hDCprn)
   MainWndProc = 0
   return
```

9.12   What is next?

In the next chapter, which discusses bitmap graphics, we will find out about memory devices and the power of special bitmap functions like BitBlt and StretchBlt for drawing bitmaps. We will also discover the potential of GDI bitmaps for creating animated effects, and we will use device-independent bitmaps for printing bitmaps.

10

Bitmap Graphics

10.1 Introduction

This chapter describes the Windows API functions that deal with bitmaps and the manipulation of raster images. Pen plotters are vector devices, and the plotter pen draws a straight line between any two given sets of x and y coordinates. Curves are constructed by drawing a series of small straight lines. On the other hand, display screens and a great many printers are raster devices. The smallest unit that can be displayed by raster devices is known as a pixel, and images are constructed from multiple horizontal lines (often called scan lines) of pixels going from one vertical edge to the opposite vertical edge of the device. In a raster device, pixels are individually addressable, and straight lines are constructed by drawing a series of pixels (or dots) in a specified color between any two given sets of x, y coordinates. Curves are constructed by drawing a series of pixels in a specified color along the path of the curve. Because this can result in ragged looking lines, techniques such as antialiasing are often used to create smoother looking lines.

Bitmaps are a way of storing data about how an image is to be displayed on a raster device. The simplest bitmap is of a monochrome image in which every pixel in the image is represented by a single bit with a value of 0 or 1. Bits that are set to 1 will usually be displayed in the current background color (e.g., white), and bits that are set to 0 will be displayed in the current foreground color (e.g., black). In color bitmaps, multiple bits represent each pixel and the number of bits per pixel governs the color displayed.

Colors displayed on a screen are combinations of the primary colors red, green, and blue, and the total number of possible colors depends on the number of shades available for each of the primary colors. True color 24-bit video display graphics cards provide 8 bits per primary color, which results in a total number of 16,777,216 possible display colors ($2^8 \times 2^8 \times 2^8$). A display monitor in 1,024 × 768 pixel resolution mode in 24-bit true color display mode would require approximately 2.36 megabytes of video memory (1,024 × 768 × 3), which is well within the capacity of current entry-level graphics cards.

Older video cards were often palette based; the palette contained a limited number (usually up to 256) of 24-bit colors. In such cards, the colors are chosen using an index value to the palette rather than directly as a color. Even though palette-based video cards could only display a limited number of colors at any one time, the actual colors in the palette were chosen from the full range of 16,777,216 possible colors.

Bitmaps are usually referred to as being either device dependent or device independent. As the name implies, the device-dependent bitmap (DDB) image must be displayed on a device that is compatible with the device that the image was created on. Thus, a DDB can be created in a compatible memory device and then copied to the screen. The value of a DDB becomes very limited when you need to display images on a display device, such as a printer, that is different from the display device that the bitmap was created for. The device-independent bitmap (DIB) format was developed so that images could be displayed or printed on any raster device. The Windows operating system will render the image of a DIB with the best quality and color support on any raster device consistent with the available device drivers.

The DIB is more versatile than a DDB when it comes to the range of display devices that it can work with; therefore, the obvious question is why use a DDB? The answer lies in the difference between the speed of the bitmap formats when it comes to rendering and manipulating images. The DIB format is slower to render because Windows needs to convert the image data to the format of the device every time the image is displayed. On the other hand, a DDB image can be moved from one location to another using the Bit Block Transfer (BitBlt) operation. Virtually all video cards support the BitBlt operation; the graphics card does all the work and the operating system can get on with other tasks.

The speed of a DDB is illustrated in this chapter through two examples, called Animate1 and Animate2, which display simple animation scenes. Animate2 represents a piston compressing air in a cylinder, and it illustrates how a memory device context can be drawn on using standard GDI vector instructions and then copied as a complete object to the screen. A timer and the ubiquitous BitBlt function are used to display the changing scenes and thus to create the animation effect.

Besides BitBlt, Windows includes three other block transfer functions: PatBlt (pattern block transfer), StretchBlt (stretch block transfer), and Plg-Blt (parallelogram block transfer). Note that PlgBlt is supported only on the Windows NT and 2000 operating systems. The use of these functions will be demonstrated through the following programs: CrossWires, BitView1, and BitView2.

10.1.1   CrossWires example program

The simplest of the block transfer functions is the pattern block transfer (PatBlt). It only has a destination device context. The syntax of PatBlt is:

```
iret = PatBlt(hdc, x, y, cx, cy, dwROP)
```

The x, y, cx, and cy arguments are in logical units. The point (x, y) specifies a corner of a rectangle that is cx units wide and cy units high. PatBlt performs raster drawing operations on this rectangular area. The last argument—dwROP—defines the logical operation that PatBlt is to perform on the brush and the destination area, which can be any one of the five raster operations listed in Table 10.1.

Note: In the normal MM_TEXT mapping mode, x, y will define the upper-left corner of the rectangle, but in other mapping modes (e.g., MM_LOENGLISH) x, y will define the lower-left corner of the rectangle. You need to specify a negative value of cy in order to define the upper-left corner.

In the application CrossWires, the PatBlt function is used to create a pair of lines that form a cross-wire cursor. As the mouse moves, a DSTIN-

Table 10.1   *Raster Operations Supported by PatBlt*

DwROP Name	Used to
BLACKNESS	draw a black rectangle.
DSTINVERT	invert the color of the rectangle.
PATINVERT	invert the rectangle if WHITE_BRUSH is the current brush.
PATCOPY	fill the rectangle using the current brush pattern.
WHITENESS	draw a white rectangle.

VERT raster operation is performed on the lines drawn using the current mouse position before updating the mouse position and redrawing the two lines. A filled rectangle is also drawn to demonstrate the effect of the cross wires as the cursor moves over an object. (See Figure 10.1.)

Note that the default CreateWindowEx function needs to be modified to include the extended style WS_EX_TOPMOST, as shown below:

```
ghwndMain = CreateWindowEx(WS_EX_TOPMOST, lpszClassName,&
            lpszAppName, INT(WS_OVERLAPPEDWINDOW), &
            CW_USEDEFAULT, &
            0,CW_USEDEFAULT, 0, NULL, ghMenu, hInstance, NULL)
```

Remove the WS_EX_TOPMOST style, if you want to demonstrate why this style is needed. Without the WS_EX_TOPMOST style, when the task bar is hidden and the screen of CrossWire fills the entire display area,

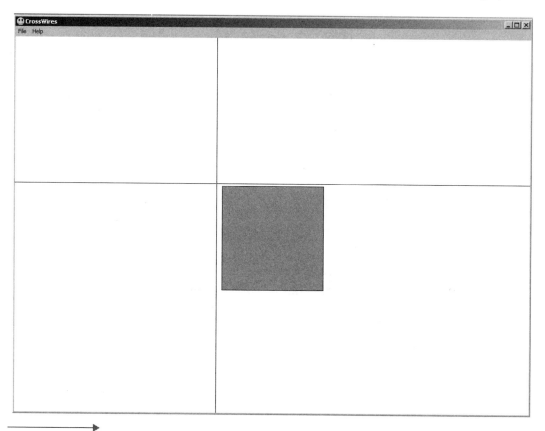

Figure 10.1   *Screen capture from application CrossWire showing the cursor created using PatBlt.*

all works well until you move the cursor to the bottom of the screen and the task bar appears. Then, when you move away from task bar, you will be left with a frozen image of the screen cursor in addition to the normal dynamic cursor. The WS_EX_TOPMOST style prevents the task bar from popping up and creating a frozen cursor. A variation on this cursor is used in Chapter 11 in the application SplitterView. The code listing is given below:

```
case (WM_CREATE)
    cxWire = 1
    xPos = 0
    ypos = 0
    hBrush = CreateSolidBrush(rgb(0,255,255))
    hdcCross = GetDC(hWnd)
    MainWndProc = 0
    return
case (WM_SIZE)
    cxClient = GetSystemMetrics (SM_CXSCREEN)
    cyClient = GetSystemMetrics (SM_CYSCREEN)
    iret = MoveWindow(hWnd ,0,0,  cxClient,cyClient, .true.)
    MainWndProc = 0
    return
case (WM_PAINT)
    hdc = BeginPaint(hwnd, ps)
    iret = SelectObject(hdc, hBrush)
    bret = Rectangle(hdc, (cxClient/2)-100, &
        (cyClient/2)-100, (cxClient/2)+100, (cyClient/2)+100)
    hBrush = SelectObject(hdc, hBrushOld)
    iret = EndPaint (hwnd, ps)
    iret = GetClientRect(hWnd, rcSplit)
    leftX = xPos-cxWire/2
    topY  = yPos-cxWire/2
    iret =PatBlt(hdcCross, leftX, 0, cxWire, rcSplit%bottom,&
            DSTINVERT)
    iret =PatBlt(hdcCross, 0, topY , rcSplit%right, cxWire,&
            DSTINVERT)
    MainWndProc = 0
        return
case (WM_MOUSEMOVE)
    ! Change the X  coordinates to match the new mouse
    ! position.
    xPos = int2(LOWORD(lParam))
    ypos = int2(HIWORD(lParam))
    iret =PatBlt(hdcCross, leftX, 0, cxWire, rcSplit%bottom,&
            DSTINVERT)
    leftX = xPos-cxWire/2
    iret =PatBlt(hdcCross, leftX, 0, cxWire, rcSplit%bottom,&
            DSTINVERT)
```

```
          iret =PatBlt(hdcCross, 0, topY , rcSplit%right, cxWire,&
                DSTINVERT)
          topY  = yPos-cxWire/2
          iret =PatBlt(hdcCross, 0, topY , rcSplit%right, cxWire,&
                DSTINVERT)
          MainWndProc = 0
          return
       case (WM_DESTROY)
          iret = ReleaseDC(hwnd,hdcCross)
          iret = DeleteObject(hBrush)
          call PostQuitMessage( 0 )
          MainWndProc = 0
          return
```

10.2 GDI device-dependent bitmaps

Images can be copied from one location to another using BitBlt. The BitBlt
function performs a bit-block transfer of the color data corresponding to a
rectangle of pixels from the specified source device context into a destination device context. The source image to be transferred can exist in memory. Alternatively, it could be a part of the screen or even the complete
screen, and the destination to which the image is to be copied can be a compatible device, such as clipboard, screen, or memory. If the color formats of
the source and destination device contexts do not match, the BitBlt function converts the source color format to match the destination format. The
syntax of the BitBlt function is as follows:

```
    bret = BitBlt(hdcDest,xDest,yDest,cWidth,cHeight, &
                  hdcSrc,xSrc,ySrc,dwRop)
```

The argument hdcDest is a handle to the destination device context.
The point (xDest, yDest) specifies the top left-hand corner of a destination
rectangle that is cWidth units wide and cHeight units high. BitBlt performs
raster drawing operations on this rectangular area. The argument hdcSrc is
a handle to the source device context. The point (xSrc, ySrc) specifies the
coordinate position of the upper left-hand corner of the source image. The
last argument, dwROP, is one of 16 possible raster-operation codes used to
define how the color data for the source rectangle are to be combined with
the color data for the destination rectangle to achieve the final color. All 16
raster-operation codes are listed in the online documentation for BitBlt and
include the five codes given in Table 10.1.

In the BitBlt function, the destination image must be the same size as
the source image, since both images share the same arguments for width

and height. The function StretchBlt is used when it is necessary to stretch or compress the size of the image being copied. The StretchBlt function copies a bitmap from a source rectangle into a destination rectangle, stretching or compressing the bitmap to fit the dimensions of the destination rectangle, if necessary. The system stretches or compresses the bitmap according to the stretching mode currently set in the destination device context. StretchBlt has the following syntax:

```
iret = StretchBlt(hdcDest, xDst, yDst, cxDst, cyDst, &
           hdcSrc, xSrc, ySrc, cxSrc, CySrc, SRCCOPY)
```

This function has two additional arguments compared with BitBlt. The function now includes separate widths and heights of the source and destination rectangles. StretchBlt creates a mirror image of a bitmap if the signs of the nWidthSrc and nWidthDest parameters or of the nHeightSrc and nHeightDest parameters differ. If nWidthSrc and nWidthDest have different signs, the function will create a mirror image of the bitmap along the x-axis. If nHeightSrc and nHeightDest have different signs, the function will create a mirror image of the bitmap along the y-axis. StretchBlt will create a mirror image when cxSrc and cxDst or cySrc and CyDst have different signs.

The function StretchBlt will duplicate rows or columns of pixels when a bitmap is to be expanded. Distortion of the image may occur for large expansions. When a bitmap is to be shrunk, StretchBlt will combine two or more rows or columns of pixels into a single row or column. It does this in one of four ways, depending on the stretching mode attribute in the device context. The function SetStretchBltMode is used to set this attribute:

```
iret = SetStretchBltMode(hdc, iStretchmode)
```

The value of iStretchmode may be one of the symbolic constants listed in Table 10.2.

Users of Windows NT4 or 2000 can also use the PlgBlt (parallelogram block transfer) function for performing a bit-block transfer from a specified rectangle in a source device context to the specified parallelogram in a destination device context:

```
iret = PlgBlt(hdcDest,lpPoint(1), hdcSrc, nXSrc, nYSrc, &
           nWidth, nHeigh, hbmMask, xMask yMask)
```

where hdcDest is a handle to the destination device context and lpPoint is a pointer to an array of three points in logical space that identify three corners of the destination parallelogram. The first point in the array corresponds to

Table 10.2   *Stretch Modes*

Symbolic Constants	Used to
BLACKONWHITE or STRETCH_ANDSCANS	perform a Boolean AND operation using the color values for the eliminated and existing pixels. For monochrome bitmaps, this mode preserves black pixels at the expense of white pixels.
WHITEONBLACK or STRETCH_ORSCANS	perform a Boolean OR operation using the color values for the eliminated and existing pixels. For monochrome bitmaps, this mode preserves white pixels at the expense of black pixels.
COLORONCOLOR or STRETCH_DELETESCAN	delete the pixels. This mode deletes all eliminated lines of pixels without trying to preserve their information.
HALFTONE or STRETCH_HALFTONE	map pixels from the source rectangle into blocks of pixels in the destination rectangle. The average color over the destination block of pixels approximates the color of the source pixels.

the upper-left corner of the source rectangle, the second point to the upper-right corner, and the third point to the lower-left corner of the parallelogram. The lower right corner of the source rectangle corresponds to the implicit fourth point in the parallelogram.

The argument hdcSrc is a handle to the source device context; nXSrc, nYSrc specify the x and y coordinates, respectively, in logical units, of the upper-left corner of the source rectangle; and nWidth and nHeight specify the width and height, respectively, in logical units, of the source rectangle. The last three arguments refer to an optional mask, and they are set to zero if no mask is required. Otherwise, hbmMask is a handle to a monochrome bitmap, which is to be used to mask the colors of the source rectangle; and the x and y coordinates of the upper-left corner of the monochrome bitmap are specified, respectively, by the arguments xMask, yMask.

10.2.1   BitView1 example program

In the program BitView1, four bitmaps are loaded from the Resource file using the LoadBitmap function. The default bitmap is set to be the blue lace bitmap. The CreateCompatibleDC function is used to create a memory device context (DC) compatible with the application's current screen. The GetObject function is used to obtain information about the bitmap. This information is returned in a bitmap structure. The bitmap is selected into the memory device context. The user may choose to copy any one of the four bitmaps from memory to the screen in normal size using BitBlt, stretched using StretchBlt, as a parallelogram using PlgBlt (Windows NT4/ 2000 only), or as a repeating pattern that fills the entire screen using BitBlt. (See Figure 10.2.)

One programming feature worth noting in BitView1 is the use of WM_USER messages. You can define your own custom Windows messages simply by declaring their names and giving them a numerical value that is an offset from the symbolic constant WM_USER. In the following code fragment, four new user messages, WM_PLGBLT, WM_STRETCHBLT, WM_BITBLT, and WM_REPEAT are declared in the global variables section:

```
Integer(4), parameter, public :: WM_PLGBLT     = WM_USER+1
Integer(4), parameter, public :: WM_STRETCHBLT = WM_USER+2
Integer(4), parameter, public :: WM_BITBLT     = WM_USER+3
Integer(4), parameter, public :: WM_REPEAT     = WM_USER+4
```

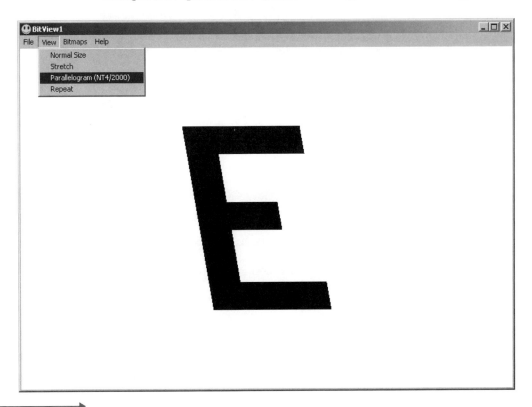

Figure 10.2   *The BitView1 program with the bitmap E displayed as a parallelogram.*

Messages can be sent to these new user messages with the normal Send-Message function, as demonstrated in the following code from BitView1. The code also demonstrates the use of the block transfer functions:

```
case (WM_CREATE)
   Draw = Normal
   magnify = 6
   hBitmap1 = LoadBitmap(ghInstance, MAKEINTRESOURCE &
             (IDB_Bitmap1))
   hBitmap2 = LoadBitmap(ghInstance, MAKEINTRESOURCE &
             (IDB_Bitmap2))
   hBitmap3 = LoadBitmap(ghInstance, MAKEINTRESOURCE &
             (IDB_Bitmap3))
   hBitmap4 = LoadBitmap(ghInstance, MAKEINTRESOURCE &
             (IDB_Bitmap4))
   hBitmap = hBitmap1
   MainWndProc = 0
   return
case (WM_SIZE)
   iret = GetClientRect(hWnd,rect)
   cxCenter = rect%right/2
   cyCenter = rect%bottom/2
   MainWndProc = 0
   return
case (WM_PAINT)
   hdc = BeginPaint(hwnd,ps)
   hdcBits = CreateCompatibleDC(Null)
   iret = GetObject (hBitmap, 24, LOC(bm))
   iret = SelectObject( hdcBits ,hBitmap)
   cxCenter = rect%right/2
   cyCenter = rect%bottom/2
   Select Case(Draw)
      Case(Normal)
         iret = SendMessage (hwnd, WM_BITBLT, 0,0)
      Case(Stretch)
         iret = SendMessage (hwnd, WM_STRETCHBLT, 0,0)
      Case(Parallogram)
         iret = SendMessage (hwnd, WM_PLGBLT, 0,0)
      Case(Repeat)
         iret = SendMessage (hwnd, WM_REPEAT, 0,0)
   end select
   iret = DeleteDC(hdcBits)
   iret = EndPaint(hwnd,ps)
   hdc = 0
   MainWndProc = 0
   return
case (WM_BITBLT)
   cxDdb = bm%bmWidth/2
   cyDdb = bm%bmHeight/2
```

```
         bret = BitBlt(hdc,cxCenter-cxDdb,cyCenter-cyDdb, &
              bm%bmWidth,  bm%bmHeight,hdcBits,0,0,SRCCOPY)
         MainWndProc = 0
         return
      case (WM_STRETCHBLT)
         cxDdb = (Magnify*bm%bmWidth)/2
         cyDdb = (Magnify*bm%bmHeight)/2
         iret = StretchBlt (hdc, cxCenter-cxDdb, cyCenter-cyDdb,&
              2*cxDdb, 2*cyDdb,hdcBits,  0, 0, bm%bmWidth,&
                   bm%bmHeight,SRCCOPY)
         MainWndProc = 0
         return
      case (WM_PLGBLT)
         cxDdb = (Magnify*bm%bmWidth)/2
         cyDdb = (Magnify*bm%bmHeight)/2
         lpPoint(1)%x = cxCenter -cxDdb
         lpPoint(1)%y = cyCenter -cyDdb
         lpPoint(2)%x = cxCenter + cxDdb
         lpPoint(2)%y = cyCenter -cyDdb
         lpPoint(3)%x = 50+(cxCenter-cxDdb)
         lpPoint(3)%y = cyCenter + cyDdb
         iret = PlgBlt (hdc,lpPoint(1),·hdcBits, 0, 0, bm%bmWidth,&
                   bm%bmHeight,0,0,0)
         MainWndProc = 0
         return
      case (WM_REPEAT)
         do y = 1, rect%bottom,bm%bmHeight
            do x = 1, rect%right,bm%bmWidth
               iret = BitBlt( hDC, x, y,  bm%bmWidth,&
                    bm%bmHeight, hdcBits, 0, 0, SRCCOPY )
            end do
         end do
         MainWndProc = 0
         return
      case (WM_DESTROY)
         iret =  DeleteObject(hBitmap1)
         iret =  DeleteObject(hBitmap2)
         iret =  DeleteObject(hBitmap3)
         iret =  DeleteObject(hBitmap4)
         call PostQuitMessage(0)
         MainWndProc = 0
         return
```

10.2.2 BitView2 example program

One obvious disadvantage of the BitView1 program is that it is limited to
displaying only bitmaps that have been previously loaded into the Resource
Editor. The application BitView2 has the ability to load bitmaps from a file

and display in normal or stretched size. A problem that occurs with loading bitmaps from disk is that only device-independent bitmaps are stored on disk. Consequently, in BitView2 we need to read in the file information of a DIB and then convert the bitmap to device-dependent bitmap (DDB) form. After that, all the operations performed on the image involve device-dependent functions such as BitBlt and StretchBlt. Later on in this chapter, we will see in BitView3 how to use the equivalent device-independent functions SetDIBitsToDevice and StretchDIBits.

Since we will be examining device-independent bitmaps later in the chapter, we will leave the techniques used in BitView2 for reading DIB files into memory until then and begin our review of BitView2 with the CreateDIBitmap function. The name CreateDIBitmap would tend to suggest that this function is used to create a device-independent bitmap, but, in fact, it is used to create a device-dependent bitmap from a DIB:

```
hbm = CreateDIBitmap(hdcSrc, LOC(pbmih), &
        CBM_INIT, pBits, LOC(pbmih), DIB_RGB_COLORS)
```

Figure 10.3   *The application BitView2 displaying the Compaq logo bitmap in normal size.*

The arguments used by CreateDIBitmap will make more sense once we have looked at device-independent bitmaps, and they are presented here for completeness rather than a detailed examination. The return value hbm is a handle to the bitmap, hdcSrc is a handle to a device context, and pbmih is a pointer to information on the bitmap size and format. The argument CBM_INIT is a flag to indicate that the data and parameters pointed to by the next two pointers should be used to initialize the bitmap's bits. The pointer pBits points to initialization data, pbmih is a pointer to color format data for the bitmap, and DIB_RGB_COLORS indicates that the color table provided contains literal RGB values rather than palette-indexed colors (DIB_PAL_COLORS).

Once a handle (hbm) is obtained for a bitmap loaded into memory, we can use the same techniques as in the BitView1 application to put BitBlt and StretchBlt images in a compatible memory device onto the display screen. Figure 10.3 shows BitView2 displaying the Compaq logo bitmap in normal size. The following code fragment shows how the three display options, Normal Size, Fit To Window, and Fit Isotropically, are achieved. If a bitmap file has been loaded, the display options in the menu are enabled through WM_INITMENUPOPUP; otherwise, they are disabled. Note the use of the functions SetMapMode, Set WindowExtEx, SetViewportExtEx, SetWindowOrgEx, and SetViewportOrgEx to achieve the isotropic stretch option (WM_STRETCHEVEN):

```
case (WM_CREATE)
   iret = Initialize()
   pheader = 0
   hdcSrc  = GetDC (hwnd)
   Draw = Normal
   MainWndProc = 0
   return
case (WM_SIZE)
   iret = GetClientRect(hWnd,rect1)
   cxClient = rect1%right
   cyClient = rect1%bottom
   cxCenter = cxClient/2
   cyCenter = cyClient/2
   MainWndProc = 0
   return
case (WM_INITMENUPOPUP)
   hMenu1 = GetSubMenu (ghMenu, 1)
   if (pheader /= 0) then
      iEnable = MF_ENABLED
   else
      iEnable = MF_GRAYED
```

```
                   end if
                   iret =   EnableMenuItem (hMenu1, IDM_NORMAL, iEnable)
                   iret =   EnableMenuItem (hMenu1, IDM_STRETCH, iEnable)
                   iret =   EnableMenuItem (hMenu1, IDM_STRETCHEVEN,iEnable)
                   MainWndProc = 0
                   return
               case (WM_PAINT)
                   if (pheader > 0) then
                      hdc = BeginPaint(hwnd,ps)
                      hdcBits = CreateCompatibleDC(Null)
                      iret = GetObject (hbm, 24, LOC(bm))
                      iret = SelectObject(hdcBits,hbm)
                      cxDdb = bm%bmWidth
                      cyDdb = abs(bm%bmHeight)
                      cxCenter = rect1%right/2
                      cyCenter = rect1%bottom/2
                      Select Case(Draw)
                         Case(Normal)
                            iret = SendMessage (hwnd, WM_BITBLT, 0,0)
                         Case(Stretch)
                            iret = SendMessage (hwnd, WM_STRETCHBLT, 0,0)
                         Case(StretchEven)
                            iret = SendMessage (hwnd, WM_STRETCHEVEN, 0,0)
                      end select
                      iret = DeleteDC(hdcBits)
                      iret = EndPaint(hwnd,ps)
                      hdc = 0
                   end if
                   MainWndProc = 0
                   return
               case (WM_BITBLT)
                   iret = BitBlt(hdc,cxCenter-cxDdb/2, cyCenter-cyDdb/2, &
                            cxDdb, cyDdb,hdcBits,0,0,SRCCOPY)
                   iret = DeleteDC(hdcBits)
                   MainWndProc = 0
                   return
               case (WM_STRETCHBLT)
                   iret = StretchBlt (hdc,0,0, cxClient,cyClient,hdcBits, &
                          0, 0, bm%bmWidth, bm%bmHeight,SRCCOPY)
                   MainWndProc = 0
                   return
               case (WM_STRETCHEVEN)
                   iret = SetMapMode (hdc, MM_ISOTROPIC)
                   iret = SetWindowExtEx (hdc, cxDdb, cyDdb, NULL)
                   iret = SetViewportExtEx (hdc, cxClient, cyClient, NULL)
                   iret = SetWindowOrgEx (hdc, cxDdb / 2, cyDdb / 2, NULL)
                   iret = SetViewportOrgEx (hdc, cxClient / 2, &
                          cyClient / 2, NULL)
```

```
iret = StretchBlt (hdc,0,0, cxDdb, cyDdb,hdcBits,  &
        0, 0, bm%bmWidth, bm%bmHeight,SRCCOPY)
MainWndProc = 0
return
```

10.3 **Animation**

So far, we have created memory devices that are compatible with the display screen, loaded bitmaps into the memory-compatible device, and used the BitBlt function to transfer the image to the screen or printer. However, we can also create our own bitmaps in memory. All we need to do is allocate an area in memory in which the image will be created. This block of memory becomes a memory bitmap using the function CreateCompatibleBitmap. The GDI allocates the memory and internal data structures for this bitmap object and supplies a handle to the bitmap. The memory bitmap is a GDI object, and it can be drawn on using GDI functions. However, since we are drawing on a bitmap in memory, we need to create a memory device context that is compatible with the display screen using the CreateCompatibleDC function so that we can ultimately view the image after it has been created. When you select the compatible bitmap into the compatible device context, you have effectively created an image area in memory that simulates the display screen. You can draw into it and perform any operation that you could perform on the actual screen.

At first that may not seem particularly useful, because you cannot view objects being drawn in memory in the same way as when they are drawn on the display screen. However, instead of displaying all the drawing steps on the screen as they occur during the creation of a complex drawing, an application can draw to the memory bitmap and then transfer a complete drawing in one operation to the screen using the BitBlt function. In this situation, the bitmap is used as a buffer for GDI drawing operations before their display on the screen. The BitBlt function is incredibly fast ,and the display is updated as one complete raster entity rather than as individual vector objects. The ability to use a memory bitmap as a shadow buffer to the display screen can be combined with a Windows timer to create animation effects. The techniques are demonstrated in two simple and similar applications—Animate1 and Animate2. In Animate1, a vertically oriented rectangle is used as a bounding box for the repeated drawing of an ellipse at different locations along the vertical axis. The ellipse is drawn green as it descends and magenta as it ascends inside the bounding rectangle. The timer is created with a time-out value (elapsed time) of 50 milliseconds. The WM_TIMER message is used to process the drawing rather than

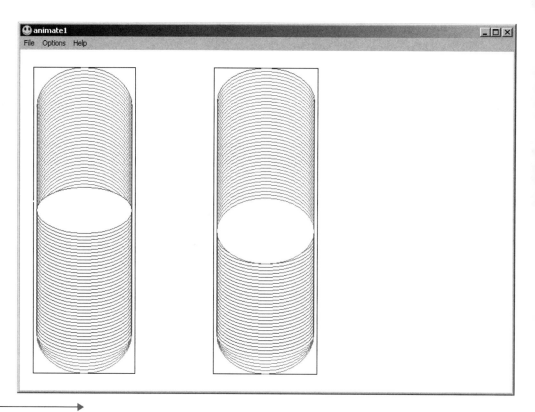

Figure 10.4   *Screen shot from the application Animate1.*

WM_PAINT. This does not cause any problems when a user resizes the client area, because all the drawing takes place in a memory and the display is updated from memory as soon as the resize action has been completed. If the window is minimized, the application will continue on its cycle of operations, and when the window is opened up, the display will reflect the display state in the memory at the elapsed point in time. In WM_TIMER, the *y* coordinates for the top and bottom of the bounding box that is used to define the ellipse are incremented in steps of plus or minus five and the new ellipse is drawn to the memory bitmap. When the timer triggers again, the memory bitmap is moved to the screen. The program also provides the user with an option to display a snapshot of the animation at any time during the animation cycle (see Figure 10.4). This is the code used to create the animation sequence in Animate1.

```
case (WM_CREATE)
    x =5
    y = 5
```

```
              Ystart = 5
              Yend = 145
              cxDdb = 160
              cyDdb = 460
              iret = SetTimer (hwnd, ID_TIMER, 50, NULL)
              hDC = GetDC( hWnd )
              hBitmap =  CreateCompatibleBitmap(hdc,cxDdb,cyDdb)
              hMemDC = CreateCompatibleDC( hDC )
              iret = SelectObject( hMemDC, hBitmap)
              hPen = CreatePen(PS_SOLID,1,rgb(0,0,0))
              iret = SelectObject( hMemDC, hPen)
              iret = Rectangle( hMemDC, 0, 0, cxDdb, cyDdb)
              MainWndProc = 0
              return
        case (WM_TIMER)
           if (hBitmap == 0) then
              MainWndProc = 0
              return
           end if
           iret = BitBlt( hDC, (cxClient/2-cxDdb/2), (cyClient/2-&
                 cyDdb/2), cxDdb, cyDdb,hMemDC, 0, 0, SRCCOPY )
           if ((Ystart >= 365).or.(Ystart<5)) then
              x = -x
           end if
           if ((Yend >455).or. (Yend <= 85)) then
              y = - y
           end if
           if( x< 0) then
              hPen = CreatePen(PS_SOLID,1,rgb(255,0,255))
              iret = SelectObject( hMemDC, hPen)
           else
              hPen = CreatePen(PS_SOLID,1,rgb(0,255,0))
              iret = SelectObject( hMemDC, hPen)
           end if
           Ystart = Ystart +x
           Yend = Yend+y
           iret = Ellipse( hMemDC, 5, Ystart,   155,Yend)
           MainWndProc = 0
           return
        case (WM_SIZE)
           cxClient = LOWORD (lParam)
           cyClient = HIWORD (lParam)
           MainWndProc = 0
           return
        case (WM_DESTROY)
           call PostQuitMessage( 0 )
           iret = DeleteDC( hMemDC )
           iret =  KillTimer (hwnd, ID_TIMER)
```

```
iret = ReleaseDC( hWnd, hDC )
MainWndProc = 0
return
```

In Figure 10.4, the shape on the left-hand side is a still captured from the animation sequence occurring in the shape in the center of the figure.

10.3.1   Animate2 example program

The application Animate1 demonstrates how the GDI device-dependent bitmap can be used to create animation effects using the GDI ellipse-drawing object. Animate2, which uses the same animation principles as Animate1, works with rectangular objects that are intended to represent a piston compressing air as it moves up a cylinder. The air, represented by a crosshatch pattern, is initially cold and drawn in blue. As the piston moves up the cylinder, the color used to represent the air is changed twice to illus-

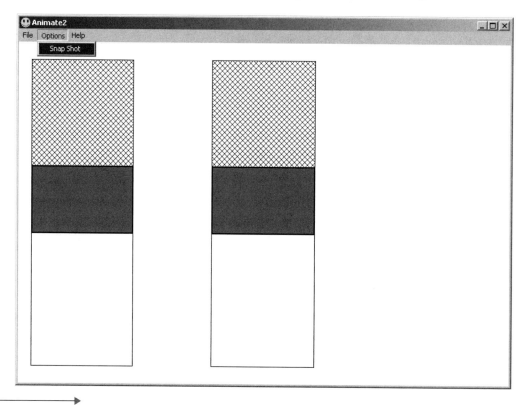

Figure 10.5   *Screen shot of animation sequence from Animate2.*

trate that the air temperature is increasing. Three rectangles are used to represent the lower cylinder, piston, and upper cylinder. Each time the piston moves, all three rectangles are redrawn. The lower cylinder is filled with a clear brush, the piston with a solid brush, and the upper cylinder with a hatch brush.

As in Animate1, the user can take a snapshot of the compression and expansion process at any time during the cycle (see Figure 10.5). The Animate2 application has considerable potential for development. One possibility is to include valves and ports for modeling the action of an air compressor; a more complex animation could be developed to model the two- and four-stroke engine cycles. This code fragment demonstrates the animation principles:

```
case (WM_CREATE)
    cxDdb = 160
    cyDdb = 460
    y = 5
    PistonTop = 200
    iret = SetTimer (hwnd, ID_TIMER, 50, NULL)
    hDC = GetDC( hWnd )
    hBitmap =  CreateCompatibleBitmap(hdc,cxDdb,cyDdb)
    hMemDC = CreateCompatibleDC( hDC )
    iret = SelectObject( hMemDC, hBitmap)
    hPen = CreatePen(PS_SOLID,1,rgb(0,0,0))
    iret = SelectObject( hMemDC, hPen)
    hBrushClear = CreateHatchBrush(HS_DIAGCROSS, &
        rgb(255,255,255))
    hBrushHot = CreateHatchBrush(HS_DIAGCROSS,rgb(255,0,0))
    hBrushWarm = CreateHatchBrush(HS_DIAGCROSS, &
        rgb(155,0,100))
    hBrushCold = CreateHatchBrush(HS_DIAGCROSS,rgb(0,0,200))
    hBrushPiston = CreateSolidBrush(rgb(255,0,255))
    iret = Rectangle( hMemDC, 0, 0, cxDdb, cyDdb )
    iret = SelectObject( hMemDC, hBrushCold)
    iret = Rectangle( hMemDC, 0, 0, cxDdb, PistonTop)
    iret = SelectObject( hMemDC, hBrushPiston)
    iret = Rectangle( hMemDC,1,PistonTop,cxDdb-1, &
        PistonTop+100)
    MainWndProc = 0
    return
 case (WM_TIMER)
    if (hBitmap == 0) then
        MainWndProc = 0
        return
    end if
```

```
      iret = BitBlt( hDC, (cxClient/2-cxDdb/2), (cyClient/2- &
         cyDdb/2), 160, 460,hMemDC, 0, 0, SRCCOPY )
      if ((PistonTop >300).or. (PistonTop <= 20)) then
         y = - y
      end if
      if( PistonTop <120) then
         iret = SelectObject( hMemDC, hBrushHot)
      else if(PistonTop>= 220) then
         iret = SelectObject( hMemDC, hBrushCold  )
      else
         iret = SelectObject( hMemDC,hBrushWarm)
      end if
      PistonTop = PistonTop +y
      iret = Rectangle( hMemDC, 0, 0, 160, PistonTop)
      iret = SelectObject( hMemDC, hBrushPiston)
      iret = Rectangle( hMemDC, 1, PistonTop, 159,&
                      PistonTop+100 )
      iret = SelectObject( hMemDC, hBrushClear)
      iret = Rectangle( hMemDC, 0, PistonTop+100, 160, 460 )
      MainWndProc = 0
      return
   case (WM_SIZE)
      cxClient = LOWORD (lParam)
      cyClient = HIWORD (lParam)
      MainWndProc = 0
      return
   case (WM_DESTROY)
      call PostQuitMessage( 0 )
      iret = DeleteDC( hMemDC )
      iret =  KillTimer (hwnd, ID_TIMER)
      iret = ReleaseDC( hWnd, hDC )
      MainWndProc = 0
      return
```

In Figure 10.5, the shape in the left of the figure is a still capture from the animation sequence occurring in the shape in the middle of the figure.

10.4 Device-independent bitmaps

The device-independent bitmap (DIB) is not a Win32 object; it does not have a handle, and it is not created by GDI functions. It is a file format that is used to describe an image contained in memory or disk. Table 10.3 provides an outline of the DIB file formats used for disk and memory images.

When a DIB is in memory, pointers to that DIB are used as arguments to the functions displaying the DIB. However, you can also convert a DIB

Table 10.3   *Device-Independent Bitmap Format*

Disk File Format Contains:	Memory Format Contains:
File header	*************
Information header	Information header
Color table (optional)	Color table (optional)
Bitmap pixel data	Bitmap pixel data

into a DDB, as we did in BitView2, or into a DIB section. DIB sections permit DIB images to be treated as GDI objects with handles and, more importantly, as objects that can be drawn on in memory. The BitBlt and StretchBlt functions can be used with DIB sections but not with a DIB. DIB sections are not covered in this book, but they are very useful for anyone working with DIB bitmaps. The information covered in this chapter should equip interested readers with the background knowledge required for an independent study of DIB sections. A good starting place would be to look up the online information for DIBSECTION and follow the links.

The information given in Table 10.3 may at first appear to be a bit of an academic exercise, but we will need to become familiar with the structures that are used to describe a DIB image in memory and on a disk. This information will equip us with the knowledge required to load DIB files from disk into memory, to save DIB files in memory onto disk, and to use the clipboard. The information is also needed when we are using DIB functions for transferring images from memory to a device context.

A DIB file on disk begins with a 14-byte file header that is defined as a structure of type BITMAPFILEHEADER, and it is composed of the following members:

- bfType—Specifies the file type; it must be BM.

- bfSize—Specifies the size, in bytes, of the bitmap file.

- bfReserved1—Must be zero.

- bfReserved2—Must be zero.

- bfOffsetBits—Specifies the offset, in bytes, from the BITMAPFILE-HEADER structure to the bitmap bits.

This information allows us to identify the file as being a bitmap file, to allocate enough memory to contain the DIB image, and to provide a pointer to the bitmap pixel bits. When the DIB file is contained in contiguous memory, it is referred to as a bitmap with a packed-DIB format. On disk, the BITMAPFILEHEADER structure is immediately followed by an information header, whereas in memory, the information header is the first structure in the bitmap. One challenge from the programmer's point of view that arises from the previous sentence occurs when you want to get a bitmap from the clipboard. You do not have the convenience of a BITMAPFILEHEADER to tell you how big the file is and the location of the bitmap bits. Applications need to work all that out before they can load a memory-based bitmap. Fortunately, that task is made easier because bitmaps to be copied from the clipboard will be in packed-DIB format.

The BITMAPINFO structure is composed of the following two members, which are themselves structures:

- bmiHeader—Bitmap information header.

- bmiColors(1)—This member contains either an array of RGBQUAD structures in which the elements of the array make up the color table or an array of 16-bit unsigned integers that specify indexes into the currently realized palette.

The information header can be one of four possibilities: It can be an OS/2 structure type BITMAPCOREINFO; it can be the Windows 3.0 structure type BITMAPINFOHEADER; it can be a Windows 95/NT structure BITMAPV4HEADER; or it can be a Windows 98, Me/2000 structure BITMAPV5HEADER. The four structures are differentiated by their structure size; this is easy to check, because it is the first entry in bmiHeader and consequently in the BITMAPINFO structure. Ideally, a bitmap application should be able to load and display a bitmap that was created using any of the four structures. However, we will focus only on the Windows 3.0 header structure, since it is still the most widely used format. The online documentation details all four of the information header structures, and the concepts demonstrated with BITMAPINFOHEADER are easily transferred to the other structures. The members of the BITMAPINFOHEADER structure are listed in Table 10.4.

If the height of a DIB, as determined from biHeight is a positive value, the DIB is of the standard bottom-up type (i.e., the origin of the pixel bits starts at the lower left-hand corner of the image). When the height of a DIB is a negative value, then the DIB is known as a top-down DIB and the origin of the pixel bits starts at the upper left-hand corner of the image. It is probably best to work with the standard bottom-up DIB, but be aware of the existence of the top-down variety.

Table 10.4   *BITMAPINFOHEADER Structure*

Member	Used to specify the:
biSize	number of bytes (40) required by the structure.
biWidth	width of the bitmap, in pixels.
biHeight	height of the bitmap, in pixels.
biplanes	number of planes for the target device. This value must be set to 1.
biBitCount	number of bits per pixel. The biBitCount member of the BITMAP-INFOHEADER structure determines the number of bits that define each pixel and the maximum number of colors in the bitmap.
biCompression	type of compression for a compressed bottom-up bitmap.
biSizeImage	size, in bytes, of the image. This may be set to 0 for BI_RGB bitmaps.
biXPelsPerMeter	horizontal resolution, in pixels per meter, of the target device for the bitmap.
biYPelsPerMeter	vertical resolution, in pixels per meter, of the target device for the bitmap.
biClrUsed	number of color indexes in the color table that are actually used by the bitmap. If this value is 0, the bitmap uses the maximum number of colors corresponding to the value of the biBitCount member for the compression mode specified by biCompression.
biClrImportant	number of color indexes that are required for displaying the bitmap. If this value is 0, all colors are required.

Note that top-down DIBs cannot be compressed. The value for biCompression can be one of the following:

- BI_RGB—An uncompressed format.

- BI_RLE8—A run-length encoded (RLE) format for bitmaps with 8 bits per pixel.

- BI_RLE4—An RLE format for bitmaps with 4 bits per pixel.

- BI_BITFIELDS—Specifies that the bitmap is not compressed and that the color table consists of three 4-byte integer color masks that specify the red, green, and blue components, respectively, of each pixel. This is valid when used with 16- and 32-bit-per-pixel bitmaps.

- BI_JPEG—Indicates that the image is a JPEG image for Windows 98 or Windows 2000 and later.

If biClrUsed is nonzero and the biBitCount member is less than 16, the biClrUsed member specifies the actual number of colors the device driver accesses. If biBitCount is 16 or greater, the biClrUsed member specifies the size of the color table used to optimize performance of the system color palettes. If biBitCount equals 16 or 32, the optimal color palette starts immediately, following the three 4-byte integer masks.

This is probably a good point at which to start applying the theory by looking look at the code used in the application BitView3. First, let us look at how DIB files are loaded and saved in BitView3. The name of the bitmap file to be opened is obtained by calling a common dialog box in IDM_OPEN. Pheader is a pointer to the memory location in which an image is located. If there is already an existing image in memory (i.e., pheader is not equal to zero), then the memory space used is freed before making a call to the function GetBitmap() to open and load the file. The CreateFile function is used to open a file for reading and to return a handle to the file:

```
hFile = CreateFile(FullName, GENERIC_READ, &
        FILE_SHARE_READ, NULL, OPEN_EXISTING, &
        FILE_FLAG_SEQUENTIAL_SCAN, NULL)
```

The arguments used in the CreateFile are self-explanatory. Fullname is the path and filename of an existing file that is to be read. The FILE_FLAG_SEQUENTIAL_SCAN can help improve the reading speed of large bitmap files. If the handle is valid, the file size (nbytes) is obtained with the function GetFileSize, and an appropriate amount of memory is reserved using malloc, starting the address pointed to by pheader:

```
nbytes = GetFileSize (hFile, NULL)
   pheader = malloc (nbytes )
```

The ReadFile function is used to read in the bitmap file. The arguments to ReadFile include a handle to the file to be read, a pointer to the location in memory that receives the data, the number of bytes (nbytes) to be read, and the location in which the number of read bytes (dwBytesRead) can be stored:

```
iret = ReadFile (hFile, pheader, nbytes, &
                 loc(dwBytesRead), NULL)
   bret = CloseHandle (hFile)
```

The Bitmap3 function GetBitmap returns a value of 1 if successful, or 0 if unsuccessful, to the calling routine. If the return value from GetBitmap is 1, then in IDM_OPEN, the pointer lpbits to the BITMAPINFO structure (bits) is set to the beginning of the information header, which is calculated as pheader plus the byte width of the BITMAPFILEHEADER structure. The variable *pBits* is used as a pointer to the location of the bitmap bits data, and it is calculated as the location of pheader plus the offset value given in the bitmap file header:

```
lpbits = pheader  + sizeof(pbmfh)
pBits = pheader   + pbmfh%bfOffBits
```

Saving a bitmap file is essentially the reverse of the process for loading a file. If the file was loaded from a disk file, it will already have a bitmap file header in memory, but if it was copied from the clipboard, then the application will need to create a bitmap file header. The following is the code used in BitView3 to load and save bitmap DIB files:

```
case (IDM_OPEN )
   bret = GETOPENFILENAME(Ofn)
   !    check to see if the OK button has been pressed
   if(bret == 0) then
      ! check for error
      call COMDLGER(ierror)
   else
      MyName = FullName(1+Ofn%NFILEOFFSET:Ofn% &
         NFILEEXTENSION-1)
      lpszHeader =" BitView3 Current File Name      "//MyName
      bret = SetWindowText(ghwndMain,lpszHeader//' 'C)
      if (pheader /= 0) then
         call free(pheader)
      end if
      iret =  GetBitmap ()
      if(iret >0) then
         bfOffBits=pbmfh%bfOffBits
         lpbits = pheader  + sizeof(pbmfh)
         pBits = pheader  +bfOffBits
      else
         iret = MessageBox(hwnd,"Cannot read this file."C, &
                   "Bitmap File"C, 0)
         MainWndProc = 0
         return
      end if
   if ( bits%bmiHeader%biSize /= 40) then
     iret = MessageBox (hwnd,"Cannot read DIB header"C, &
              "DIB information header"C, 0)
   end if
```

```
            end if
         iret = InvalidateRect (hwnd, NULL_RECT, .TRUE.)
         MainWndProc = 0
         return
   case (IDM_SAVEAS)
         bret = GETSAVEFILENAME(Ofn)
         ! check to see if the OK button has been pressed
         if(bret == 0) then   !   check for error
            call COMDLGER(ierror)
            ! ierror is the returned error value
         else
            MyName = FullName(1+Ofn%NFILEOFFSET:Ofn% &
               NFILEEXTENSION-1)
            lpszHeader =" BitView3 Current File Name        "&
               //MyName
            bret = SetWindowText(ghwndMain,lpszHeader//' 'C)
            iret = SaveBitmap()
            if(iret == 0) then
               iret = MessageBox (hwnd,"Cannot write Bitmap &
                  file"C, "Write DIB file"C, 0)
            end if
         end if
         MainWndProc = 0
         return
```

The following functions are used to read and write DIB files:

```
integer(4) function GetBitmap ()
use BitView2Globals
implicit none
integer(4) iret
integer(4) dwBytesRead
integer(4) hFile
logical(4) bret
integer(4) nbytes
hFile = CreateFile (FullName, GENERIC_READ, &
   FILE_SHARE_READ, NULL, OPEN_EXISTING, &
   FILE_FLAG_SEQUENTIAL_SCAN, NULL)
   if (hFile == INVALID_HANDLE_VALUE) then
      GetBitmap = NULL
      return
   end if
   nbytes = GetFileSize (hFile, NULL)
   pheader = malloc (nbytes )
   if (pheader == 0) then
      bret = CloseHandle (hFile)
      GetBitmap = 0
      return
   end if
```

```
         iret = ReadFile (hFile, pheader, nbytes, &
                          loc(dwBytesRead), NULL)
         bret = CloseHandle (hFile)
         GetBitmap = 1
         return
      end
      integer(4) function SaveBitmap ()
      use BitView2Globals
      implicit none
      integer(4) iret
      integer(4) dwBytesWritten
      integer(4) hFile
      logical(4) bret
         hFile = CreateFile (FullName, GENERIC_WRITE, 0, NULL, &
                 CREATE_ALWAYS, FILE_ATTRIBUTE_NORMAL, NULL)
         if (hFile == INVALID_HANDLE_VALUE) then
            SaveBitmap = 0
            return
         end if
         bret = WriteFile(hFile, pheader, pbmfh%bfSize, &
                    loc(dwBytesWritten), NULL)
         iret = CloseHandle (hFile)
         if (dwBytesWritten /= pbmfh%bfSize) then
            iret = DeleteFile (FullName)
            SaveBitmap = 0
            return
         end if
         SaveBitmap = 1
         return
         end
```

Once the bitmap has been loaded into memory, we can use the SetDI-BitsToDevice function to display a DIB without shrinking or stretching, or the StretchDIBits function if shrinking or stretching is required. Looking first at the SetDIBitsToDevice function, each pixel of the DIB is mapped to a pixel of the output device. The image is always displayed correctly oriented—that is, with the top row of the image on top. Any transforms that might be in effect for the device context determine the starting position in which the DIB is displayed but otherwise have no effect on the size or orientation of the image. This is the function:

```
      iret = SetDIBitsToDevice(hdc,xDest,yDest,dwWidth, &
             dwHeight,xSrc, ySrc, uStartScan, cScanLines, &
             lpvBits, lpbmi, fuColorUse)
```

where hdc is a handle to device context and xDest and yDest are the x and y coordinates of the upper left-hand corner of the destination rectangle. The source image is of width dwWidth and height dwHeight, and x and y coordinates of the lower left-hand corner of the image are given by xSrc and ySrc, respectively. The first scan line to draw is given by uStartScan and the number of scan lines to draw is given by cScanLines. The address of the array of DIB pixel bits is pointed to by lpvBits, and lpbmi is a pointer to the bitmap information structure. Arguments uStartScan and cScanLines can be used when an application wishes to reduce the amount of memory required to set bits from a large device-independent bitmap on a device surface. The application can band the output by repeatedly calling SetDIBitsToDevice, placing a different portion of the bitmap into the lpvBits array each time. The values of the uStartScan and cScanLines parameters identify the portion of the bitmap contained in the lpvBits array. (See Figure 10.6.)

The argument fuColorUse is a color use flag and may be either DIB_PAL_COLORS, to indicate that the color table contains an array of 16-bit indexes into the currently selected logical palette, or DIB_RGB_COLORS, to mean that the color table contains literal RGB values.

Figure 10.6   *Bitmap displayed by the application BitView3 in the Fit Isotropically option.*

The StretchDIBits function copies the color data for a rectangle of pixels in a device-independent bitmap (DIB) to the specified destination rectangle. The rows and columns of color data of the source rectangle will be stretched or compressed by the StretchDIBits function as required to fit the destination rectangle using the specified raster operation. This is the function:

```
iret = StretchDIBits &
(hdc,xDest,yDest,dwWidth,dwHeight,xSrc, ySrc, &
nScrWidth, nScrHeight lpvBits, lpbmi, fuColorUse, dwRop)
```

The arguments nScrWidth and nScrHeight specify the width and height of the source rectangle, respectively, and the dwRop is a raster code operation (see online documention for BitBlt). The other arguments with the same names as those used in the SetDIBitsToDevice function have identical meanings to those of their counterparts:

```
case (WM_PAINT)
    if (pheader /= 0) then
        hdc = BeginPaint(hwnd,ps)
        cxCenter = rect1%right/2
        cyCenter = rect1%bottom/2
        cxDib = bits%bmiHeader%biWidth
        cyDib = abs(bits%bmiHeader%biHeight)
        Select Case(Draw)
            Case(Normal)
                iret = SendMessage (hwnd, WM_BITBLT, 0,0)
            Case(Stretch)
                iret = SendMessage (hwnd, WM_STRETCHBLT, 0,0)
            Case(StretchEven)
                iret = SendMessage (hwnd, WM_STRETCHEVEN, 0,0)
        end select
        iret = EndPaint(hwnd,ps)
    end if
    MainWndProc = 0
    return
case (WM_BITBLT)
    iret = SetDIBitsToDevice (hdc,cxCenter-cxDib/2,&
        cyCenter-cyDib/2,cxDib, cyDib, 0, 0, 0, cyDib, &
        pbits, bits, DIB_RGB_COLORS)
    MainWndProc = 0
    return
case (WM_STRETCHBLT)
    iret = SetStretchBltMode (hdc, COLORONCOLOR)
    iret = StretchDIBits (hdc,0,0,cxClient,cyClient, 0, 0, &
        cXDib,cyDib, pbits, bits, DIB_RGB_COLORS, SRCCOPY)
    MainWndProc = 0
    return
```

```
case (WM_STRETCHEVEN)
   iret = SetStretchBltMode (hdc, COLORONCOLOR)
   iret = SetMapMode (hdc, MM_ISOTROPIC)
   iret = SetWindowExtEx (hdc, cxDib, cyDib, NULL)
   iret = SetViewportExtEx (hdc, cxClient, cyClient, NULL)
   iret = SetWindowOrgEx (hdc, cxDib / 2, cyDib / 2, NULL)
   iret = SetViewportOrgEx (hdc, cxClient / 2, &
               cyClient / 2, NULL)
   iret = StretchDIBits (hdc, 0, 0, cxDib, cyDib,0, 0,&
      cxDib, cyDib,pBits, bits, DIB_RGB_COLORS, SRCCOPY)
   MainWndProc = 0
   return
```

Note: Note the use of the WM_INITMENUPOPUP message, which is sent when a drop-down menu or submenu is about to become active. This allows an application to modify the menu before it is displayed. In the case of BitView3, menu items for manipulating bitmaps are enabled or disabled according to whether or not a bitmap has been loaded. The code used is as follows:

```
case (WM_INITMENUPOPUP)
   hMenu = GetSubMenu (ghMenu, 0)
   hMenu1 = GetSubMenu (ghMenu, 1)
   if (pheader /= 0) then
      iEnable = MF_ENABLED
   else
      iEnable = MF_GRAYED
   end if
   iret =   EnableMenuItem (hMenu, IDM_SAVEAS,iEnable)
   iret =   EnableMenuItem (hMenu, IDM_PROPERTIES, iEnable)
   iret =   EnableMenuItem (hMenu1, IDM_NORMAL, iEnable)
   iret =   EnableMenuItem (hMenu1, IDM_STRETCH, iEnable)
   iret =   EnableMenuItem (hMenu1, IDM_STRETCHEVEN,iEnable)
   MainWndProc = 0
   return
```

10.4.1 BitView4 example program

As we have already learned in Chapter 8, outputting information to a printer is essentially a process similar to that used to output information to a display screen. A PRINTDLG structure (prndlg) needs to be initialized and then a handle to a printer device context obtained (hdcprn = prndlg%hdc) for the printing operations. A call should be made to the function GetDeviceCaps to determine whether the current printer has raster capabilities.

```
iret = GetDeviceCaps (hdcPrn, RASTERCAPS)
```

The return value needs be tested against the appropriate symbolic constants to determine whether the printer can provide raster features such as BitBlt (RC_BITBLT), StretchBlt (RC_STRETCHBLT), SetDIBitsToDevice (RC_DI_BITMAP), or StretchDIBits (RC_STRETCHDIB). The online information for GetDeviceCap gives details of all the symbolic constants to be used when checking for particular raster capabilities. The function GetDeviceCap is also called to determine the pixel dimensions of a page, and this information is used to position the bitmap image as required on the printed page. A document information structure (di) is initialized and selected into the printer device context so that printing can commence.

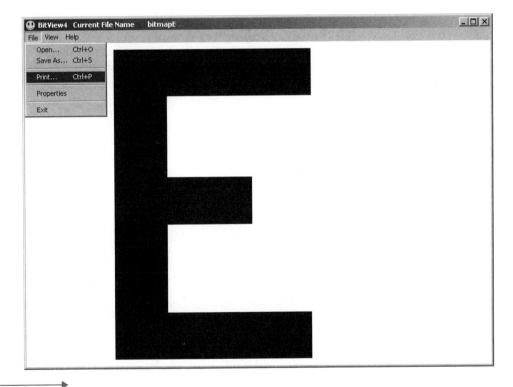

Figure 10.7   *A print option is included in BitView4.*

(See Figure 10.7.) This is how the code for printing a bitmap appears in
BitView4:

```
case (IDM_Print)
   if(pheader == 0)then
      iret = MessageBox (NULL,'Open Bitmap first'C, &
        'Print Bitmap Error'C ,IOR(MB_OK ,MB_ICONQUESTION))
      return
   end if
   ! initialize PRINTDLG structure
   prndlg%lStructSize = sizeof(prndlg)
   prndlg%hwndOwner = hWnd
   prndlg%Flags = IOR(PD_RETURNDC ,IOR(PD_NOSELECTION, &
                   PD_NOPAGENUMS))
   !  Open up print dialog box
   bret = PrintDlg(prndlg)
   if(bret == 0) then
      return
   end if
   hdcPrn = prndlg%hDC
   if(hdcPrn == 0) then
      iret = MessageBox (NULL,'Cannot get a printer DC'C, &
        'Print Bitmap Error'C ,IOR(MB_OK ,MB_ICONQUESTION))
      return
   end if
   ! Check if the printer can print bitmaps
   iret = GetDeviceCaps (hdcPrn, RASTERCAPS)
   if ( (IAND(iret,RC_DI_BITMAP) == 0).or. &
      (IAND(iret,RC_STRETCHDIB) == 0) ) then
      iret = MessageBox (hwnd, "Printer cannot &
         print bitmap"C,'Print Bitmap Error'C ,&
         IOR(MB_OK ,MB_ICONQUESTION))
      ! iret =  DeleteDC (hdcPrn)
      MainWndProc = 0
      return
   end if
   di%cbSize = sizeof(di)
   di%lpszDocName = loc(MyName//''C)
   di%lpszOutput = Null
   di%lpszDatatype = 'bmp'
   di%fwType  = 0
   !  Get size of printable area of page
   cxPage = GetDeviceCaps (hdcPrn, HORZRES)
   cyPage = GetDeviceCaps (hdcPrn, VERTRES)
   !  Send the bitmap to the printer
   iret  = StartDoc(prndlg%hDC, di)
   iret = StartPage(prndlg%hDC)
   cxDib = bits%bmiHeader%biWidth
```

```
      cyDib = abs(bits%bmiHeader%biHeight)
      Select Case(Draw)
         Case(Normal)
            iret = SetDIBitsToDevice(hdcPrn,0,0,cxDib, &
                     cyDib,0,0,0, cyDib, pbits, bits, &
                     DIB_RGB_COLORS)
         Case(Stretch)
            iret = StretchDIBits (hdcPrn,0,0,cxPage,cyPage, &
                     0, 0, cXDib,cyDib, pbits, bits, &
                     DIB_RGB_COLORS, SRCCOPY)
         Case(StretchEven)
            iret = SetStretchBltMode (hdcPrn, COLORONCOLOR)
            iret = SetMapMode (hdcPrn, MM_ISOTROPIC)
            iret = SetWindowExtEx (hdcPrn, cxDib, cyDib, NULL)
            iret = SetViewportExtEx (hdcPrn, cxPage, cyPage, &
                     NULL)
            iret = SetWindowOrgEx (hdcPrn, cxDib / 2, cyDib / &
                     2, NULL)
            iret = SetViewportOrgEx (hdcPrn, cxPage / 2, &
                     cyPage / 2, NULL)
            iret = StretchDIBits (hdcPrn, 0, 0, cxDib, cyDib,&
                     0, 0, cxDib, cyDib,pBits, bits, &
                     DIB_RGB_COLORS, SRCCOPY)
      end select
      if(EndPage(hDCPrn) > 0) then
         iret = EndDoc(hDCprn)
      else
         iret = MessageBox (NULL,'Cannot print bitmap'C, &
            MyName//''C ,IOR(MB_OK ,MB_ICONQUESTION))
      end if
      bret = DeleteDC(hDCprn)
      MainWndProc = 0
      return
```

10.4.2   BitView5 example program

BitView5 provides an Edit menu with options to Copy a bitmap from the application to the clipboard and Paste a bitmap from the clipboard to the application. The clipboard is opened for data transfer with the following instruction:

```
      iret = OpenClipboard (hwnd)
```

and closed with the instruction:

```
      iret = CloseClipboard ()
```

There are various predefined clipboard formats (see SetClipboardData in the online documentation), all of which have identifiers beginning with the prefix CF. Predefined clipboard formats relating to bitmaps include the following:

- CF_BITMAP—A handle to a device-dependent bitmap. The bitmap is transferred to the clipboard using the bitmap handle. The program should not continue to use the bitmap after giving it to the clipboard.

- CF_DIB—A memory block defining a device-independent bitmap. The memory object contains a BITMAPINFO structure followed by the bitmap bits.

- CF_DIBV5—A memory block defining a device-independent bitmap. The memory object contains a BITMAPV5HEADER structure followed by the color space information for the bitmap and the bitmap bits (Windows 98, 2000, and later).

A handle to a bitmap in memory is passed to the clipboard using the instruction:

```
iret = SetClipboardData (CF_BITMAP,hbmCopy)
```

and a handle to a bitmap in the clipboard is obtained using:

```
hBitmapClip = GetClipboardData (CF_BITMAP)
```

The process of copying a device-independent bitmap to the clipboard is straightforward. The memory location where the bitmap is stored becomes the property of the clipboard, so we must make a copy of the bitmap, and then the copy becomes the property of the clipboard. Otherwise, all that is required is for the application to open the clipboard, pass a pointer to the image copy in memory using the SetClipboardData function, and then close the clipboard. The process is illustrated in the following code from BitView5:

```
case (IDM_Copy)
   if (pheader == 0) then
      MainWndProc = 0
      return
   end if
   hGlobal = GlobalAlloc (GHND.or.GMEM_SHARE, &
             pbmfh%bfSize - sizeof (pbmfh))
   pGlobal = GlobalLock (hGlobal)
   call CopyMemory(pGlobal,pheader + sizeof (pbmfh),&
                pbmfh.bfSize - sizeof (pbmfh))
   iret = GlobalUnlock (hGlobal)
   !  Transfer it to the clipboard
```

```
iret = OpenClipboard (hwnd)
iret = EmptyClipboard ()
iret = SetClipboardData (CF_DIB, hGlobal)
iClipboard = 1
iret = CloseClipboard ()
MainWndProc = 0
return
```

The process of pasting from the clipboard to an application is essentially the reverse of copying to the clipboard. It involves opening the clipboard, getting a pointer to the bitmap in the clipboard, making a copy of the image for use by the application, and then closing the clipboard. The problem is to determine the size of memory that needs to be copied and where the actual bitmap bits begin. This involves getting a pointer to the beginning of the image in clipboard memory and checking the size of the bitmap information header. If it is equal to 40, we are dealing with a BITMAP-INFO structure and all is well, but if it is a different value, we exit gracefully because BitView5 does not handle other headers. Note that BitView5 can easily be extended to deal with the other headers and even bitmaps in compressed form as well if you want to read them.

To calculate the offset from the pointer at the beginning of the image in memory and the beginning of the bitmap bits, we need to know whether a mask is included and the size of the color table if one is present. The mask size is 12 if the compression value corresponds to the symbolic constant BI_BITFIELDS, but otherwise it is zero. Each entry in the color table corresponds to an RGBQUAD structure, which is 4 bytes long. For 4- and 8-bit pixel values, the color table will be 16×4 or 256×4, whereas for monochrome images it will always be 2×4. An easy way to perform the calculation for a number of color entries is to do a left-bit shift on the number 1 according to the bit pixel value, as follows:

```
dwColorSize = ishft(1,clipbits%bmiHeader%biBitCount)*4
```

If the bit pixel value is above 8, it is assumed to be 24-bit color without a color table. The value of the bmiHeader structure member biClrUsed is checked first, and if it is a nonzero value, this value is used for determining the length of the color table. The beginning of the bitmap data can now be calculated. The final step is to determine the size of the bitmap bit data. Often, but not always, the bmiHeader structure member biSizeImage will contain the value; therefore, it is necessary to calculate the number of bytes per scanline from the bitmap image pixel width and number of bits per pixel. The only thing to remember is that scanlines must align on a 32-bit boundary. An easy way of doing this is to add three to the number (effec-

3

Figure 10.8   *The Compaq logo bitmap has been pasted from the clipboard to BitView5.*

tively rounding up) and perform a logical AND operation with the hexadecimal value FFFFFFFC. The number of bytes per scanline is multiplied
by the pixel height of the image to get the total number of bytes used. With
this information, a copy can be made of the image in clipboard and the
clipboard can be closed. The beginning of the image copy in memory is
pointed to by pheader, and the beginning of the bitmap bits is pointed to
by pbits. Since we may wish to save an image copied from the clipboard, a
file header structure is inserted at the beginning of the image and the values
set for the members. The header file structure member bfType is set to
"BM" (#4D42) to indicate that it is a bitmap file. (See Figure 10.8.)

The code to perform a paste from clipboard operation in BitView5 is as
follows:

```
case (IDM_PASTE)
   iret = OpenClipboard (hwnd)
   hGlobal = GetClipboardData (CF_DIB)
   lpclip  = GlobalLock (hGlobal)
   dwInfoSize = clipbits%bmiHeader.biSize
```

```
if(dwInfoSize /= 40) then
   iret = MessageBox (hwnd,"Cannot paste this bitmap"C,&
     "Bitmap Paste"C, MB_ICONEXCLAMATION .or. MB_OK)
else if( clipbits%bmiHeader%biCompression == &
            BI_BITFIELDS) then
   dwMaskSize = 12
else
   dwMaskSize = 0
end if
if( clipbits%bmiHeader%biClrUsed > 0) then
   dwColorSize = clipbits%bmiHeader%biClrUsed*4
else if( clipbits%bmiHeader%biBitCount <=8 &
       .AND.clipbits%bmiHeader%biBitCount>=1) then
   dwColorSize = ishft(1,clipbits%bmiHeader%biBitCount)*4
else
   dwColorSize = 0
end if
pBits = lpclip + dwInfoSize+dwMaskSize +dwColorSize
if (pheader /= 0) then
   call free(pheader)
   lpbits = 0
   pheader = 0
end if
Select case(clipbits%bmiHeader%biBitCount)
   Case(1)
      BytePerScanLine = (int((7+clipbits%bmiHeader% &
         biWidth)/8)+3).AND.#FFFFFFFC
   Case(4)
      BytePerScanLine = (int((1+clipbits%bmiHeader% &
         biWidth)/2)+3).AND.#FFFFFFFC
   Case(8)
      BytePerScanLine = ((clipbits%bmiHeader%biWidth) &
         +3).AND.#FFFFFFFC
   Case Default
      BytePerScanLine = ((clipbits%bmiHeader% &
             biWidth*3)+3).AND.#FFFFFFFC
   end Select
   SizeImage = BytePerScanLine*clipbits%bmiHeader% &
      biHeight
   SizeImage = max(clipbits%bmiHeader%biSizeImage, &
      SizeImage)
   pheader = malloc (sizeof(pbmfh)+dwInfoSize+ &
      dwMaskSize+dwColorSize+SizeImage)
   call CopyMemory (pHeader +sizeof(pbmfh),lpclip,&
   dwInfoSize+ dwMaskSize+dwColorSize+ SizeImage)
   lpbits = pHeader +sizeof(pbmfh)
   pBits = pheader+sizeof(pbmfh) + dwInfoSize+ &
      dwMaskSize +dwColorSize
```

```
      pbmfh%bfType = #4D42
      pbmfh%bfSize = sizeof(pbmfh)+dwInfoSize+dwMaskSize+ &
         dwColorSize+SizeImage
      pbmfh%bfReserved1 = 0
      pbmfh%bfReserved2 = 0
      pbmfh%bfOffBits = sizeof(pbmfh)+dwInfoSize+ &
         dwMaskSize+dwColorSize
      iret = InvalidateRect (hwnd, NULL_RECT, .TRUE.)
      lpszHeader =" BitView2   Current File Name &
                     Clipboard"C
      FullName = "Clipboard.bmp"C
      bret = SetWindowText(ghwndMain,lpszHeader//' 'C)
   end if
   iret = GlobalUnlock (hGlobal)
   iret = CloseClipboard ()
   MainWndProc = 0
   return
```

Note: Note the use of the function IsClipboardFormatAvailable to determine whether the clipboard has any bitmaps available for pasting. This
function is used in BitView5 to enable or disable the Paste menu item, as
follows, when a WM_INITMENUPOPUP message is sent:

```
   bret = IsClipboardFormatAvailable(CF_DIB)
      if (bret /=0) then
         iEnable = MF_ENABLED
      else
         iEnable = MF_GRAYED
      end if
         iret =   EnableMenuItem (hMenu1, IDM_PASTE,iEnable)
```

10.5   What is next?

The next chapter is on Win32 common controls. We will learn to use controls such as animation control, tab control, tree view control, and list view
control. In addition, we will discover how to use PatBlt to help create a
splitter window view effect when we create an application that combines a
tree view and a list view control.

11

More Common Controls

11.1 Common control basics

The 22 common controls listed in Table 11.1 can be used to help create applications with a professional-looking user interface. We have already met four of these controls in Chapter 7 (up-down, status bar, tool bar, and tool tips), and in this chapter we will learn how to use six more common controls—animation control, month calendar control, date and time picker control, tab control, tree view control, and list view control. Once you have grasped the programming techniques used with all ten of these common controls, you will have gained enough knowledge to be able to include any of the remaining available common controls with your applications. Detailed information about each control can be obtained from the online documentation under the topic "Common Controls," which also contains some sample code (in C) for each control.

The interface definitions of the controls supported by Visual Fortran are contained in the COMCTL32.f90 file. Any Visual Fortran application that uses a common control must contain USE COMCTL32 in addition to the

Table 11.1   *Common Controls*

Animation control	Hot key control	Progress bar control	Tool tip control
Combo box control	Image list	Property sheet	Track bar control
Date and time picker control	IP address control	Rebar control	Tree view control
Drag list box	List view control	Status bar	Up-Down control
Flat scroll bar	Month calendar control	Tab control	
Header control	Pager control	Tool bar control	

normal USE DFWIN. The program should declare a variable of the structure type INITCOMMONCONTROLSEX and make a call to the Windows InitCommonControlsEx function to load COMCTL32.dll, as illustrated in the following code fragment:

```
type (T_INITCOMMONCONTROLSEX) iccex
   iccex%dwSize = sizeof(iccex)
   iccex%dwICC = ICC_WIN95_CLASSES
   call initcommoncontrolsex(iccex)
```

The structure field dwICC should be set either to the symbolic constant ICC_WIN95_CLASSES, which provides access to all the controls, or to the symbolic constant that is specific to the common control (see Table 11.2) that you wish to use.

Common controls can be created with the Resource Editor when the control is to be used in a dialog box. Alternatively, call either the CreateWindow or CreateWindowsEx function and specify the name of the window class appropriate to the common control that you wish to create.

Table 11.2   *Symbolic Constants for Common Controls*

Symbolic Constant	Provides Access to the Following Common Controls:
ICC_ANIMATE_CLASS	Animation
ICC_BAR_CLASSES	Tool bar, status bar, track bar, tool tips
ICC_COOL_CLASSES	Rebar (cool bar)
ICC_DATE_CLASSES	Month calendar, date and time picker, up-down
ICC_HOTKEY_CLASS	Hot key
ICC_LISTVIEW_CLASSES	List view, header
ICC_PROGRESS_CLASS	Progress bar
ICC_TAB_CLASSES	Tab, tool tips
ICC_TREEVIEW_CLASSES	Tree view, tool tips
ICC_WIN95_CLASSES	All classes
ICC_UPDOWN_CLASS	Up-Down
ICC_USEREX_CLASSES	Comboex

The window class names are listed in the online documentation under the heading "Common Control Window Classes."

Note: When using common controls in a dialog box, it is a good idea to specify the style No fail create. This ensures that the dialog box will always appear and any common controls not initialized will be displayed as a white rectangle. Without the No fail create style, dialog boxes are not be displayed when the common controls have not been initialized properly.

11.1.1 Common control messages

The normal Win32 functions for sending or posting message are used to send messages to a common control. Since common controls are windows, you can send them normal window messages, but additionally each common control also has a set of control-specific messages for communication with that particular control. For example, you can send the list view message LVM_GETITEMCOUNT to obtain the number of items in a list view. Likewise, a tree view message would begin with the letters TVM_.

Events such as user input will cause common controls to send a notification message about the event to their parent windows. It is up to an application to trap these notification messages so that it can ascertain what action the user wants to occur. All common controls notify their parents about changes to their state using WM_NOTIFY messages with the exception of the track bar control, which uses WM_HSCROLL and WM_VSCROLL messages. The lParam parameter of the WM_NOTIFY message is either the address of an NMHDR structure or the address of a structure that has NMHDR as its first member. The NMHDR structure contains the following members:

- hwndFrom—Window handle to the control sending a message.

- idFrom—Identifier of the control sending a message.

- code—Notification code. This member can be a control-specific notification code or it can be one of the common notification codes.

For example, a list view notification LVN_COLUMNCLICK would be sent by the system to an application when a user had clicked on a column of a list view. An application would receive this information as a WM_NOTIFY message and take the appropriate action.

Note: Consult the online documentation for each control to determine which WM_NOTIFY messages it sends and which are the notification codes used by that control.

11.1.2 Common control styles and structures

The online help under the title "Common Control Styles" provides information about a set of styles that is common to the controls. Examples of these styles include CCS_ADJUSTABLE and CCS_TOP. In addition, most common controls have a set of individual control styles, which can be used to vary the appearance and behavior of the control. The individual control style options available are detailed with the information provided for each common control in the online documentation.

Some of the common controls require one or more structures to be filled in. For example, an application with a list view control must use the LVCOLUMN structure to provide information about the columns. The online information for each of the common controls will specify the name of any structure that is to be used with that control.

11.2 Animation controls

Animation controls are created using the CreateWindow or CreateWindowEx function and specifying the window class as ANIMATE_CLASSA. You may also use the Resource Editor if the animation control is to run in a dialog box. In the latter case, use the dialog box editor to place an animation control in the dialog box, and then set the styles of the control through the control properties. Any animation control that is created as part of a dialog box resource is destroyed automatically when the user closes the dialog box, but an animation control created using CreateWindow or CreateWindowEx must be destroyed by the application.

The following styles can be used with animation controls:

- ACS_AUTOPLAY—To start playing the animation when the animation clip is opened.

- ACS_CENTER—To center the animation in the animation control's window.

- ACS_TRANSPARENT—To draw the animation using a transparent background rather than the background color specified in the animation clip.

- ACS_TIMER—To override the default of creating a thread for playing an AVI clip. When this style is set, the control uses a Win32 timer to synchronize playback.

The sample application, Viewer, demonstrates the use of an animation control in a window. It can play AVI files, including any of the AVI files that come with the Windows operating system or were created by certain screen capture tools. To illustrate the use of Viewer, two sample animation AVI files were created using proprietary software. The first animation sequence consists of the steps that are used in Visual Fortran to create a Win32 application. This is illustrated in Figure 11.1. The second animation sequence is

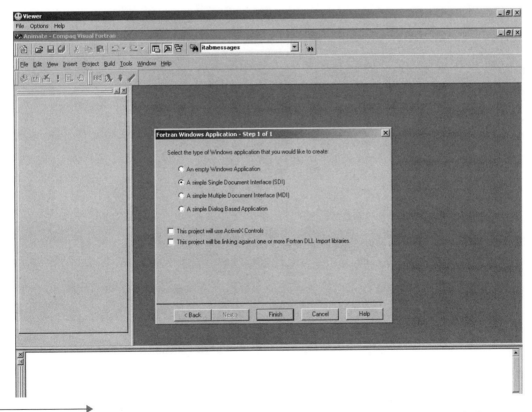

Figure 11.1   *Displaying an AVI file that shows steps in creating a Win32 application called Animate.*

Figure 11.2
*In Viewer, the
animation control
adjusts to the size of
the AVI file.*

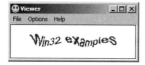

a small banner displaying the message "Win32 examples." This can be seen in Figure 11.2 and illustrates that the application Viewer will automatically size to fit the AVI file.

The animation control messages ACM_OPEN, ACM_PLAY, and ACM_STOP can be sent, respectively, to open, play, and stop playing an AVI file. The use of these three control messages and the way to create an animation control is illustrated in the following code fragment from Viewer:

```
case (WM_CREATE)
   hWndAnimate = CreateWindowEx(0, ANIMATE_CLASSA, ""C, &
   ior(WS_CHILD, ior(WS_BORDER,ior(ACS_AUTOPLAY, &
      WS_VISIBLE))), 0,0,0,0, hwnd, IDC_ANIMATE2, &
      ghinstance, Null)
   iret = InitializeOpen()
   MainWndProc = 0
   return
   ! WM_DESTROY: PostQuitMessage() is called
   case (WM_DESTROY)
      iret = DestroyWindow(hWndAnimate)
      call PostQuitMessage( 0 )
      MainWndProc = 0
      return
      ! WM_COMMAND: user command
   case (WM_COMMAND)
      select case (loword(wParam) )
         case (IDM_OPEN)
            ! get open file dialog box
            Ofn%Flags = null
            bret = GETOPENFILENAME(Ofn)
            ! check to see if the OK button has been pressed
            if(bret == 0) then   !   check for error
               call COMDLGER(ierror)
               ! ierror is the returned error value
               MainWndProc  = 0
               return
            end if
            iret = SendMessage(hWndAnimate , ACM_OPEN, &
                0, loc(szFileName))
```

```
            iret = GetWindowRect(hWndAnimate,rcClient)
            Width = rcClient%right-rcClient%left
            Length = rcClient%bottom-rcClient%top
            if (Width < 200) then
                Width = 200
                iret = MoveWindow(hWndAnimate ,0,0,Width, &
                        Length , redraw)
            else
                Width = Width + 10
            end if
            Length = Length+48
            iret = MoveWindow(hWnd ,0,0,Width,Length, &
                redraw)
            MainWndProc = 0
            return
        case (IDM_Play)
            iret = SendMessage(hWndAnimate, ACM_PLAY, &
                    4, MAKELONG(0, -1) )
            MainWndProc = 0
            return
        case (IDM_STOP)
            iret = SendMessage(hWndAnimate , ACM_STOP, 0,0)
            MainWndProc = 0
            return
        case (IDM_EXIT)
            iret = SendMessage( hWnd, WM_CLOSE, 0, 0 )
            MainWndProc = 0
            return
```

Note that the resource identifier IDC_ANIMATE2 was added manually to the resource.h and resource.fd files. This is the case with all the examples in this chapter that use either the CreateWindow or CreateWindowEx functions.

11.3   Calendar and date time picker controls

The calendar and date time picker controls are very easy to implement in any application. For the sample program Calendar, these two controls are placed in a standard dialog box and initialized in the dialog box procedure associated with the dialog box. The important point to remember is to initialize the common control library using:

```
type (T_INITCOMMONCONTROLSEX) iccex
iccex&dwSize = sizeof(iccex)
iccex&dwICC = ICC_DATE_CLASSES
call initcommoncontrolsex(iccex)
```

Figure 11.3
*Month calendar
and date time
picker controls.*

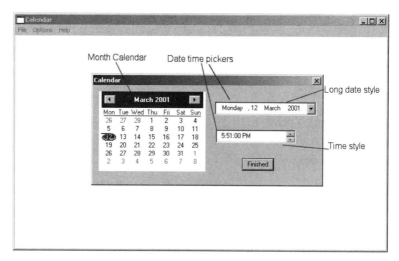

Remember to set the No fail create style for the dialog box so that any common controls that are not initializing properly will appear as a white rectangle instead of preventing the dialog box from appearing.

Figure 11.3 shows the month calendar and date time pickers created by the program Calendar. Referring to Figure 11.3, the left and right arrow buttons on the month calendar permit the month to change one month at a time. Click on the month to display all 12 months, and click on the year to display a spin button for changing years between 1752 and 9999. Clicking the button with the downward facing arrow in the date time picker with the long date style will produce a month calendar, while for the date time picker with the time style, the spin buttons permit the time to be adjusted.

Readers wishing to develop applications around either the month calendar or the date and time picker controls should consult the online documentation for information about the various control and notification messages associated with these controls.

11.4   Tab controls

Tab controls provide a useful way of grouping related data together as separate sections of information similar to the dividers in address books, which separate information in alphabetical order. With a tab control, an application has multiple pages that occupy the same display area. Each page of the tab control would be composed of a group of controls such as edit boxes, list boxes, and the like that are available to the user when the appropriate tab is selected. Like most of the common controls, a tab control can be cre-

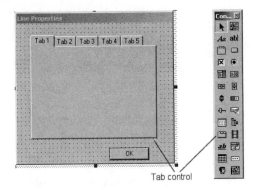

Figure 11.4
Dialog box and tab control from viewer example.

Tab control

ated by calling either the CreateWindows or the CreateWindowsEx functions or by using the Resource Editor. Tab control styles must be specified when a tab control is created. If a tab control has a large numbers of tabs, they can be displayed as multiple rows of tabs using the TCS_MULTILINE style.

Applications with tab controls are required to specify the attributes for each individual tab in the control using either a TCITEM or a TCITEM-HEADER structure. The two structures TCITEM and TCITEM-HEADER are very similar. The main difference between them is that TCITEM contains a field for lParam, which is used for supplying user-defined data associated with each tab item. The value of lParam can be data if only four bytes of information are required; otherwise, it must be a pointer to a user-defined data structure.

The application MultiTab illustrates the process of creating a tab control and responding to user selections. The main dialog box is a modal box, and the page of each tab is a modeless dialog box. The first step is to create a dialog box in the Resource Editor and then place a tab control in the dialog box, as shown in Figure 11.4.

Then create a page for each of the tabs to be used in the tab control. The pages of a tab control are normal dialog boxes with the style set to pop-up and no border specified (see Figure 11.5). Pages of a tab control must not contain a close or cancel button, because it is the function of the dialog box containing the tab control to close a tab control.

Finally, the code needs to be written for each dialog box procedure. The main dialog box containing the tab control is created using DialogBox-Param in the normal method for a modal dialog box. The dialog procedure for the main dialog box is responsible for the creation of the dialog boxes that are to be used as pages of the tab control. Each page of the tab control

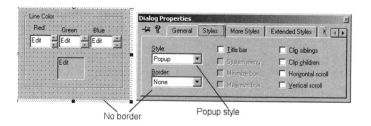

Figure 11.5
*Tab control pages
are normal dialog
boxes without
Cancel or OK
buttons.*

No border   Popup style

will also have its own dialog box procedure. Since pages are modeless dialog boxes, they are created in the main dialog box procedure using CreateDialogParam. A TCITEMHEADER structure named Tabhead is used to define the names Style and Color for the two tabs. Information concerning each tab is placed into the tab control by sending a TCM_INSERTITEM message. The index number for a tab in the tab control is specified with wParam, and lParam is a pointer to a TCITEMHEADER or TCITEM structure. The following code illustrates these points:

```
case (WM_INITDIALOG) ! initialize dialog box
   iccex%dwSize = sizeof(iccex)
   iccex%dwICC = ICC_TAB_CLASSES
   Call initCommonControlsEx (iccex)
   hTab = GetDlgItem(hdlg,IDC_TAB1)
   if (hTab == 0) then
      iret = MessageBox(Null, "error getting tab dialog"C,&
         "Multi Tabs"C, IOR(MB_OK, MB_ICONHAND))
   end if
   Tabhead%mask = TCIF_TEXT
   Tabhead%cchTextMax = 6
   szTab = "Style"C
   Tabhead%pszText = loc(szTab)
   iret = SendMessage (hTab, TCM_INSERTITEM , 0, &
      loc(Tabhead))
   szTab = "Color"C
   Tabhead%pszText = loc(szTab)
   iret = SendMessage (hTab, TCM_INSERTITEM , 1, &
      loc(Tabhead))
   !  initialise first page of dialog
   hTabs1 = CreateDialogParam(ghInstance,IDD_LineType, &
            hTab,loc(StyleDlgProc),0)
   hTabs2 = CreateDialogParam(ghInstance,IDD_LineColor, &
            htab,loc(ColorDlgProc),0)
   iret = ShowWindow(hTabs1,SW_SHOW)
   call CenterTabs (hTabs1, hTab)
   TabDlgProc = 1
   return
```

MultiTab uses a modified version of the generic center window routine to ensure that each page is correctly located in its corresponding tab control. The following WM_MOVE routine is included so that if the user moves the main dialog box, the page will not be left behind.

```
case (WM_MOVE)
call CenterTabs (hTabs1, hTab)
call CenterTabs (hTabs2, hTab)
TabDlgProc = 1
return
```

Tab controls send a TCN_SELCHANGE notification message every time a user selects a different tab. Applications read notification messages in WM_NOTIFY. Applications use the lParam parameter of the WM_NOTIFY to obtain the address of an NMHDR structure. The members in an NMHDR structure are:

- hwndFrom—Handle of the window sending the message

- idFrom—Identifier of the control sending the message

- code—Notification code

When a user has selected a tab different from the one currently in use, the notification code for the code member in the NMHDR structure will correspond to TCN_SELCHANGE. If a TCN_SELCHANGE notifica-

Figure 11.6
MultiTab dialog box.

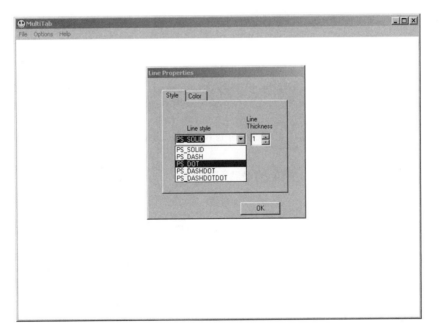

tion message has been sent, then the hwndFrom member of the NMHDR structure will provide a handle to the tab controls sending the message. Once the handle to the control is obtained, it is a straightforward process to send a TCM_GETCURSEL message to determine which tab has been selected. The TCM_GETCURSEL message returns the index of the tab that has been chosen. In the following code fragment, lptabm is a pointer to an NMHDR structure named itabmessages.

```
case(WM_NOTIFY)
lptabm = lparam
if(itabmessages%code == TCN_SELCHANGE) then
    hTab = itabmessages%hwndFrom
    iTabNo = SendMessage( hTab ,TCM_GETCURSEL,0,0)
        if(iTabNo == 0) then
            hTabs1 = CreateDialogParam(ghInstance, &
                   IDD_LineType,htab,loc(StyleDlgProc),0)
            iret = ShowWindow(hTabs1,SW_SHOW)
            iret = ShowWindow(hTabs2,SW_HIDE)
            call CenterTabs (hTabs1, hTab)
        elseif(iTabNo == 1) then
            hTabs2 = CreateDialogParam(ghInstance, &
                   IDD_LineColor,htab,loc(ColorDlgProc),0)
            iret = ShowWindow(hTabs1,SW_HIDE)
            iret = ShowWindow(hTabs2,SW_SHOW)
            call CenterTabs (hTabs2, hTab)
        end if
end if
TabDlgProc = 1
return
```

The remaining dialog box procedures, StyleDlgProc and ColorDlgProc belonging to the two pages of the tab control, are standard and need no discussion. The working tab control can be seen in Figure 11.6. In MultiTab, the user can scribble on the screen by holding the left mouse button down. The tab control is used to set line style, thickness, and color.

11.5 Tree view controls

Figure 11.7 illustrates how tree view controls provide a convenient way of visually displaying relationships that exist within hierarchical groups of data. In tree controls, the top item is called a root item while other items are referred to as parents and children according to their position in the hierarchy. Child items are displayed indented below their associated parent item. Items are displayed with connecting lines for a tree view control with the

Figure 11.7
Tree view control.

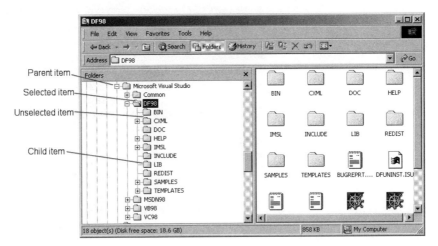

TVS_HASLINES style. A tree view control can have a pair of bitmaps associated with an item's label, one bitmap being displayed when the item is selected and the other when the item is not selected.

An example named TreeView was created to illustrate the principle of using a tree view control in an application. In this example, the tree view control is created using the CreateWindowEx function and specifying WC_TREEVIEW as the window class. The control is also available in the Resource Editor. The application TreeView contains the fictitious names and addresses of eight people, and it is used to illustrate how a tree view control could be used to navigate an address database. The following code calls a subroutine, DataFile, in which the details of eight people are filled into an array, Info. This array is of the type People, which is defined in the module TreeViewGlobals.f90. A tree view and an image list containing two bitmaps are both created. The image list is then associated with the tree view:

```
Case(WM_CREATE)
   iccex%dwSize = sizeof(iccex)
   iccex%dwICC = ICC_TREEVIEW_CLASSES !ICC_WIN95_CLASSES
   call initcommoncontrolsex(iccex)
   call DataFile(Info,n)
   hWndTree = CreateWindowEx(WS_EX_CLIENTEDGE, &
      WC_TREEVIEWA, " "C,IOR (WS_VISIBLE, &
      IOR(WS_CHILD,IOR(WS_BORDER, ior(TVS_HASLINES, &
      ior(TVS_HASBUTTONS, TVS_LINESATROOT)))))), 0,0, &
          300,300,hwnd, ID_TREEVIEW, ghInstance, NULL)
   BITMAP_WIDTH = 16
   BITMAP_HEIGHT = 16
```

```
hIml = ImageList_Create(BITMAP_WIDTH,BITMAP_HEIGHT , &
    ILC_COLOR ,0,2)
hBmp1 = LoadBitmap(ghInstance, &
   MAKEINTRESOURCE(IDB_BITMAP1))
idbOpenFolder = ImageList_Add(hIml,hBmp1,Null)
hBmp2 = LoadBitmap(ghInstance, &
   MAKEINTRESOURCE(IDB_BITMAP2))
idbPage = ImageList_Add(hIml,hBmp2,Null)
iret = SendMessage(hWndTree, &
   TVM_SETIMAGELIST,TVSIL_NORMAL, hIml)
```

11.5.1 Adding items to a tree view control

Items are added to a tree view control by entering the field details of
the structures TVITEM and TVINSERTSTRUCT and then sending a
TVM_INSERTITEM message. The TVITEM structure contains information about the item and the images to be associated with it, and the TVIN-
SERTSTRUCT contains information about the parent of the item and
where it should be placed in relation to the other items in its group. In the
next code section, a root item called Addresses and five children of the root
item are created. The children have labels B, C, E, L, and M. Then for the
letters C, E, L, and M, the surnames of the eight people are entered into the
tree view structure, as follows:

```
TVitem%mask = ior(TVIF_TEXT,ior (TVIF_IMAGE, &
              ior(TVIF_SELECTEDIMAGE, TVIF_PARAM)))
TVitem%pszText = loc("Addresses"C)
TVitem%cchTextMax = 40
TVitem%iImage = idbPage
TVitem%iSelectedImage = idbOpenFolder
TVIns%item = TVitem
TVIns%hParent = Null
TVIns%hInsertAfter = TVI_ROOT
iAdd = SendMessage (hWndTree, TVM_INSERTITEMA , 0, &
   loc(TVIns))
TVitem%pszText = loc('C'C)
TVIns%hParent = iAdd
TVIns%item = TVitem
TVIns%hInsertAfter = TVI_SORT
iC = SendMessage (hWndTree, TVM_INSERTITEMA , 0, &
   loc(TVIns))
TVitem%pszText = loc('L'C)
TVIns%item = TVitem
iL = SendMessage (hWndTree, TVM_INSERTITEMA , 0, &
  loc(TVIns))
TVitem%pszText = loc('B'C)
TVIns%item = TVitem
```

```
iB = SendMessage (hWndTree, TVM_INSERTITEMA , 0, &
   loc(TVIns))
TVitem%pszText = loc('M'C)
TVIns%item = TVitem
iM = SendMessage (hWndTree, TVM_INSERTITEMA , 0,
loc(TVIns))
TVitem%pszText = loc('E'C)
TVIns%item = TVitem
iE = SendMessage (hWndTree, TVM_INSERTITEMA , 0,
loc(TVIns))
do I = 1 ,n
   TVitem%pszText = loc(Info(I)%surname)
   TVIns%item = TVitem
   if(index(Info(I)%surname,'M') /= 0) then
      TVIns%hParent = iM
   else if(index(Info(I)%surname,'B') /= 0) then
      TVIns%hParent = iB
   else if(index(Info(I)%surname,'C') /= 0) then
      TVIns%hParent = iC
   else if(index(Info(I)%surname,'E') /= 0) then
      TVIns%hParent = iE
   else if(index(Info(I)%surname,'L') /= 0) then
      TVIns%hParent = iL
   end if
   iChild = SendMessage (hWndTree, TVM_INSERTITEMA , 0, &
            loc(TVIns))
end do
```

When a user selects any tree view item, the control sends a TVN_SELCHANGED notification message through WM_NOTIFY. Applications should check to see whether the wParam of the WM_NO-TIFY message corresponds to the tree view ID. If that is the case, the lParam parameter of the WM_NOTIFY message will be the address of an NMTREEVIEW structure. The first member of the NMTREEVIEW structure is an NMHDR structure, and the application should verify that the code member of this structure corresponds to TVN_SELCHANGED. If a TVN_SELCHANGED notification message has been sent, then information about either the new item or the old item can be obtained from the two TVITEM structures (olditem and newitem), which are also members of the NMTREEVIEW structure. In the following code fragment, lptree-view is a pointer to an NMTREEVIEW structure named ptvdis. When a surname item is selected, a dialog box will display the information known about that person, as illustrated in Figure 11.8.

```
case (WM_NOTIFY)
   if( wParam == ID_TREEVIEW) then
      lptreeview = lparam
```

```
if( ptvdis%hdr%code == TVN_SELCHANGEDA) then
   szText = " "C
   TVitem%hItem = ptvdis%itemNew%hItem
   TVitem%mask = TVIF_TEXT
   TVitem%pszText = loc(szText)
   TVitem%cchTextMax = 40
   iChild = SendMessage (hWndTree, TVM_GETITEMA, &
            0, loc(TVitem))
   Icount = 0
   do I = 1, n if(Trim(Info(I)%surname) == &
      Trim(szText)) then
         Icount = I
      end if
   end do
   if(Icount > 0) then
      lpszName = "Address"C
      iret = DialogBoxParam(ghInstance, &
      LOC(lpszName), hWnd, LOC(AddressDlgProc), 0)
   end if
end if
MainWndProc = 0
return
end if
```

Figure 11.8
TreeView used to display address information.

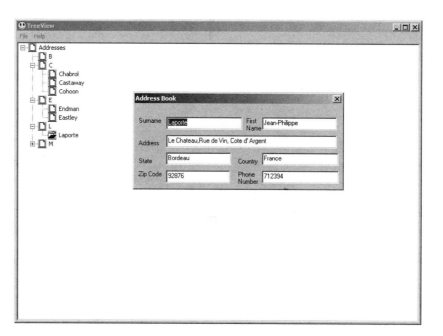

11.5.2   List view controls

The right-hand pane of Windows Explorer shown in Figure 11.9 is an example of a list view. A list view control can display items in one of four views: in large icon view, in small icon view, in list view, or in details view (also known as report view).

In the sample application DataView, we will see how the address information from the previous example can be displayed in a list view using the report (or details) style. In details view, a column header, containing a title for each column, is positioned above columns of text or numbers. The header control is divided into parts, called header items, whose width can be set by the user. A header item can behave like a command button, performing some actions, such as sorting data, when the user clicks it.

The first step is to create a list view by using the CreateWindow or CreateWindowEx function and specifying WC_LISTVIEW as the class name. The list view style LVS_REPORT is specified because it is more appropriate for this application. The other list view styles are LVS_ICON (large icon), LVS_SMALLICON, and LVS_LIST. A column header structure is initialized, and, for each of the columns, the appropriate string from the string table is loaded into the structure and the messages LVM_INSERTCOLUMN and LVM_SETCOLUM are sent. An image list is created for a small icon by calling ImageList_Create. An icon is loaded by calling LoadIcon and then added to the image list by calling the macro ImageList_ReplaceIcon. The icon is associated with the list view by sending

Figure 11.9

A list view control from Windows Explorer in large icon display view.

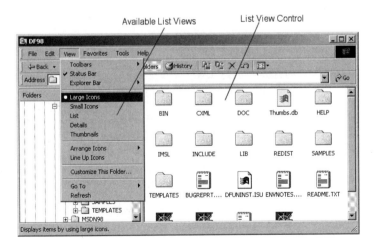

the message LVM_SETIMAGELIST. A call is then made to the subroutine AddDataToList, where each address item is placed into the list view control. In the following code fragment, the variable *col* is an LVCOLUMN structure:

```
case (WM_CREATE)
   call DataFile(Info,n)
   iret = GetClientRect(hWnd, rcList)
   hWndList = CreateWindowEx(WS_EX_CLIENTEDGE, &
       WC_LISTVIEWA, " "C, IOR(WS_VISIBLE, &
       IOR(WS_VSCROLL,IOR(WS_CHILD, &
       LVS_REPORT))), 0,16, rcList%right,rcList%bottom, &
       hwnd, ID_LISTVIEW, ghInstance, NULL)
   col%MASK = IOR(LVCF_FMT , IOR(LVCF_SUBITEM, &
       IOR(LVCF_TEXT, LVCF_WIDTH)))
   col%FMT = LVCFMT_LEFT
   col%CX = (rcList%right - rcList%left )/7
   do index = 1, 7
      iret  = LoadString(ghinstance, index, szHeading, &
             sizeof(szHeading))
      col%PSZTEXT = loc(szHeading)
      col%iSubItem = index-1
      iret = SendMessage (hWndList, LVM_INSERTCOLUMNA, &
          index-1, loc(col))
      iret = SendMessage (hWndList, LVM_SETCOLUMNA, &
          index-1, loc(col))
   end do
   hSmall = ImageList_Create(16,16 ,ILC_COLOR ,0,2)
   hIcon = LoadIcon(ghInstance, &
          MAKEINTRESOURCE(IDI_Icon1))
   idSmall = ImageList_ReplaceIcon(hSmall,-1,hIcon)
   iret = SendMessage(hWndList, LVM_SETIMAGELIST, &
          LVSIL_SMALL, hSmall )
   call AddDataToList(hWndList,item,Info,n)
   MainWndProc = 0
   return
```

In the AddDataToList subroutine, an LVITEM structure called item is filled out for each of the items (addresses) to be added to the list view. The LVITEM structure has a number of fields, including the item (row) number, the subitem (column) number, and the text associated with the subitem. The subroutine is listed below:

```
subroutine AddDataToList(hWndList,item,Info,n)
use DataViewGlobals
use dfwin
implicit none
character(25) szValue
```

```
character(40)sztext
character(80)szAddress
integer(4) hWndList
logical(4) bret
integer(4) iret
integer(4) i, n
type (T_LVITEM) item
type (People) Info(n)
   item%MASK = LVIF_text
   item%state = 0
   item%stateMask = 0
   iret = SendMessage (hWndList, LVM_DELETEALLITEMS, 0,0)
   do i = 1,n
      item%iItem = i-1
      item%iSubItem = 0
      sztext = Info(I)%surname
      item%pszText =  loc(sztext)
      item%cchTextMax = sizeof(szText)
      iret = SendMessage (hWndList, LVM_INSERTITEMA, 0, &
               loc(item))
      item%iSubItem = 1
      sztext = Info(I)%FirstName
      item%cchTextMax = sizeof(szText)
      bret = SendMessage (hWndList, LVM_SETITEMA, 1, &
               loc(item))
      item%iSubItem = 2
      szAddress = Info(I)%Address
      item%pszText = loc(szAddress)
      item%cchTextMax = sizeof(szAddress)
      bret = SendMessage (hWndList, LVM_SETITEMA, 1, &
               loc(item))
      item%iSubItem = 3
      sztext = Info(I)%State
      item%pszText = loc(sztext)
      item%cchTextMax = sizeof(szText)
      bret = SendMessage (hWndList, LVM_SETITEMA, 1, &
               loc(item))
      item%iSubItem = 4
      sztext = Info(I)%Country
      item%pszText = loc(szText)
      item%cchTextMax = sizeof(szText)
      bret = SendMessage (hWndList, LVM_SETITEMA, 1, &
               loc(item)
      item%iSubItem = 5
      szValue = Info(I)%ZipCode
      item%pszText = loc(szValue)
      item%cchTextMax = sizeof(szValue)
      bret = SendMessage (hWndList, LVM_SETITEMA, 1, &
            loc(item))
```

```
            item%iSubItem = 6
            szValue = Info(I)%PhoneNo item%pszText = loc(szValue)
            item%cchTextMax = sizeof(szValue)
            bret = SendMessage (hWndList, LVM_SETITEMA, 1, &
                loc(item))
        end do
    end subroutine AddDataToList
```

Each of the column headers looks like a button, and when it is clicked, a list view notification message, LVN_COLUMNCLICK, is sent. The wParam of the WM_NOTIFY message contains the identity of the list view control, and the lParam provides the address of an NM_LISTVIEW structure. The NMHDR structure contained in this structure is checked to confirm that it is a column-click message. If so, then the subitem member of the NM_LISTVIEW provides the information about which column header has been clicked. The code used in DataView to identify which column has been clicked is as follows:

```
case(WM_NOTIFY)
    if( wParam == ID_LISTVIEW) then
        plistview = lparam
        if( colclick%hdr%code == LVN_COLUMNCLICK) then
            !  The user clicked a column header
            !  sort by this criterion.
            n = SendMessage( hWndList,LVM_GETITEMCOUNT,0,0)
            if(n == 0 ) then
                MainWndProc = 0
                return
            end if
            select case (colclick%isubItem)
                case(0)! sort by surname
                    call SortOrder(Info,n,0)
                case(1)! sort by first name
                    call SortOrder(Info,n,1)
                case(2) ! sort by address
                    call SortOrder(Info,n,2)
                case(3) ! sort by state
                    call SortOrder(Info,n,3)
                case(4) ! sort by country
                    call SortOrder(Info,n,4)
                case(5) ! sort by zip code
                    call SortOrder(Info,n,5)
                case(6) ! sort by phone number
                    call SortOrder(Info,n,6)
            end select
            call AddDataToList(hWndList,item,Info,n)
            MainWndProc = 0
            return
```

```
        end if
        MainWndProc = 0
        return
    end if
```

Once the program has determined which column header has been clicked, then some predetermined action can be performed on the data in that column. In the DataView application, the action is to sort out the information in a column in either alphabetic or numeric order. The sorting routine is a simple one using the Fortran intrinsic function LLT. This useful function determines whether a string is lexically less than another string, based on the ASCII collating sequence. The code for the sorting routine is listed below:

```
subroutine SortOrder(Info,n,iSort)
use DataViewGlobals
use dfwin
implicit none
logical(4) bret
integer(4) i,j
integer(4) pmin
integer(4) n, iSort
type (People) Info(n)
type (People) Temp
   do i = 1,n-1
       pmin = i
       do j = i+1, n
          Select Case(iSort)
          Case(0)
             bret = LLT(Info(J)%surname, Info(pmin)%surname)
          Case(1)
             bret = LLT(Info(J)%FirstName, &
                 Info(pmin)%FirstName)
          Case(2)
             bret = LLT(Info(J)%Address, Info(pmin)%Address)
          Case(3)
             bret = LLT(Info(J)%State, Info(pmin)%State)
          Case(4)
             bret = LLT(Info(J)%Country, Info(pmin)%Country)
          Case(5)
             bret = LLT(Info(J)%ZipCode, Info(pmin)%ZipCode)
          Case(6)
             bret = LLT(info(J)%PhoneNo, Info(pmin)%PhoneNo)
          end select
          if( bret == .true.) then
             pmin = j
          end if
       end do
```

Figure 11.10
ListView used to
display address
information.

Click headers to
sort data order   Adjustable width columns

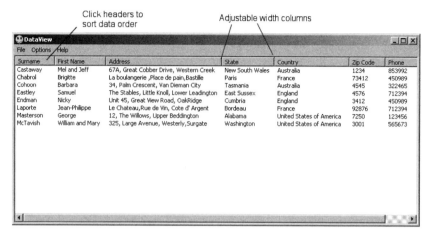

```
      if( i /= pmin) then
          Temp = Info(i)
          Info(i) = Info(pmin)
          info(pmin) = Temp
      end if
  end do
end subroutine SortOrder
```

Figure 11.10 is a screen capture from the DataView application showing
the column headers and displaying the eight fictitious addresses that we
used in the previous tree view example.

11.6   Splitter view

The final program does not demonstrate any new common controls, but it
does show how to combine a tree view with a list view and create adjustable
width (or splitter view) windows. The program also uses three of the
extended list view styles: LVS_EX_FULLROWSELECT, LVS_EX_HEAD-
ERDRAGDROP, and LVS_EX_GRIDLINES. With the first style, when
an item is selected, that item and all the subitems will be highlighted. For
the second style, a user can drag a header and its column from one location
on the header bar to another. The third style provides a spreadsheet-style
grid over the list view. All three of these styles are meaningful only with a
list view that is in the details (report) style. The following piece of code
illustrates how to create the two controls and set the extended list view
styles:

```
case (WM_CREATE)
    iccex%dwSize = sizeof(iccex)
```

```
iccex%dwICC = ICC_WIN95_CLASSES
call initcommoncontrolsex(iccex)
do i = 1, 26
    Letters(i) = char(64+i)
end do
cxSplitter = GetSystemMetrics(SM_CXEDGE)
if (cxSplitter == 0) then
    cxSplitter = 2
end if
call DataFile(Info,n)
iret = GetClientRect(hWnd, rcList)
hWndList = CreateWindowEx(WS_EX_CLIENTEDGE, &
    WC_LISTVIEWA, " "C, IOR(WS_VISIBLE, &
    IOR(WS_VSCROLL,IOR(WS_CHILD, LVS_REPORT))), 0,0, &
    rcList%right,rcList%bottom,hwnd, &
    IDC_LISTVIEW, ghInstance, NULL)
hWndTree = CreateWindowEx(WS_EX_CLIENTEDGE, &
    WC_TREEVIEWA, " "C, IOR(WS_VISIBLE, IOR(WS_CHILD, &
    IOR(WS_BORDER, ior(TVS_HASLINES, ior(TVS_HASBUTTONS, &
    TVS_LINESATROOT)))))), 0,16,300,300,hwnd, &
    IDC_TREEVIEW, ghInstance, NULL)
lvStyle = ior(LVS_EX_FULLROWSELECT, &
        ior(LVS_EX_HEADERDRAGDROP,LVS_EX_GRIDLINES))
iret = SendMessage (hWndList, &
        LVM_SETEXTENDEDLISTVIEWSTYLE, lvStyle, lvStyle)
col%MASK = IOR(LVCF_FMT, IOR(LVCF_SUBITEM, &
        IOR(LVCF_TEXT, LVCF_WIDTH)))
col%FMT = LVCFMT_LEFT
col%CX = (rcList%right - rcList%left )/7
do index = 1, 7
    iret = LoadString(ghinstance, index, szHeading, &
            sizeof(szHeading))
    col%PSZTEXT = loc(szHeading)
    col%iSubItem = index-1
    iret = SendMessage (hWndList,LVM_INSERTCOLUMNA, &
            index-1, loc(col))
    iret = SendMessage (hWndList,LVM_SETCOLUMNA, &
            index-1, loc(col))
end do
BITMAP_WIDTH = 16
BITMAP_HEIGHT = 16
hImage = ImageList_Create(BITMAP_WIDTH,BITMAP_HEIGHT, &
        ILC_COLOR ,0,2)
hBmp1 = LoadBitmap(ghInstance, &
    MAKEINTRESOURCE(IDB_BITMAP1))
idxOpenFolder = ImageList_Add(hImage,hBmp1,Null)
hBmp2 = LoadBitmap(ghInstance, &
    MAKEINTRESOURCE(IDB_BITMAP2))
idxPage = ImageList_Add(hImage,hBmp2,Null)
```

```
iret = SendMessage(hWndTree, &
        TVM_SETIMAGELIST,TVSIL_NORMAL, hImage)
TVitem%mask = ior(TVIF_TEXT,ior (TVIF_IMAGE, ior &
        (TVIF_SELECTEDIMAGE, TVIF_PARAM)))
TVitem%pszText = loc("Addresses"C)
TVitem%cchTextMax = 40
TVitem%iImage = idxPage
TVitem%iSelectedImage = idxOpenFolder
TVIns%item = TVitem
TVIns%hParent = Null
TVIns%hInsertAfter = TVI_ROOT
iAdd = SendMessage (hWndTree, TVM_INSERTITEMA , 0, &
        loc(TVIns))
! Add the letters of the alphabet to tree view.
do i = 1,26
    szText = letters(i)//char(0)
    TVitem%pszText = loc(szText)
    TVIns%hParent = iAdd
    TVIns%item = TVitem
    TVIns%hInsertAfter = TVI_FIRST
    iret = SendMessage (hWndTree, TVM_INSERTITEMA, 0, &
            loc(TVIns))
end do
iret = SendMessage (hWndTree, TVM_SORTCHILDREN, 0, iAdd)
MainWndProc = 0
return
```

Here is how the splitter window effect is achieved. When the list view control is created, a gap of two pixels wide is left between this control and the tree view control. This two pixel–wide strip of the window class originally registered at the program startup provides feedback on mouse movements through messages such as WM_LBUTTONDOWN, WM_MOUSEMOVE, and so on. The WM_MOUSEMOVE message is used to change the normal arrow cursor into a double-headed arrow when the mouse is over the two pixel–wide strip. If the left mouse button is clicked at this point, a thin vertical line is created using patblt (pattern block transfer) with the raster operation code set to DSTINVERT, which causes the destination rectangle to be inverted. The line may be moved to a new location, and when the mouse button is released, the tree view and list view windows will be redrawn so that the tree view ends at the line and the list view begins at the line:

```
case (WM_LBUTTONDOWN)
   ! Change the X  coordinates to match the new mouse
   ! position.
   xPos = int2(LOWORD(lParam))
   iret = SetCapture(hWnd)
```

```
        iret = GetClientRect(hWnd, rcSplit)
        rcSplit%left = min(max(50,xPos-cxSplitter/2), &
                      rcSplit%right -50)+1
        if(hdcSplit /=0) then
           iret = ReleaseDC(hwnd,hdcSplit)
        end if
        hdcSplit = GetDC(hWnd)
        iret =PatBlt(hdcSplit, rcSplit%left, 0, cxSplitter, &
            rcSplit%bottom,DSTINVERT)
        MainWndProc = 0
        return
     case (WM_MOUSEMOVE)
        ! Change the X coordinates to match the new mouse
        ! position.
        xPos = int2(LOWORD(lParam))
        if(hdcSplit /= 0) then
           iret =PatBlt(hdcSplit, rcSplit%left, 0, cxSplitter, &
               rcSplit%bottom,DSTINVERT)
           rcSplit%left = min(max(50,xPos-cxSplitter/2), &
               rcSplit%right -50)+1
           iret =PatBlt(hdcSplit, rcSplit%left, 0, cxSplitter, &
                rcSplit%bottom,DSTINVERT)
        end if
        if (xPos >= rcTree%right .AND. &
            xPos <= rcTree%right+2) then
           iret = SetCursor(LoadCursor(NULL, IDC_SIZEWE))
        else
           iret = SetCursor(LoadCursor(NULL, IDC_ARROW))
        end if
        MainWndProc = 0
        return
     case (WM_LBUTTONUP)
        ! Change the X  coordinates to match the new mouse
        ! position.
        xPos = int2(LOWORD(lParam))
        if(hdcSplit /=0) then
           iret = PatBlt(hdcSplit, rcSplit%left, 0, cxSplitter,&
               rcSplit%bottom,DSTINVERT)
           rcSplit%left = min(max(50,xPos-cxSplitter/2), &
               rcSplit%right -50)+1
           iret = ReleaseCapture()
           iret = ReleaseDC(hwnd,hdcSplit)
           hdcSplit = 0
           rcSplit%left = rcSplit%left -cxSplitter/2
           rcTree%right = rcSplit%left
           if (hWndTree /= 0) then
               iret = SetWindowPos(hWndTree,Null,0,0, &
                   rcSplit%left, rcSplit%bottom, SWP_NOZORDER)
           end if
```

```
                rcSplit%left = rcSplit%left + cxSplitter
                if (hwndList /=0) then
                   iret = SetWindowPos(hwndList,Null,rcSplit%left,0, &
                       rcSplit%right - rcSplit%left, rcSplit%bottom, &
                       SWP_NOZORDER)
                end if
             end if
             MainWndProc = 0
             return
```

Figure 11.11 is a screen capture from the SplitterView application. The list view control has the LVS_EX_GRIDLINES style. The program uses only the original eight fictitious names and addresses from the previous two examples. It would, however, be very easy to include a data entry facility into the program and to store the database information on disk. The enhancement of the SplitterView application is left to the creativity of the reader.

You may be thinking that the list view control with the gridline style looks like a spreadsheet and wondering if it could be used for data entry. The answer is yes. One restriction when using list view controls for data

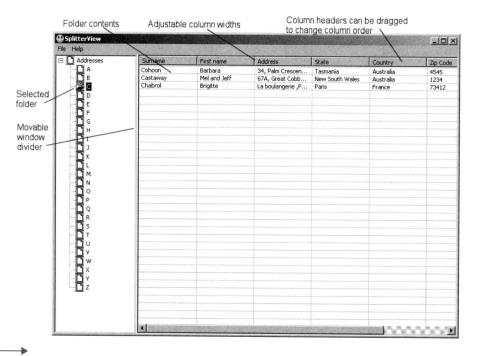

Figure 11.11   *Combined TreeView and list view controls separated by a splitter column.*

entry is that selections can be made only one row at a time, unlike a spreadsheet in which individual cells can be selected. For this reason, a list view cannot behave exactly like a spreadsheet for data entry, but it can be made to provide functionality that is very similar to a spreadsheet. Spreadsheets need only a single edit box for data entry, whereas a list view must have the same number of edit boxes as cells in a row of the list view control. This creates a practical limitation on the width of a list view control if it is to be used for editing the displayed data. Some possibilities for using a list view control as a spreadsheet look-alike are demonstrated in the application called GridDataEntry, which is located in the "Extras" section of the software on the companion Web site.

Note: The examples TreeView, DataView, and SplitterView were inspired by the CHICOAPP example described by Nancy Cluts in her book, *Programming the Windows 95 User Interface*. It is worthwhile to either get a copy of the book or to look it up in the book section of the MSDN library, because it describes (using the C language) how to use lots more of the common controls. The spreadsheet lookalike application, GridDataEntry, in the Extras section on the Web site is a natural, logical extension of the basic idea.

11.7 What is next?

In the next chapter, we will create a multiple-document interface application based on an edit box as used by Scribe. Multiple-document interfaces require some special housekeeping methodology to track each child window. Fortunately, as we will learn, Windows does most of the hard work for us.

12

Multiple Document Interface (MDI) Applications

12.1 Introduction

Multiple document interface (MDI) applications allow a user to create and work with multiple documents within a single application. The MDI applications described here must be of the Fortran Windows project type, since they need to use the full set of Win32 APIs, including graphics (GDI) functions. The multiple documents can be of a single type, such as text documents in word processing, or of several types—for example a spreadsheet and a chart. The main window of an MDI application is called the "frame window" (see Figure 12.1). It is a conventional window with a title bar, a menu, a sizing border, and a system menu icon plus minimize, maximize, and close buttons.

In Figure 12.1, the client area of the frame window is filled with a client window (workspace) whose color is the system color COLOR_APP-WORKSPACE. This client window provides most of the MDI support, and it is where child windows are displayed. The client window of an MDI application is created in WM_CREATE by calling the function CreateWindow, but on this occasion, the window class is the predefined type MDI-CLIENT.

Child windows are created by sending the client window a WM_MDICREATE message with a pointer to a structure of type MDI-CREATESTRUCT. These child windows are used for displaying documents, and, as can be seen in Figure 12.1, they essentially look like any single-document window. Child windows can never appear outside the application window, because they are clipped to the workspace area. Only one document window is active (indicated by a highlighted title bar) at any particular time, and this document appears in front of all the other document windows. A menu for the document window with the current focus is displayed on the main application window.

Figure 12.1
*Multiple document
interface window.*

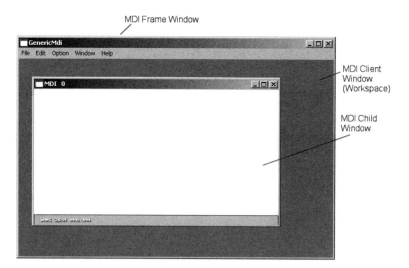

There are 12 messages that are specific to MDI applications, and they are listed in Table 12.1. Each message begins with the prefix WM_MDI. A frame window sends one of these messages to the client window to perform operations on a child window or to obtain information about a child window.

Table 12.1   *Multiple Document Interface Messages*

Message	This message is sent to an MDI client window to
WM_MDIACTIVATE	instruct the client window to activate a different MDI child window.
WM_MDICASCADE	arrange all its child windows in a cascade format.
WM_MDICREATE	create an MDI child window.
WM_MDIDESTROY	close an MDI child window.
WM_MDIGETACTIVE	retrieve the handle to the active MDI child window.
WM_MDIICONARRANGE	have an application send the WM_MDIICON-ARRANGE message to a MDI client window to arrange all minimized MDI child windows.
WM_MDIMAXIMIZE	maximize an MDI child window.
WM_MDINEXT	activate the next or previous child window.
WM_MDIREFRESHMENU	refresh the window menu of the MDI frame window.

Table 12.1 *Multiple Document Interface Messages (continued)*

Message	This message is sent to an MDI client window to
WM_MDIRESTORE	restore an MDI child window from maximized or minimized size.
WM_MDISETMENU	replace the entire menu of an MDI frame window, to replace the Window menu of the frame window, or both.
WM_MDITILE	arrange all of its MDI child windows in a tile format.

The concept of a multiple document interface application is easy to comprehend. However, there are some important points to be considered during the programming stage, as will be demonstrated through the MDI application MultiPad.

12.2 MultiPad example

We shall go through the steps of creating a generic multiple document window application and then modify the code to provide an MDI application of our own design.

Select File from the Visual Studio menu and click on New. Type in the project name slot MultiPad, and set the directory in the slot marked location. You may need to click on the button at the end of the slot to choose a directory. Select Fortran Windows Application from the radio buttons, and then click on the OK button.

A new dialog box appears offering a choice of window applications. Check the options labeled, "A simple Multiple Document Interface (MDI)" and select Finish. The next dialog box gives information about the type of application that will be created and the project directory that it will be created in. Click OK to complete the process.

Select Build, and then click on Execute MultiPad.exe. A warning message is displayed stating that the file does not exist, and it asks if you want to build it. Choose Yes, and, after successfully compiling and linking, the MultiPad frame window will be displayed, as shown in Figure 12.2.

Now click on New in the File menu several times to generate a number of child windows. Notice that an extra menu named Option has appeared in the top menu. The Option menu displays a list of open child windows

Figure 12.2
*Generic MDI
application
showing MDI
frame and client
windows.*

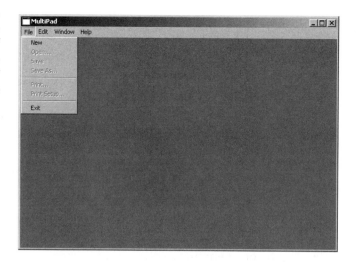

and the currently active window is checked. Selecting any of the upper four
menu items (see Figure 12.3) will cause text to be displayed in the text window at the bottom of the active child window.

Options in the Windows menu permit the child windows to be tiled or
cascaded when in their normal state, and, if they are minimized, the icons
can be arranged. Programmingwise, this is achieved by sending the appropriate WM_MDITITLE, WM_MDICASCADE, and WM_MDIICON-

Figure 12.3
*MultiPad example
child window.*

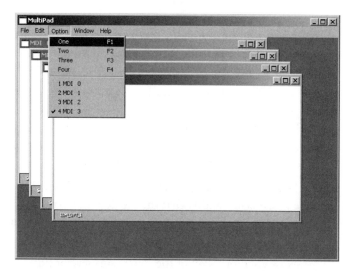

ARRANGE messages to the client window. For example, the syntax to send a message to cascade the child windows would be:

```
iret = SendMessage(ghwndClient, WM_MDICASCADE, 0, 0)
```

A look through the source code for MultiPad reveals that it contains the following functions:

- WinMain—Entry point for the application. A window class (and window procedure) is defined for the frame window and for each type of child window supported by the application. A window procedure for the client window is not needed, because this window class is preregistered. The main window is displayed and the message loop is processed.

- MainWndProc—Processes messages for the main window.

- MDIWndProc—Processes messages for MDI child windows.

- TextWndProc—Processes messages for text child of MDI child windows.

- CenterWindow—Centers one window over another.

- AboutDlgProc—Processes messages for the about box.

Although this generic application illustrates useful programming techniques for multiple document interface applications, it has only limited capabilities. We shall modify the program so that each document window will contain a multiline edit box with the capabilities of loading text to—and saving text from—the document windows. The function TextWndProc is well worth studying as an example of working with a child window of an MDI child window. In addition, it also illustrates how to create 3D transparent text. However, for our application, it is not required, and consequently it should be deleted from the project. The functions WinMain, MainWndProc, and MDIWndProc are modified as follows.

In the following listing, WinMain remains as originally created but with any references to TextWndProc deleted. Two window classes and their callback procedures, MainWndProc and MDIWndProc, are defined and registered. Two menus are loaded, one for the frame window and one for the child windows. The line of code

```
ghChildMenuWindow = GetSubMenu(ghChildMenu, 2)
```

is used to identify which of the child windows' menus will display the list of active child windows. In this case, it is the menu, with an index value of 2 (zero based). In Figure 12.3, this corresponds to Window in the top menu of the child window.

Note: The use of the function TranslateMDISysAccel processes accelerator keystrokes for window menu commands of the multiple document interface child windows associated with the specified MDI client window. The function translates WM_KEYUP and WM_KEYDOWN messages to WM_SYSCOMMAND messages and sends them to the appropriate MDI child windows.

Here is the listing for WinMain.

```
integer(4) function WinMain( hInstance, hPrevInstance, &
      lpszCmdLine, nCmdShow )
! Variables
type (T_WNDCLASS) wc
type (T_MSG)  mesg
    ghInstance = hInstance
    ghModule = GetModuleHandle(NULL)
    ghwndMain = NULL
    lpszClassName ="MultiPadMain"C
    lpszMDIClassName ="MultiPad"C
    lpszAppName ="MultiPad"C
    lpszIconName ="MultiPad"C
    lpszMenuName ="MultiPad"C
    lpszAccelName ="MultiPad"C
    ! If this is the first instance of the application,
    ! register the window class(es)
    if (hPrevInstance .eq. 0) then
        !  Main window
        wc%lpszClassName = LOC(lpszClassName)
        wc%lpfnWndProc = LOC(MainWndProc)
        wc%style = CS_OWNDC
        wc%hInstance = hInstance
        wc%hIcon = LoadIcon( hInstance, LOC(lpszIconName))
        wc%hCursor = LoadCursor( NULL, IDC_ARROW )
        wc%hbrBackground = ( COLOR_WINDOW+1 )
        wc%lpszMenuName = NULL
        wc%cbClsExtra = 0
        wc%cbWndExtra = 4
        if (RegisterClass(wc) == 0) goto 99999
        !  MDI Child window
        wc%lpszClassName = LOC(lpszMDIClassName)
        wc%lpfnWndProc = LOC(MDIWndProc)
        if (RegisterClass(wc) == 0) goto 99999
    end if
```

```
! Load the window's menu, accelerators and create
! the window
ghMenu = LoadMenu(hInstance, LOC(lpszMenuName))
if (ghMenu == 0) goto 99999
haccel = LoadAccelerators(hInstance, &
        LOC(lpszAccelName))
if (haccel == 0) goto 99999
! Load the child window's menu
lpszMDIMenuName = "MultiPadChild"C
ghChildMenu = LoadMenu(hInstance, LOC(lpszMDIMenuName))
if (ghMenu == 0) goto 99999
ghChildMenuWindow = GetSubMenu(ghChildMenu, 2)
ghwndMain = CreateWindowEx(0,lpszClassName, &
            lpszAppName, IOR(WS_OVERLAPPED, &
            IOR(WS_CAPTION,IOR(WS_BORDER, &
            IOR(WS_THICKFRAME,IOR(WS_MAXIMIZEBOX, &
            IOR(WS_MINIMIZEBOX, IOR(WS_CLIPCHILDREN, &
            IOR(WS_VISIBLE, WS_SYSMENU)))))))), &
            CW_USEDEFAULT,0,CW_USEDEFAULT,0, &
            NULL,ghMenu,hInstance,NULL)
if (ghwndMain == 0) goto 99999
lret = ShowWindow( ghwndMain, nCmdShow )
! Read and process messages
do while( GetMessage (mesg, NULL, 0, 0) )
  if ((TranslateAccelerator(ghwndMain, haccel, &
      mesg) == 0) .AND. &
      (TranslateMDISysAccel(ghwndClient, mesg) .EQV. &
      .FALSE. )) then
    lret = TranslateMessage( mesg )
    iret = DispatchMessage( mesg )
  end if
end do
WinMain = mesg.wParam
return
99999 iret = MessageBox(ghwndMain, "Error initializing &
            application MultiPad"C,"Error"C, MB_OK)
WinMain = 0
end
```

12.3   MainWndProc, Main windows messages entry point

Looking now at the listing that follows for MainWndProc, we can see that in WM_CREATE, a client window is created through a call to the function CreateWindow. The window class specified in the argument is MDICLI-ENT, which is the preregistered class for an MDI client window. Note that the last argument for the function CreateWindow is a pointer to a structure of the type CLIENTCREATESTRUCT. There are two fields in a CLI-ENTCREATESTRUCT structure. The first field is the handle for the sub-menu to which the document list will be appended, and the other is the menu ID that is to be associated with the first document window in the list. In our application, MultiPad, this is given the value 1.

It is usual for MDI applications to have a minimum menu displayed when there are no active child windows. MultiPad needs to be modified so that the frame, top-level menu displays only two options, File and Help, as well as the function MainWndProc edited to reflect these options. The File menu offers a choice of New, Open, or Exit. The Exit option from the File menu is achieved by the sending of a WM_CLOSE message, which is han-dled by MainWndProc. The menu items New and Open must both create a document window when they are selected. The code written by the Visual Studio Wizard as part of the generic MDI application to enable the menu item New to create new document windows needs only minor modifica-tions to also perform the extra tasks of Open. The sequence used in New to create a new window is outlined below.

A data structure, Info, which is of the type PERWNDINFO (declared in the file containing global variables), is used to contain information about handles to the parent and the edit windows, the size of the window, and the window's title caption. Memory is allocated to an associated info structure each time a new child window is created.

New document windows are created by sending the client window a WM_MDICREATE message with lParam set to a pointer to a MDICRE-ATESTRUCT structure. For MainWndPro, the following code is used.

```
hwndChildWindow = SendMessage(ghwndClient, &
                WM_MDICREATE, INT4(0), LOC(mdicreate))
```

In the above line, mdicreate is the name of a MDICREATESTRUCT. The MDICREATESTRUCT structure contains an lParam field that is used to point to a memory block containing a handle to the data structure info.

When the client window creates a child document window, it adds the title of the window to the bottom of the submenu specified in the MDI-CLIENTSTRUCTURE. A maximum of nine documents are listed on the menu. Any more than nine windows open will cause a More Windows item to be displayed on the menu. Selecting the More Windows item will cause a list box to be displayed that contains a list of all the document windows.

Any messages that have not been processed by the function MainWnd-Proc must be offered to the default procedure for frame windows, Def-

FrameProc, for processing, rather than the normal window default procedure, DefWindowProc. Also, note in the listing for MainWndProc that all unprocessed WM_COMMAND messages are sent to the active child window so that the child window can process any messages relating to its window.

Note: Some messages, such as the WM_MENUCHAR, WM_SET-FOCUS, or WM_SIZE messages, must also be offered to DefFrameProc even when they have been processed by the frame window procedure.

This is the listing for MainWndProc.

```
integer(4) function MainWndProc ( hWnd, mesg, wParam, &
            lParam )
type (T_CLIENTCREATESTRUCT) clientcreate
type (T_MDICREATESTRUCT)     mdicreate
type (PERWNDINFO)    Info
integer(4) hwndChildWindow
integer(4) hInfo
integer(4) pInfo
integer(4) hActiveChild
logical(4) lret
integer(4) iret
logical(4) bret
integer(4) ierror
integer(4)   hwndEdit
    select case ( mesg )
     ! Create the MDICLIENT window that contains the MDI
     ! children
      case (WM_CREATE)
         gloadFile = .false.
         iret = InitializeOpen()
         lpszName = "MDICLIENT"C
         clientcreate%hWindowMenu = ghMenuWindow
         clientcreate%idFirstChild = 1
         ghwndClient = CreateWindow(lpszName, ""C, &
         IOR(WS_CHILD, IOR(WS_CLIPCHILDREN, WS_VISIBLE)), &
             0, 0, 0, 0, hwnd, NULL,&
             ghInstance,LOC(clientcreate))
         MainWndProc = 0
         return
      case (WM_DESTROY)
         call PostQuitMessage( 0 )
         MainWndProc = 0
         return
```

```fortran
            case (WM_COMMAND)
              select case ( loword(wParam) )
                case (IDM_OpenFile)
                ! get open file dialog box
                    Ofn%Flags = null
                    bret = GETOPENFILENAME(Ofn)
                ! check to see if the OK button has been pressed
                    if(bret == 0) then   ! check for error
                        call COMDLGER(ierror)
                            ! ierror is the returned error value
                            MainWndProc  = 0
                            return
                    else
                        lpszCaption = &
                            szFileName(1+Ofn%NFILEOFFSET: &
                            Ofn%NFILEEXTENSION-1)
                        ext = szFileName(Ofn%NFILEEXTENSION+1: &
                                    Ofn%NFILEEXTENSION+3)
                    end if
                ! Creates new MDI child. Allocate memory for
                ! INFO to be associated with the new child
                hInfo = LocalAlloc(LHND, SIZEOFINFO)
                if (hInfo .NE. 0) then
                    pInfo = LocalLock(hInfo)
                    if (pInfo == NULL) then
                        iret = MessageBox(ghwndMain,"Failed &
                            in LocalLock"C,"Error"C, MB_OK)
                    end if
                    Info%CaptionBarText = lpszCaption
                    Info%hParent      = ghwndClient
                    call CopyMemory(pInfo, LOC(Info), &
                        SIZEOFINFO)
                    lpszTitle = Info%CaptionBarText // ""C
                    lpszName ="MultiPad"C
                    mdicreate%szClass = LOC(lpszName)
                    mdicreate%szTitle = LOC(lpszTitle)
                    mdicreate%hOwner  = ghModule
                    mdicreate%x       = CW_USEDEFAULT
                    mdicreate%y       = CW_USEDEFAULT
                    mdicreate%cx      = CW_USEDEFAULT
                    mdicreate%cy      = CW_USEDEFAULT
                    mdicreate%style   = 0
                    ! Pass the handle of the per MDI child
                    ! INFO to the child MDI window for
                    ! storage mdicreate%lParam  = hInfo
                    ! Create Child Window
                    gloadFile = .true.
                    hwndChildWindow = SendMessage(ghwndClient,&
                     WM_MDICREATE, INT4(0), LOC(mdicreate))
```

```
            if (hwndChildWindow == NULL) then
                iret = MessageBox(ghwndMain,"Failed &
                in Creating Child Window"C, &
                "Error"C, MB_OK)
                gloadFile = .false.
                MainWndProc  = 0
                return
            end if
            hwndEdit = Info%hEditWnd
            lret = LocalUnlock(hInfo)
        else
            iret = MessageBox(ghwndMain,"Failed to &
              Allocate INFO data!"C, "Error"C, MB_OK)
        end if
        MainWndProc  = 0
        return
    case (IDM_NEW)
    ! Creates new MDI child. Allocate memory for
    ! INFO to be associated with the new child
        hInfo = LocalAlloc(LHND, SIZEOFINFO)
        if (hInfo .NE. 0) then
            pInfo = LocalLock(hInfo)
            if (pInfo == NULL) then
                iret = MessageBox(ghwndMain,"Failed &
                    in LocalLock"C,"Error"C, MB_OK)
            end if
            write (lpszCaption,"('doc', &
              I4)")giMDICount
            Info%CaptionBarText = lpszCaption
            Info%hParent       = ghwndClient
            call CopyMemory(pInfo, LOC(Info), &
                 SIZEOFINFO)
            lpszTitle = Info%CaptionBarText // ""C
            lpszName ="MultiPad"C
            mdicreate%szClass = LOC(lpszName)
            mdicreate%szTitle = LOC(lpszTitle)
            mdicreate%hOwner  = ghModule
            mdicreate%x       = CW_USEDEFAULT
            mdicreate%y       = CW_USEDEFAULT
            mdicreate%cx      = CW_USEDEFAULT
            mdicreate%cy      = CW_USEDEFAULT
            mdicreate%style   = 0
    ! Pass the handle of the per MDI child INFO
    ! to the child MDI window for storage
            mdicreate%lParam  = hInfo
            ! Create Child Window
            gloadFile = .false.
            hwndChildWindow = &
                SendMessage(ghwndClient,&
```

```
                            WM_MDICREATE, INT4(0), LOC(mdicreate))
                    if (hwndChildWindow == NULL) then
                        iret = MessageBox(ghwndMain,&
                         "Failed in Creating Child Window"C,&
                         "Error"C, MB_OK)
                        MainWndProc = 0
                        return
                     end if
                    giMDICount = giMDICount + 1
                    lret = LocalUnlock(hInfo)
                else
                    iret = MessageBox(ghwndMain,"Failed to &
                     Allocate INFO data!"C, "Error"C, MB_OK)
                end if
                MainWndProc = 0
                return
            case (IDM_EXIT)
                iret = SendMessage( hWnd, WM_CLOSE, 0, 0 )
                MainWndProc = 0
                return
            case (IDM_ABOUT)
                lpszName = "AboutDlg"C
                iret = DialogBoxParam(ghInstance,&
                    LOC(lpszName), hWnd,LOC(AboutDlgProc), 0)
                MainWndProc = 0
                return
            case DEFAULT
            ! Pass WM_COMMAND messages to the appropriate
            ! active child window proc for processing
                hActiveChild = SendMessage(ghwndClient, &
                        WM_MDIGETACTIVE, 0, 0)
                if (hActiveChild .NE. 0) then
                    iret = SendMessage(hActiveChild, &
                        WM_COMMAND, wParam, lParam)
                end if
                MainWndProc = DefFrameProc( hWnd, &
                    ghwndClient, mesg, wParam, lParam )
                return
        end select
    ! Let the default window proc handle all other messages
    case default
        MainWndProc = DefFrameProc( hWnd, ghwndClient, &
                    mesg, wParam, lParam )
    end select
end
```

12.4 MDIWndProc, MDI windows messages entry point

When working with multiple windows, it is sometimes necessary to store information that is unique to each window. The technique used in Multi-Pad is to reserve memory space for storing these unique data by setting the cbWndExtra field of the WNDCLASS structure to a nonzero value when the window class is being registered. In the MultiPad application, 4 bytes are used to store a handle to the PERWNDINFO structure info. This memory is reserved during the WM_CREATE message of the function MDIWndProc, where an edit text box is created in the current document window. A handle to the PERWNDINFO information (hInfo) is stored using SetWindowLong:

```
iret = SetWindowLong(hwnd, 0, hInfo)
```

The handle to the PERWNDINFO structure is retrieved from the memory storage location with the function GetWindowLong:

```
hInfo = GetWindowLong(hwnd, 0)
```

The WM_MDISETMENU message can be used to set the menu of a client window based on the information received from a WM_MDIACTIVE message. The WM_MDIACTIVE message sends the handles of the windows being deactivated and activated as wParam and lParam, respectively. In the MultiPad application if any windows are open, the menu will be set to MultiPadChild, and when all the windows are closed, the menu will be MultiPad.

```
case (WM_MDIACTIVATE)
   if (lParam == hwnd) then
      iret = SendMessage(GetParent(hwnd), &
         WM_MDISETMENU, ghChildMenu, ghChildMenuWindow)
      iret = DrawMenuBar(GetParent(GetParent(hwnd)))
   end if
```

All unprocessed messages should be sent to DefMdiChildProc and not DefWindowProc for default processing, but the messages WM_CHILD-ACTIVE, WM_GETMINMAXINFO, WM_MENUCHAR, WM_MOVE, WM_SETFOCUS, WM_SIZE, and WM_SYSCOMMAND must always be sent on to the function DefMdiChildProc.

Figure 12.4
*MultiPad screen
with four child
windows opened.*

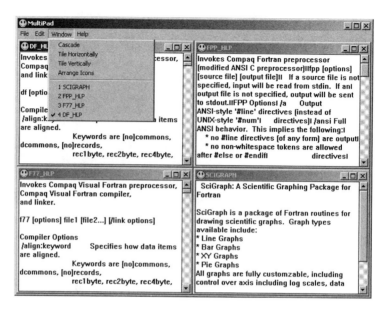

Figure 12.4 shows MultiPad with four screens in the tiled position; a listing for MDIWndProc follows:

```fortran
integer(4) function MDIWndProc (hwnd, message, wParam,
lParam)
type (PERWNDINFO) Info
type (T_MDICREATESTRUCT)   mdicreate
character(SIZEOFAPPNAME)   lpszName
character(SIZEOFAPPNAME)   lpszTitle, lpszCaption
logical(4) bret
integer(4) hInfo
integer(4) pInfo
integer(4) hTextWnd
integer(4) iret
logical(4) lret
integer(4) hwndEdit
integer(4) hwndChild
integer(4) ierror
integer(4) hwndChildWindow
integer(4) length
integer(4) ilength
   select case (message)
      case (WM_COMMAND)
       ! Retrieve this child window's INFO data for
       ! displaying messages in the text window
          hInfo = GetWindowLong(hwnd, 0)
          if (hInfo .NE. 0) then
              pInfo = LocalLock(hInfo)
```

```
            if (pInfo == NULL) then
                MDIWndProc  = 0
                return
            end if
    call CopyMemory(LOC(Info), pInfo, SIZEOFINFO)
        hwndEdit = Info%hEditWnd
        lret = LocalUnlock(hInfo)
    else
        iret = MessageBox(ghwndMain, "Can't get &
            hInfo!"C, "Can't get hInfo!"C, MB_OK)
    end if
    select case ( loword( wParam) )
    ! File menu
        case(IDM_SAVE)
            if(Info%CaptionBarText(1:3) == 'doc') then
                Ofn%flags = OFN_OVERWRITEPROMPT
                szFileName(1:40)= Info%CaptionBarText
                length = Len(Trim(szFileName(1:39)))
                ilength = length-3
                do while(szFileName(ilength:ilength)== &
                        ' ')
                    szFileName(ilength:length-1) = &
                    szFileName(ilength+1:length)
                        length = length -1
                end do
                szFileName(length+1:length+4) = '.txt'
                bret = GETSAVEFILENAME(Ofn)
                ! check if the OK button has been
                ! pressed
                if(bret == 0) then   ! check for error
                    call COMDLGER(ierror)
                    ! ierror is the returned error value
                else
                    lpszCaption = szFileName(1+ &
                    Ofn%NFILEOFFSET: Ofn%NFILEEXTENSION-1)
                    ext = szFileName(Ofn%NFILEEXTENSION+ &
                        1:Ofn%NFILEEXTENSION+3)
                    Info%CaptionBarText = lpszCaption
                    hwndChild = SendMessage(GetParent &
                        (hwnd), WM_MDIGETACTIVE,0,0)
                    bret = SetWindowText(hwndChild, &
                        lpszCaption//' 'C)
                end if
            end if
            call SaveFile(hWndEdit)
            MDIWndProc = 0
            return
        case (IDM_SAVEFileAs)
```

```
              ! get save file dialog box
              Ofn%flags = OFN_OVERWRITEPROMPT
              bret = GETSAVEFILENAME(Ofn)
              ! check if the OK button has been pressed
              if(bret == 0) then   ! check for error
                call COMDLGER(ierror)
                ! ierror is the returned error value
              else
                lpszCaption = szFileName(1+ &
                Ofn%NFILEOFFSET: Ofn%NFILEEXTENSION-1)
                ext = szFileName(Ofn%NFILEEXTENSION+1:&
                      Ofn%NFILEEXTENSION+3)
                Info%CaptionBarText = lpszCaption
                hwndChild = SendMessage&
                        (GetParent(hwnd),&
                        WM_MDIGETACTIVE,0,0)
                bret = SetWindowText(hwndChild,&
                        lpszCaption//' 'C)
                call SaveFile(hWndEdit)
              end if
              MDIWndProc = 0
              return
          case (IDM_FileClose)
              hwndChild = SendMessage&
                      (GetParent(hwnd),&
                      WM_MDIGETACTIVE,0,0)
              iret = SendMessage(hwndChild, WM_CLOSE, &
                      hwndChild,0)
              MDIWndProc  = 0
              return
      ! Edit menu
          case (IDM_UNDO)
              iret = SendMessage (hwndEdit, &
                      WM_UNDO, 0, 0)
              MDIWndProc  = 0
              return
          case (IDM_CUT)
              iret = SendMessage (hwndEdit, &
                      WM_CUT, 0, 0)
              MDIWndProc  = 0
              return
          case (IDM_COPY)
              iret = SendMessage (hwndEdit, &
                      WM_COPY, 0, 0)
              MDIWndProc  = 0
              return
          case (IDM_PASTE)
              iret = SendMessage (hwndEdit, &
                      WM_PASTE, 0, 0)
```

```
                      MDIWndProc  = 0
                      return
                   case (IDM_Clear)
                      iret = SendMessage (hwndEdit, &
                              WM_CLEAR, 0, 0)
                      MDIWndProc  = 0
                      return
                   case (IDM_SelectAll)
                      iret = SendMessage (hwndEdit,EM_SETSEL,&
                              0,-1)
                      MDIWndProc  = 0
                      return
                   ! Handle standard MDI messages
                   case (IDM_HTILE)
                      iret = SendMessage(ghwndClient,&
                              WM_MDITILE,&
                              MDITILE_HORIZONTAL, 0)
                      MDIWndProc = 0
                      return
                   case (IDM_VTILE)
                      iret = SendMessage(ghwndClient, &
                              WM_MDITILE, MDITILE_VERTICAL, 0)
                      MDIWndProc = 0
                      return
                   case (IDM_CASCADE)
                      iret = SendMessage(ghwndClient, &
                              WM_MDICASCADE, 0, 0)
                      MDIWndProc = 0
                      return
                   case (IDM_ARRANGE)
                      iret = SendMessage(ghwndClient, &
                              WM_MDIICONARRANGE, 0, 0)
                      MDIWndProc = 0
                      return
                   case DEFAULT
                       MDIWndProc = 0
                       return
                end select
         ! different MDI children can require menus
         ! set menu for child that is currently active.
         case (WM_MDIACTIVATE)
            if (lParam == hwnd) then
               iret = SendMessage(GetParent(hwnd), &
                        WM_MDISETMENU, ghChildMenu, &
                        ghChildMenuWindow)
               iret = DrawMenuBar(GetParent(GetParent(hwnd)))
            end if
            MDIWndProc = 0
            return
```

```
case (WM_SIZE)
! Whenever the MDI child window is resized,
! its children have to be resized accordingly.
! first, get the edit window's handle from
! the per MDI child INFO data structure
    hInfo = GetWindowLong(hwnd, 0)
    if (hInfo .NE. 0)  then
        pInfo = LocalLock(hInfo)
        if (pInfo == NULL) then
            iret = MessageBox(ghwndMain,"Failed in &
                    LocalLock"C, "Error"C, MB_OK)
        end if
        call CopyMemory(LOC(Info), pInfo, SIZEOFINFO)
        hwndEdit = Info%hEditWnd
        lret = LocalUnlock(hInfo)
    else
        iret = MessageBox(ghwndMain,"Can't get &
                hInfo!"C,"Error"C, MB_OK)
    end if
    iret = GetClientRect(hwnd, Info%rcClient)
    iret = MoveWindow(hwndEdit,0,0, &
            Info%rcClient%right, &
            Info%rcClient%bottom,.TRUE.)
case (WM_CREATE)
  ! Creates the edit window for this MDI child and
  ! saves its handle in the per MDI child INFO
  ! data structure.   INFO was allocated in the
  ! MDIWndProc at IDM_NEW time and is
  ! passed to us at WM_CREATE time
  hInfo = SetHandle (lParam)
  if (hInfo .NE. 0 )  then
      pInfo = LocalLock(hInfo)
      if (pInfo == NULL) then
          iret = MessageBox(ghwndMain, "Failed &
              in LocalLock"C, "Error"C, MB_OK)
      end if
      call CopyMemory(LOC(Info), pInfo, SIZEOFINFO)
      if (GetClientRect(hwnd, Info%rcClient) &
          .EQV. .FALSE.) then
          iret = MessageBox(ghwndMain,"Failed in &
                  GetClientRect!"C, "Error"C, MB_OK)
      end if
      hwndEdit = CreateWindow("EDIT"C, "  "C, &
          IOR(WS_VISIBLE,IOR(WS_CHILD, &
          IOR(WS_VSCROLL, IOR(ES_LEFT, &
          IOR(WS_BORDER ,IOR(ES_Multiline, &
          IOR(ES_NOHIDESEL,IOR(ES_Autovscroll, &
          WS_CLIPSIBLINGS)))))))),0,0,0 ,0, &
          hwnd, NULL, ghInstance, NULL)
```

```
                        Info%hEditWnd = hwndEdit
                        call Copymemory(pInfo, LOC(Info), SIZEOFINFO)
                         ! Save the handle to INFO in our window
                         ! structure
                        if(gloadFile == .true.) then
                            call LoadFile(hWndEdit)
                            gloadFile = .false.
                        end if
                        iret = SetWindowLong(hwnd, 0, hInfo)
                        iret = LocalUnlock(hInfo)
                    else
                        iret = MessageBox(ghwndMain,"Can't allocate &
                                hInfo!"C,"Error"C, MB_OK)
                    end if
                case (WM_CLOSE)
                ! Free the INFO data that associates with this
                ! window also, reset the menu.
                    iret = messagebox(null,"OK to close window?"C, &
                            "MultiPad"C, MB_ICONQUESTION.OR. &
                            MB_OKCANCEL)
                    if(iret == IDCANCEL) then
                            MDIWndProc = 0
                            return
                    else
                        iret = SendMessage(GetParent(hwnd), &
                            WM_MDISETMENU, ghMenu,ghMenuWindow)
                        iret = DrawMenuBar(GetParent(GetParent(hwnd)))
                        hInfo = GetWindowLong(hwnd, 0)
                        iret = LocalFree(hInfo)
                    end if
                case DEFAULT
                    MDIWndProc = DefMDIChildProc(hwnd, message, &
                                    wParam, lParam)
                    return
            end select
        MDIWndProc = DefMDIChildProc(hwnd, message, wParam, &
                    lParam)
        return
    end
```

Note: In the MultiPad application we have retained some functions such as
LocalAlloc and LocalLock that were initially created by the Visual Studio
Wizard. The online information for these functions states that they are provided only for compatibility with 16-bit versions of Windows. When developing your own MDI applications, you may prefer to use HeapAlloc.

12.5   What is next?

In the next chapter, we will look at creating combo and list boxes using the "owner draw" feature. We will be using the registry to keep a list of the most recently used files as well as the user's preference for the display of tip of the day at startup time.

13

Finishing Touches

13.1 Introduction

The emphasis in this chapter is to develop techniques that will add a touch of professionalism to our applications. We will use the owner draw option to customize list and combo boxes and thus provide a degree of individualism for our applications. We will examine how to provide a tip of the day dialog box at startup. In addition, we will be using the Registry to maintain a list of recently used files for an application and display that list on the application's File menu.

13.2 Owner draw controls

One particularly important feature of the Windows environment is the degree of standardization of user interfaces for most, if not all, applications. Users have becomes familiar with a particular sequence of top-level menus, File at the beginning and Help at the end. They expect that for options such as cut, copy, or paste the respective accelerator keys will be Ctrl+X, Ctrl+C, or Ctrl+V. Dialog boxes and tabbed dialog boxes are an accepted method for making choices and entering data. The left-hand button of the mouse is used for selecting, while context menus are invoked by clicking the right-hand mouse button. However, the Windows environment also permits software developers to exercise control over the appearance of a control or menu item through an owner draw feature. Owner draw capabilities are available for buttons, combo boxes, list boxes, list view controls, menu items, static controls, and tab controls. However, a note of caution is also necessary. Having the ability to redefine the look of standard user interface items does not necessarily mean that all possible controls should be created using the owner draw facility.

We will use the owner draw capabilities of a combo box and two list boxes to illustrate the process and obtain an idea of the potential available to software developers. The technique follows a similar pattern for all the controls. Essentially, either in the Resource Editor or in WM_CREATE, the owner draw style is specified for the control. Then, as the control is being created, a WM_DRAWITEM message is sent. The application must be able to act on this message and draw the control. When the WM_DRAWITEM message is sent, the lParam message parameter will be a pointer to a structure of the type DRAWITEMSTRUCT. The user code is required to fill in the fields of this structure. The structure supplies the information required by the owner window for painting (drawing) the control or menu item. This is a list of the fields in the DRAWITEMSTRUCT structure:

- ctlType—Specifies the control type (ODT_BUTTON, ODT_COMBOBOX, ODT_MENU, etc.).

- ctlID—Specifies the identifier of the Combo box, list box, button, or static control. Not used for a menu item.

- itemID—The menu item identifier or the index of the item in a list box or combo box. A value of −1 indicates that the control is empty and only a focus rectangle can be drawn.

- itemAction—Specifies the drawing action required. This can be one of three values:

  - ODA_DRAWENTIRE—The entire control is to be drawn.
  - ODA_FOCUS—Control has lost or gained focus.
  - ODA_SELECT—Selection state has changed.

- itemState—Specifies the visual state of an item after the current drawing action takes place. This can be a combination of the following values:

  - ODS_CHECKED—Menu item is to be checked.
  - ODS_COMBOBOXEDIT—Drawing takes place in selection field (edit control).
  - ODS_DEFAULT—The item is the default item.
  - ODS_DISABLED—The item is to be disabled.
  - ODS_FOCUS—The item has the keyboard focus.
  - ODS_GRAYED—The item is to be grayed (menu only).
  - ODS_SELECTED—Menu item's status is selected.

- hwndItem—Handle to the control for combo boxes, list controls, buttons, and static controls. For menus, this member identifies the menu containing the item.

- hdc—Handle to a device context; this device context must be used when performing drawing operations on the control.

- rcItem—Specifies a rectangle that defines the boundaries of the control to be drawn. This rectangle is in the device context specified by the HDC member. Menu items must not be drawn outside this area since automatic clipping works only for the other controls.

- itemData—Application-defined 32-bit value.

The process is illustrated in the program FreeDraw. The screen capture from FreeDraw, in Figure 13.1, shows a dialog box with an owner-drawn combo box used to select pen colors and a list box for selecting pen thickness. A second list box illustrates how hatch brushes could be selected. In this case, that functionality is not used since a hatch brush has no meaning in the context of drawing lines.

While building the dialog box in the Resource Editor, it is important to make sure that the following styles are set for the combo and list boxes. For

Figure 13.1
Owner-drawn controls can provide users with a visual cue of choices available.

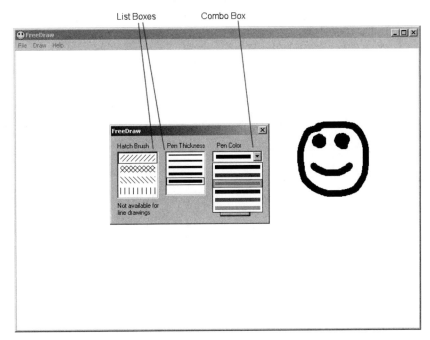

the Pen Color combo box, the type should be drop down, owner draw should be set to Fixed, and make sure that the Has strings box is not checked. For the Hatch Brush list box, the owner draw style is Fixed, whereas for the Pen Thickness list box it is Variable. Both list boxes should be Single selection and again make sure that the Has strings box is not checked. In the dialog box procedure, the WM_INITDIALOG message is used to set the color for each item in the list and the combo boxes and to set the initial values. The code fragment below, used to fill and set the combo box, is identical to that used for the list boxes, except that the CB used here is replaced with LB.

```
do i = 1, 6
   iret = SendMessage(ghWndCombo1, CB_ADDSTRING,0, &
          LineColor(i))
end do
iret = SendMessage(ghWndCombo1, CB_SETCURSEL, &
       currentcolor-1, 0)
```

The value of the member itemID of a DRAWITEMSTRUCT is determined in WM_DRAWITEM. If there is an item in the box, the DRAW-ITEMSTRUCT member itemAction is tested to select which of the three possible actions has been requested, and one of the following three user-written subroutines will be called: HandleFocusState, DrawEntireItem, or HandleSelectionState. In the code fragment shown below, lpdis had been previously declared as a pointer to the DRAWITEMSTRUCT structure dis.

```
case (WM_DRAWITEM)
   lpdis = lParam
   if (dis%itemID == -1) then
     ! no items in the box, so only show focus.
     call HandleFocusState(lpdis, -2)
   else
     select case (dis%itemAction)
     case (ODA_DRAWENTIRE)
     call DrawEntireItem(lpdis, -4)
     case (ODA_SELECT)
     call HandleSelectionState(lpdis, 0)
     case (ODA_FOCUS)
     call HandleFocusState(lpdis, -2)
     end select
   end if
   DrawDlgProc = .TRUE.
   Return
```

A WM_MEASUREITEM message is sent to the owner window of an owner-drawn button, combo box, list box, list view control, or menu item when the control or menu is created. Once a WM_MEASUREITEM message is received, the control owner must fill in the MEASUREITEM-STRUCT structure pointed to by the lParam part of the message and return. Through the information provided by the user in the MEASURE-ITEMSTRUCT structure, the system will now have the control dimensions. Normally a WM_MEASUREITEM message is sent once per control, but if a list box or combo box is created using the LBS_OWNER-DRAWVARIABLE or CBS_OWNERDRAWVARIABLE style, this message is sent to the owner for each item in the control.

The height of an item in a list or combo box is set using the itemHeight field of a MEASUREITEMSTRUCT structure. In the following code fragment from the dialog box procedure, all the list items in the Pen Color combo box and the Hatch Brush list box are set with the same height. The items in the Pen Thickness list box are set to have variable heights according to the thickness of the line that they display. In the code, lpmis has been previously declared as a pointer to the MEASUREITEMSTRUCT structure mis.

```
case (WM_MEASUREITEM)
   lpmis = lParam
   if (mis%itemID == -1) then
      !If -1 for item, then setting height of the always
      !visible static item part of the dropdown combo box.
      mis%itemHeight = 15
      DrawDlgProc = .TRUE.
      return
   end if
   if (mis%CtlID == IDC_COMBO1) then
      ! Fixed height for Pen Combo box
      mis%itemHeight = 15
      else if (mis%CtlID == IDC_LIST2) then
      ! Fixed height for Hatch brush box
      mis%itemHeight = 20
      else
      ! Pen thickness box has variable height property
      mis%itemHeight = mis%itemID+10
   end if
   DrawDlgProc = 1.
   Return
```

The three possible actions to be requested by the WM_DRAWITEM are that the entire control is to be drawn (ODA_DRAWENTIRE), the control has lost or gained focus (ODA_FOCUS), and the selection state has been changed (ODA_SELECT). The owner draw routines must perform all three of these actions when requested. The following three subroutines are used in FreeDraw to perform the drawing routines. The code uses standard graphical techniques for drawing using solid and hatch brushes. Comments are included to indicate the purpose of certain code lines.

```fortran
subroutine HandleSelectionState(lpdis, inflate)
use dfwin
use FreeDrawGlobals
integer(4) inflate
type (T_DRAWITEMSTRUCT) dis
pointer( lpdis,dis)
type (T_RECT) rc
integer(4) hbr
integer(4) iret
logical(4) bret
   ! Resize rectangle to place selection frame outside
   ! of the focus frame and the item.
   bret = CopyRect (rc, dis%rcItem)
   bret = InflateRect (rc, inflate, inflate)
   if (iand(dis%itemState , ODS_SELECTED .NE. 0)) then
   ! selecting item so use black frame
   hbr = GetStockObject(BLACK_BRUSH)
   else
   ! de-selecting item so remove frame
   hbr = CreateSolidBrush(GetSysColor(COLOR_WINDOW))
   end if
   iret = FrameRect(dis%hDC, rc, hbr)
   bret = DeleteObject (hbr)
end
subroutine HandleFocusState(lpdis, inflate)
use dfwin
use FreeDrawGlobals
integer(4) inflate
type (T_DRAWITEMSTRUCT) dis
pointer(lpdis,dis)
type (T_RECT) rc
integer(4) hbr
integer(4) iret
logical(4) bret
   ! Resize rectangle to place focus frame between the
   ! selection
   ! frame and the item.
   bret = CopyRect (rc, dis%rcItem)
   bret = InflateRect (rc, inflate, inflate)
   if (iand(dis%itemState , ODS_FOCUS) .NE. 0) then
   ! gaining input focus so use gray frame
   hbr = GetStockObject(GRAY_BRUSH)
   else
```

```
            ! losing input focus so remove (paint over) frame
            hbr = CreateSolidBrush(GetSysColor(COLOR_WINDOW))
            end if
            iret = FrameRect(dis%hDC, rc, hbr)
            bret = DeleteObject (hbr)
end
subroutine DrawEntireItem(lpdis, inflate)
use dfwin
use FreeDrawGlobals
integer(4) inflate
type (T_DRAWITEMSTRUCT) dis
pointer( lpdis, dis)
type (T_RECT) rc
integer(4) hbr
logical(4) bret
integer(4) iret
            ! Resize rectangle to leave space for frames
            bret = CopyRect (rc, dis%rcItem)
            bret = InflateRect (rc, inflate, inflate)
            ! Create a brush using the value in the item data
            ! field.
            ! This value was initialized, when the item was added
            ! to the list/combo box.
            if ( dis%hwndItem == ghWndCombo1) then
            hbr = CreateSolidBrush (dis%itemData)
            else if ( dis%hwndItem == ghWndList1) then
            hbr = CreateSolidBrush (dis%itemData)
            else
            hbr = CreateHatchBrush (BrushHatch(dis%itemID &
                        +1),LineColor(1))
            end if
            iret = FillRect (dis%hDC, rc, hbr)
            bret = DeleteObject (hbr)
            bret = DeleteObject (hbr)
            ! Draw or erase appropriate frames
            call HandleSelectionState(lpdis, inflate + 4)
            call HandleFocusState(lpdis, inflate + 2)
      end
```

Note: The techniques used in FreeDraw were inspired by the OwnCombo example in the Win32 sample code that ships with CVF6.6. You may also want to look at the Menu example in the Win32 section to see how to create owner draw menus.

13.3 Registry

The Registry is a centralized database that applications can use for storing configuration data. The Registry completely replaces the initialization files previously used in the 16-bit versions of Windows. Since individual users can store their preferences in the Registry, it is possible for applications to customize their user interface according to the preferences of the current user. Another advantage is that the Registry supports networking; thus, user Registry data can be stored in a central location and imported into a local computer Registry when a user logs on.

The Registry Editor shown in Figure 13.2 is invoked by calling REDEDIT.exe. The hierarchical structure of the information stored in the Registry can be clearly seen in Figure 13.2.

The data elements shown in the left pane of Figure 13.2 are known as keys (HKEY_CLASSES_ROOT, HKEY_CURRENT_USER, and so on). Each key can contain children that are known as subkeys. In Figure 13.2, Printer is one of a number of subkeys of HKEY_CURRENT_USER, and Settings is a subkey of Printer. In its turn, Wizard is a subkey of Settings. Data entries, which are contained in the right-hand pane, are called values (Additional Driver, Default Attributes, and so on). Each value consists of a value name, data type, and associated data.

Figure 13.2
The Registry Editor.

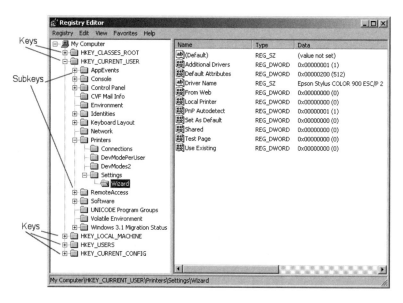

Table 13.1 *Data Types for Registry Values*

Data Type	Description
REG_BINARY	Binary data in any form.
REG_DWORD	Double word (32-bit) number.
REG_DWORD_BIG_ENDIAN	Double word number and the most significant byte is the low-order byte.
REG_DWORD_LITTLE_ENDIAN	Double word number, and the most significant byte is the high-order byte. Same as REG_DWORD.
REG_EXPAND_SZ	NULL-terminated string containing unexpanded reference to environment variables (e.g., "%path%").
REG_LINK	Symbolic link.
REG_MULTI_SZ	Array of NULL-terminated strings, terminated by two NULL characters.
REG_NONE	No defined value type.
REG_RESOURCE_LIST	Device driver resource list.
REG_SZ	NULL-terminated string.

Keys and their values are specific to individual applications. Some applications may need to associate many values with a specific key, while other applications may simply need to know that a key exists. For example, the Wizard key shown in Figure 13.2 has ten specified values associated with it. A key can have any number of values associated with it, and the values may be one of the data types described in Table 13.1.

The Registry has five predefined root (or top-level) keys as shown in Figure 13.2. These keys are to be used for the following purposes.

- HKEY_CLASSES_ROOT—Used for storing definitions of document types, file associations, and the shell interfaces.

- HKEY_CURRENT_USER—Current user preferences are stored in this key, including the settings of environment variables and data about program groups, colors, printers, network connections, and application preferences. This key makes it easier to establish the current user's settings. The key maps to the current user's branch in

HKEY_USERS; software vendors store the current user-specific preferences to be used within their applications.

- HKEY_LOCAL_MACHINE—Hardware configuration, network protocol, and software classes (HKEY_CLASSES_ROOT) are stored in this key.

- HKEY_USERS—Used to store information about the default user configuration and contains a branch for each user of the computer. The default configuration is supplied for new users on the local computer and for the default current user if the user has not changed preferences.

- HKEY_CURRENT_CONFIG—This is a link of the display subkey of the selected configuration of the config subkey of the root HKEY_LOCAL_MACHINE.

The method used for writing to, and reading from, the Registry is illustrated in the next section by means of the program TipOfTheDay, which is described next.

13.4   Tip of the day example

Many programs have a "Tip of the Day" feature in which a tip concerning the application is displayed at startup time. Figure 13.3 shows a typical tip of the day dialog box, complete with a display area for the tip, a Next Tip button, and a check box to switch the tips on and off. Creating the dialog is straightforward. The purpose of this program is to show how to use the Registry for keeping a record of whether or not the user wants the tips to be displayed at startup time.

The TipOfTheDay application uses the RegCreateKeyEx function to create a Tips key. If the key already exists in the Registry, the function will open it. The function RegSetValueEx is used to set the value of the tip to either YES or NO, and then the Registry is closed using the function Reg-CloseKey. The technique is illustrated in the following code fragment for the Close button routine in the dialog box procedure.

Figure 13.3
Tip of the day
dialog box.

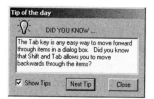

```
      if (LoWord(wParam) .EQ. IDOK) then
         ! Close tips dialog box. Is show tips box checked
         if ((SendMessage( GetDlgItem(hDlg, IDC_CHECK_Tips),&
                BM_GETCHECK, 0, 0)) ==FALSE ) then
            TipsFlag = 0
            TipValue = 'NO'
         else
            TipsFlag = 1
            TipValue = 'YES'
         end if
         iret = RegCreateKeyEx(HKEY_CURRENT_USER, &
                "Software\\Smiley\\Tips"C, 0," "C, &
                REG_OPTION_NON_VOLATILE,KEY_ALL_ACCESS,&
                Null,loc(hKey),Null)
         iret = RegSetValueEx(hKey,"Show Tips at Startup"C,&
                0,REG_SZ,loc(TipValue),3)
         iret = RegCloseKey(hKey)
         ! Don't need brush to paint edit box any more
         iret = DeleteObject(hStaticBrush)
         iret = EndDialog(hDlg, TRUE)
         TipsProc = 1
         return
      end if
```

It is, then, a simple process during a WM_CREATE message to call the subroutine GetTips listed below and open the Registry key with the function RegOpenKeyEx. The function RegQueryValueEx is used to check the key value and determine whether the user would like tips to be displayed at startup. The key is then closed.

```
integer(4) function GetTips(hwnd)
use TipOfTheDayGlobals
implicit none
character(4) TipString
integer(4) dataType,cbdata
integer(4) hwnd
integer(4) hKey
integer(4) iret
   GetTips = 0
   iret = RegOpenKeyEx(HKEY_CURRENT_USER, &
          "Software\\Smiley\\Tips"C, 0, &
          KEY_ALL_ACCESS,loc(hKey))
   iret = RegQueryValueEx(hKey,"Show Tips at Startup"C,&
          0,loc(dataType),loc(TipString),loc(cbdata))
   ! this line is repeated deliberately
   ! if not successful, try once more
   if( iret /= 0) then
   iret = RegQueryValueEx(hKey,"Show Tips at Startup"C,&
          0,loc(dataType),loc(TipString),loc(cbdata))
```

Figure 13.4
Registry entry for tip key showing that tips are to be shown at startup.

```
        end if
        iret = RegCloseKey(hKey)
        if (index(TipString,'YES') /= 0) then
            TipsFlag = 1
        else
            TipsFlag = 0
        end if
    return
    end function GetTips
```

Start the TipOfTheDay program. The first time the program is run, there is no Registry entry for the display of tips and so the tip of the day dialog box will not be displayed. Now select Tip of the Day in the Help menu. Set the show tips check box and then close the program down. A value of YES will be written to the Registry concerning the display of tips at startup (see Figure 13.4). Restart the program, and the tip of the day dialog box will be displayed at startup. From now on, the program will either display or not display the tip of the day dialog box depending on the state of the show tips check box when the program was last shut down.

13.5   Recently used list

Most commercial programs display a list of the most recently used programs in the File menu, similar to that shown in Figure 13.5 for the Scribe3 program. If you wish to display the full path to the application, it is a good idea to have the filenames displayed as a submenu to the main File menu, as shown in Figure 13.5. Alternatively, if you wish to display the file names in the main File menu, it is better to use a shortened path or even just the name of the file alone. That way, the width of the File menu does not expand to an unreasonable size.

There are three subroutines used in Scribe3 to:

- Maintain an updated list of the most recently used files.
- Display the updated list in the menu.
- Save the list in the Registry.

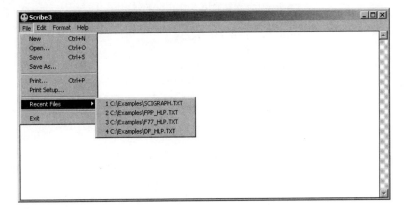

Figure 13.5
*List of recently
used files.*

The global character array IniString contains up to four names on the current list of recently used files. The first subroutine UpdateFileMenu tests to determine whether the new file is already a member of the list and to return if that is the case. Otherwise, UpdateFileMenu will call the subroutines WriteRecentFiles and UpdateMRUMenu.

The subroutine WriteRecentFiles uses the RegCreateKeyEx function to create or open a Recent File List key. The function RegSetValueEx is used to set the value of the data names MRU1 to MRU4 to correspond to the full name of each file including the directory path. Information is also set concerning the wishes of the user about displaying the tip of the day at startup. The Registry is closed using the function RegCloseKey.

The subroutine UpdateMRUMenu is used to set the menu names for menu items IDM_MRU1 to IDM_MRU4, using the function ModifyMenu. The menu items IDM_MRU1 to IDM_MRU4 were defined while creating the recent file list section of the File menu. The subroutine listings are as follows.

```
subroutine UpdateFileMenu(hwnd)
use Scribe3Globals
implicit none
! Local variables
integer(4) hwnd
integer(4) i
    do i = 1,4
    if (IniString(i) == szFileName) then
    return
    end if
    end do
    call WriteRecentFiles
    call UpdateMRUMenu(hwnd)
```

```
end subroutine UpdateFileMenu
subroutine WriteRecentFiles
use Scribe3Globals
implicit none
! Local variables
Character(256) MenuString
Character(3) TipValue
integer(4) retval
integer(4) hKey
integer(4) iret
integer(4) Tcount
   iret = RegCreateKeyEx(HKEY_CURRENT_USER, &
   "Software\\Smiley\\Scribe3 &
           \\3.0\\Recent File List"C,0," "C, &
   REG_OPTION_NON_VOLATILE, KEY_ALL_ACCESS, &
           Null,loc(hKey),Null)
   MenuString = IniString(3)
   IniString(4) = IniString(3)
   iret = RegSetValueEx(hKey,"MRU4"C,0, REG_SZ, &
   loc(MenuString),256)
   MenuString = IniString(2)
   IniString(3) = IniString(2)
   iret = RegSetValueEx(hKey,"MRU3"C,0,REG_SZ, &
   loc(MenuString),256)
   MenuString = IniString(1)
   IniString(2) = IniString(1)
   iret = RegSetValueEx(hKey,"MRU2"C,0,REG_SZ, &
   loc(MenuString),256)
   MenuString = szFileName
   IniString(1) = szFileName
   iret = RegSetValueEx(hKey,"MRU1"C,0,REG_SZ, &
   loc(MenuString),256)
   TCount = 4
   ! save tip of the day status
   If (TipsFlag == 1) then
      TipValue = 'YES'
   else
      TipValue = 'NO'
   end if
   iret = RegSetValueEx(hKey,"Total Count"C,0,&
         REG_DWORD, loc(Tcount),4)
   iret = RegSetValueEx(hKey,"Show Tips at &
      Startup"C,0,REG_SZ, loc(TipValue),3)
   iret = RegCloseKey(hKey)
   return
end subroutine WriteRecentFiles
subroutine UpdateMRUMenu(hwnd)
use Scribe3Globals
```

```
implicit none
include 'resource.fd'
! Local variables
logical(4) bret
integer(4) hwnd
integer(4) iret
integer(4) hmenu,File
character(259) MenuString
    MenuString ='1 '//IniString(1)//' 'C
    File = 0
    hMenu = GetSubMenu (GetMenu (hwnd), File)
    bret = ModifyMenu(hMenu, IDM_Mru1, MF_BYCOMMAND, &
            IDM_Mru1, LOC(MenuString))
    MenuString = IniString(2)//' 'C
    MenuString ='2 '//IniString(2)
    bret = ModifyMenu(hMenu, IDM_Mru2, MF_BYCOMMAND, &
            IDM_Mru2,LOC(MenuString))
    MenuString = IniString(3)
    MenuString = '3 '//IniString(3)//' 'C
    bret = ModifyMenu(hMenu, IDM_Mru3, MF_BYCOMMAND, &
            IDM_Mru3,LOC(MenuString))
    MenuString = IniString(4)
    MenuString = '4 '//IniString(4)//' 'C
    bret = ModifyMenu(hMenu, IDM_Mru4, MF_BYCOMMAND, &
            IDM_Mru4,LOC(MenuString))
    iret = DrawMenuBar(hWnd)
end subroutine UpdateMRUMenu
```

During the startup process of Scribe3, a call is made in WM_CREATE to the subroutine GetRecentFiles listed below. The subroutine opens the Recent File List Registry key with the function RegOpenKeyEx. The function RegQueryValueEx is used for reading in the strings containing the file names (see Figure 13.6) and also to determine whether the user would like tips to be displayed at startup. The key is then closed, and the list of recently used files is displayed on the menu through a call to UpdateMRU-Menu.

Figure 13.6
Registry entry showing the recent file list of Scribe3.

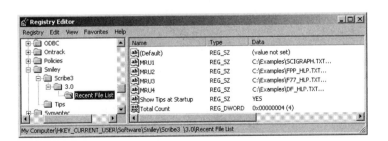

```fortran
subroutine GetRecentFiles(hwnd)
use Scribe3Globals
implicit none
character(4) TipString
character(5),parameter:: MenuKey(4)= (/ &
        "MRU1"C,"MRU2"C,"MRU3"C,"MRU4"C/)
logical(4) bret
integer(4) hwnd
integer(4) iret
integer(4) hmenu,File,i
integer(4) hKey,Tcount
integer(4) dataType,cbdata
    iret = RegOpenKeyEx(HKEY_CURRENT_USER, &
            "Software\\Smiley\\Scribe3 &
            \\3.0\\Recent File List"C,0, &
            KEY_ALL_ACCESS,loc(hKey))
    iret = RegQueryValueEx(hKey,"Total Count"C,&
            0,loc(dataType),loc(Tcount),loc(cbdata))
    if(iret /= 0) then
    iret = RegQueryValueEx(hKey,"Total Count"C,&
            0,loc(dataType),loc(Tcount),loc(cbdata))
    end if
    do i = 1, Tcount
    iret = RegQueryValueEx(hKey,MenuKey(i),0 , &
            loc(dataType),loc(IniString(i)),loc(cbdata))
    if( iret /= 0) then
    iret = RegQueryValueEx(hKey,MenuKey(i),0, &
            loc(dataType),loc(IniString(i)),loc(cbdata))
    end if
    end do
    iret = RegQueryValueEx(hKey,"Show Tips at Startup"C,&
            0, loc(dataType),loc(TipString),loc(cbdata))
    if( iret /= 0) then
    iret = RegQueryValueEx(hKey,"Show Tips at Startup"C,&
            0, loc(dataType),loc(TipString),loc(cbdata))
    end if
    iret = RegCloseKey(hKey)
    if (index(TipString,'YES') /= 0) then
       TipsFlag = 1
    else
       TipsFlag = 0
    end if
    call UpdateMRUMenu(hwnd)
    return
end subroutine GetRecentFiles
```

13.6   What is next?

In the next chapter, we continue developing our "finishing touch skills" by creating Help files. We will learn to create full-featured help files that have a contents list, text with jumps, pop-up definition windows, and index-searchable keywords. We will create a context-sensitive help file to provide information about controls in a dialog box.

14

Creating Help Files

14.1 Help Workshop

Help files add an air of professionalism to an application by providing users with online product information just like any commercial Windows program. Many commercial programs now use the HyperText Markup Language (HTML) format for Help files, and Chapter 4 described how to add such files to an application (QuickWin or Win32) using the Resource Editor. In this chapter, we will create Help files using the program Windows Help Workshop, which comes as part of the CVF Visual Studio package. Appendix B contains information about a newer Help version known as HTML Help.

The creation of a basic Help system requires the following steps:

- Collate the information to be included in a Help file.
- Create and edit a Rich Text Format (extension .rtf) file of the topics using any suitable word processor.
- Enter the required control codes into the topic text files.
- Include any graphics.
- Create and edit a Help project file (extension .hpj) using Help Workshop.
- Compile the source files to produce a Help file (extension .hlp)
- Iterate the preceding steps until the Help file meets your application requirements.

We will now develop some Help files to illustrate these steps. Initially we will create a very basic Help file, before going on to examine more advanced options.

Figure 14.1
*Scribe1 file menu
used as an example
for our first Help
file.*

14.2   First Help project

Our first Help project will be to create a Help file for the File menu of
Scribe1, as illustrated in Figure 14.1.

It is easy to plan and collate the information for a single menu item such
as the File menu. For our Help1 project, we will put the entries for the individual menu items on a single page. The first step is to type the contents of
Table 14.1 into a word processor and save the file as FirstHelp.RTF. The
examples in this chapter have been generated using Microsoft Word 97/
2000, but other word processors with the capability of saving in Rich Text
Format can be used.

The topic heading File Menu will be created as a nonscrolling region.
This means when a topic has more text or graphics than will fit into the
main Help window, the nonscrolling region will stay at the top of the
screen while the user scrolls through the topic information. The nonscrolling region must be the first paragraph in the topic. To create a nonscrolling
region, you need to select the paragraphs that belong to the nonscrolling

Table 14.1   *File Menu Help Contents*

File Menu

The File menu consists of the following four commands.

- New—Clears memory and starts a new document. If there is any existing information in memory, the program will prompt to determine whether you wish to save the existing document before the memory is cleared.
- Open—Opens an existing text file. The file can be one that has been created using either Scribe or any standard word processor, providing that it has been saved as a text file.
- Save—Saves a copy of the current window as a text file. The file is in ASCII format and can be read by Scribe or any standard text editor.
- Exit—Stops execution of the program. The program will prompt to determine whether the document is to be saved before the window is closed.

Figure 14.2
Help workshop screen.

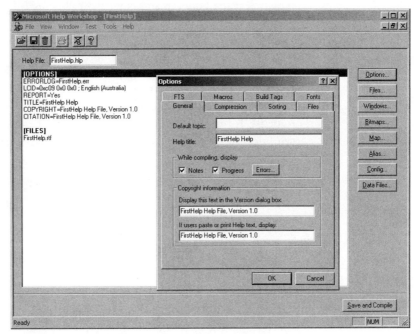

region and format the selected paragraphs with a "Keep With Next" paragraph attribute. In this example, for the nonscrolling region text, the font color has been changed from black to light blue, and the typeface set to Arial bold with a 14-point font.

Start up Help Compiler and select New in the File menu. You will be given the choice of a new Help Project or a Help Contents. Select Help Project and press OK. Type in FirstHelp.hpj in response to the prompt for a name, and press OK. Your screen should look something like that shown in Figure 14.2 but without as many text entries.

Click on the Options button and the options tabbed dialog box will appear, as shown in Figure 14.2. Select the General tab and enter the following information:

```
Help title:  FirstHelp Help
```

Display this text in the Version Dialog box:

```
FirstHelp Help File, Version 1.0
```

If users print or paste Help text, display this text:

```
FirstHelp Help File, Version 1.0
```

Now select the Files tab and enter the following information:

```
Help File:    FirstHelp.hlp
Log File:     FirstHelp.err
```

Click on the Change button, and you will be presented with a blank list box. Click on the Add button, and you should be presented with an Open dialog box showing the names of RTF file(s). Select FirstHelp.rtf, and press the Open\OK button as required to get back to the tabbed dialog box. The entry under Rich Text Format files should show FirstHelp.rtf.

Close the dialog box, then press the Save and Compile button at the bottom right-hand corner of the screen. You will be presented with the read-only screen of the Help compiler, as shown in Figure 14.3.

Some information will be displayed about the progress of the compiler during the compilation stage. For this simple Help application, the only likely negative message would be a warning concerning nonscrolling regions being defined after scrolling regions. The presence of this type of warning does not normally cause any problems with the way the Help file is displayed. However, check that the nonscrolling region in the RTF file does not have any white space before it is defined as a nonscrolling region (e.g., maybe you started on line two and not line one.). It is also useful to select all the text after the nonscrolling region and make sure that the "Keep With Next" attribute is switched off.

To run the Help file, either click the tool bar question mark button or click on the File menu of Help Workshop. Then select Run WinHelp and

Figure 14.3
*Entering file data
into the Options
dialog box.*

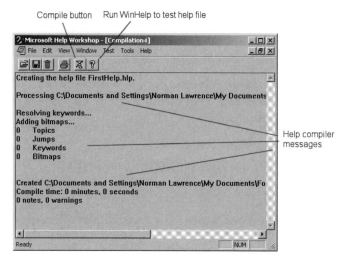

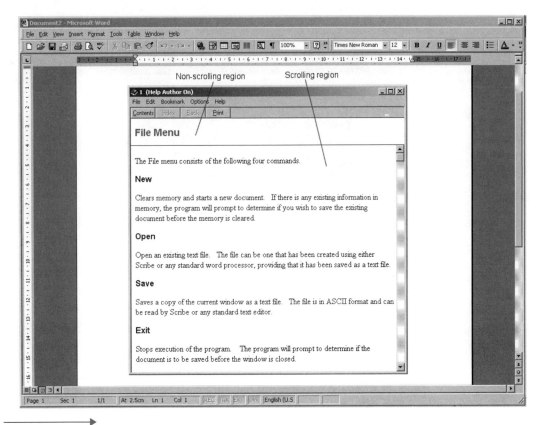

Figure 14.4   *How WinHelp displays the File Menu topic from FirstHelp.hlp.*

in the View Help File dialog box that appears, select the radio button Double-clicked file icon, and press enter. You should be presented with the FirstHelp Help file, as shown in Figure 14.4.

14.3   Scribe3 Help

Now that we have developed a simple Help file and have become familiar with creating both Rich Text Format files and Help project files, it is time to build a fully featured Help file. For our example, we will go through the process of creating a Help file for use with Scribe3. Figure 14.5 shows one of the topic pages from the finished Help file. This page illustrates some Help file techniques that can be used.

Notice the browse buttons for moving through the topics in a group. Pop-up windows can be used to Help clarify terminology, and topic jumps

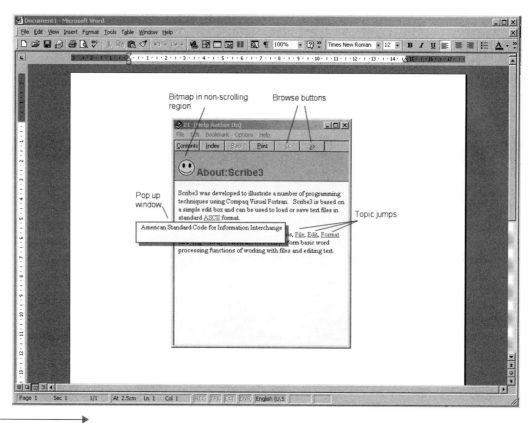

Figure 14.5   *A topic page from the Scribe3 Help file.*

are useful when a reader wants to get some extra information. Now that we have seen the possibilities, let us look at the techniques used. The process of creating the Help file for Scribe3 involves inserting compiler code controls as footnotes to each topic according to the desired outcome. Figures 14.6 and 14.7 show how the process looks to the Help file author.

Help files contain numerous topic entries similar to the ones illustrated in Figures 14.6 and 14.7. To ensure that each topic can be identified within

Figure 14.6
*The File menu
item New for
Scribe3 showing
footnote control
codes.*

#$K+**File:New**¶

¶
Use·this·command·to·clear·memory·and·start·a·new·document.···If·there·is·any·existing·information·in·memory,·the·program·will·prompt·to·determine·if·you·wish·to·save·the·existing·document·before·the·memory·is·cleared.¶
-------------------------------------Page Break-------------------------------------

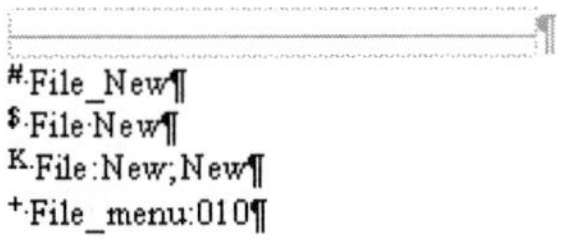

Figure 14.7
The footnote entries
for the footnote
codes for the File
menu topic New.

```
#·File_New¶
$·File·New¶
K·File:New;New¶
+·File_menu:010¶
```

a file, every topic must be separated by a hard page break, and all topics must be given a unique identifier. Optionally, a topic may also have a title, or a browse sequence, or a list of keywords attached to it. The following section describes how to assign these control codes to topics within the Rich Text Format file. The control codes used by the Help compiler for particular tasks are listed in Table 14.2.

14.3.1 Topic ID

Topic IDs are strings that provide a unique identity for each topic in a Help file. They can be used for displaying information in a pop-up window and to provide a target identity for any jumps to that topic. Topic IDs are case insensitive strings and can contain any combination of alphabetical characters (A–Z), numeric characters (0–9), a period (.), and underscore (_). In previous versions of the Microsoft Help Workshop, spaces were not permitted in a

Table 14.2 *Help Control Codes*

Control Code	Use to
#	specify a topic ID string, which provides a unique identity for a topic. Any topic that does not have a topic ID can only be accessed using keywords or browse sequences.
$	specify the topic title. Topic titles are displayed in the list box associated with the Help Index.
K	define a keyword that can be used to search for a topic.
+	define the order in which a user may browse through a set of topics.
Strikethrough or double-underlined text	define text, which a user can select when they wish to jump to another topic.
Underlined text	provide a pop-up window for displaying associated information whenever a user clicks on the text using the left mouse button.
Hidden text	specify the topic ID string for the topic, which will be displayed when the user selects the text that immediately precedes it.

topic ID; but the online Help for Version 4.0 states that topic IDs can contain spaces providing that they are not leading or trailing spaces. I have experienced some difficulties when using spaces in topic ID strings and suggest that it is best to stay with the previous practice of using an underscore.

A topic ID is added to a Help topic as follows:

- Place the cursor (caret) to the left of the topic heading.

- Select the sequence Insert -> Footnote -> Custom Mark, and assign the number sign (#) as the footnote reference mark.

- Type in the topic ID string as the footnote (e.g., File_New).

- In the footnote, a single space is placed between the number sign (#) and the topic ID string.

14.3.2   Topic titles

Topic titles are optional. If included, they are displayed in the Bookmark section of WinHelp; when a topic also includes an index keyword, that topic title will be displayed in the Index dialog box.

A topic title is added to a Help topic as follows:

- Place the caret to the left of the topic heading.

- Use a dollar sign ($) as the footnote reference mark.

- Type the title string as the footnote (e.g., File New). Note that spaces are permitted.

- A single space is placed between the dollar sign and the title.

Topic titles can also be displayed at the beginning of a topic. To place the title at the beginning of the topic, type it as the first paragraph and then define the code for the title in a footnote for the title.

14.3.3   Keywords

Topics cannot contain keywords unless they have a topic title. Keywords are used in WinHelp just like the index of a book. All keywords are displayed in the Help Index, and a user may select a topic to view by choosing a keyword. Keywords should be assigned to all the topics in a Help file, since a keyword search can provide a very quick way for users to access Help topics. Keywords can be any combination of characters, including spaces. When the first character is the letter K, it must be preceded with an extra space or a semicolon.

A keyword is added to a Help topic as follows:

- Place the caret to the left of the topic heading.

- Use an uppercase K as the footnote reference mark.

- Type the keyword, or keywords, as the footnote (e.g., File:New; new;clear;memory). Multiple words should be separated with a semicolon (;).

- Allow only one space between the K and the first keyword.

14.3.4   Browse sequences

Browse forward (>>) and Browse back (<<) buttons on the WinHelp toolbar permit a user to browse through topics in a linear fashion, just like reading the pages of a book. The author of the Help files determines the order (or browse sequence) a Help user must follow when moving from topic to topic. For example, in the File menu of Scribe3, a logical browse sequence would be to go through the File menu topics in the order that they appear in the Scribe 3 menu. The linear order between topics is established using a browse sequence code, which has two parts, a group code and an order code. Table 14.3 lists the browse sequence used for the File menu in Scribe3.

Each browse sequence code consists of a group name (File_menu) followed by a colon and an order string (010...080). The order string establishes the order of topics within the File_menu browse group.

Table 14.3   *Browse Sequence Code for File Menu in Scribe3*

Command	Browse Sequence Code
New	File_menu:010
Open	File_menu:020
Save	File_menu:030
Save As	File_menu:040
Print	File_menu:050
Page Setup	File_menu:060
Recent Files	File_menu:070
Exit	File_menu:080

A browse sequence is added to a Help topic as follows:

- Place the caret to the left of the topic heading.

- Use the plus sign (+) as the footnote reference mark.

- Type the group name, a colon, and the order string as the footnote (e.g., File_Menu:010).

14.3.5 Topic jumps

Selected text in topics can be created as "hot spots" to enable a user to jump to other related topics. Related topics are linked together through topic ID strings. Jumps between topics in WinHelp applications provide a facility similar to cross referencing in a book. To the Help user, jump text is underlined and green in color.

Incorporating jumps into a Help file requires the ability to use the double-underline (or strikethrough) and hidden text features of your word processor. Figure 14.8 shows how these features can be utilized in Microsoft Word 97/2000. Users of other word processors may need to consult the manual for their product to determine how to switch these features on and off.

To code a word or phrase as a jump in the topic file:

- Place the caret at the place in the text where you want to enter the jump term.

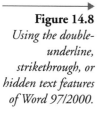

Figure 14.8
Using the double-underline, strikethrough, or hidden text features of Word 97/2000.

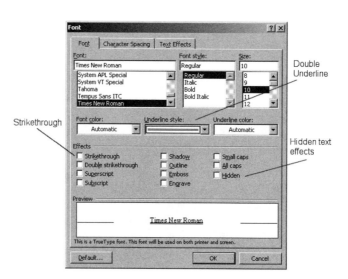

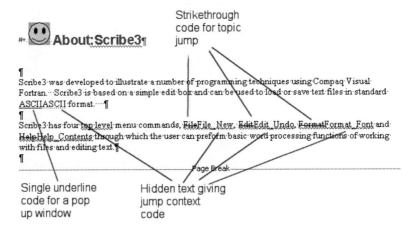

Figure 14.9
The About:Scribe3 topic as it appears to the Help file author.

- Select the strikethrough or double-underline feature of your word processor.

- Type the jump word or words in strikethrough or double-underline mode.

- Turn off the strikethrough or double-underline mode, and select the editor's hidden text feature.

- Type the topic ID string assigned to the topic that is the target of the jump.

Note that no spaces are permitted between the strikethrough (or double underlined) text and the hidden text.

Compare the text in Figure 14.9 with that in Figure 14.5, which shows how the page appears to the user.

14.3.6 Pop-up windows

Jumps to a pop-up window can be used to clarify words or phrases that may be unfamiliar to the user. To display the definition of a word or phrase, the user selects the word and then clicks the left mouse button or presses the Enter key, causing the definition to appear in a pop-up window within the Help window.

These are the steps used to create a definition topic:

- Place the caret where you want to place the term that needs defining.

- Select the underline features of your word processor.

- Type the term that will be defined.

- Turn off the underline feature, and then select the editor's hidden-text feature.

- Type the topic ID string assigned to the topic that contains the definition of the term.

14.4   Building the Scribe3 Help file

Creating the Scribe3 Help file follows the same basic procedure as was used for the FirstHelp example. Start up the Help Compiler, and select New in the File menu. Select New Help Project and press OK. Type in Scribe3.hpj in response to the prompt for a name and press OK. Click on the Options button and select the General tab and enter the following information:

```
Help title:  Scribe3 Help
```

Display this text in the Version Dialog box:

```
Scribe3 Help File, Version 1.0
```

If users print or paste Help text, display this text:

```
Scribe3 Help File, Version 1.0
```

Then select the Files tab and enter the following information:

```
Help File:  Scribe3.hlp
Log file:   Scribe3.err
```

Click on the Change button, and you will be presented with a blank list box. Click on the Add button, and you should be presented with an Open dialog box showing the names of RTF file(s). Select Scribe3.rtf, and press the Open\OK button as required to get back to the tabbed dialog box. The entry under Rich Text Format files should show Scribe3.rtf.

Now, in the main Help Workshop screen, click on the Window button and enter main in response to the request for a window type. In the tabbed dialog control, select buttons and check the browse button option. The position and color tabs permit you to customize the size and look of the Help window that will be presented to the user.

14.4.1   Contents file

We also need to build a contents file so that the user can navigate through the Help file. The steps are straightforward.

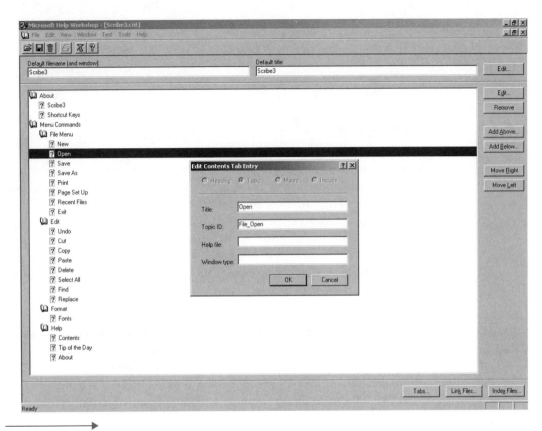

Figure 14.10   *Creating a contents list for Scribe3.*

Select New in the Help Compiler File menu. Choose New Help Contents and press OK. The Help contents dialog window will appear, as shown in Figure 14.10. The contents list is created using the Add Above and Add Below buttons and filling in the prompt box. In the prompt box, check the radio button labeled Headings when entering the headings About, Menu Commands, File Menu, and Edit because they are to be displayed in the list as a book. Otherwise, in the prompt box check the Topics radio button for such topics as New, Open, and Save, and enter the Topic ID (context string) in the edit box provided. Click on the compile button, and then finally on the Run WinHelp button.

When the Help file is complete, the final stage is to include it in the Scribe3 program using the following code:

```
case (IDM_HELPCONTENTS)
    if (WinHelp (hWnd,"\\Scribe3.hlp"C, HELP_FINDER, &
        loc( " "C )) .EQV. .FALSE.) then
```

```
              lpszMessage = "Unable to activate help"C
              iret = MessageBox (hWnd,lpszMessage,"Scribe3", &
                 IOR(MB_SYSTEMMODAL,IOR(MB_OK, MB_ICONHAND)))
        end if
        MainWndProc = 0
        return
```

14.5   Context Help

Applications that support context-sensitive Help messages permit the user
to select a control and by pressing the F1 key, invoke a pop-up message box
that provides Help information about the selected item. Alternatively, if an
application displays a context-sensitive question mark in its menu bar, the
user clicks onto the question mark, moves it across to the control about
which the Help information is sought, and then clicks on the item to display the Help message. The process is shown in Figure 14.11. Providing
your applications with context-sensitive Help is straightforward, as will be
demonstrated with the ContextHelp program.

The context Help messages are contained in a standard Help file along
with Help information for the application. Each message is created as a
separate topic in a Rich Text Format file. That is, every message is typed
in at the start of a new page and a footnote is placed using the number
sign (#). The value of the footnote is a Help resource identifier allocated
by the Resource Editor. It will be something like HIDC_CHECK1,

Figure 14.11

*A context-sensitive
Help message being
displayed for a list
box control.*

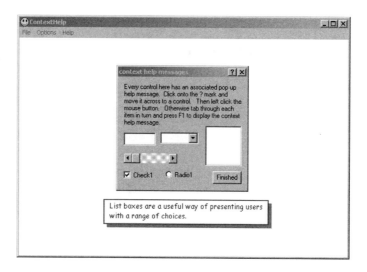

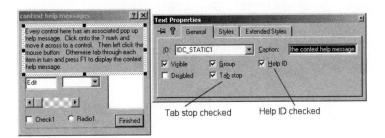

Figure 14.12
Setting the Help ID for a static text box.

HIDC_COMBO1, or HIDC_EDIT1, depending on the control being used. We shall see in a moment exactly where to find the Help resource identifier.

Figure 14.12 shows the dialog box and controls used for theContextHelp example. It is important to ensure that all the Help ID and Tab stop check boxes are checked.

In this application, a modal dialog box was created, but the principles are the same for modeless dialog boxes, other than the normal differences regarding the message loop and how the dialog box is closed. The dialog box procedure is listed below. The context Help messages are handled through a WM_HELP message, as follows:

```
case(WM_HELP )
phelp = lparam
bret = WinHelp(hi%hItemHandle,"\\ContextHelp.hlp"C,&
            HELP_CONTEXTPOPUP,hi%dwContextId)
```

The arguments used in the call to WinHelp are:

- `hi%hItemHandle`: handle to the window requesting help

- `"\\ContextHelp.hlp"C`: location of the help file

- `HELP_CONTEXTPOPUP`: display the information requested in a pop-up window

- `hi%dwContextId`: identity of the item requesting help

Note that the variable *hi* is a HELPINFO structure (Fortran type T_HELPINFO) and that phelp is used as a pointer to the structure. Readers may wish to look up the HELPINFO structure using the online documentation to obtain information about the other fields of this structure. The code used in the dialog procedure is as follows:

```fortran
integer(4) function &
   ContextDlgProc(hDlg,message,wParam,lParam )
!DEC$ IF DEFINED(_X86_)
!DEC$ ATTRIBUTES STDCALL, ALIAS :  &
         '_ContextDlgProc@16':: ContextDlgProc
!DEC$ ELSE
!DEC$ ATTRIBUTES STDCALL, ALIAS :  $
         'ContextDlgProc' :: ContextDlgProc
!DEC$ ENDIF
use dfwina
use ContextHelpGlobals
implicit none
integer     hDlg
integer     message
integer     wParam
integer     lParam
include 'resource.fd'
integer(4) iret
logical bret
type (T_HELPINFO) hi
pointer (phelp, hi)
   select case (message)
      case (WM_INITDIALOG)
         ContextDlgProc = 1
         return
      case(WM_HELP )
         phelp = lparam
         bret = WinHelp(hi%hItemHandle,&
              "\\ContextHelp.hlp"C, &
              HELP_CONTEXTPOPUP,hi%dwContextId)
         ContextDlgProc = 1
         return
      case(WM_Close )! dialog system menu close button
         iret = EndDialog(hDlg, TRUE)
         ContextDlgProc = 1
         return
      case (WM_COMMAND) ! Dialog finish (OK) button
         if (loword(wParam) .EQ. IDOK) then
            iret = EndDialog(hDlg, TRUE)
            ContextDlgProc = 1
            return
         end if
   end select
   ContextDlgProc = 0 ! Didn't process the message
   return
end
```

Note: In the preceding code, the lines beginning with !DEC$ ATTRIBUTES are compiler directives and are shown with Fortran continuation signs (&) at the end of each line, indicating that the code continues onto a second line. This is for typographical convenience only. If you type these lines, they must be entered as a single line.

When the Help ID box is checked in a control property box, as shown in Figure 14.12, the Resource Editor creates a new resource file called resource.hm, which is used to store the Help identity code for that control. The Help ID is based on the control's normal ID; therefore, if a control had the identity of IDC_CHECK1, it would be allocated a Help identity of HIDC_CHECK1. This value must be used to identify the Help topic when creating a Help file.

After the program has been created and the Rich Text Format Help file written, then all that remains is to use Help Workshop to build a Help project and compile the final Help file. This follows the same procedure as

Figure 14.13

Including a Resource.hm file in the map section of the Help project.

for the previous two Help files. In addition, the resource.hm file needs to be included as a part of the Help project. Build the Help project as normal, and then, referring to Figure 14.13, click on the Map button. Select the Include button and browse to find the resource.hm file. Then select the file, and click OK to include it in the project. Then save and compile the project as normal. You can check the behavior of the pop-up Help within Help Workshop by clicking on the question mark button. In the selection options offered, chose a mapped Help ID from the combo box and select the open Help as pop-up window option.

The final step is to run the application and confirm that the response of the controls in the dialog box is correct. Click on any of the controls in the dialog box and press the F1 key, and a message appropriate to that control will pop up. You can achieve the same result by clicking on the context Help button (question mark) and moving the cursor over to any one of the controls and clicking that control.

14.6   What is next?

In the next chapter, we will be looking at how to create some interesting graphical effects using the OpenGL graphics language. We will examine animation effects using double buffering and lighting effects and creating three-dimensional objects.

15

Open GL Basics

15.1 Introduction

OpenGL was originally developed by Silicon Graphics, Inc., as a 3D graphics API to be used with Silicon's workstations, but today OpenGL is a cross-platform graphics standard under the control of the OpenGL Architecture Review Board (ARB). Members of the ARB, who represent leading hardware and software companies, meet regularly to review and revise OpenGL standards. OpenGL is a library of graphic functions that can be used to create applications with animated or interactive two- and three-dimensional graphics based on geometric primitives such as points, lines, and polygons. OpenGL provides the means for generating images that use wire frame displays, shading, shadows, and texture mapping. Every window in OpenGL uses a pixel format, and the attributes of each pixel include, among other things, RGB values, opacity values, and depth values so that pixels with a shallow depth overwrite deeper pixels. It is important to note that OpenGL functions should be used only with an OpenGL window. However, Graphics Device Interface (GDI) functions can be used with an OpenGL window once you have finished rendering the OpenGL scene.

The basic steps in creating OpenGL applications are as follows:

- Specify the pixel format.
- Specify how the pixels will be rendered on the video device.
- Call OpenGL commands to construct objects and to define viewing volume, lighting, and colors.

The OpenGL library follows the C calling convention, and Visual Fortran provides a set of interface functions in DFOPNGL.MOD so that OpenGL functions are available within Fortran. Hence, Visual Fortran

applications using OpenGL functions must include a `use dfopngl` statement. OpenGL symbolic constants and state variables are prefixed with GL,
whereas functions are prefixed with gl; consequently, they are easy to identify in a code listing. In Visual Fortran, all OpenGL symbolic constants and
state variables (e.g., GL_LINES, GL_POINTS, GL_CULL_FACE) are
used without modification. The Visual Fortran OpenGL functions are the
same as the equivalent C functions, except that the gl prefix is changed to
fgl. So, for example, the OpenGL function glColor3f becomes fglColor3f in
Visual Fortran and glBegin becomes fglBegin.

The OpenGL API implementation consists of three distinct libraries:

- The OpenGL functions as specified by the OpenGL ARB, are contained in the library opengl32.dll. Functions from this library are prefixed with gl.

- Second is an OpenGL utility library, glu32.dll. Functions from this
  library are prefixed with glu.

- Finally, there is an Auxiliary or AUX library, glaux.lib. The AUX
  library provides a platform-independent window along with some
  basic keyboard and mouse input abilities, which can be used with
  OpenGL functions. Functions from this library are prefixed with aux.

All the functions in the opengl32 and openglu32 libraries are described
in the "Platform SDK" section of the online documentation. The AUX
routines are not listed in the online documentation, and readers wanting
more information on these routines will need to consult the *OpenGL Programmer's Guide, Release 1* (the red book, 1st edition). Virtually all the AUX
routines concerned with the creation and use of OpenGL Windows are
used in this chapter; Appendix C contains a list of the AUX library ready-
made three-dimensional objects.

The OpenGL samples that come with Visual Fortran use either the
AUX library or Win32 APIs, but an alternative option for developing
OpenGL applications is to use the OpenGL Utility Toolkit (GLUT).
GLUT has the advantage over the Win32 approach of being operating sys-
tem–independent, and it has a significantly greater number of features than
the AUX library, thereby enabling the creation of more complex interfaces.
Only the AUX and Win32 approaches to developing OpenGL applications
will be described in the next three chapters, but readers interested in using
GLUT will find further information in Appendix D and in the latest version of the red book (3rd edition).

15.2 Getting started

OpenGL is a set of platform-independent graphics APIs, and, consequently, it does not have any functions for creating windows or managing user input from a keyboard. The AUX library was created as a toolkit to provide basic capabilities for creating a window and for reading keyboard and mouse input. Internally, the AUX library makes use of the native environment APIs for these functions. The functions provided by the AUX library are the same on all platforms.

The AUX library is a useful introduction to writing OpenGL programs, because only a few lines of code are needed to create an OpenGL window and then any of the OpenGL functions can be used for drawing to that window. Using the AUX library means that we can get on with the task of using OpenGL commands and leave the issues involved with creating an OpenGL window using the Win32 API until the following chapter. The AUX library contains only a handful of functions for window management and the handling of input events but saves the trouble of managing these tasks in Fortran through the Window API.

The following program listing is the very simplest possible OpenGL program, and it illustrates the techniques for creating an OpenGL window and setting the background color. You should create an empty Fortran Windows Application project called OpenGL1 and then add two free format files to the project, one named main.f90 and the other named drawit.f90. Then enter the following code for the function WinMain into the file main.f90 and the code for the function drawit into the file drawit.f90. Compile and run the program, which should display an OpenGL window, as shown in Figure 15.1.

Figure 15.1
An OpenGL window created by the application OpenGL1.

OpenGL Window created using AUX Library

```
integer(4) function WinMain (hInstance, hPrevInstance, &
                  lpszCmdLine, nCmdShow)
!DEC$ ATTRIBUTES STDCALL, DECORATE, ALIAS: 'WinMain' &
           :: WinMain
! OpenGL1 creates a basic OpenGL window
use dfopngl
implicit none
interface
   integer function drawit
   end function
end interface
integer(4) hInstance,hPrevInstance, lpszCmdLine
integer(4) nCmdShow
integer(4) iret
   call fauxInitDisplayMode (IOR(AUX_SINGLE , AUX_RGBA))
   call fauxInitPosition (0, 0, 330, 300)
   iret = fauxInitWindow ("OpenGL Window created using &
         AUX Library"C)
   call fauxMainLoop(loc(drawit))
   WinMain = 0
   return
end Function WinMain
integer function drawit
use dfopngl
   call fglClearColor(0.9, 0.8, 0.6, 1.0)
   call fglClear(GL_COLOR_BUFFER_BIT)
end function drawit
```

Note: In the preceding code, the line beginning with !DEC$ ATTRIBUTES is a compiler directive and is shown with the Fortran continuation sign (&) at the end of the line, indicating that the code continues onto a second line. This is for typographical convenience only. If you type these lines, they must be entered as a single line.

Let us now examine the program line by line to see what is happening. The following code is used to create an empty WinMain shell:

```
integer(4) function WinMain (hInstance, hPrevInstance, &
                  lpszCmdLine, nCmdShow)
!DEC$ ATTRIBUTES STDCALL, DECORATE, ALIAS: 'WinMain' ::
WinMain
   ... OpenGL code goes in here.
   WinMain = 0
   return
end Function WinMain
```

In all our Win applications so far, whenever we have used the WinMain function we went on and called the Win32 API functions to create a window. For the applications in this chapter, however, our window will be created using the AUX library functions.

The display mode of the OpenGL window is set using the function aux-InitDisplayMode, as follows:

```
call fauxInitDisplayMode (IOR(AUX_SINGLE , AUX_RGBA))
```

In this example, a single-buffered window will be created with a color mode of red, green, blue, and alpha. In a single-buffered window all the drawing commands are carried out directly on the display window. Windows can be either single-buffered or double-buffered (AUX_DOUBLE). With a doubled-buffered window, the drawing commands are carried out in memory on a second window (or frame buffer). The buffers can be quickly swapped so that the frame buffer contents are displayed on the screen. Double-buffering is the basis for creating animation scenes in addition to providing smooth screen updates.

The position of the OpenGL window is set using the function auxInit-Position to define the position of the upper-left corner of the window (in pixel units) together with its width and height, as follows:

```
call fauxInitPosition (0, 0, 330, 300)
```

In this example, an OpenGL window will be created that has its upper-left corner at pixel location 0 for x and 0 for y. It will have a width and height of 330×300 pixels, respectively.

Note: The values of y in the argument for auxInitPosition relates to the normal Windows convention of having $y = 0$ at the top of the screen. However, the coordinate system used in the OpenGL window just specified will have $y = 0$ at the bottom of the OpenGL window.

Finally, our OpenGL window is created with the caption, "OpenGL Window created using AUX Library" using the function auxInitWindow, as follows:

```
iret = fauxInitWindow ("OpenGL Window created using AUX &
                        Library"C )
```

These three functions from the AUX library are all we need to create an OpenGL window that can be used to draw on with any of the OpenGL API functions.

The remaining function, auxMainLoop, is used to keep the program in a loop until the window is closed. The single argument with the function auxMainLoop is a pointer to a function that the program should call when it needs updating. In our program, this is the function drawit, and it is here that the actual drawing is done.

Currently our OpenGL window would have a black background, but in our drawit function we will use our first true OpenGL functions to change the background to a wheat color, as follows:

```
call fglClearColor(0.9, 0.8, 0.6, 1.0)
call fglClear(GL_COLOR_BUFFER_BIT)
```

The glClearColor is used to define the color that is to be used when clearing the window. The first three numbers represent the colors red, green and blue. In Win32, the RGB colors are represented by integers between 0 and 255, but in OpenGL the RGB colors are represented by floating-point values between 0 and 1. The fourth argument in glClearColor is the alpha component. The alpha component is used for defining the translucency of a surface. Translucent objects allow light to pass through while opaque objects do not let light pass through. The glClear function clears one or more buffers according to the argument passed. In this example, the color buffer is to be cleared. The red, green, and blue colors of a drawing have separate buffers, which are collectively referred to as the color buffer.

15.3 Lines and points

Now that we can create an OpenGL window, we shall extend the program OpenGL1 so it will draw points and lines to the window, as shown in Figure 15.2. In our program, we need only to modify the function drawit, as follows:

```
integer Function drawit
use dfopngl
integer(2) pattern
real(4) i,ipoint, iline
   call fglClearColor (1.0, 1.0, 1.0, 1.0)
   call fglClear(GL_COLOR_BUFFER_BIT)
   ! Draw points
   ipoint = 1
   call fglColor3f (1.0, 0.0, 0.0)
   do i = 50, 450, 25
      call fglPointSize(ipoint)
      call fglBegin(GL_POINTS)
         call fglVertex2f(i, 400)
```

```
      call fglEnd
      ipoint = ipoint+1.0
   end do
   ! Draw solid lines
   iline = 1.0
   call fglColor3f (1.0, 0.0, 1.0)
   do i = 100,350, 50
      call fglLineWidth (iline)
      call fglBegin(GL_LINES)
         call fglVertex2f(50, i)
         call fglVertex2f(450,i)
         iline = iline + 1.0
      call fglEnd
   end do
   ! Draw patterned line
   pattern = Z'4F0F' ! alternatively #4f0f
   call fglLineStipple (2, pattern)
   call fglEnable (GL_LINE_STIPPLE)
   call fglLineWidth (1.0001)
   call fglBegin(GL_LINES)
      call fglColor3f (0.0, 0.0, 1.0)
      call fglVertex2f(50, 50)
      call fglVertex2f(450, 50)
   call fglEnd
   call fgldisable (GL_LINE_STIPPLE)
   call fglColor3f (0.0, 1.0, 1.0)
   call fglLineWidth (1.5)
   call fglBegin(GL_LINE_LOOP )
      call fglVertex2f(30, 10)
      call fglVertex2f(480,10)
      call fglVertex2f(480,430)
      call fglVertex2f(30,430)
   call fglEnd
   call fglFlush
end Function drawit
```

Now, to examine the code in drawit, the function glColor is used to set the color that is to be used for drawing objects. In the following example, the color is set to be red:

```
call fglColor3f (1.0, 0.0, 0.0)
```

All objects drawn after this call will be drawn in red until a new color is specified through a call to glColor. In OpenGL, function names provide a lot of information, as can be seen by looking at the above line of code. The gl indicates that it is an OpenGL function, the Color indicates the general function task, and the 3f indicates that three floating-point numbers will follow. Many OpenGL functions are flexible in the number of arguments

Figure 15.2
*A variety of point
and line sizes
drawn by using the
program's lines.*

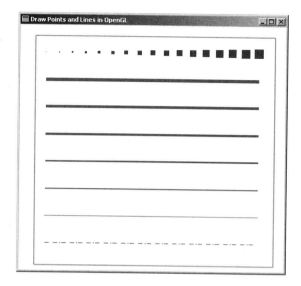

required and as to whether they are floating-point or integer values. For example, glVertex2i(), glVertex2f(), glVertex3i(), and glVertex3f() are valid ways of specifying integer or floating-point values for two- and three-dimensional coordinates using the generic function glVertex. All OpenGL functions can be referenced in the online Help documentation using their generic function names.

OpenGL is often referred to as a state machine—that is, once it is put into various modes (or states), they remain in effect until changed. For example, the current color is a state variable. The current color is only one of many state variables that OpenGL preserves. Others control such things as the current viewing and projection transformations, polygon drawing modes, positions and characteristics of lights, and material properties of the objects being drawn. Many state variables refer to modes that are enabled or disabled with the functions glEnable or glDisable. All OpenGL state variables begin with GL_, and they are listed in the online Help.

Points and lines are created from a list of vertex (point coordinates) values contained between fglBegin and fglEnd. The appropriate symbolic constant (GL_POINTS, GL_LINES, GL_LINE_STRIP, or GL_LINE_LOOP) is sent as the argument for fglBegin. Internally, each vertex is represented as a three-dimensional floating-point coordinate. However, when the user specifies only the *x* and *y* values, OpenGL will provide a zero value for the *z* coordinate. The following OpenGL code illustrates how to set the size of a point to 2.5 and then to draw the point in the current color at the vertex position of $x = 200.0$ and $y = 400.0$. The default point size is 1.0.

```
call fglPointSize(2.5)
call fglBegin(GL_POINTS)
   call fglVertex2f(200.0, 400.0)
call fglEnd()
```

Lines are created in a similar way; this time we need to supply two vertices for each line to define the start and end of the line.

```
call fglLineWidth (1.5)
call fglBegin(GL_LINES)
   call fglVertex2f(50, 100)
   call fglVertex2f(450,100)
call fglEnd()
```

Note that the default line width is changed from 1.0 to 1.5 in the preceding example. Other line types are line strips, which need two vertices for the first line and then one vertex for each subsequent line, and line loop, which automatically supplies the final line to close a given set of lines. Here are examples of their use in drawing a rectangle.

```
call fglBegin(GL_LINE_STRIP )
   call fglVertex2f(30, 10)
   call fglVertex2f(480,10)
   call fglVertex2f(480,430)
   call fglVertex2f(30,430)
   call fglVertex2f(30, 10)
call fglEnd()
call fglBegin(GL_LINE_LOOP )
   call fglVertex2f(30, 10)
   call fglVertex2f(480,10)
   call fglVertex2f(480,430)
   call fglVertex2f(30,430)
call fglEnd()
```

Lines can be drawn either solid or with a recurring pattern called stippling in OpenGL. The following code segment shows how to use line stippling in OpenGL:

```
! Draw patterned line
pattern = Z'4F0F' ! alternatively #4f0f
call fglLineStipple (2, pattern)
call fglEnable (GL_LINE_STIPPLE)
Code to draw lines goes in here
call fgldisable (GL_LINE_STIPPLE)
```

In the foregoing code, the variable pattern is a 16-bit value that specifies the pattern to use when drawing a line. A hexadecimal value of FFFF represents a solid line, while a value of 0F0F represents a dashed line, and 0000 represents no line. Note that in this pattern, the zero bit is used first. The line stipple pattern is set with a call to glLineStipple, which has two arguments. The second argument specifies the pattern to be used, while the first argument specifies a multiplier to be used for each bit in the line stipple pattern. The number 2 in the example code means that each bit in the pattern will be used twice before the next bit in the pattern is used. Values for this factor can be set in the range 1–256. Try changing the value in the program OpenGL2 for both the stipple and repeat factor to test out the line effects that you can create.

15.4 Resizing windows

Our next example, OpenGL3, draws two filled triangles and two filled rectangles. In addition to demonstrating how to draw triangles and rectangles, this program also introduces a number of important AUX functions that can be used to enhance the capabilities of the AUX window. In the previous program, the window could be resized but the graphical objects did not alter their size to fit the new dimensions of the window. In OpenGL3, the window can now be resized and the objects alter their size accordingly while still keeping their original proportions. This is achieved by the following AUX function, which is used to point the AUX library to a user-defined routine that resizes the actual window.

```
call fauxReshapeFunc(LOC(Resize))
```

The argument for the function is a pointer to the user-defined reshape routine. Values for the width and height of the current window are supplied by the AUX library routines to the user-defined reshape routine. These values are used to set the width and height of the current viewport through a call to the function glViewport, as follows:

```
call fglViewport(100, 100, width, height)
```

The first two values define the location in pixels for the upper-left corner of the viewport rectangle on the screen. The next two values define the width and height of the viewport, respectively. The value of height is a maximum at the top of the screen. The viewport defines the area within the window in actual screen coordinates that OpenGl can use to draw in. OpenGL offers a variety of projections for mapping the viewport to real-world units. These include 2D and 3D orthographic projections as well as a perspective projection (by definition this is 3D). OpenGL3 uses a 2D orthographic projection, but later examples illustrate the other projections. Thus, the viewport is mapped to a viewing (or clipping) area that has left and right dimensions of –1.0 and 1.0, respectively, and bottom and top dimensions of –1.0 and 1.0, respectively, through a call to the OpenGL Utility library function gluOrtho2d, as follows:

```
call fgluOrtho2d(DBLE(-1.0), DBLE(1.0), DBLE(-1.0), &
                 DBLE(1.0))
```

One problem is that the user may resize the window to some arbitrary shape and so change the aspect ratio of the viewport. For example, if the viewport is set to be 480 by 480 square and the orthographic viewing area is mapped to be square, then squares will be drawn square. When the viewport is resized by the user to be narrow and tall or wide and short, our square will be drawn distorted. The way around this is to maintain the aspect ratio of our orthographic viewing area. This is illustrated in the following code, where the dimensions of the viewport width are tested against height and, depending on the result, either the height of the window is modified by the aspect ratio height/width or the width is modified by the aspect ratio width/height. Note that when the window height is zero, it is reset to a value of 1 to avoid a divide-by-zero error. There is no need to perform the same check for the window width, because it is impossible to reduce the width of a window to zero. This is the code:

```
if(height == 0) height = 1
call fglLoadIdentity
if (width <= height) then
    call fgluOrtho2d(DBLE(-1.0), DBLE(1.0), &
    DBLE(-1.0)*height/width, DBLE(1.0)*height/width)
else
    call fgluOrtho2d(DBLE(-1.0)*width/height, &
    DBLE(1.0)*width/height, DBLE(-1.0), DBLE(1.0))
end if
```

The call to glLoadIdentity is used to reset the coordinate system by replacing the current matrix with the identity matrix before carrying out the matrix operations required by the call to gluOrtho2d. An identity matrix is one that has all zeros except for the leading diagonals, which have a value of 1.

Users can also use the input to the program using the keyboard by calling the function auxKeyFunc or a mouse by calling the function auxMouse-

Func. The function auxKeyFunc has two arguments; the first is a symbolic constant indicating which key is to be used, and the second is a pointer to the routine that is to be called when the chosen key is pressed. Use one of the following symbolic constants to specify the key required: AUX_A to AUX_Z for upper case, AUX_aa to AUX_zz for lower case, AUX_0 to AUX_9, AUX_LEFT, AUX_RIGHT, AUX_UP, AUX_DOWN, AUX_ES-CAPE, AUX_SPACE, or AUX_RETURN.

Use of auxKeyFunc is illustrated in the following code for the space bar and upper- and lower-case f. When the space bar is pressed, the routine KeySpace is called, and when either upper- or lower-case f is pressed, the routine Fill is called. KeySpace is used to close the program, and Fill is used for drawing filled triangles and polygons.

```
call fauxKeyFunc(AUX_SPACE,loc(KeySpace))
call fauxKeyFunc(AUX_F, LOC(Fill))
call fauxKeyFunc(AUX_ff, LOC(Fill))
```

The auxMouseFunc has three arguments. The first is to specify which button is to be used (AUX_LEFTBUTTON, AUX_MIDDDLEBUTTON, or AUX_RIGHTBUTTON); the second is to test whether the button has been clicked (AUX_MOUSEDOWN) or released (AUX_MOUSEUP); and the third is a pointer to the routine to be called when the event occurs.

```
call fauxMouseFunc(AUX_LEFTBUTTON,AUX_MOUSEDOWN,Fill)
```

In the above example, the routine Fill (draw filled triangles and polygons) will be called when the left mouse button is clicked. A complete listing follows for the part of our program that creates the window for the application OpenGL3.

```
integer(4) function WinMain (hInstance, hPrevInstance, &
                     lpszCmdLine, nCmdShow)
!DEC$ ATTRIBUTES STDCALL, DECORATE, ALIAS: 'WinMain' &
         :: WinMain
! OpenGL3 a program to draw polygons using OpenGL
use dfopngl
implicit none
integer(4) hInstance,hPrevInstance, lpszCmdLine
integer(4) nCmdShow
interface
   integer(4) function  KeySpace
   end function
   integer(4) function  Drawit
   end function
   subroutine Resize(width, height)
```

```
            !DEC$ ATTRIBUTES STDCALL, DECORATE, ALIAS: 'Resize' &
                    :: Resize
            integer(4)  width, height
            end subroutine Resize
            subroutine Fill
            end subroutine Fill
            subroutine Lines
            end subroutine Lines
        end interface
        integer(4) iret
            call fauxInitDisplayMode (IOR(AUX_SINGLE , AUX_RGBA))
            call fauxInitPosition (100, 100, 585, 480)
            iret = fauxInitWindow ("Press     Space Bar to Quit, &
                    F or f or left mouse button for fill, &
                    L or l or right mouse for lines"C)
            call fauxReshapeFunc(LOC(Resize))
            call fgluOrtho2d(DBLE(-1.0), DBLE(1.0), DBLE(-1.0), &
                            DBLE(1.0))
            call fauxKeyFunc(AUX_SPACE,loc(KeySpace))
            call fauxKeyFunc(AUX_F, LOC(Fill))
            call fauxKeyFunc(AUX_L, LOC(Lines))
            call fauxKeyFunc(AUX_ff, LOC(Fill))
            call fauxKeyFunc(AUX_ll, LOC(Lines))
            call fauxMouseFunc(AUX_LEFTBUTTON,AUX_MOUSEDOWN,Fill)
            call fauxMouseFunc(AUX_RIGHTBUTTON, &
                            AUX_MOUSEDOWN,Lines)
            call CreateScene
            call fauxMainLoop(LOC(drawit))
            WinMain = 0
            return
        end Function WinMain
        integer Function KeySpace
        use dfopngl
        call fauxQuit()
        end Function KeySpace
        subroutine Resize(width, height)
        !DEC$ ATTRIBUTES STDCALL, DECORATE, ALIAS: 'Resize' &
                  :: Resize
        use dfopngl
        integer(4)  width, height
            call fglViewport(0, 0, width, height)
            if(height == 0) height = 1
            call fglLoadIdentity
            ! define clipping area (left, right, bottom, top)
            if (width <= height) then
                call fgluOrtho2d(DBLE(-1.0), DBLE(1.0), &
                DBLE(-1.0)*height/width, DBLE(1.0)*height/width)
            else
```

```
          call fgluOrtho2d(DBLE(-1.0)*width/height, &
                DBLE(1.0)*width/height, DBLE(-1.0), &
                DBLE(1.0))
     end if
end
subroutine Fill
use dfopngl
     call fglPolygonMode(GL_FRONT_AND_BACK,GL_FILL)
end
subroutine Lines
use dfopngl
     call fglPolygonMode(GL_FRONT_AND_BACK,GL_LINE)
end
```

Note: In the preceding code, the lines beginning with !DEC$ ATTRIBUTES
are compiler directives and are shown with Fortran continuation signs (&) at
the end of each line, indicating that the code continues onto a second line.
This is for typographical convenience only. If you type these lines, they
must be entered as a single line.

Typical output from OpenGL3 is as illustrated in Figure 15.3. The triangle and square on the left are filled with a single color, and the triangle
and square on the right are smooth and are filled using multiple colors.

Figure 15.3
*Output from
OpenGL3 showing
filled polygons.*

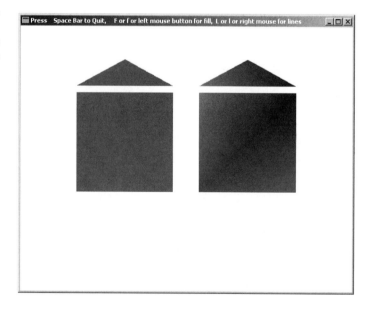

15.5   Triangles and quadrilaterals

Let us now look at the individual subroutines used to create the triangles and polygons in OpenGL3. The simplest two-dimensional shape is a triangle, which is constructed by specifying three vertices per triangle within a set of glBegin and glEnd functions, as follows:

```
call fglBegin(GL_TRIANGLES)
   ! first triangle
   call fglColor3f (1.0, 0.0, 1.0)
   call fglVertex2f(-0.85, 0.55)
   call fglVertex2f(-0.475, 0.75)
   call fglVertex2f(-0.10, 0.55)
   ! second triangle
   call fglColor3f (0.0, 1.0, 0.0)
   call fglVertex2f(0.10, 0.55)
   call fglColor3f (1.0, 0.0, 0.0)
   call fglVertex2f(0.475, 0.75)
   call fglColor3f (0.0, 0.0, 1.0)
   call fglVertex2f(0.85, 0.55)
call fglEnd
```

In the first triangle, only one fill color is used, but in the second triangle, each vertex has been assigned a different color. OpenGL calculates how the three colors are blended within the fill area of the triangle. This process is called smooth shading (or Gouraud shading). Shading can be set for lines, triangles, polygons, and so on as flat (one color) or smooth (blend of colors) using the function glShadeModel with GL_FLAT or GL_SMOOTH, respectively, as the argument. The default shade model is smooth. We will make use of this useful feature of OpenGL in the Animation application later in this chapter and with the GridView application described in Chapter 16.

One important characteristic of all polynomials, including triangles, is the order used in defining their vertices, and this is usually referred to as the winding of the polynomial. When the vertices of a polynomial are defined in a counterclockwise order, they are said to have counterclockwise winding. The choice of winding direction is either clockwise or counterclockwise. In OpenGL, by default, polygons are assumed to have a counterclockwise winding. This is important when you are using the OpenGL cull face function to cull backward-facing polygons. If you are not consistent in the order that you use for defining the polygons, you may find some polygons remain unfilled. You can use the OpenGL function glFront-

Face to tell OpenGL which winding order is to be considered as defining a front-facing polygon, as follows:

```
call fglFrontFace(GL_CW)    ! Clockwise winding
```

or

```
call fglFrontFace(GL_CCW)   ! Counterclockwise winding
```

If you need to draw many triangles, you will find it easier to use triangle strips (GL_TRIANGLE_STRIP) or triangle fans (GL_TRIANGLE_FAN) rather than GL_TRIANGLES, because once the first triangle is defined, each subsequent triangle requires only one vertex to define it.

OpenGL offers a variety of ways to draw a four-sided figure, the simplest being glRect, which requires only the x and y locations of two opposing corners. Other possibilities are to draw quadrilaterals (GL_QUADS) or four-sided polygons (GL_POLYGON). The following piece of code illustrates how to create a quadrilateral:

```
call fglBegin(GL_QUADS)
   call fglColor3f (1.0, 0.0, 1.0)
   call fglVertex2f(-0.85, -0.25)
   call fglVertex2f(-0.85, 0.5)
   call fglVertex2f(-0.10, 0.5)
   call fglVertex2f(-0.10, -0.25)
call fglEnd
```

You can also create quadrilateral strips (GL_QUAD_STRIP), which require only a pair of vertices once the initial quadrilateral has been defined. The following code illustrates how to create a four-sided polygon:

```
call fglBegin(GL_POLYGON)
   call fglVertex2f(0.10, -0.25)
   call fglVertex2f(0.10, 0.5)
   call fglVertex2f(0.85, 0.5)
   call fglVertex2f(0.85, -0.25)
call fglEnd
```

15.6   Display lists

OpenGL is fast when it comes to drawing and filling shapes such as triangles and polygons, but it can perform these tasks even faster when you use display lists. Display lists are groups of OpenGL commands that have been stored for subsequent execution. To optimize performance, OpenGL display lists cannot be modified; thus, they are best suited to drawing code sections that are, "write once, use many times" in nature. Display lists are easy to create, as the following code fragment illustrates with the name 1:

```
call fglNewList (name, GL_COMPILE)
...OpenGL instructions go here
call fglEndList
```

The first argument to glNewList (in this example, name) is an integer value used to identify the list. It is usual to give the list a name that identifies its purpose, such as circle or wing_section. The second argument provides instructions to either compile the list (GL_COMPILE) or to compile and execute the list (GL_COMPILE_AND_EXECUTE). This is the code in the application OpenGL3, which creates two triangles and two rectangles using a display list.

```
subroutine CreateScene
use dfopngl
   call fglNewList (1, GL_COMPILE)
    ! First Rectangle
    call fglBegin(GL_QUADS)
       call fglColor3f (1.0, 0.0, 1.0)
       call fglVertex2f(-0.85, -0.25)
       call fglVertex2f(-0.85, 0.5)
       call fglVertex2f(-0.10, 0.5)
       call fglVertex2f(-0.10, -0.25)
    call fglEnd
    ! Second Rectangle
    call fglBegin(GL_POLYGON)
       call fglColor3f (1.0, 0.0, 0.0)
       call fglVertex2f(0.10, -0.25)
       call fglColor3f (0.0, 1.0, 0.0)
       call fglVertex2f(0.10, 0.5)
       call fglColor3f (0.0, 0.0, 1.0)
       call fglVertex2f(0.85, 0.5)
       call fglColor3f (1.0, 0.0, 1.0)
       call fglVertex2f(0.85, -0.25)
    call fglEnd
      call fglBegin(GL_TRIANGLES)
        ! first triangle
        call fglColor3f (1.0, 0.0, 1.0)
        call fglVertex2f(-0.85, 0.55)
        call fglVertex2f(-0.475, 0.75)
        call fglVertex2f(-0.10, 0.55)
        ! second triangle
        call fglColor3f (0.0, 1.0, 0.0)
        call fglVertex2f(0.10, 0.55)
        call fglColor3f (1.0, 0.0, 0.0)
```

```
                call fglVertex2f(0.475, 0.75)
                call fglColor3f (0.0, 0.0, 1.0)
                call fglVertex2f(0.85, 0.55)
           call fglEnd
        call fglEndList
     end
```

A call is made once only to the subroutine CreateScene to set up the display list; after that call, the scene can be drawn or redrawn at any time by using the function drawit, which calls the display list, as follows:

```
integer Function drawit
use dfopngl
implicit none
   call fglClearColor(1.0, 1.0, 1.0, 1.0)
   call fglClear(GL_COLOR_BUFFER_BIT)
   call fglCallList (1)
   call fglFlush()
end Function drawit
```

15.7 Double-frame buffers

When we looked at bitmaps in Chapter 10, we discovered that, by drawing to memory and then bit blitting the memory contents to the screen, we could create animation effects. In this example, we will make use of the

Figure 15.4
Output from the program AnimateGL.

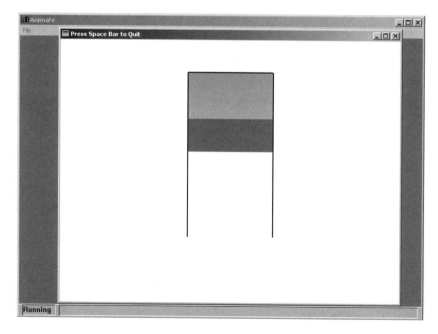

double-buffering capabilities of OpenGL to demonstrate its animation possibilities. The AUX library function, auxIdleFunction, makes it easy to set up simple animation sequences. The auxIdleFunction requires one argument, which is the name of the function to call when the program is idle. The example AnimateGL represents a piston moving up and down inside a cylinder, compressing some air. The polygon representing the air has its lower two vertices colored red and its upper two vertices colored blue. The polygon is filled with a blend of these two colors to simulate the effect of cold air at the top of the cylinder and hot air around the piston. A sample screen display is shown in Figure 15.4.

The program section for creating the window is essentially similar to the previous programs, with the notable exceptions of AUX_DOUBLE being specified as an argument for auxInitDisplayMode, the use of the function auxIdleFunc, and the need to use two global variables—deltay and Piston-Top. This is the code used to create the window:

```
integer(4) function WinMain (hInstance, hPrevInstance, &
                 lpszCmdLine, nCmdShow)
!DEC$ ATTRIBUTES STDCALL, DECORATE, ALIAS: 'WinMain' &
          :: WinMain
! An OpenGL program to simulate air being compressed
! in a cylinder.
use dfopngl
use Globals
implicit none
integer(4) hInstance,hPrevInstance, lpszCmdLine, &
          nCmdShow
interface
   integer(4) function  KeySpace
   end function
end interface
interface
   integer(4) function  Drawit
   end function
end interface
interface
   subroutine Resize(width, height)
   !DEC$ ATTRIBUTES STDCALL,DECORATE, ALIAS : 'Resize' &
             :: Resize
   integer(4)  width, height
   end subroutine Resize
end interface
integer(4) iret
   call fauxInitDisplayMode (IOR(AUX_DOUBLE, AUX_RGBA))
   call fauxInitPosition (0, 0, 640, 480)
   iret = fauxInitWindow ("Press Space Bar to Quit"C)
```

```
            call fauxReshapeFunc(LOC(Resize))
            call fgluOrtho2D(DBLE(-1.0), DBLE(1.0), DBLE(-1.0), &
                            DBLE(1.0))
            deltay = + 0.010
            PistonTop = 0.0
            call fauxKeyFunc(AUX_SPACE,loc(KeySpace))
            call fauxIdleFunc(LOC(drawit))
            call fauxMainLoop(0)
            WinMain = 0
            return
        end Function WinMain
        integer Function KeySpace
        use dfwin
        use dfopngl
         call fauxQuit
        end Function KeySpace
        subroutine Resize(width, height)
        !DEC$ ATTRIBUTES STDCALL,DECORATE, ALIAS : 'Resize' &
                :: Resize
        use dfopngl
        integer(4)  width, height
            call fglViewport(0, 0, width, height)
            if(height == 0) height = 1
            call fglLoadIdentity();
            ! define the clipping area (left, right, bottom, top)
            if (width <= height) then
               call fgluOrtho2D(DBLE(-1.0), DBLE(1.0), &
                  DBLE(-1.0)*height/width, DBLE(1.0)*height/width)
            else
               call fgluOrtho2D(DBLE(-1.0)*width/height, &
                  DBLE(1.0)*width/height, DBLE(-1.0), DBLE(1.0))
            end if
        end
```

Note: In the preceding code, the lines beginning with !DEC$ ATTRIBUTES are compiler directives and are shown with Fortran continuation signs (&) at the end of each line, indicating that the code continues onto a second line. This is for typographical convenience only. If you type these lines, they must be entered as a single line.

When the scene has been drawn to the frame buffer, the buffers are swapped, and the new scene is displayed on the screen. As the following listing demonstrates, the drawit routine is straightforward. Each time the routine is called, the current value of PistonTop is checked. If it is outside the specified limits, the sign of the variable *deltay* is changed. The value (100) passed in the call to the sleep routine can be changed to vary the speed of the animation effect.

```
integer Function drawit
use dfopngl
use Globals
implicit none
    call fglClearColor(1.0, 1.0, 1.0, 1.0)
    call fglClear(GL_COLOR_BUFFER_BIT)
    if ((PistonTop >0.72).or. (PistonTop <= -0.20)) then
        deltay = -deltay
    end if
    PistonTop = PistonTop + deltay
    call fglColor3f(0.0, 0.0, 0.0)
    call fglLineWidth (1.50)
    call fglBegin(GL_LINE_STRIP)
        call fglVertex2f(-0.25, -0.5)
        call fglVertex2f(-0.25, 0.753)
        call fglVertex2f(0.252, 0.753)
        call fglVertex2f(0.252, 0-.5)
    call fglEnd
    call fglLineWidth (1.50)
    call fglPolygonMode(GL_FRONT,GL_FILL)
    call fglColor3f(0.75, 0.75, 0.75)
    call fglRectf( -0.248, PistonTop-0.25, 0.25, &
                    PistonTop)
    call fglBegin(GL_POLYGON)
        call fglColor3f (1.0, 0.25, 0.0)
        call fglVertex2f(-0.248, PistonTop)
        call fglVertex2f(0.25, PistonTop)
        call fglColor3f(0.0, 0.75, 1.0)
        call fglVertex2f(0.25, 0.75)
        call fglVertex2f(-0.248, 0.75)
    call fglEnd
    call fglFlush
    call fauxSwapBuffers
    call sleep(100)
end Function drawit
```

15.8 OpenGL in three dimensions

So far, we have drawn only two-dimensional shapes, but the AUX Library has a collection of 3D shapes that are available as wireframe or solid objects. We will use the AUX Library teapot to demonstrate some techniques for working in three-dimensional space, but you can use any of the available shapes listed in Appendix C. In 2D space we used a clipping area, but when working in 3D space, we need to define a clipping volume. For this example, we will work with an orthographic projection, which means that two parallel lines going into the distance will be drawn the same distance apart rather than tending to taper toward each other, as happens with a perspective projection. Since we now have a viewing volume, we are required to specify values for near and far on the z-axis (the axis normal to the screen). The following line of code sets the clipping volume to be a cube that has sides of two-dimensional units with 0,0,0 at the center of the cube.

```
call fglOrtho(DBLE(-1.0), DBLE(1.0), DBLE(-1.0), &
              DBLE(1.0), DBLE(-1.0), DBLE(1.0))
```

In the following listing for Teapot1, the auxIdleFunc is used to repeatedly call the function drawit so that the teapot will be redrawn in a new rotated position.

```
integer(4) function WinMain (hInstance, hPrevInstance, &
                lpszCmdLine, nCmdShow)
!DEC$ ATTRIBUTES STDCALL, DECORATE, ALIAS: 'WinMain' &
            :: WinMain
! Program to draw a wireframe 3-D Teapot
! in an OpenGL window
use dfopngl
implicit none
integer(4) hInstance,hPrevInstance, lpszCmdLine
integer(4) nCmdShow
interface
    integer(4) function   KeySpace
    end function
    integer(4) function   Drawit
    end function
    subroutine Resize(width, height)
    !DEC$ ATTRIBUTES STDCALL,DECORATE, ALIAS : 'Resize' &
                :: Resize
        integer(4)   width, height
    end subroutine Resize
end interface
integer(4) iret
    call fauxInitDisplayMode (IOR(AUX_DOUBLE , AUX_RGBA))
    call fauxInitPosition (0, 0, 640, 480)
    iret = fauxInitWindow ("Press Space Bar to Quit"C)
    call fauxReshapeFunc(LOC(Resize))
    call fglOrtho(DBLE(-1.0), DBLE(1.0), DBLE(-1.0), &
                DBLE(1.0), DBLE(-1.0), DBLE(1.0))
    call fauxKeyFunc(AUX_SPACE,loc(KeySpace))
    call fauxIdleFunc(LOC(drawit))
    call fauxMainLoop(0)
    WinMain = 0
    return
```

```
end Function WinMain
integer Function KeySpace
use dfopngl
   call fauxQuit
end Function KeySpace
subroutine Resize(width, height)
!DEC$ ATTRIBUTES STDCALL, DECORATE, ALIAS : 'Resize' &
         :: Resize
use dfopngl
integer(4)  width, height
   call fglViewport(0, 0, width, height)
   if(height == 0) height = 1
   call fglLoadIdentity();
   ! define clipping volume (left, right, bottom, top,
   ! near, far)
   if (width <= height) then
      call fglOrtho(DBLE(-1.0), DBLE(1.0), &
         DBLE(-1.0)*height/width, &
         DBLE(1.0)*height/width, DBLE(-1.0), DBLE(1.0))
   else
      call fglOrtho(DBLE(-1.0)*width/height, &
                    DBLE(1.0)*width/height, DBLE(-1.0), &
                    DBLE(1.0), DBLE(-1.0), DBLE(1.0))
   end if
end
```

Note: In the preceding code, the lines beginning with !DEC$ ATTRIBUTES are compiler directives and are shown with Fortran continuation signs (&) at the end of each line, indicating that the code continues onto a second line. This is for typographical convenience only. If you type these lines, they must be entered as a single line.

Each call to the drawit function creates a rotation of the teapot by 30 degrees in the *y*-axis. This is achieved by using the function glRotate, as follows

```
call fglRotatef(30.0, 0.0, 1.0, 0.0)
```

The first number in the argument list of glRotate is the angle of rotation, while the other three arguments represent the *x*-, *y*-, and *z*-axes, respectively. A value of 1.0 indicates which axis the rotation is to be performed around. When you want to rotate around more than one axis, it is recommended that you make one call for each axis that you wish to rotate around rather than trying to combine the rotations into one single call. The actual code to draw the teapot is a simple one-line call to the AUX Library, as follows:

```
call fauxWireTeaPot(0.5)
```

The argument passed to auxWireTeaPot is the diameter of the teapot. The following is a listing of the drawit routine used to create the teapot shown in Figure 15.5.

```
integer Function drawit
use dfopngl
    call fglClearColor (1.0, 1.0, 1.0, 1.0)
    call fglClear(GL_COLOR_BUFFER_BIT)
    call fglColor3f (1.0, 0.5, 0.0)
    call fauxWireTeaPot(0.5)
    call fglFlush
    call fglRotatef(30.0, 0.0, 1.0, 0.0)
    call fauxSwapBuffers
end Function drawit
```

Figure 15.5   *WireFrame teapot drawn using the AUX Library.*

15.9 Lighting

The example Teapot1 can be modified to draw a solid teapot by replacing the line that makes a call to auxWireTeaPot with the following line of code:

```
call fauxSolidTeaPot(0.5)
```

However, if that is the only modification that you make to Teapot1, the results will be disappointing because the solid teapot will look like a filled two-dimensional shape. Some form of lighting needs to be applied to the scene so that a more realistic 3D object can be created. First, we need to gain an appreciation of the techniques used by OpenGL for lighting a scene.

In OpenGL, light sources are characterized by the percentage of red, green, and blue light that they emit, whereas surfaces are characterized by the amount of the incoming red, green, and blue that they reflect. The light in an OpenGL scene comes from several sources, which can be individually turned on and off. Lighting is treated as four independent components that are computed separately and then added together. The four separate components of light are emitted, ambient, diffuse, and specular. Unless a surface emits it own light (e.g., a red-hot object), it will normally be illuminated by three different kinds of light: ambient, diffuse, and specular.

Ambient light is light that has bounced off so many surfaces that it no longer has any particular direction. Objects that are in ambient lighting conditions are evenly lit on all surfaces. When ambient light strikes a surface, it will be scattered equally in all directions. Diffuse light comes from a particular direction. Fluorescent lighting is an example of diffuse lighting. Once diffuse lighting hits a surface, it will be scattered equally in all directions. Specular light comes from a particular direction and it tends to bounce off a surface in a preferred direction. A spotlight or torch beam is an example of a specular light source.

Single-light sources are often composed of varying intensities of ambient, diffuse, and specular light. OpenGL allows you to independently set the red, green, and blue values for the ambient, diffuse, and specular components of a light source. In the following code fragment, RGBA values are defined for the ambient, diffuse, and specular components of light number 0 using the OpenGL function glLightfv. The arguments passed to glLightfv are, respectively, the light number (GL_LIGHT0–GL_LIGHT7), a symbolic constant representing the light source type (check online documentation for other alternatives), and a pointer to the data values to be used. Finally, two calls are made to glEnable. The first call enables lighting (fglEnable (GL_LIGHTING)), while the second call switches on light number 0 (fglEnable (GL_LIGHT0)).

```
real(4) glfLightAmbient(4)
real(4) glfLightDiffuse(4)
real(4) glfLightSpecular(4)
data glfLightAmbient /0.1, 0.1, 0.1, 1.0/
data glfLightDiffuse /0.7, 0.7, 0.7, 1.0/
data glfLightSpecular / 1.0, 0.0, 0.0, 1.0/
! Add a light to the scene
call fglLightfv (GL_LIGHT0, GL_AMBIENT,
loc(glfLightAmbient))
call fglLightfv (GL_LIGHT0, GL_DIFFUSE,
loc(glfLightDiffuse))
call fglLightfv
(GL_LIGHT0,GL_SPECULAR,LOC(glfLightSpecular))
call fglEnable (GL_LIGHTING)
call fglEnable (GL_LIGHT0)
```

A surface in OpenGL is characterized as a material that has different ambient, diffuse, and specular colors. The values set for each of these colors will determine how much ambient, diffuse, and specular light is reflected from the material. Thus, a perfectly green surface will reflect all the green light and absorb all the red and blue light that strikes it. When a green surface is viewed under either a white (red, green, and blue) or green light, it will appear green, but when it is viewed under either a red or blue light, it will appear black, because all the incident light is absorbed. The values used for ambient and diffuse surface reflectivity will define the color of the material, and normally they will be the same. The specular reflectivity is usually chosen to be white (sometimes gray). This means that a specular highlight on an object will have a white appearance. For example, when a white light is shone on a blue plastic surface, most of the surface will appear blue, but any shiny highlights will be white.

In the following code fragment, the RGBA values are defined for the ambient and diffuse components of light to be reflected from the material using the OpenGL function glMaterialfv. The arguments passed to glMaterialfv, respectively, define which surface the data applies to (GL_FRONT_AND_BACK), the type of reflection (GL_AMBIENT, GL_DIFFUSE, GL_SPECULAR) or emisson (GL_EMISSION), and a pointer to the data values to be used. When the reflection type is specular, then a value must be specified regarding the shininess of the surface (0 for a matte surface and 128 for maximum shininess). The final line of code shows how the call is made to set the shininess level of a surface.

```
real(4) glfMaterialColor(4)
data glfMaterialColor / 0.0, 0.0, 1.0, 1.0 /
call fglMaterialfv (GL_FRONT_AND_BACK, &
                    GL_AMBIENT_AND_DIFFUSE, &
                    loc(glfMaterialColor))
call fglMaterialfv (GL_FRONT_AND_BACK, GL_SPECULAR , &
                    loc(glfMaterialColor))
call fglMaterialfv(GL_FRONT, GL_SHININESS, loc(180.0))
```

15.9.1 Positioning lights

The position of a light in an OpenGL scene can be set using the function glLightfv, as follows:

```
real(4) glfLightPosition(4)
data glfLightPosition / 1.0, 1.0, 0.0, 1.0 /
call fglLightfv(GL_LIGHT0,GL_POSITION, &
                loc(glfLightPosition))
```

The arguments used with glLightfv to set the light position specify, respectively, which light to set (GL_LIGHT0), what to do with the light (GL_POSITION), and a pointer to the data to be used. The data contains four values—the coordinates x, y, and z plus a fourth number that provides information about the light characteristics. If the fourth number is zero, it means that the light source is directional and the x, y, and z values describe its direction. The default position for lights in an OpenGL scene is at [0, 0, 1, 0], which means that the light source is directional; all the light rays are parallel to and in the direction of the z-axis. A nonzero value for the fourth number indicates that the light is positional, which means that the light rays radiate in all directions from the light source. The following two lines of code define a positional light source (GL_LIGHT1) as a spotlight with a cutoff angle and set the intensity to 45.0.

```
call fglLightf(GL_LIGHT1, GL_SPOT_CUTOFF, 60.0)
call fglLightf(GL_LIGHT1, GL_SPOT_EXPONENT, 45.0)
```

The intensity value can be set in the range 0–128. Note that the value given for the GL_SPOT_CUTOFF parameter is half the angle at the cone apex. In the above code, the angle at the cone apex will be 120 degrees. Values for the GL_SPOT_CUTOFF parameter are in the range 0–90 or the default value of 180, which represents a cone apex angle of 360 degrees.

15.10 Normal vectors

Shapes such as triangles, rectangles, quadrilaterals, and polygons are defined using a set of vertices, and they take their color from the color assigned to each vertex. It is necessary to know the angle that a directional light makes with a surface before you can calculate the angle at which light will leave a surface. The way this is done in OpenGL is by specifying a line that is perpendicular (at 90 degrees) to each vertex in an upward direction. The starting point for the line is the vertex; thus, it is necessary only to specify the end point of the line. This line is usually referred to as the normal vector. Once the normal vector is set, it stays in operation until a new value is specified. In the following piece of code, the normals for all three vertices are set in the same z direction.

```
call fglNormal3f(0.0, 0.0, -1.0)
call fglBegin(GL_TRIANGLES)
   call fglVertex3f(0.0, 0.0, 0.0)
   call fglVertex3f(15.0, 0.0, 0.0)
   call fglVertex3f(10.0, 20.0, 0.0)
call fglEnd()
```

If you do not wish to calculate the normal vectors for the vertices, a simple solution is to let OpenGL do it automatically for you, as follows:

```
call fglEnable(GL_AUTO_NORMAL)
```

Figure 15.6
Effect of two light sources on teapot.

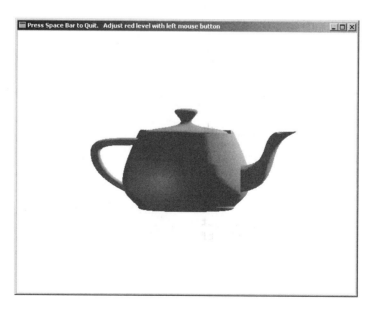

The example Teapot2 illustrates the use of lighting to light a three-dimensional object. The teapot is initially displayed in shades of cyan, and the user can click the left mouse button to increase the level of red in the light source from zero to one in increments of 0.1. The main light source is positioned at the upper-right corner, and one unit in the *z*-axis into the screen. This light position produces a shadow in the front of the teapot. A spotlight is positioned one unit in the *z*-axis out of the screen and slightly to the left and down from the center position. The shadow and spotlight effects can be clearly seen in the screen display shown in Figure 15.6. Try experimenting with the lighting and surface material properties by changing data values and by commenting out a single line relating to either ambient or diffuse lighting for the light source or material.

This is the code used in Teapot2 to set the lighting and draw the scene:

```
subroutine SetScene:
use dfopngl
use Globals
implicit none
real(4) glfLightPosition(4)
real(4) glfSpotPosition(4)
data glfLightPosition / 1.0, 1.0, 1.0, 0.0 /
data glfSpotPosition / -0.150, -0.150, -1.0, 1.0 /
   ! Initial RGB components of light
   glfLightSpot = 1.0
   glfLightAmbient(1) = 0.0
   glfLightAmbient(2) = 0.5
   glfLightAmbient(3) = 0.5
   glfLightAmbient(4) = 1.0
   ! Add a light to the scene
   call fglEnable (GL_LIGHTING)
   call fglLightfv(GL_LIGHT0,GL_POSITION, &
                   loc(glfLightPosition))
   call fglLightfv(GL_LIGHT1,GL_POSITION, &
                   loc(glfSpotPosition))
   call fglEnable (GL_LIGHT0)
   call fglEnable (GL_LIGHT1)
   call fglEnable (GL_AUTO_NORMAL)
   call fglLightf(GL_LIGHT1, GL_SPOT_CUTOFF, 60.0)
   call fglLightf(GL_LIGHT1, GL_SPOT_EXPONENT, 45.0)
end
integer Function drawit
use dfopngl
use Globals
implicit none
real(4) glfMaterialColor(4)
real(4) glfMaterialColor1(4)
```

```
data glfMaterialColor / 0.75, 0.25, 0.25, 1.0 /
data glfMaterialColor1 / 0.2, 0.2, 0.2, 1.0 /
   call fglLightfv (GL_LIGHT0, GL_DIFFUSE, &
           LOC(glfLightAmbient))
   call fglLightfv (GL_LIGHT0, GL_AMBIENT, &
           LOC(glfLightAmbient))
   call fglLightfv (GL_LIGHT1, GL_SPECULAR, &
           LOC(glfLightSpot))
   call fglMaterialfv(GL_FRONT, GL_AMBIENT, &
           LOC(glfMaterialColor))
   call fglMaterialfv(GL_FRONT, GL_DIFFUSE, &
           LOC(glfMaterialColor))
   call fglMaterialfv(GL_FRONT, GL_SPECULAR, &
           LOC(glfMaterialColor1))
   call fglMateriali (GL_FRONT, GL_SHININESS, 80)
   call fglClearColor (1.0, 1.0, 1.0, 1.0)
   call fglClear(GL_COLOR_BUFFER_BIT)
   call fauxSolidTeaPot(0.5)
   call fglFlush
   call fauxSwapBuffers
end Function drawit
```

15.11 Bezier curves

In Chapter 9, we used the Win32 GDI to create a Bezier curve by specifying four points—a starting point for the line, two control points, and an end point for the line. We discovered that by varying the position of the two control points, a range of curves could be generated between the end points of the line. In this section, we will use OpenGL to create a Bezier curve, and in Chapter 16, we will extend the technique to include Bezier surfaces.

In OpenGL, Bezier curves and surfaces are created using evaluators. Evaluators provide a way to specify points on a surface or curve using only control points. A curve or surface can be subdivided at any required level of precision, and the normal vectors of a surface are calculated automatically. The points generated by an evaluator are used just as if you had supplied a list of vertices, so you can draw points or draw lines to join the points or draw a fully light surface. The glMap1f and glMap1d functions are used to define a one-dimensional evaluator using single or double precision values, respectively. The syntax of use is:

```
glMap1f(target, u1, u2, stride, order, points)
```

where the terms are defined as follows:

- Target—One of nine symbolic constants used to indicate what kind of control points are contained in points. The value GL_MAP1_VERTEX_3 indicates that each control point has three floating-point values representing x, y, and z. See the online documentation for details of the other options.

- u1, u2—The lower and upper limits of the parametric value u for the curve. The values in between correspond to the other points along the curve in increments of one. Setting u1 = 10 and u2 = 30 would cause 21 points to be generated along the curve, the starting point being number 10 and the final one being number 30.

- Stride—The number of floating-point values between the beginning of one control point and the beginning of the next one in the data structure array. For a vertex consisting of three values (representing x, y, and z) this value would be 3.

- Order—The order of the spline. This is the degree plus one. For our Bezier curve, the degree is three because the curve is cubic, and so the order is four. It represents the number of control points.

- Points—Pointer to the array that contains the control points for defining the curve.

The following code fragment illustrates how to create a Bezier curve composed of 81 points through a call to the function glMap1 and then to draw the curve as a set of line strips joining the 81 points generated.

```
call fglMap1f(GL_MAP1_VERTEX_3, 0.0, 80.0,3,4, &
        loc(ctrPoints(1,1)))
call fglEnable(GL_MAP1_VERTEX_3)
call fglColor3f(0.0, 0.0, 0.0)   ! Black
call fglBegin(GL_LINE_STRIP)
   do i = 0,80
      call fglEvalCoord1f(i)
   end do
call fglEnd()
```

The function glEvalCoord1 is used to generate the x, y, and z coordinates of the points generated. Note the call to glEnable to inform OpenGL that we want the evaluator to generate x, y, and z coordinates. The actual coordinates are generated in the do loop, which is bracketed by the calls to glBegin and glEnd.

Figure 15.7
*Output from
BezierGL1
program.*

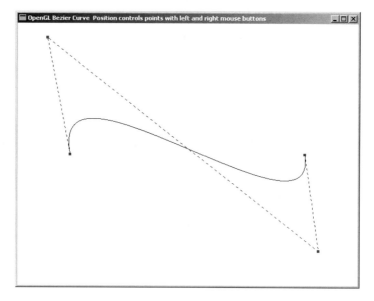

Readers who wish more detail on the mathematical basis used by evaluators should study the online documentation. The example BezierGL1 illustrates how to create and display a single Bezier curve. The actual curve is drawn in a solid black line, and a dashed line is drawn through the control points, as shown in Figure 15.7. The following two subroutines are from BezierGL1. Routine CreateScene is used to create a display containing the information for drawing the Bezier curve, and routine drawit is used to display the curve.

```
subroutine CreateScene()
use dfopngl
use Bezier1dGlobals
implicit none
integer(4) i
integer(4), parameter :: List1 = 1
   call fglClearColor(1.0, 1.0, 1.0, 0.2)
   call fglNewList (List1, GL_COMPILE)
      call fglMap1f(GL_MAP1_VERTEX_3, 0.0, 80.0, &
           3,4,loc(ctrPoints(1,1)) )
      call fglEnable(GL_MAP1_VERTEX_3)
      call fglColor3f(0.0, 0.0, 0.0)   ! Black
      call fglBegin(GL_LINE_STRIP)
         do i = 0,80
            call fglEvalCoord1f(i)
         end do
      call fglEnd()
      call fglColor3f(1.0, 0.0, 0.0)   ! Red
```

```
                call fglPointSize(5.0)
                call fglBegin(GL_POINTS)
                   do i = 1,4
                      call fglVertex3f(ctrPoints(1,i), &
                         ctrPoints(2,i), ctrPoints(3,1))
                   end do
                call fglEnd()
                call fglLineStipple(1, Z'0F0F')
                call fglLineWidth(1.001)
                call fglEnable(GL_LINE_STIPPLE)
                call fglColor3f(0.0, 0.0, 1.0)   ! Blue
                call fglBegin(GL_LINE_STRIP)
                   do i = 1,4
                      call fglVertex3f(ctrPoints(1,i), &
                            ctrPoints(2,i), ctrPoints(3,1))
                   end do
                call fglEnd()
                call fgldisable(GL_LINE_STIPPLE)
          call fglEndList ()
       end
       subroutine Drawit
       use dfopngl
       implicit none
       integer(4), parameter :: List1 = 1
          call fglClearColor(1.0, 1.0, 1.0, 0.2)
          call fglClear(GL_COLOR_BUFFER_BIT )
          call fglCallList (List1)
          call fglFlush()
          call fauxSwapBuffers()
       end
```

15.12 Getting cursor location

The AUX function auxMouseFunc can be used to provide the x and y coordinates of the present cursor position when a mouse button is clicked. So far, when we used a mouse callback function, we have not passed any argument to the callback routine since we wanted to know only whether the button had been clicked. Now we are going to pass a structure of type AUX_EVENTREC. This structure contains two members:

- Event—Integer specifying which event took place (AUX_MOUSEUP or AUX_MOUSEDOWN)

- Data(4)—Integer containing the following information about the event:

  - Data(1)—Mouse position in x direction.

- Data(2)—Mouse position in y direction.
- Data(3)—Integer related to mouse up or down.
- Data(4)—Which mouse button (left = 1, middle = 4, R = 2).

The symbolic constants AUX_MOUSEX and AUX_MOUSEY cannot be used because they have values of 0 and 1, respectively; therefore, we need to use integer values of 1 and 2 directly for reading the data array. The following routines are used in BezierGL1 to get the coordinates or the cursor when the right and left mouse buttons are clicked. The coordinates are then used to define the control points for the Bezier curve. Note that the coordinates value for y is converted from the window system with $y = 0$ at the top of the OpenGL system and $y = 0$ at the bottom.

```
subroutine ControlR(mousedata)
use dfopngl
use Bezier1dGlobals
type(AUX_EVENTREC) mousedata
   ctrPoints(1,3) = mousedata%data(1)
   ctrPoints(2,3) = ySize-mousedata%data(2)
   call CreateScene
end
subroutine ControlL(mousedata)
use dfopngl
use Bezier1dGlobals
type(AUX_EVENTREC) mousedata
   ctrPoints(1,2) = mousedata%data(1)
   ctrPoints(2,2) = ySize-mousedata%data(2)
   call CreateScene
end
```

15.13 What is next?

In the next chapter, we will create OpenGL applications using Win32 API functions. We will learn how to write text to the OpenGL window, display bitmap files, use the mouse to select points, and create Bezier surfaces.

16

More OpenGL

16.1 Introduction

As discussed in Chapter 15, the AUX library offers an easy approach to learning OpenGL, because only a few lines of code are needed to create an OpenGL window. Once the window is created, you can use any of the OpenGL functions to draw to that window. However, the window created by the AUX library has very limited capabilities.

In this chapter, we move on and use Win32 routines to create a conventional window with menus, dialog boxes, and so on for use with OpenGL functions. We need to specify a window that provides the rendering context for use with Open GL functions and this is achieved in the following sequence of events:

- Set the pixel format of the device context using the function SetPixel-Format.

- Create a rendering context with wglCreateContext.

- Select the rendering context as the current context with wglMake-Current.

- Call OpenGL functions.

- When finished with the rendering context, remove it with the function wglDeleteContext.

A rendering context is not the same as a device context. A device context stores details of drawing instructions and drawing modes for GDI, whereas a rendering context stores information about OpenGL instructions and states.

Some of the OpenGL functions that we will use begin with *wgl* rather than *gl*. The *w* preceding the *gl* indicates that these are not true OpenGL

functions; rather, they are functions especially written for the Windows
operating system and hence they are nonportable to other operating systems. Interested readers can use the online documentation to explore the
complete list of the *wgl* functions and their intended use. Recall from Chapter 15 that all OpenGL functions are preceded with the letter *f* when coded
in Visual Fortran, so wglCreateContext will become fwglCreateContext.
The following piece of code illustrates how the preceding sequence of events
is used to create and destroy a rendering context:

```
case (WM_CREATE)
   ! Create a rendering context.
   hdc = GetDC(hwnd)
   call SetDCPixelFormat(hdc)
   hrc = fwglCreateContext(hdc)
   bret = fwglMakeCurrent(hdc, hrc)
   MainWndProc = 0
   return
case (WM_DESTROY)
   ! release OpenGL rendering context
   bret = fwglMakeCurrent(null, null)
   ! delete handle to the OpenGL rendering context
   bret = fwglDeleteContext(hrc)
   bret = DeleteDC(hdc) !handle to device context
   call PostQuitMessage( 0 )
   MainWndProc = 0
   return
```

Note that the wglDeleteContext function (coded in Visual Fortran as
fwglDeleteContext) does not delete the device context associated with the
OpenGL rendering context through the call to wglMakeCurrent. After calling wglDeleteContext, you must also call DeleteDC to delete the associated
device context.

In the preceding code for WM_CREATE, the call to SetDCPixelFor-
mat(hdc) is made to a user-written subroutine in which the pixel format is
set. The pixel format is a part of the Win32 API, which provides support
for OpenGL. The pixel format is set for a device context with regard to
OpenGL properties such as color (e.g., 24-bit color), whether the window
is to be single- or double-buffered, and the depth (*z*-axis) of the buffer. The
starting point is to fill out a PIXELFORMATDESCRIPTOR and then pass
this structure to the function ChoosePixelFormat. This function returns an
integer index to an available pixel format for the given device context,
which is in turn passed to the function SetPixelFormat. Finally, the function
DescribePixelFormat is called to obtain information on the pixel format
identified by the integer index with regard to an available pixel format. The

following piece of code illustrates the process using a PIXELFORMATDE-SCRIPTOR structure named *pfd*.

```
nPixelFormat = ChoosePixelFormat(hdc, pfd)
bret = SetPixelFormat(hdc, nPixelFormat, pfd)
iret = DescribePixelFormat (hdc, nPixelFormat, 40, pfd)
```

For more information on setting the device context's pixel format, see the online information for SetPixelFormat function, and follow the PIXEL-FORMATDESCRIPTOR link. This can all seem complex, but, in practice, the same piece of code can be used with every application. The following subroutine SetDCPixelFormat has been taken from the OpenGL Cubes example, which ships as part of the Visual Fortran examples. I have saved it in a file called EssentialGL.f90 and used it in all the examples described in this chapter. The subroutine SetDCPixelFormat contains USE statements to include the Visual Fortran OpenGL interface definitions (dfopngl, as in Chapter 15) and the normal Visual Fortran interface definitions (dfwina). Note that dfwina is used instead of dfwin due to the call made to SelectPalette in the subroutine. In addition to setting the pixel format, this subroutine also provides for situations in which a color palette is to be used.

```
subroutine SetDCPixelFormat(hdc)
!DEC$  ATTRIBUTES VALUE :: hdc
use dfwina
use dfopngl
integer(4) hdc
integer(4) hHeap
integer(4) nColors,i
integer(4) iret
integer(4) lpPalette
integer(4) ibyRedmask, ibyGreenMask,ibyBlueMask
integer(4) nPixelFormat
BYTE  byRedMask, byGreenMask, byBlueMask
type(T_LOGPALETTE)  logpal
type(T_PIXELFORMATDESCRIPTOR)    pfd
type(T_PALETTEENTRY)   palette(256)
logical(4)  bret
    DATA pfd / T_PIXELFORMATDESCRIPTOR (  &
        sizeof(PIXELFORMATDESCRIPTOR), &
        1,                    IOR(PFD_DRAW_TO_WINDOW , &
                              IOR(PFD_SUPPORT_OPENGL, &
                              PFD_DOUBLEBUFFER)), &
                              PFD_TYPE_RGBA, &
        24,                   &
        0, 0, 0, 0, 0, 0,     &
        0, 0,                 &
        0, 0, 0, 0, 0,        &
```

```
                    32,                  &
                    0,                   &
                    0,                   &
                    PFD_MAIN_PLANE,      &
                    0,                   &
                    0, 0, 0              &
              ) /
          nPixelFormat = ChoosePixelFormat(hdc, pfd)
          bret = SetPixelFormat(hdc, nPixelFormat, pfd)
          iret = DescribePixelFormat (hdc, nPixelFormat, 40, pfd)
          if (IAND(pfd%dwFlags , PFD_NEED_PALETTE)) then
              nColors = ISHL(1, pfd%cColorBits)
              hHeap = GetProcessHeap()
              lpPalette = HeapAlloc (hHeap, 0, 8 + (nColors * 4))
              logpal%palVersion = #300
              logpal%palNumEntries = nColors
              logPal%palPalEntry(1) = palette(1)
              byRedMask   = ISHL(1, pfd%cRedBits) - 1
              ibyRedMask = byRedMask
              byGreenMask = ISHL(1, pfd%cGreenBits) - 1
              ibyGreenMask = byGreenMask
              byBlueMask  = ISHL(1, pfd%cBlueBits) - 1
              ibyBlueMask = byBlueMask
              byRedMask = ibyRedMask
              byGreenMask = ibyGreenMask
              byBlueMask = ibybluemask
              do i = 1, nColors
                 palette(i)%peRed = (IAND((ISHL(i , &
                         -pfd%cRedShift)),  &
                         byRedMask) * 255) / byRedMask
                         ibyRedMask = palette(i)%peRed
                 palette(i)%peGreen =(IAND((ISHL(i , &
                         -pfd%cGreenShift)), &
                         byGreenMask) * 255) / byGreenMask
                         ibyGreenMask = palette(i)%peGreen
                 palette(i)%peBlue = (IAND((ISHL(i , &
                         -pfd%cBlueShift)), &
                         byBlueMask) * 255) / byBlueMask
                         ibyBlueMask = palette(i)%peBlue
              end do
              call CopyMemory (lpPalette, LOC(logpal),8 + &
                          (nColors * 4))
              hPalette = CreatePalette (logpal)
              if (hPalette .NE. NULL) then
                  i = SelectPalette (hdc, hPalette, .FALSE.)
                  i = RealizePalette (hdc)
              end if
          end if
      end
```

The MainWndProc for an OpenGL application will contain all the normal messages to create, destroy, size, or paint a window. We have already considered how to create and destroy a window, and now we need to look at sizing and painting a window. Then we will be looking at two new palette messages. First, we look at the following typical OpenGL WM_SIZE message:

```
case (WM_SIZE)
   ! Redefine the viewing volume and the viewport when
   ! the window size changes.
   glnWidth = LOWORD(lParam)
   glnHeight = HIWORD(lParam)
   call fglMatrixMode(GL_PROJECTION)
   call fglLoadIdentity()
   call fgluOrtho2D( DBLE(0.0),DBLE(8.0),DBLE(0.0),&
                     DBLE(8.0))
   call fglViewport(0, 0, glnWidth, glnHeight)
   MainWndProc = 0
   return
```

The contents of the WM_SIZE message are very similar to the statements found in the ReshapeFunction routine used in the AUX applications of Chapter 15. The main difference is that we have called the function glMatrixMode, which is used to specify which matrix is the current matrix. In the preceding code, the function glMatrixMode is used with the argument GL_PROJECTION, to set the projection matrix as the current matrix. The three possible choices of arguments for glMatrixMode are listed in Table 16.1.

In the foregoing case, the function glMatrixMode, with the argument GL_PROJECTION and the identify matrix, is loaded to reset the projection matrix and then the function gluOrtho2D is used to define a new 2D orthographic projection matrix. The sequence of events in the above WM_SIZE message should serve for all occasions; the main differences will

Table 16.1   *Matrix Mode Symbolic Constants*

Symbolic Constants	Subsequent matrix operations will apply to the
GL_MODELVIEW	Modelview matrix stack.
GL_PROJECTION	Projection matrix stack.
GL_TEXTURE	Texture matrix stack.

Table 16.2   *Projection Functions*

Projection Functions	Multiply the current matrix by a
gluOrtho2D	2D orthographic projection matrix.
GlOrtho	3D orthographic projection matrix.
GluPerspective	Perspective projection matrix.
GlFrustum	Projection matrix.

relate to which of the projections we choose to use. The available options are listed in Table 16.2.

In our OpenGL examples we use the first three projections, and readers should have no difficulty in developing applications using glFrustum. Further information on these projection matrices can be found in the online Platform SDK documentation for the OpenGL routines.

As with any Win32 application, all the drawing is performed within a WM_PAINT message, as follows:

```
case (WM_PAINT)
  ! Draw the scene
  iret = BeginPaint (hwnd, ps)
  call DrawScene (hdc, nAngle)
  bret = EndPaint (hwnd, ps)
  MainWndProc = 0
  return
```

The subroutine SetDCPixelFormat described previously makes provision for situations in which a color palette is to be used, but we also need to include in MainWndProc, the following two window messages, which relate specifically to palettes.

The first of these is the WM_QUERYNEWPALETTE message, which informs a window that it is about to receive the keyboard focus, and, in doing so, it provides the window with an opportunity to realize its logical palette when it receives the focus. Once an application's window has the focus and the application calls the function RealizePalette, the system will attempt to realize the maximum possible number of requested colors. The following code fragment shows its use:

```
case (WM_QUERYNEWPALETTE)
  ! If the program is using a color palette,
  ! realize the palette and update the client
  ! area when the windows receives the
```

```
    ! input focus.
    if (hPalette .NE. NULL) then
        n = RealizePalette (hdc)
        if (n) then
            bret = InvalidateRect (hwnd, NULL_RECT, .FALSE.)
        end if
        MainWndProc = n
        return
    end if
```

The WM_PALETTECHANGED message is sent to all top-level and overlapped windows after the window with the keyboard focus has realized its logical palette and, hence, has changed the system palette. This message enables any window without keyboard focus that uses a color palette to realize its logical palette and update its client area. The UpdateColors function is called after a WM_PALETTECHANGED message is received to update the client area of the specified device context by remapping the current colors in the client area to the currently realized logical palette. The code is used as follows:

```
case (WM_PALETTECHANGED)
    ! If the program is using a color palette, realize
    ! the palette and update the colors in the client area
    ! when another program realizes its palette.
    if ((hPalette .NE. NULL) .AND. (wParam .NE. hwnd)) then
        if (RealizePalette (hdc)) then
            bret = UpdateColors (hdc)
        end if
        MainWndProc = 0
    end if
```

The background of a window is erased and repainted with the class background brush (specified in the function WinMain for the hbrBackground member of the WNDCLASS structure) every time it is resized. This action can produce an annoying flicker when resizing OpenGL applications that have colored backgrounds or that are displaying large colored objects. The way to avoid the annoying flicker is for the application to process the WM_ERASEBKGND message and return a non-zero background. This indicates to the operating system that the application is responsible for erasing the background and that no further erasing is needed. Here is the code used:

```
case (WM_ERASEBKGND)
    ! Prevent flickering during resizing
    MainWnd Proc = .true.
    return
```

Now that we know how to create an OpenGL window for rendering, let's start exploring the possibilities.

16.2 OpenGL vendor and version

It is often useful to get information about the implementation of OpenGL on the current computer, and this is easily done with the function glGet-String using the following syntax:

```
lpstring =fglGetString(GL_VENDOR)
```

Any one of the four symbolic constants listed in Table 16.3 can be passed as the argument to glGetString, and the function will return a pointer to a string that contains information about the requested item.

When an error is generated, glGetString returns zero. A similar function, gluGetString, is used to get a string that describes the GLU version number or supported GLU extension calls. This function returns a pointer to a static, NULL-terminated string. The two symbolic constants used with the gluGetString function are:

- GLU_VERSION—Used to obtain the GLU version number.

- GLU_EXTENSIONS—Used to obtain a list of supported GLU extensions.

In our first example, which is called AboutOpenGL, a dialog box is used to display the information returned by the glGetString and gluGetString functions. A typical output is shown in Figure 16.1; the details displayed will depend on the graphics card and driver that is installed on the

Table 16.3 *Symbolic Constants Used with the glGetString Function*

Symbolic Constant	Use to obtain
GL_VENDOR	the company responsible for this OpenGL implementation.
GL_RENDERER	the name of the renderer. This is specific to a particular configuration of a hardware platform.
GL_VERSION	a version or release number.
GL_EXTENSIONS	a space-separated list of supported extensions to OpenGL.

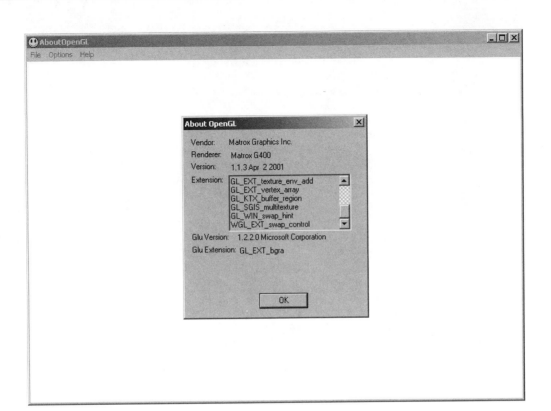

Figure 16.1   *Information about OpenGL drivers used.*

computer. The function AboutOpenGLDlgProc listed below is used to create the dialog box and display the information. This is the code listing:

```
integer(4) function AboutOpenGLDlgProc( hDlg, message, &
            uParam, lParam )
!DEC$ ATTRIBUTES STDCALL,DECORATE,ALIAS : &
            'AboutOpenGLDlgProc' :: AboutOpenGLDlgProc
use dfopngl
use dfwin
implicit none
integer(4) hDlg
integer(4) message
integer(4) uParam
integer(4) lParam
include 'resource.fd'
! Variables
character(256) szName,szRenderer,szVersion,szExtensions
character(256) szGluVersion,szGluExtensions
pointer(lpstring1,szName)
```

```
pointer(lpstring2,szRenderer)
pointer(lpstring3,szVersion)
pointer(lpstring4,szExtensions)
pointer(lpstring5,szGluVersion)
pointer(lpstring6,szGluExtensions)
integer(4) iret
   select case (message)
      case (WM_INITDIALOG)
         call CenterWindow (hDlg, GetWindow (hDlg,GW_OWNER))
         lpstring1 =fglGetString(GL_VENDOR)
         lpstring2 =fglGetString(GL_RENDERER)
         lpstring3 =fglGetString(GL_VERSION)
         lpstring4 =fglGetString(GL_EXTENSIONS)
         iret=  SetDlgItemText(hDlg,IDC_OPENGL_VENDOR, &
                   szName)
         iret=  SetDlgItemText(hDlg,IDC_OPENGL_RENDERER, &
                   szRenderer)
         iret=  SetDlgItemText(hDlg,IDC_OPENGL_VERSION, &
                   szVersion)
         iret=  SetDlgItemText(hDlg,IDC_OPENGL_EXTENSIONS, &
                   szExtensions)
         lpstring5 =fgluGetString(GLU_VERSION)
         lpstring6 =fgluGetString(GLU_EXTENSIONS)
         iret=  SetDlgItemText(hDlg,IDC_GLU_VERSION, &
                   szGluVersion)
         iret=  SetDlgItemText(hDlg,IDC_GLU_EXTENSIONS, &
                   szGluExtensions)
         AboutOpenGLDlgProc = 1
         return
      case (WM_COMMAND)
         if (LOWORD(uParam) .EQ. IDOK) then
            iret = EndDialog(hDlg, TRUE)
            AboutOpenGLDlgProc = 1
            return
         end if
   end select
   AboutOpenGLDlgProc = 0
   return
end
```

Note: In the preceding code, the line beginning with !DEC$ ATTRIBUTES
is a compiler directive and is shown with the Fortran continuation sign (&)
at the end of the line, indicating that the code continues onto a second line.
This is for typographical convenience only. If you type these lines, they
must be entered as a single line.

16.3 Bitmap fonts

Writing text in an OpenGL window is a more complicated process than using text in Win32, because we need to create glyphs (letters and characters) as bitmaps. This very daunting task is made simple through the function wglUseFontBitmap, which generates the appropriate bitmaps from the currently selected font. Each character (font bitmap) is contained in a single display list. The basic steps to be followed are as follows:

- Select the required font using the GDI32 function SelectObject.

- Create glyph (bitmap) display lists using wglUseFontBitmaps.

- Specify the start of the glyph display lists using the function glListBase.

- Position the start of text using the function glRasterPos.

- Write the required text using the glCallLists function.

- Delete the display lists using glDeleteLists when finished using them.

In this code fragment, the system font is selected as the device context's selected font; bitmap display lists are created of glyph images in the range ASCII 0 to 255; the desired text is displayed at a specified location on the screen; and, finally, the display lists are deleted:

```
! Make the system font the device context's selected font.
bret = SelectObject(hdc, GetStockObject (SYSTEM_FONT))
! Create the bitmap display lists, make images of glyphs
! 0-255.
! The display list numbering starts at 1000, an arbitrary
! choice.
bret = fwglUseFontBitmaps(hdc, 0, 255, 1000)
! Specify the start of glyph display lists.
call fglListBase (1000)
! Specify starting position for displaying the text.
Call fglRasterPos3d(2.0,4.0,0.0)
Text = 'Hello World from OpenGL'
! Now write the text to screen.
call fglCallLists (LEN_TRIM(text), GL_UNSIGNED_BYTE, &
                   loc(Text))
! Delete the display lists when finished using them.
call fglDeleteLists(1000,255)
```

Every font that we want to use must be created as a set of display lists following the above procedures. For example, if we wished to use some bold characters in addition to normal characters, we need to create a bold font version of the normal font. This also applies if we need italic characters or

Figure 16.2   *Using a variety of bitmap fonts in OpenGL.*

characters of a different font size. The use of multiple fonts is demonstrated in the HelloGL1 example. In this example, four fonts are created from two font sizes (40 and 60) with normal and italic versions of each size. Four symbolic constants—FontLarge, FontLargeItalic, FontHuge, and Font-HugeItalic with values of 1,000, 2,000, 3,000, and 4,000—are declared as global parameters. These symbolic constants are used to define the starting base for each font. Each font is created by calling the MakeFont routine from WM_CREATE, as follows:

```
case (WM_CREATE)
    ! Create a rendering context.
    hdc = GetDC(hwnd)
    call SetDCPixelFormat(hdc)
    hrc = fwglCreateContext(hdc)
    bret = fwglMakeCurrent(hdc, hrc)
    call fglClearColor(0.9, 0.8, 0.6, 1.0)
    size = 40
    italic = .false.
```

```
        call MakeFont (hdc, FontLarge, size, italic)
        size = 40
        italic = .true.
        call MakeFont (hdc, FontLargeItalic, size, italic)
        size = 60
        italic = .false.
        call MakeFont (hdc, FontHuge, size, italic)
        size = 60
        italic = .true.
        call MakeFont (hdc, FontHugeItalic, size, italic)
        MainWndProc = 0
        return
```

A typical screen display is shown in Figure 16.2. The MakeFont routine
is used to create a font according to values passed to it for the arguments
size and italic. The font bitmaps are stored in a display list starting at the
number specified by the argument FontBase. The is the code for MakeFont:

```
subroutine MakeFont(hdc,FontBase, size, italic)
use gdi32
use dfopngl
use HelloGL1Globals
implicit none
integer(4) hdc
logical(4) bret
integer(4) size
logical(4) italic
integer(4) oldfont,fonts
integer(4) iret
integer(4) FontBase
    fonts = CreateFont(      &
    size,                    &   ! Height Of Font
    0,                       &   ! Width Of Font
    0,                       &   ! Angle Of Escapement
    0,                       &   ! Orientation Angle
    FW_NORMAL,               &   ! Font Weight
    italic,                  &   ! Italic
    .FALSE.,                 &   ! Underline
    .FALSE.,                 &   ! Strikeout
    ANSI_CHARSET,            &   ! Character Set Identifier
    OUT_TT_PRECIS,           &   ! Output Precision
    CLIP_MASK,               &   ! Clipping Precision
    ANTIALIASED_QUALITY,     &   ! Output Quality
    ior(FF_DONTCARE,DEFAULT_PITCH), &  ! Family And Pitch
    'Times New Roman'C )                ! Font Name
    oldfont = SelectObject(hDC, fonts)  ! Selects The Font
                                        ! We Want
    ! the display list numbering starts at FontBase
```

```
      bret = fwglUseFontBitmaps(hdc, 0, 255,FontBase)
      ! restore old font
      iret = SelectObject(hdc, oldfont)
   end
```

The routine DrawScene is used to write the words "Hello World from OpenGL" in the four different fonts. Note that the text is positioned using the raster positioning function glRasterPos. The following is a listing of the routine:

```
subroutine DrawScene (hdc)
use gdi32
use dfopngl
use HelloGL1Globals
implicit none
integer(4) hdc
logical(4) bret
integer(4) oldfont,fonts
character(50) text
   call fglColor3f(1.0, 0.0, 1.0)   ! Magenta
   call fglListBase (FontLarge)     ! start of glyph display
                                    ! lists
   call fglClear(GL_COLOR_BUFFER_BIT )
   Call fglRasterPos3d(1.0,6.0,0.0)
   Text = 'Hello World from OpenGL'
   call fglCallLists (LEN_TRIM(text), GL_UNSIGNED_BYTE, &
         loc(Text))
   call fglListBase (FontLargeItalic)! start of glyph &
         display lists
   Call fglRasterPos3d(1.0,5.0,0.0)
   Text = 'Hello World from OpenGL'
   call fglCallLists (LEN_TRIM(text), GL_UNSIGNED_BYTE, &
            loc(Text))
   call fglColor3f(0.0, 0.0, 1.0)   ! Blue
   call fglListBase (FontHugh)! start of glyph display lists
   Call fglRasterPos3d(1.0,4.0,0.0)
   Text = 'Hello World from OpenGL'
   call fglCallLists (LEN_TRIM(text), GL_UNSIGNED_BYTE, &
            loc(Text))
   call fglListBase (FontHughItalic)! start of glyph &
            display lists
   Call fglRasterPos3d(1.0,3.0,0.0)
   Text = 'Hello World from OpenGL'
   call fglCallLists (LEN_TRIM(text), GL_UNSIGNED_BYTE, &
            loc(Text))
   bret = SwapBuffers(hdc)
end
```

> **Note:** When the raster position is clipped, the specified position becomes invalid. Consequently, any text whose starting position is defined by a clipped raster position will not be displayed.

16.4   TrueType fonts

Bitmap fonts are raster fonts, and they serve well for displaying text on the screen. However, if you want to label the *y*-axis of a graph with the letters oriented in a vertical direction, you need fonts that can be manipulated with the normal OpenGL vector functions. This is where the function wglUseFontOutlines is very useful; not only can the fonts be translated and rotated, but you can create three-dimensional characters by extruding the font in the *z* direction. The use of wglUseFontOutlines is restricted to True-Type fonts only; it will not work with stroke and raster fonts. This function is used to create display lists of the currently selected font. Each display list describes a glyph outline in floating-point coordinates. Each display list consists of either line segments or polygons, and, as with raster font display lists, it has a unique identifying number, which is an offset from the list base number.

The function wglUseFontOutlines requires a pointer to a GLYPHMET-RICSFLOAT structure. A GLYPHMETRICSFLOAT contains information about the placement and orientation of each glyph in a character cell. Fortunately, Win32 fills in all the details. and all we need to do is declare a GLYPHMETRICSFLOAT structure and pass its location to wglUse-FontOutlines. Readers seeking more information on either the wglUse-FontOutlines function or the GLYPHMETRICSFLOAT structure are encouraged to consult the online documentation.

> **Note:** The routine MakeFont listed below will not compile in the current version of CVF 6.6 because of the duplicate declarations of the GLYPH-METRICS structure. You will need to remove one of the duplicate declarations before you can compile this routine and run the program. The simplest way is to add the directive ignore =>T_GLYPHMETRICSFLOAT to the line USE DFOPNGL. The alternative method is to remove the definition for TYPE T_GLYPHMETRICSFLOAT from DFOPNGLT.F90 and recompile the code. If you choose to follow this approach, I recommend that you save a copy of the original code (.f90 and mod files) before you make any

modifications to DFOPNGLT.F90. That way you will be able to recover the situation if your modifications do not work out as expected. The symbolic constants WGL_FONT_LINES and WGL_FONT_POLYGONS are also duplicated, but this is not a problem since you can use their values instead, which are 0 and 1, respectively.

The following MakeFont routine is used in the HelloGL2 example to create two extruded TrueType fonts; one is a solid font constructed from polygons, and the other is an outline font constructed from line segments:

```
subroutine MakeFont(hdc)
use gdi32
use dfopngl
use dfopngl, ignore =>T_GLYPHMETRICSFLOAT
use HelloGL2Globals
implicit none
integer(4) hdc
logical(4) bret
integer(4) oldfont,fonts
integer(4) iret
type (T_GLYPHMETRICSFLOAT) gmf(1:256)
    FontBaseSolid = fglGenLists(256)
    FontBaseOutline = fglGenLists(256)
    fonts = CreateFont( &
        -12, &                        ! Height Of Font
        0, &                          ! Width Of Font
        0, &                          ! Angle Of Escapement
        0, &                          ! Orientation Angle
        FW_NORMAL, &                  ! Font Weight
        .FALSE., &                    ! Italic
        .FALSE., &                    ! Underline
        .FALSE., &                    ! Strikeout
        ANSI_CHARSET, &               ! Character Set Identifier
        OUT_TT_PRECIS, &              ! Output Precision
        CLIP_MASK, &                  ! Clipping Precision
        ANTIALIASED_QUALITY, &        ! Output Quality
        ior(FF_DONTCARE,DEFAULT_PITCH), &  ! Family And Pitch
        'Times New Roman'C ) ! Font Name
    oldfont = SelectObject(hDC, fonts) ! Selects The Font
                                       ! We Want
    iret = fwglUseFontOutlines( &
        hDC, & ! Select The Current DC
        1,   & ! Starting Character
        256, & ! Number Of Display Lists To Build
        FontBaseSolid, & ! Starting Display Lists
        1.0, & ! Deviation From The True Outlines
        1.40, & ! Font Thickness In The Z Direction
```

```
              ! use 1 and not WGL_FONT_POLYGONS in next line
              ! due to duplicate declarations in CVF files
              1,    & ! Use Polygons: Use 0 for Lines
              loc(gmf))
      iret = fwglUseFontOutlines(  &
          hDC,  & ! Select The Current DC
          1,    & ! Starting Character
          256,  & ! Number Of Display Lists To Build
          FontBaseOutline, & ! Starting Display Lists
          1.0,  & ! Deviation From The True Outlines
          1.40, & ! Font Thickness In The Z Direction
          ! use 0 and not WGL_FONT_LINES  in next line
          ! due to duplicate declarations in CVF files
          0,    & ! create font as lines
          loc(gmf))
      ! restore old font
      iret = SelectObject(hdc, oldfont)
end
```

Hidden surface removal

Every pixel to be drawn is allocated a value, referred to as the z value, to indicate the distance from the viewer's perspective. The higher the value, the closer the pixel is to the viewer. When any pixels are to be drawn at the same location, the z values for each pixel will be checked, and the one with a higher z value will be displayed, since it will be closer to the viewer. This process of depth testing is enabled and disabled by calling glEnable and glDisable and using GL_DEPTH_TEST as the argument. Initially, depth testing is disabled. The glDepthFunc function is used to specify the function used to compare each incoming pixel's z value with the z value present in the depth buffer. The online documentation contains a list of the symbolic constants that may be used. The depth buffer can be cleared using the function glClearDepth and specifying a clear value. Clear values are clamped to be in the range 0 to 1. Here is a short code fragment from HelloGL2 to illustrate the use:

```
call fglClearDepth(1.0) ! Enables Clearing Of The Depth
                        ! Buffer
call fglDepthFunc(GL_LESS)  ! The Type Of Depth Test To Do
call fglEnable(GL_DEPTH_TEST) ! Enables Depth Testing
```

The output from HelloGL2 is shown in Figure 16.3. The subroutine for drawing the text is a modified version of that used in the HelloGL1 example. Text created with this type of font is positioned with Cartesian coordinates, and it can be manipulated using any of the vector transformations. In this example, the functions glRotate and glTranslate are used to cause the

Figure 16.3   *Extruded TrueType font.*

text to rotate about its center, and the size of the text is controlled using the function glScale. This function can be used to individually adjust the height, width, and depth of the font characters. Two choices of font are offered—solid and outline. Here is the updated listing for DrawScene:

```
subroutine DrawScene (hdc)
use gdi32
use dfopngl
use HelloGL2Globals
implicit none
integer(4) hdc, i
logical(4) bret
character(50) text
    call fglColor3f(1.0,0.5,0.5)
    call fglClearColor(1.0, 1.0, 1.0, 0.2)
    if(wireframe  == .true.) then
       call fglListBase (FontBaseOutline-1)
    else
       call fglListBase (FontBaseSolid-1)
```

```
      end if
      do i = 1, 360
         ! Clear The Screen And The Depth Buffer
         call fglClear(ior(GL_COLOR_BUFFER_BIT, &
             GL_DEPTH_BUFFER_BIT))
         call fglLoadIdentity()              ! Reset The View
         call fglRotatef(30,1.0,0.0,0.0) ! Rotate On The X Axis
         call fglRotatef(20,0.0,1.0,0.0) ! Rotate On The Y Axis
         call fglRotatef(i,0.0,0.0,1.0)  ! Rotate On The Z Axis
         call fglTranslatef(scale*(-5.0), 0.0, 0.0)
         call fglScalef(scale*1.0,scale*2.0,scale*1.0)
         ! Print GL Text To The Screen
         Text = 'Hello World from OpenGL'
         ! Now draw the text
         call fglCallLists(LEN_TRIM(text), GL_UNSIGNED_BYTE, &
             loc(text))
         bret = SwapBuffers(hdc)
      end do
   end
```

16.5   Three-dimensional shapes

In OpenGL we have only a small set of two-dimensional primitives, such as points, lines, rectangles, and polygons, and we must use these primitives when we want to construct three-dimensional shapes. A simple shape such as a cube is constructed using six polygons, quads, or rectangles to form the sides, while an object such as a dodecahedron would be constructed from 12 five-sided polygons.

When the vertices of a polygon are specified in a clockwise order, they are said to have a clockwise winding; conversely, when the vertices are specified in a counterclockwise direction, they have a counterclockwise winding. By default, in OpenGL, the front face of a polygon will have a counterclockwise winding. The function glFrontFace can be used to define whether the front face of a polygon has clockwise or counterclockwise windings. Passing the symbolic constant GL_CCW sets counterclockwise polygons as front facing; and the symbolic constant GL_CW sets clockwise polygons as front facing. The following line causes the front face of polygons to be defined as clockwise from this point on:

```
call fglFrontFace(GL_CW)
```

Although it may seem rather academic whether the front face of a polygon is drawn counterclockwise or clockwise, it is a very useful feature as we will now discover. Consider drawing a cube composed of opaque surfaces;

quite clearly we expect to see the front face of the cube, but we would not expect to see the face that is opposite the current front face of the cube. With no problems from the visibility side, we can enable the depth buffer and only the front face will be drawn. However, the face that is not drawn is a back-facing polygon, and it has to go through the rendering stage before being rejected. If we can eliminate these invisible polygons from the rendering process, the time to draw an image will be reduced significantly. The technique is to cull all polygons that we know will not be visible, and in this example, we should cull all polygons that are back facing. You can enable and disable the elimination of back-facing polygons with glEnable and glDisable passing GL_CULL_FACE as the argument. The default faces to be culled are back-facing polygons, but you can use the function glCullFace with either of the symbolic constants GL_FRONT or GL_BACK to define the faces you want culled.

```
call fglEnable(GL_CULL_FACE)
call fglCullFace(GL_BACK)
```

In the example Cube, a simple cube shape is constructed from Quads, each of the six sides being allocated a different color using the following code to create the cube:

```
subroutine CreateScene ()
use dfopngl
use Cube1Globals
real(4) size
   size = 1.0
   call fglEnable(GL_CULL_FACE)
   call fglCullFace(GL_BACK)
   call fglFrontFace(GL_CCW)
   call fglNewList (DRAWCUBE, GL_COMPILE)
      call fglBegin(GL_QUADS)
         call fglColor3f(0.0,0.0,1.0)    !Front face
         call fglVertex3f(size, size, size)
         call fglVertex3f(-size, size, size)
         call fglVertex3f(-size, -size, size)
         call fglVertex3f(size, -size, size)
         call fglColor3f(1.0,0.5,0.0)       ! Back face
         call fglNormal3f (0.0, 0.0, -size)
         call fglVertex3f(size, size, -size)
         call fglVertex3f(size, -size, -size)
         call fglVertex3f(-size, -size, -size)
         call fglVertex3f(-size, size, -size)
         call fglColor3f(1.0,0.0,0.0)   ! Left face
         call fglVertex3f(-size, size, size)
         call fglVertex3f(-size, size, -size)
         call fglVertex3f(-size, -size, -size)
```

```
                  call fglVertex3f(-size, -size, size)
                  call fglColor3f(1.0,1.0,0.0)   ! Right face
                  call fglVertex3f(size, size, size)
                  call fglVertex3f(size, -size, size)
                  call fglVertex3f(size, -size, -size)
                  call fglVertex3f(size, size, -size)
                  call fglColor3f(0.0,1.0,1.0)   !  Top face
                  call fglVertex3f(-size, size, -size)
                  call fglVertex3f(-size, size, size)
                  call fglVertex3f(size, size, size)
                  call fglVertex3f(size, size, -size)
                  call fglColor3f(1.0,0.0,1.0)   !  Bottom face
                  call fglVertex3f(-size, -size, -size)
                  call fglVertex3f(size, -size, -size)
                  call fglVertex3f(size, -size, size)
                  call fglVertex3f(-size, -size, size)
            call fglEnd()
      call fglEndList ()
   end
```

For the Cube example, a timer is used to continually provide a new value for the variable *nAngle*, which is used to update the position of the cube. As can be seen in Figure 16.4, the user can select which of the *x*-, *y*-, and *z*-axes the cube is to rotate around. The cube is drawn using the following routine.

```
subroutine DrawScene (hdc, nAngle)
use dfwin
use dfopngl
use Cube1Globals
integer(4)  hdc, nAngle
integer(4) i, j, k
logical(4)  bret
    call fglClearColor(1.0, 1.0, 1.0, 1.0)
    call fglClear(IOR(GL_COLOR_BUFFER_BIT, &
          GL_DEPTH_BUFFER_BIT))
    ! Define the modelview transformation
    call fglMatrixMode(GL_MODELVIEW)
    call fglLoadIdentity()
    call fglTranslatef(0.0, 0.0, -22.0)
    call fglRotatef(10.0, 1.0, 0.0, 0.0)
    call fglRotatef(10.0, 0.0, 1.0, 0.0)
    call fglRotatef(10.0, 0.0, 0.0, 1.0)
    if(RotateX == .true. ) then
       call fglRotatef(REAL(nAngle), 1.0, 0.0, 0.0)
    end if
    if(RotateY == .true. ) then
       call fglRotatef(REAL(nAngle), 0.0, 1.0, 0.0)
    end if
```

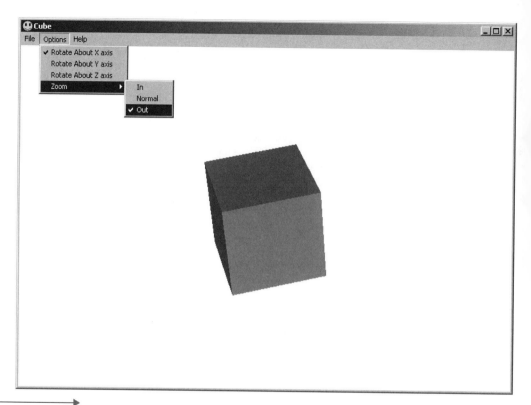

Figure 16.4 *Rotating cube.*

```
        if(RotateZ == .true. ) then
           call fglRotatef(REAL(nAngle), 0.0, 0.0, 1.0)
        end if
        call fglCallList (DRAWCUBE)
        bret = SwapBuffers(hdc)
    end
```

Zoom in and out

The menu in the cube example provides the user with the choice to zoom in
or out on the cube. This feature is easy to include when you use the gluPer-
spective function to define the projection matrix, because it requires only
four arguments: the angle specifying the field of view, the aspect ratio of the
viewing volume, and the distances to the near and far clipping planes.
Changing the field of view angle is the way to create the effect of zooming
in and out of a scene. In the cube example, the projection matrix is created
in WM_SIZE; then, when the relevant menu item is selected, a new field of
view angle is set and a WM_SIZE message is sent to force a redraw using

the new field of view angle. The code used in WM_SIZE to create the projection matrix is as follows:

```
case (WM_SIZE)
    !  Redefine the viewing volume and the viewport when the
    !  window size changes.
    glnWidth = LOWORD(lParam)
    glnHeight = HIWORD(lParam)
    if(glnHeight == 0) glnHeight = 1.0
    gldAspect = DBLE(DBLE(glnWidth) / DBLE(glnHeight))
    call fglMatrixMode(GL_PROJECTION)
    call fglLoadIdentity()
    call fgluPerspective(DBLE(ViewAngle), & ! Field of view
                                            ! angle
    gldAspect,              & ! Aspect ratio of viewing volume
    DBLE(1.0),              & ! Distance to near clipping plane
    DBLE(100.0))             ! Distance to far clipping plane
    call fglViewport(0, 0, glnWidth, glnHeight)
    MainWndProc = 0
    return
```

16.6 Bezier surfaces

Creating a Bezier surface is much like creating the Bezier curve, with the obvious addition of an extra dimension (v) associated with the functions that we use. Therefore, we must define points along both the u and v domains. In the drawing routine, we call glMap2f instead of glMap1f to specify control points along the two domains (u and v). The two-dimensional evaluator is enabled with a call to glEnable just like the one-dimensional evaluator. Then we call glMapGrid2f with the number of divisions in the u and v directions. After the evaluator is set up, we can call the two-dimensional version of glEvalMesh1 to evaluate our surface grid as follows:

```
call fglEvalMesh2(GL_LINE,0,12,0,12) ! mesh of lines
```

In this line of code, a surface mesh of lines is to be created and the u and v domain values are set to range from 0 to 12. The symbolic constants GL_POINTS, GL_LINE, or GL_FILL are used to specify, respectively, a surface of points, lines, or polygons.

In our example, Bezier3d, the control points are the same for the z value, which produces a uniform surface—that is, an extrusion of a Bezier curve along the z-axis. The surface is constructed from three Bezier surfaces, which can be displayed as wireframe or filled polygons. The coordinates of the control points are varied using a timer to generate a wave effect on the surface. Figure 16.5 shows surfaces that are constructed from filled polygons. A very

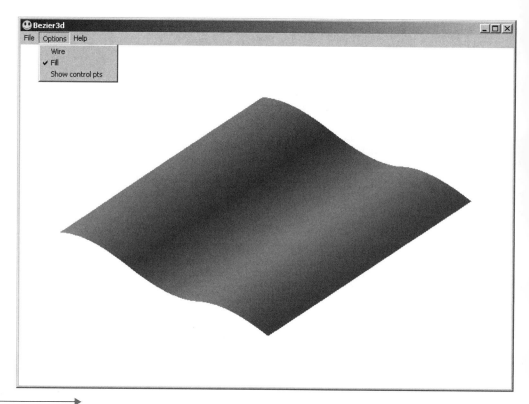

Figure 16.5   *Surface created using three Bezier surfaces.*

useful feature of evaluators is that surface normals can be generated automatically by calling glEnable and passing GL_AUTO_NORMAL as the argument. This is the code used to render the scene:

```
subroutine DrawScene (hdc,ctrPoints1,ctrPoints2,ctrPoints3)
use dfwin
use dfopngl
use Bezier3dGlobals
implicit none
integer(4) hdc
logical(4) bret
integer(4) iret,i,j
real(4) glfMaterialColor(4)
data glfMaterialColor / 0.0, 1.0, 1.0, 1.0 /
real(4), dimension(3,3,3) :: &
   ctrPoints1,ctrPoints2,ctrPoints3
   call fglClearColor(1.0, 1.0, 1.0, 1.0)
   call fglEnable(GL_AUTO_NORMAL)
   call fglMaterialfv (GL_FRONT_AND_BACK, &
         GL_AMBIENT_AND_DIFFUSE, LOC(glfMaterialColor))
```

```fortran
call fglMaterialfv (GL_FRONT_AND_BACK, GL_SPECULAR ,&
      LOC(glfMaterialColor))
call fglMaterialfv(GL_FRONT, GL_SHININESS, loc(180.0))
call fglClear(GL_COLOR_BUFFER_BIT)
call fglMatrixMode(GL_MODELVIEW)
call fglPushMatrix()
! create first bezier surface
call fglMap2f(GL_MAP2_VERTEX_3, 0.0, 12.0,3,3, 0.0, &
   12.0,9,3,loc(ctrPoints1(1,1,1)) )
call fglEnable(GL_MAP2_VERTEX_3)
call fglMapGrid2f(12,0.0,12.0,12,0.0,12.0)
call fglColor3f(0.0, 1.0, 1.0)  ! cyan
! Evaluate the grid, using lines
if ( wireframe == 1 ) then
   call fglEvalMesh2(GL_LINE,0,12,0,12) !mesh of lines
else
   call fglEvalMesh2(GL_FILL,0,12,0,12) ! fill with color
end if
! create second bezier surface
call fglMap2f(GL_MAP2_VERTEX_3, 0.0, 12.0,3,3, 0.0, &
   12.0,9,3,loc(ctrPoints2(1,1,1)) )
call fglEnable(GL_MAP2_VERTEX_3)
call fglMapGrid2f(12,0.0,12.0,12,0.0,12.0)
if ( wireframe == 1 ) then
   call fglEvalMesh2(GL_LINE,0,12,0,12) !mesh of lines
else
   call fglEvalMesh2(GL_FILL,0,12,0,12) ! fill with color
end if
! create third bezier surface
call fglMap2f(GL_MAP2_VERTEX_3, 0.0, 12.0,3,3, 0.0, &
   12.0,9,3,loc(ctrPoints3(1,1,1)))
call fglEnable(GL_MAP2_VERTEX_3)
call fglMapGrid2f(12,0.0,12.0,12,0.0,12.0)
if ( wireframe == 1 ) then
   call fglEvalMesh2(GL_LINE,0,12,0,12) !mesh of lines
else
   call fglEvalMesh2(GL_FILL,0,12,0,12) ! fill with color
end if
if(showcontrolpts == 1) then
   call fglColor3f(1.0, 0.0, 0.0)  ! Red
   call fglPointSize(5.0)
   call fglBegin(GL_POINTS)
   do i = 1,3
      do j = 1, 3
         call fglVertex3f(ctrPoints1(1,j,i), &
           ctrPoints1(2,j,i), ctrPoints1(3,j,i))
         call fglVertex3f(ctrPoints2(1,j,i), &
            ctrPoints2(2,j,i),ctrPoints2(3,j,i))
```

```
            call fglVertex3f(ctrPoints3(1,j,i), &
                ctrPoints3(2,j,i),ctrPoints3(3,j,i))
          end do
        end do
        call fglEnd()
        call fglEnd()
      end if
      call fglPopMatrix()
      call fglFlush()
      bret = SwapBuffers(hdc)
    end
```

16.7   Bitmaps

We have already covered bitmaps in Chapter 10, and now all we need to do is to learn what the differences are between displaying bitmaps using GDI32 and using OpenGL. A bitmap in OpenGL is a pixel that is either zero or one—that is, it is literally a map of pixel bits. Pictures that have pixels with more than two colors are referred to as "images" or sometimes "pix-

Figure 16.6   *Displaying bitmaps in OpenGL.*

maps" (short for pixel maps). The example BitmapGL demonstrates how to load Windows-style 24-bit color bitmaps into memory and display the image on the screen. Once we have loaded the bitmap into memory, we need to swap the red and blue pixels, because OpenGL works with the order BGR and not RGB for displaying images from memory. The following piece of code demonstrates how to swap the red and blue pixels in memory:

```
if ( bits%bmiHeader%biBitCount == 24) then
   iret = InvalidateRect (hwnd, NULL_RECT, .TRUE.)
   bfOffBits=pbmfh%bfOffBits
   pBits = loc(pbmfh) +bfOffBits
   ! swap red and blue in bitmap
   width = bits%bmiHeader%biWidth * 3
   width = int((width + 3) / 4) * 4
   do ny=1,bits%bmiHeader%biHeight
      noffset = (ny-1) * width
      do nx=1,bits%bmiHeader%biWidth
         nred = noffset + (nx-1) * 3  + 1
         nblue = nred + 2
         redpixels = pixels(nred)
         bluepixels = pixels(nblue)
         pixels(nred) = bluepixels
         pixels(nblue) = redpixels
      end do
   end do
else
   pBits = 0
   iret = MessageBox (hWnd,'Current Version supports &
      only 24 bit color bitmaps'C, 'Cannot display this &
      bitmap'C, MB_OK)
   return
   MainWndProc = 0
end if
```

Once the pixel color order has been sorted out, all that remains to do is to draw the image to the screen, as illustrated in Figure 16.6 for the sample bitmap. Note in the following code that the function glPixelTransferf has been used to scale the value of the red, green, and blue pixels. Menu selection items of Bright, Normal, and Dark, which correspond to scale values of 1.3, 1.0, and 0.7, respectively, permit the user to lighten or darken the image displayed. The function glPixelZoom is used to scale the bitmap to fit the available window size. This is the code used to draw the image:

```
subroutine DrawScene (hdc)
use dfwin
use dfopngl
```

```
use BitViewGLGlobals
implicit none
integer(4) hdc
integer(4) iret
integer(4) xoffset,yoffset
integer(4) xsize,ysize
real(4) xscale,yscale
logical(4) bret
type(T_RECT) rect1
   iret = GetClientRect(ghwndMain,rect1)
   call fglViewport(0, 0, rect1.right,rect1.bottom)
   call fglMatrixMode(GL_PROJECTION)
   call fglLoadIdentity()
   call fgluOrtho2D( DBLE(0.0),DBLE(rect1.right- &
            1),DBLE(0.0),DBLE(rect1.bottom-1))
   call fglMatrixMode(GL_MODELVIEW)
   call fglClearColor(1.0, 1.0, 1.0, 1.0)
   call fglClear(GL_COLOR_BUFFER_BIT)
   if (pBits /= 0) then
      xsize = rect1%right
      ysize = int(float(bits%bmiHeader%biHeight * &
            xsize) /float(bits%bmiHeader%biWidth))
      if (ysize > rect1%bottom) then
         ysize = rect1%bottom
         xsize = int(float(bits%bmiHeader%biWidth * &
            ysize) /float(bits%bmiHeader%biHeight))
      end if
      xscale = float(xsize) / float(bits%bmiHeader%biWidth)
      yscale = float(ysize) / float(bits%bmiHeader%biHeight)
      xoffset = int((rect1%right - xsize) * 0.5)
      yoffset = int((rect1%bottom- ysize) * 0.5)
      call fglPixelStorei(GL_UNPACK_ALIGNMENT, 4)
      call fglPixelZoom(xscale, yscale)
      call fglRasterPos2i(xoffset, yoffset)
      call fglPixelTransferf(GL_RED_SCALE, RedScale)
      call fglPixelTransferf(GL_GREEN_SCALE, GreenScale)
      call fglPixelTransferf(GL_BLUE_SCALE, BlueScale)
      call fglDrawPixels(bits%bmiHeader%biWidth, &
        bits%bmiHeader%biHeight, GL_RGB, GL_UNSIGNED_BYTE, &
        pBits)
      call fglFinish()
      bret = SwapBuffers(hdc)
   end if
end
```

The function glReadPixels is used to read a block of pixels from the frame buffer and store the information at a specified location. The arguments used with the function are as follows:

```
glReadPixels(x,y, & ! Window coordinates of the
                   ! lower-left corner of the pixel block
width, height,  &  ! Dimensions of the pixel block to be
                   ! read.
format, & ! Format of pixel data
type, &   ! Type of pixel data
pixels)   ! pointer to where pixel data is to be stored
```

The online documentation lists the alternatives symbolic constants that can be specified for format and type. This is the code used in BitmapGL to obtain the current viewport dimensions, to use these dimensions to capture the screen, and then to swap the red and blue pixels around:

```
integer(4) function CaptureScreen (hwnd)
use dfopngl
use BitViewGLGlobals
implicit none
integer(4) hwnd
integer(4) hFile
integer(4) iret
integer(4) viewport(4)
integer(4) xpixels,ypixels
integer(4) xrow,ycol
integer(4) infosize
integer(4) filesize
integer(4) noffset
integer(4) ny, nx
integer(4) nred,nblue
integer(1) redpixels, bluepixels
integer(4) dwBytesWritten
   ! get viewport dimensions
   call fglGetIntegerv (GL_VIEWPORT, viewport)
   xpixels = viewport(3)
   ypixels = viewport(4)
   xrow = xpixels * 3
   xrow = int((xrow + 3) / 4) * 4
   ycol = ypixels
   imagelength = (4+xrow) * ycol
   ! set bitmap information header values
   bminfoheader%biSize         = sizeof (bminfoheader)
   bminfoheader%biWidth        = xpixels
   bminfoheader%biHeight       = ypixels
   bminfoheader%biPlanes       = 1
   bminfoheader%biBitCount     = 24
   bminfoheader%biCompression  = BI_RGB
   bminfoheader%biSizeImage    = imagelength
   bminfoheader%biXPelsPerMeter = 2952 ! 75 dpi
   bminfoheader%biYPelsPerMeter = 2952 ! 75 dpi
```

```
bminfoheader%biClrUsed       = 0
bminfoheader%biClrImportant  = 0
headersize = sizeof(bmfilehead)
infosize = sizeof(bminfoheader)
filesize = headersize + infosize + imagelength
! set bitmap file header information
bmfilehead%bfType        = 'BM'
bmfilehead%bfSize        = imagelength
bmfilehead%bfReserved1 = 0
bmfilehead%bfReserved2 = 0
bmfilehead%bfOffBits     = headersize + infosize
lpbits = loc(bminfoheader)
! allocate memory for bitmap
pSavebits = malloc(imagelength)
! read pixel information
call fglFinish()
call fglpixelStorei(GL_PACK_ALIGNMENT, 4)
call fglPixelStorei(GL_PACK_ROW_LENGTH, 0)
call fglPixelStorei(GL_PACK_SKIP_ROWS, 0)
call fglPixelStorei(GL_PACK_SKIP_PIXELS, 0)
call fglReadPixels (viewport(1),viewport(2), &
   viewport(3),viewport(4),GL_RGB, &
   GL_UNSIGNED_BYTE,pSavebits)
! swap red and blue in bitmap
do ny=1,ypixels
   noffset = (ny-1) * xrow
   do nx=1,xpixels
      nred = noffset + (nx-1) * 3  + 1
      nblue = nred + 2
      redpixels = SavePixels(nred)
      bluepixels = SavePixels(nblue)
      SavePixels(nred) = bluepixels
      SavePixels(nblue) = redpixels
   end do
end do
CaptureScreen = 1
return
end
```

Once an image has been captured from the screen and stored in memory, BitmapGL uses the techniques developed in Chapter 10 to save the information to a file or send it to a printer for rendering.

The development of this application is left as an exercise for the reader. For example, we used glPixelTransferf to scale the value of the red, green, and blue pixels in step values of 1.3, 1.0, and 0.7 to lighten or darken the image displayed. Using a dialog box and providing three slider controls would give the user greater precision in adjusting the individual balance of colors in an image. By incorporating mouse selection techniques described in Chapter 17, you could create a feature to remove the red eye effect from photographs.

16.8   What is next?

In Chapter 17, we will use the mouse to create interactive OpenGL applications that permit the user to draw selection boxes, join selected points in a grid with lines, and rotate an object by moving the mouse.

17

Interactive OpenGL Applications

17.1 Using a mouse

Many graphics applications, including computer-aided drawing (CAD) programs, computational fluid dynamics programs, and finite element analysis programs, permit the user to interact with the displayed graphics by means of a mouse. Typical interactions include using the mouse to rotate, pan, and zoom the display. Additionally, users can select points to construct objects such as lines, areas, and volumes. In this final chapter, we will learn how to use the mouse for making selections and controlling viewports.

The first example in this chapter, GridView, evolved from the rotating cube example of Chapter 16. In Chapter 16, the rotation of the cube was obtained using a timer to increment the angles of rotation at predetermined intervals of time. For the cube example, it is easy to remove the timer and increment the rotation angles according to whether the mouse is moved from side to side or up and down. When the mouse movement is in the direction of increasing or decreasing x (side to side), the angle of rotation around the z-axis can be incremented or decremented accordingly. The same test is also applied to the y direction (up and down) and the rotation angle around the x-axis is incremented or decremented accordingly. The code required is as follows:

```
case (WM_MOUSEMOVE)
    ix = LOWORD(lParam)
    iy = HIWORD(lParam)
    if(RotateX) then
        if ((iy - oldY) >=0) then
            nAngleX = nAngleX + 2
        else
            nAngleX = nAngleX - 2
        end if
        bret = InvalidateRect (hwnd, NULL_RECT, .FALSE.)
```

```
      end if
      if(RotateZ) then
         if ((ix - oldX) >=0) then
            nAngleZ = nAngleZ + 2
         else
            nAngleZ = nAngleZ - 2
         end if
         bret = InvalidateRect (hwnd, NULL_RECT, .FALSE.)
      end if
      oldX = ix
      oldY = iy
      MainWndProc = 0
      return
```

A cube that can be rotated by moving the mouse is interesting but not very useful. I wanted an application that would not only illustrate the principle but would also provide readers with some ideas for applications; thus, the GridView example was conceived. In Figure 17.1, GridView displays

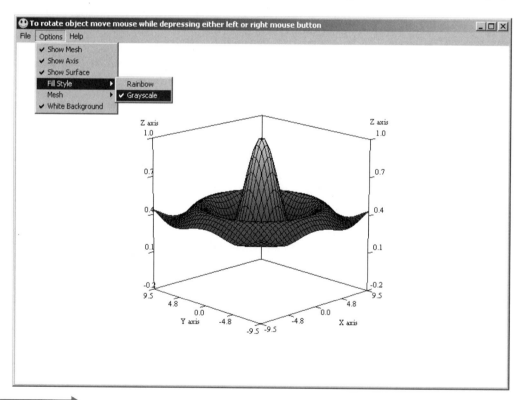

Figure 17.1   *Displaying contour grid information.*

contour-type information for an *x-y* grid. The program creates a two-dimensional *x-y* grid based on given maximum and minimum values of *x* and *y* and then generates *z* elevation data according to a specified function.

The axis is constructed from the three sides of a cube. The zero point for the screen axis is in the center of the cube, and the cube is extended out by unit value in the positive and negative directions for all three axes. A simple routine is used to construct an *x-y* mesh to fit within the cube, and then the *z* elevation is calculated using the following code:

```
do  ix=1,pointsTotal
   Rad = sqrt((x(ix))**2+(y(ix))**2)+0.00001
   z(ix) = sin(Rad)/ Rad
end do
```

Menu items in GridView provide the user with options to display any combination of mesh, axis, and solid surface. The user can also select the mesh density (coarse, medium, or fine), choose between rainbow and gray-scale for fill colors, and select white or wheat (default) as the background color. This is the code used in the routine DrawScene, where the appropriate display lists are called and the rotation angles are updated:

```
subroutine DrawScene (hdc, nAngleX, nAngleY)
use dfwin
use dfopngl
use GridViewGlobals
integer(4)  hdc, nAngleX, nAngleY
logical(4)  bret
   if(WhiteBkgnd == .true.) then
      ! white background
      call fglClearColor(1.0, 1.0, 1.0, 0.50)
   else
      ! set background color to wheat
      call fglClearColor(0.9, 0.8, 0.6, 0.50)
   end if
   call fglClear(IOR(GL_COLOR_BUFFER_BIT, &
               GL_DEPTH_BUFFER_BIT))
   ! Define the modelview transformation
   call fglMatrixMode(GL_MODELVIEW)
   call fglLoadIdentity()
   call fglTranslatef(0.0, 0.0, -25.0)
   call fglRotatef(10.0, 1.0, 0.0, 0.0)
   call fglRotatef(REAL(nAngleX), 1.0, 0.0, 0.0)
   call fglRotatef(REAL(nAngleY), 0.0, 1.0, 0.0)
   if(AxisOn == .true.) then
      call fglCallList (AxisLabels)
   end if
```

```
         if(SurfaceOn == .true.) then
            if(RainbowOn == .true.) then
               call fglCallList (Rainbow)
            else
               call fglCallList (Grayscale)
            end if
         end if
         if(MeshOn == .true.) then
            call fglCallList (Mesh)
         end if
         bret = SwapBuffers(hdc)
      end
```

17.1.1   Rainbow and grayscale colors

The code used to construct the plot and the associated axis is straightforward and does not need to be repeated here. One exception is the routine to create the rainbow and grayscale colors. This useful routine can be used in a variety of applications, and it is worthwhile spending a few moments to understand how it works. The routine creates a range of 60 colors with magenta/red at one end and blue/black at the other end, which corresponds to an RGB value of 1,0,1 for magenta and 0,0,0.1 for blue/black. The three colors, red, green, and blue permit the following six combinations:

- Change magenta to red by reducing the blue value from 1 to 0.
  (RGB(1,0,1) to RGB(1,0,0))

- Change red to yellow by increasing the green from 0 to 1.
  (RGB(1,0,0) to RGB(1,1,0))

- Change yellow to green by decreasing the red from 1 to 0.
  (RGB(1,1,0) to RGB(0,1,0))

- Change green to cyan by increasing the blue from 0 to 1.
  (RGB(0,1,0) to RGB(0,1,1))

- Change cyan to blue by decreasing the green from 1 to 0.
  (RGB(0,1,1) to RGB(0,0,1))

- Change the blue to blue/black by reducing the blue from 1 to 0.
  (RGB(0,0,1) to RGB(0,0,0.1))

The trick is to have two variables, one of which goes from 0 to 1 while the other is going from 1 to 0 for each of these six steps. In GridView, equal increments are used to go from 0 to 1 and 1 to 0. The following code fragment will help to clarify the process:

```
do iloop = 1, ContourNumber
   IndexValue = (6*(1/float(ContourNumber))* iloop)- 0.1
   Iselect =  int(IndexValue)
   ColorValue1 = IndexValue-Iselect
   ColorValue2 = 1-ColorValue1
   Select Case(Iselect)
      CASE(0)
         ! Magenta/Red end
         RedValue    = 1
         GreenValue  = 0
         BlueValue   = ColorValue2
... remaining code omitted
```

When the variable *iloop* is equal to 1 and ContourNumber is set to 60, IndexValue will be 0. The variable *Iselect* will have a value of 0; therefore, ColorValue1 will be equal to 0, ColorValue2 will be equal to 1.0, and hence our starting value for magenta will be RGB(1,0,1). For an iloop value of 60, the IndexValue will be 5.9 and Iselect will have a value of 5. This means that ColorValue1 will be equal to 0.9, and ColorValue2 will be equal to 0.1, which will give a blue value of RGB(0,0,0.1). The colors are stored in the array starting with blue/black in row 1 and finishing with magenta in row 60.

Grayscale is easy to generate, since all RGB colors have the same value. A gray corresponding to RGB(0.3,0.3,0.3) gives a good dark gray, and a good value for a light gray would be RGB(0.9,0.9,0.9). All you need to do is increment the values in equal steps. In GridView the 60 colors are stored in the array ContourColours, which is 60 rows by 8 columns. The first two columns are used to store the minimum and maximum elevation values represented by each color; the next three columns are used to store the color RGB values as well as the final three columns containing the grayscale RGB values. The routine as used in GridView is as follows:

```
subroutine Contour_Colour(ContourColours)
use GridViewGlobals
implicit none
real(8) RedValue, GreenValue, BlueValue
real(8) ColorValue1,ColorValue2,GrayValue
real(8) IndexValue
integer(4) Iselect,Iloop
real(8) ContourColours(ContourNumber,8)
   ContourColours = 0
   do Iloop = 1, ContourNumber
      IndexValue = (6*(1/float(ContourNumber))* iloop )- 0.1
      Iselect =  int(IndexValue)
      ColorValue1 = IndexValue-Iselect
```

```
            ColorValue2 = 1-ColorValue1
            Select Case(Iselect)
               CASE(0)
                  ! Magenta/Red end
                  RedValue    =  1
                  GreenValue  =  0
                  BlueValue   =  ColorValue2
               CASE(1)
                  RedValue    =  1
                  GreenValue  =  ColorValue1
                  BlueValue   =  0
               CASE(2)
                  RedValue    =  ColorValue2
                  GreenValue  =  1
                  BlueValue   =  0
               CASE(3)
                  RedValue    =  0
                  GreenValue  =  1
                  BlueValue   =  ColorValue1
               CASE(4)
                  RedValue    =  0
                  GreenValue  =  ColorValue2
                  BlueValue   =  1
               CASE(5)
                  ! Blue/dark blue end
                  RedValue    =  0
                  GreenValue  =  0
                  BlueValue   =  ColorValue2
            end select
         ContourColours(1+ContourNumber-Iloop,3) = RedValue
         ContourColours(1+ContourNumber-Iloop,4) = GreenValue
         ContourColours(1+ContourNumber-Iloop,5) = BlueValue
         end do
         GrayValue   = 0.3
         do Iloop = 1, ContourNumber
            ContourColours(Iloop,6) = GrayValue
            ContourColours(Iloop,7) = GrayValue
            ContourColours(Iloop,8) = GrayValue
            GrayValue = GrayValue + 0.6/float(ContourNumber)
         end do
      end subroutine Contour_Colour
```

17.1.2   Polygon offset

In GridView, a mesh of unfilled polygons is drawn superimposed on the surface created from filled polygons. The overlapping of these lines and the filled polygons (both share the same Z vertex value) can produce a visual effect known as Z fighting, which results in the lines being only partly visible. OpenGL 1.1 and later versions have a function, glPolygonOffset, that can be used to provide an offset between coplanar polygons.

```
call fglPolygonOffset (factor, units)
```

The first argument factor is used to scale the maximum Z slope with respect to X or Y of the polygon, while the argument's units are used to scale the minimum resolvable depth buffer value. This function, glPolygonOffset, is enabled by:

```
call fglenable(GL_POLYGON_OFFSET_FILL)
```

and is disabled by:

```
call fgldisable(GL_POLYGON_OFFSET_FILL)
```

In GridView, both factor and units are set to 1.0 (values may be positive or negative), and the polygon offset is enabled for fill mode. The surface is constructed first from polygons drawn in fill mode, and then the polygons are redrawn in line mode.

Note: The glPolygonOffset can be used only with polygons; it cannot be used with lines (e.g., GL_LINES) and points (GL_POINTS).

The GridView example is a simple application with scope for further development. Consider the splitter view example in Chapter 11; GridView could be incorporated into a splitter window application with a list view as the other window. The values generated by the function could be displayed in the list view. With a little bit of work, it would be possible to let the user enter in a function for z in terms of x and y, then parse the user input, and, finally, plot the function.

17.2 Rubber banding

Rubber banding is the name given to the operation for drawing a single line or rectangle in such a way that one end of the line or a corner of the rectangle follows the movement of the mouse cursor. We have already demonstrated the principal of rubber banding to create a selection box in Chapter 3 with the QuickWin example Select. Now, all we need to do is find out how it is done in OpenGL. As in the QuickWin example, we draw a line, and, when a new line needs to be drawn, we rub out the old line by XOR-ing a line over the old line and drawing our new line at the desired location.

In OpenGL, the following functions are used first to enable logical drawing operations, then to specify the required logical operation, and, finally, to turn off the logical operation:

```
call fglEnable(GL_COLOR_LOGIC_OP)
call fglLogicOp(GL_XOR)
call fglDisable(GL_COLOR_LOGIC_OP)
```

The symbolic constants for other logical operations are listed in the online documentation for glLogicOp. The application SelectionBox demonstrates how easy it is to use rubber-banding methods to create a selection box in OpenGL. In this example, the mouse coordinates are displayed in the top of the window, and, when the left mouse button is released, a yellow rectangle is drawn. Figure 17.2 shows a selection box being created by the application. One use for a selection box would be to incorporate it into the bitmap example from Chapter 16 and use the box to select a part of the displayed bitmap that is to be enlarged, sent to the printer, or saved. The fol-

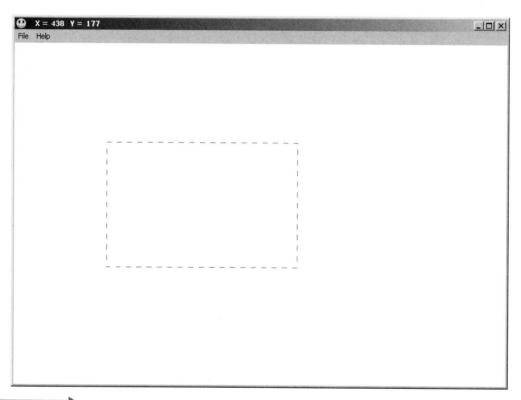

Figure 17.2   *Selection box created using OpenGL.*

lowing code fragment shows how the mouse actions are coordinated to produce the rubber-banding effect:

```
case (WM_LBUTTONDOWN)
    box = .true.
    iret = setcapture(0)
    call fglEnable(GL_COLOR_LOGIC_OP)
    call fglLogicOp(GL_XOR)
    MouseX = LOWORD(lParam)
    MouseY = glnHeight  - HIWORD(lParam)
    xstart = MouseX
    ystart = MouseY
    MainWndProc = 0
    return
case (WM_LBUTTONUP)
    box = .false.
    iret = releasecapture()
    call fglDisable(GL_COLOR_LOGIC_OP)
    xend = LOWORD(lParam)
    yend = glnHeight - HIWORD(lParam)
    bret = InvalidateRect (hwnd, NULL_RECT, .FALSE.)
    MainWndProc = 0
    return
case (WM_MOUSEMOVE)
    MouseX = LOWORD(lParam)
    MouseY = glnHeight - HIWORD(lParam)
    if(box == .true.) then
        call fglLineWidth(1.2)
        call fglEnable(GL_LINE_STIPPLE)
        call fglLineStipple(2,#ofof)
        call fglColor3d(0.5, 0.5, 0.5)
        call fglBegin(GL_LINE_LOOP)
            call fglVertex3f(xstart,ystart,0.0)
            call fglVertex3f(MouseX,ystart,0.0)
            call fglVertex3f(MouseX,MouseY,0.0)
            call fglVertex3f(xstart,MouseY,0.0)
        call fglEnd()
        iret = swapbuffers(hdc)
        call fglBegin(GL_LINE_LOOP)
            call fglVertex3f(xstart,ystart,0.0)
            call fglVertex3f(MouseX,ystart,0.0)
            call fglVertex3f(MouseX,MouseY,0.0)
            call fglVertex3f(xstart,MouseY,0.0)
        call fglEnd()
        write(text,'(4x,"X = ",I4,3x,"Y = ",I4)')MouseX,MouseY
        iret = SetWindowText(hwnd, text//' 'C)
    end if
    MainWndProc = 0
    return
```

17.3 Picking

A very useful feature is the ability to pick an object using the mouse. It may be just to select a point displayed on a graph and query the value, or it could be points in a CAD drawing that we want to connect with a series of lines. OpenGL provides a selection mode to automatically track all objects drawn within a specified region of the window. This selection mode, together with some additional code, enables an application to identify which object a user has picked (selected).

OpenGL has three rendering modes, which are set by calling the function glRenderMode(mode). The argument mode may be one of the following symbolic constants:

- GL_RENDER—Set the normal (this is also the default) render mode, in which the pixels are written into the frame buffer for display.

- GL_SELECT—Set the selection mode, in which no change is made to the frame buffer; instead, a record of the names of primitives that would have been drawn in GL_RENDER mode is returned to the selection buffer. The selection buffer must be created before the selection mode is entered.

- GL_FEEDBACK—Set the feedback mode, and again no changes are made to the frame buffer. Instead, the coordinates and attributes of vertices that would have been drawn in the GL_RENDER mode are returned in a feedback buffer. The feedback buffer must be created before the feedback mode is entered.

We will illustrate use of the selection mode in our example, but the feedback mode is used in a similar manner.

For picking in OpenGL, the scene is drawn as normal into the frame buffer and displayed. Then a call is made to glRenderMode, and the render mode is set to selection. The scene is redrawn but the contents of the frame buffer are not changed. When you exit from selection mode, OpenGL returns a list of the primitives (points, lines, etc.) that would have been drawn in the viewing volume. This list contains only the primitives drawn in the viewing volume that are also contained in the name stack. The list is stored in the selection buffer. The function glSelectBuffer is used to specify a buffer for selection mode values. The two arguments passed to the function are a pointer to an unsigned integer array and the size of the array. The following call to glSelectBuffer specifies that the size of the array to be used is 20 and that the name of the array is SelectionBuffer.

```
call fglSelectBuffer(20,loc(SelectionBuffer))
```

Naming a group of primitives involves nothing more than assigning a unique integer to each primitive. The name list is maintained on the name stack. The function glLoadName(name) causes the integer value represented by name to be placed on the top of the name stack. The functions glPushName and glPopName are used to push and pop the name stack. The name stack is always empty when the render mode is anything other than GL_SELECT. The name stack is used during selection mode to allow sets of rendering commands to be uniquely identified. It consists of a set of ordered unsigned integers. The name stack is initialized using the function glInitNames, and then names are either pushed on or loaded to the stack. The following code fragment illustrates how the name stack is initialized and a zero value pushed onto the stack before loading the names for a set of points. The names would start at 1 and finish at 24. The following would be part of the rendering code for a scene:

```
call fglInitNames()
call fglPushName(-1)
do i = 1,24
   call fglLoadName(i )
   call fglBegin(GL_POINTS)
      call fglVertex3f(X(i),Y(i),0.0)
   call fglEnd()
end do
```

Note: The function glLoadName should not be placed between a call to glBegin and the corresponding call to glEnd. Furthermore, the function glLoadName should not be called when the name stack is empty. Since glInitNames, glPushName, and glLoadName are active only when the render mode is GL_SELECT, the foregoing code can also be used for doing the normal rendering as well.

Hit records placed by OpenGL in the selection buffer consist of four pieces of information:

- The first is the number of names on the name stack when the hit was called. In our example, this will always be 1, since each point is a single entity without any hierarchical association. One example of a hierarchical association would be a house. The house would be the root level; then we could have rooms at the next level and the contents of the room at the next level. In such a case, the first name would be placed on top of the stack with a call to glLoadName, and the remaining names would be pushed onto the stack with calls to glPushName.

■ The next two numbers are the minimum and maximum window-coordinate z values. The actual values of these coordinates lie between 0 and 1, but they are both scaled by the multiplier (2^32)-1 and rounded to the nearest unsigned integer before being stored.

■ The fourth entry is the contents of the name stack at the time of the hit, and the bottom-most element is given first. In our example, this entry will be the point number. If it was a hierarchical association and the number of names (first entry) was three, then we would expect three numbers here. Using the house example, the first number would tell us which house, the next number which room, and the next number which piece of furniture was chosen.

In our example, we want to make only a single selection; therefore, only one entry will be made in the selection buffer per mouse click. In other instances, we may want to select a group of named items, and each selection operation would generate multiple hit entries that follow the above format. In such a case, the selection array should be large enough to deal with all the names on the name list.

In OpenGL a distinction is made between selection and picking. With selection, the viewing volume by default is the whole screen and so we would expect all the names on the name list to be contained in the selection buffer. This sort of information is unlikely to be useful, and normally the viewing volume is redefined to be a smaller part of the viewing volume. Typically, a mouse would be used to create a selection box (see previous example), and the coordinates obtained would be used to redefine a new viewing volume for the selection process. For example, in a graphical application, a selection box could be used to select a group of objects such as lines for deleting. Picking occurs when you create a very small viewing volume at the current mouse position for use during selection. Again, only objects that would be drawn within that viewing volume will generate hit records. The selection buffer is examined as normal to determine which objects (if any) the mouse clicked on. The function gluPickMatrix is used to create a matrix describing the new viewing volume.

```
call fgluPickMatrix(float(mouseX),float(mouseY), &
          SelectionBoxX ,SelectionBoxY, vwp)
```

The first two arguments for gluPickMatrix define the center of the viewing volume in window coordinates. Since the mouse coordinates are passed in this example, the viewing volume will be centered underneath the mouse. The third and fourth arguments define, respectively, the width and the height of the viewing volume in window pixels. The final argument, vwp, is an array containing the window coordinates of the currently defined viewport. This is obtained by calling:

```
call fglGetIntegerv(GL_VIEWPORT, loc(vwp))
```

To use gluPickMatrix, first call glMatrixMode and save the current Projection matrix state. This action also saves the current viewing volume. Then call glLoadIdentity to create a unit-viewing volume. The function gluPickMatrix is called to translate this viewing volume to the correct location. You must apply any further perspective projections used with the original scene to complete the mapping process. This may all seem quite abstract, but the following code from the Select example will help to illustrate the process involved.

```
integer(4) function MouseSelect(mouseX, mouseY)
! function to select object with mouse
use dfopngl
use SelectGlobals
implicit none
integer(4) mouseX, mouseY
integer(4) hdc
integer(4) vwp(4)
real(4) mat(16)
real(4) SelectionBoxX
real(4) SelectionBoxY
   SelectionBoxX   = 30.0
   SelectionBoxY   = 30.0
   MouseSelect  = 0
   hdc = fwglGetCurrentDC ()
   SelectionBuffer = 0
   call fglGetIntegerv(GL_VIEWPORT, loc(vwp))
   call fglSelectBuffer(12,loc(SelectionBuffer))
   call fglRenderMode(GL_SELECT)
   call fglMatrixMode(GL_PROJECTION)
   call fglGetFloatv(GL_PROJECTION_MATRIX, loc(mat))
   call fglPushMatrix()
   call fglLoadIdentity()
   call fgluPickMatrix(float(mouseX),float(mouseY), &
             SelectionBoxX , SelectionBoxY, vwp)
   call fglMultMatrixf(loc(mat))
   call fglMatrixMode(GL_MODELVIEW)
   call fglClear(GL_COLOR_BUFFER_BIT)
```

```
call DrawScene (hdc)
call fglMatrixMode(GL_PROJECTION)
call fglPopMatrix()
call fglFlush()
call fglRenderMode(GL_RENDER)
call fglMatrixMode(GL_MODELVIEW)
if(SelectionBuffer(1) >0) then
   SelectedNode = SelectionBuffer(4)
   if (SelectedNode > 0) then
      MouseSelect = 1
   end if
endif
end function MouseSelect
```

The preceding function will return a value of 1 for a hit and 0 to indicate no hit. The routine calling the function, MouseSelect, should then check the hit information contained in the selection buffer and store or act on the information according to the functionality required from the picking process.

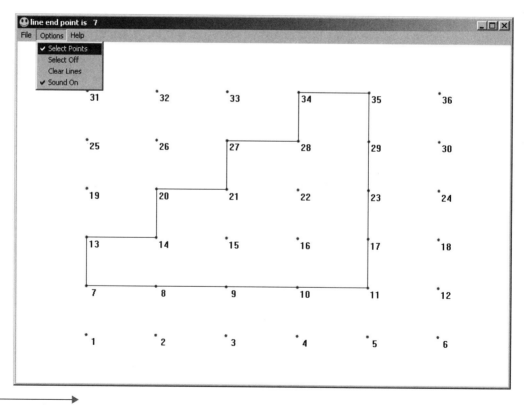

Figure 17.3   *Using the mouse to join the dots and create lines in OpenGL.*

In the example Select, any two points picked by the mouse are joined with a line. Figure 17.3 shows a situation in Select where many points have already been joined. This is what happens in the Select example. When the left mouse button is pressed, the following code gets the mouse coordinates from lParam and passes them to GetPoint:

```
case (WM_LBUTTONDOWN)
   if(SelectPoint == .true.) then
      MouseX = LOWORD(lParam)
      MouseY = glnHeight - HIWORD(lParam)
      call GetPoint(MouseX,MouseY )
   end if
```

Note that the mouse value for $y = 0$ starts at the top of the screen. In OpenGL, $y = 0$ starts at the bottom of the screen; hence, the value for MouseY needs to be converted to OpenGL coordinates. The routine Get-Point listed below is used to do the housekeeping by calling the function MouseSelect, getting the hit information from the selection buffer, and, finally, joining two points with a line:

```
subroutine GetPoint(mouseX,mouseY )
use dfwina
use dfopngl
use SelectGlobals
implicit none
character(40) text
logical(4) bret
integer(4) mouseX, mouseY
integer(4) MouseSelect
integer(4) SelectionKeep(2)
integer(4) ValidHit
integer(4) iloop
integer(4) iret
   ValidHit = 0
   ValidHit = MouseSelect(mouseX,mouseY)
   if ( ValidHit > 0 ) then
      if(SelectionBuffer(1) >0) then
         SelectedNode = SelectionBuffer(4)
         do iloop = 1, SelectCount
            if ( SelectionKeep(iloop)==SelectedNode) THEN
               call beepqq(200, 200)
               iret = messagebox(null,'This point has &
                  already been selected 'C,  &
                  'Duplicate Point &
                  Warning'C, MB_ICONINFORMATION)
               return
            end if
         end do
```

```
               if (  SelectedNode  > 0 ) then
                  if(SoundOn == .true.) then
                     call beepqq(440, 200)
                  end if
                  ! track points that have been selected
                  SelectCount = SelectCount + ValidHit
                  SelectionKeep(SelectCount)= SelectedNode
                  if(SelectCount == 1) then
                     text = 'line start point is'
                    write(text(20:24), '(I4)') SelectedNode
                  else
                     text = 'line end point is'
                    write(text(18:22), '(I4)') SelectedNode
               end if
                  iret = SetWindowText(ghwndMain, text//''C)
               end if
               if(SelectCount >= 2) then
                  linesTotal = linesTotal+1
                  Lines(linesTotal)%Start = SelectionKeep(1)
                  Lines(linesTotal)%End = SelectionKeep(2)
                  SelectionKeep = 0
               SelectCount = 0
                  bret = InvalidateRect (null, NULL_RECT, &
                         .FALSE.)
            end if
         endif
      endif
   end
```

17.3.1   How round is round?

The OpenGL function glPointSize is used to specify the size to which a point is to be drawn. By default, points are drawn as a collection of pixels aligned in a square region of height and width corresponding to the value in pixels passed in glPointSize. Points are drawn round in OpenGL by using a process called antialiasing. With antialiasing enabled, a circular group of pixels is drawn, and the pixels on the boundary are drawn at less than full intensity to give an appearance of a smooth boundary. Point antialiasing is controlled by passing the argument GL_POINT_SMOOTH to glEnable and glDisable. You can also use the glHint function to tell OpenGL how you would like the point to be rendered. You should check the online documentation for the range of primitives covered by glHint and the hint options that can be used. Here is how you would request points to be drawn round:

```
call fglEnable(GL_POINT_SMOOTH)
call fglHint( GL_POINT_SMOOTH_HINT,GL_NICEST)
```

I have found that the roundness of points can usually be improved by turning blending on as follows:

```
call fglEnable(GL_BLEND)
call fglBlendFunc(GL_SRC_ALPHA, GL_ONE_MINUS_SRC_ALPHA)
```

Not all point sizes are supported when point antialiasing is enabled; only size 1.0 is guaranteed to be supported. Other supported sizes depend on the particular OpenGL implementation. I have used one graphics card with its own drivers that did not support round large points. In such a case, possible options would be to live with square points, to contact the manufacturers and ask them to provide support for large round points, to get a different card, or to force OpenGL to use the standard OpenGL driver that comes with the operating system. The method that I used to force the use of the default OpenGL driver was to set the AlphaBits in the PIXELFORMAT-DESCRIPTOR to a nonzero value. However, remember that your software will not be able to take advantage of any hardware acceleration offered by the graphics card.

17.4 What is next?

The objective of this book is to demonstrate how to create graphical user interfaces (GUI) in Visual Fortran through a variety of examples. If you can now confidently use Visual Fortran to develop applications in a Windows environment that have graphical user interfaces and good display graphics, then the book has fulfilled its intended objectives. It is now time for you to fly solo and develop your own applications.

For readers who wish to gain further information about using Win32 APIs for developing graphical user interfaces, I strongly recommend Charles Petzold's book, *Programming Windows* (5th ed.), published by Microsoft Press.

For readers wanting to develop applications with OpenGL display graphics, I recommend Richard Wright and Michael Sweet's book, *OpenGL Superbible* (2nd ed.), published by Waite Group Press.

The sample code in both books is written in the C programming language, but if you have worked through the examples in this book and reviewed the material in Appendix A, you should have few, if any, difficulties following the program code.

17.5 Finally

We have come to the end of this book on using Visual Fortran to create Windows Interfaces, and I hope that you will be as impressed as I am with the range of capabilities that Visual Fortran offers to Fortran programmers. There are some additional programs located in the extras section of the software on the companion Web site. The extra OpenGL examples include how to work with textures and how to tessellate concave polygons.

Please feel free to contact me through the publishers, if there are any comments that you would like to make about the book or programs and, in particular, if there any other topics that you believe should be included in a subsequent edition.

Overview of C for Fortran Programmers

As with Fortran 90/95, C is a free-format language. The end of a statement is signified by means of a semicolon (;), and a user can have multiple statements on one line separated by semicolons, or a single statement may go over a number of lines. Comments may be everything between the pair of symbols /* and */.

In C, the parts of a program that are enclosed by two curly brackets {} are called blocks. The start of a block, {, may be on the same line as the expression where the block starts, or it may be on the start of the following line and aligned with the other statements in the block. The conclusion of the block is signaled by the block-end curly bracket } positioned on its own and indented slightly to the right.

Unlike Fortran, C does not differentiate between subroutines and functions; C has only functions. The structure for a program written in C is made up of many functions, one of which must always be present and named main. There can be only one main for each program. Every function must contain at least one block to define the start and the end of the function. In the following example, the word void preceding the function main indicates that there is no return value from this function:

```
void main ()
/
************************************************************
*    Code fragment of a simple C program
************************************************************/
   {
   int number1, number2, sum;
   number1 = 15;   /* setting the value of number1 */
   number2 = 20;   /* setting the value of number2 */
   sum = number1 + number2;
   /* remaining code omitted for brevity */
   }
```

A.1   Variables

The four predefined basic types of variables in C are char, int, float, and double. A variable is declared to be of a certain type at the time that it is defined:

```
char c;      /* c is a variable type char */
int i;       //* i is a variable type int */
float f;     /*  f is a variable type float */
double d;    /* d is a variable type double (float) */
```

A char variable is used to contain a single character. A character constant is formed by enclosing the character within a pair of single quote marks. So c = 'a', or c = ';' would be valid uses of the char variable *c* declared above. A character constant is not the same as a character string, which is any number of characters enclosed in double quotes. The integer type can be further subdivided by using the modifiers signed or unsigned, short or long.

A.2   Operators

C includes a unary *increment operator* (++) and a unary *decrement operator* (--). Increment and decrement operators increase or decrease the value stored in an integer variable by one. Hence, the following two statements achieve the same result.

```
a = a + 1;
a++;
```

C includes several assignment operators that combine an assignment and a binary operation in a single expression. Thus, the assignment statement:

```
a = a + 5;
```

Table A.1   *Assignment Operations in C*

Assignment Operator	C Expression	Fortran Equivalent
+=	a+=3	a = a+3
-=	a -= 3	a = a-3
*=	a *= 3	a = a*3
/=	a /= 3	a = a/3

can be abbreviated using the addition assignment operator += to give:

```
a += 5;
```

The += operator adds the value of the variable on the left of the operator to the value on the right of the operator and stores the result in the variable to the left of the operator. Other assignments are given in Table A.1.

A.3 Looping

In C there are three ways to carry out iterative cycles: for, while, and do while.

A.3.1 For

The general format of the for statement is as follows:

```
for (init_expression; loop_condition; loop_expression)
```

The first component within the brackets of the for statement, init_expression, is used to set the initial values before the loop begins. The initial conditions can be made up of one or more expressions separated by a comma. It is thus possible to assign an initial value to several variables before beginning the iterative cycle. The second component inside the brackets of the for statement specifies the condition, or conditions, that are necessary in order for the loop to continue. The final component within the brackets of the for statement contains an expression that is evaluated each time after the body of the loop is executed.

The statement break may be used to interrupt the iterative cycle where it is located and to shift control to the first statement immediately following the cycle. In the following example, the variable *max* is assigned the value 20 and the counter variable *i* is assigned the starting value 1. The for loop will cycle through the program statements until the exit condition of i < 10 is reached or if the value of sum is greater than max:

```
for (int max = 20, int i = 1; i < 10; i++)
    {
    int sum;
    sum = sum + i;
    if(sum>max) break;  /* interrupts the cycle and
                         /* executes the statement
                         /* a = 10.0 */

        {
```

```
     statements;      /* only if sum < max */
     }
  }
a = 10.0;
```

A.3.2 While

The while statement has the syntax while(*test expression*). Statements contained in the block following the while statement are repeated
until the test expression is true (different from zero). When the expression is
false (equal to 0), the iterative cycle is interrupted. In the following example, the library function getchar() reads a character keyed in from the keyboard and the cycle is repeated until the character q is typed in. The !=
expression in C is the same as the Fortran expression /=.

```
while (getchar( ) != 'q')
  {
    statements;
  }
```

A.3.3 Do while

The do while statement will always be executed at least once. The do statement proceeds a block of code and the while statement immediately follows the same block of code. The statements within the code block are
repeated while the test expression is true. Once the test expression is false
(equal to 0), the iterative cycle is interrupted:

```
do
  {
    statements;    /* are executed at least once */
  }while(getchar( ) != 'q');
```

A.4   If statements

In C, decision-making structures can be developed using if, else if, and
else statements that are conceptually similar to the equivalent ones in Fortran, as follows:

```
if(Test1)
  {
    statements;     /* Test1 true*/
  }
  else if (Test2)
  {
```

```
        statements;    /* Test1 false Test2 true*/
        }
    else     /* otherwise default*/
      {
        statements;    /* Test1 false    Test 2 false*/
      }
```

A.5   Switch constructs

The switch construct is equivalent to the Select Case construct in Fortran. It is made up as follows:

```
Switch(j)      /* switch type int */
{
    case 1;
        statements;    /* when j = 1 */
        break;
    case 2;
        statements;    /* when j = 2 */
        break;
    default;
        statements;    /* in other cases */
        break;
}
```

A.6   Structures

The struct statement used in C to collect variables together in convenient groups called structures is similar to the Fortran type statement. For example, a structure called mytime in C is defined in the rather straightforward method:

```
struct mytime
{
 int seconds;
 int minutes;
 int hours;
};
```

Variables of the structure type mytime can then be declared and the internal variables set in a fashion similar to their Fortran counterpart:

```
struct mytime myclock;
myclock.seconds = 30;
myclock.minutes = 20;
myclock.hours = 9;
```

B

HTML Help Files

In Chapter 14 we used the WinHelp 4.0 compiler, HCW.exe, that comes with Visual Studio, but you may prefer to work with HTML Help files, which have the file suffix chm. These Compiled HTML (chm) and Compiled HTML Index (chi) files are the standard help system for the Windows 2000 and Windows 98 and ME operating systems.

The Microsoft HTML Help 1.3 authoring system is based on Microsoft's WinHelp 4.0; users of WinHelp and Help Workshop will be familiar with many of the features of HTML Help and HTML Help Workshop. As with WinHelp, HTML Help uses a project file to combine topic, contents, index, image, and other source files into a single compiled Help file. The HTML Help Workshop is an authoring tool that makes it easy for viewing and editing files and provides an HTML Help for compressing HTML, graphic, and other files into a relatively small compiled Help (.chm) file. These compiled Help files can then be distributed with a software application. There is also an online HTML Help Authoring Guide, which provides guidance with the creation of a help system.

The Microsoft HTML Help Workshop can be freely downloaded from http://msdn.microsoft.com/library/default.asp?URL=/library/tools/html-help/chm/hh1start.htm.

B.1   Converting existing Help projects

The New Project Wizard of HTML Help Workshop can be used to convert existing WinHelp projects into HTML Help projects. HTML Help Workshop will convert only complete WinHelp projects. Assuming that all the

Figure B.1
The HTML Help Workshop Wizard can convert WinHelp projects to HTML projects.

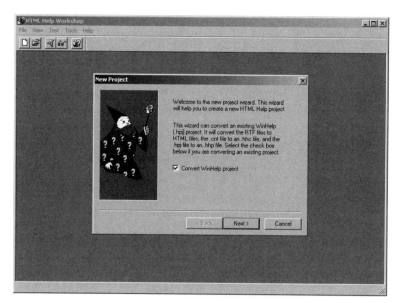

files referenced by the existing Help (.hpj) file are in the locations specified, the Wizard performs the following conversions to WinHelp files:

- WinHelp project (.hpj) file—Converted to an HTML Help project (.hhp) file.

- WinHelp topic (.rtf) files—Converted to HTML Help topic (.htm, .html) files.

- WinHelp contents (.cnt) files—Converted to HTML Help contents (.hhc) files.

- WinHelp index—Converted to HTML Help index (.hhk) files.

    To convert an existing help project to an HTML Help project:

- On the File menu, click New, and then click Project.

- Select the Convert WinHelp project check box, and then click Next.

- Specify the location of the existing Help project (.hpj) file you want to convert.

- Specify a location and name for the new HTML Help project you are creating, click Next, and then click Finish.

    As an example of the conversion process, I converted the Scribe3 WinHelp project into HTML Help project format. After converting the WinHelp project for Scribe3, the keywords were displayed in the HTML

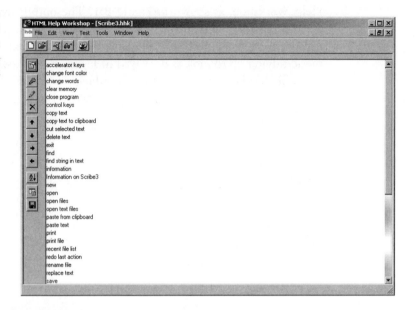

Figure B.2
HTML Help Workshop showing list of keywords for Scribe3 Help.

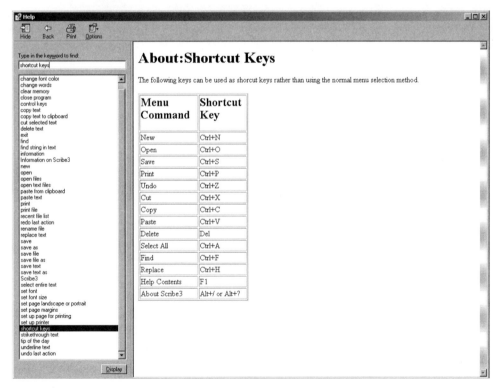

Figure B.3   *HTML Help viewer showing list of shortcut keys for Scribe3 Help.*

Help Workshop, as shown in Figure B.1. The output from the converted Scribe3 HTML Help file as it appears in the HTML Help Viewer to a Help user is given in Figure B.2. The converted table needed a little bit of cosmetic tidying up to look as displayed in Figure B.3. Needless to say, once a Help file has been converted from WinHelp to HTML Help format, you would want to modify the appearance to take advantage of the new display capabilities.

C

Auxiliary Library OpenGL Three-Dimensional Models

It is sometimes useful to be able to use an OpenGL three-dimensional object without having to write your own code. Fortunately, the auxiliary library contains the following ready-made three-dimensional objects. Each three-dimensional model is available in two varieties: (1) wireframe or (2) solid with shading and surface normals. The solid versions are great when you want to test lighting effects. All arguments passed to the routines are double-precision real variables.

```
auxWireSphere(radius)
auxSolidSphere(radius)

auxWireCube(size)
auxSolidCube(size)

auxWireBox(width, height, depth)
auxSolidBox(width, height, depth)

auxWireTorus(innerRadius, outerRadius)
auxSolidTorus(innerRadius, outerRadius)

auxWireCylinder(radius, height)
auxSolidCylinder(radius, height)

auxWireIcosahedron(radius)
auxSolidIcosahedron(radius)

auxWireOctahedron(radius)
auxSolidOctahedron(radius)

auxWireTetrahedron (radius)
auxSolidTetrahedron(radius)

auxWireDodecahedron(radius)
auxSolidDodecahedron(radius)
```

```
auxWireCone(radius, height)
auxSolidCone(radius, height)

auxWireTeapot(size)
auxSolidTeapot(size)
```

GLUT and f90gl

GLUT is an OpenGL Utility Toolkit that makes the creation of OpenGL applications easier, because it provides a simple OpenGL window environment that is operating system independent. This means you can write a single OpenGL program that will work on both Win32 PCs and UNIX workstations. Mark J. Kilgard developed GLUT; Nate Robins and Paul Mayfield, with help from Layne Christensen, were responsible for porting GLUT to the Windows 95 and NT environments. GLUT is well suited for users who are learning OpenGL and developing simple OpenGL applications; however, if your application needs a more sophisticated user interface, you should use the Win32 APIs.

When developing applications using GLUT, you need to use it in conjunction with f90gl. f90gl provides the official Fortran 90 bindings for OpenGL and GLU as well as the application of those bindings to GLUT. It is a public domain implementation by the National Institute of Standards and Technology. f90gl is not included with Visual Fortran, but you can download the f90gl compiled libraries from the Visual Fortran Web site. Go to http://www.compaq.com/fortran/ and look under "Downloads."

Note that all inquiries and bug reports for f90GL or GLUT should be sent to the address below or to william.mitchell@nist.gov and not to the Visual Fortran Web site.

William F. Mitchell
Mathematical and Computational Sciences Division
100 Bureau Dr. Stop 8910
National Institute of Standards and Technology
Gaithersburg, MD 20899-8910

william.mitchell@nist.gov

The f90gl web page is at http://math.nist.gov/f90gl/.

D.1   What happens after I download f90gl?

This section will help to get you started once you have downloaded the f90gli.zip file from the Visual Fortran Web site, unzipped the file, and read the various information text files. The following instructions regarding the unzipped files are for users building applications within the Developer Studio environment.

- Copy the file glut32.dll in the lib folder to your Windows System folder.

- Copy the files f90GL.lib, f90GLU.lib, f90GLUT.lib, and glut32.lib from the lib folder to your Visual Fortran LIB folder—for example, C:\Program Files\Microsoft Visual Studio\DF98\LIB. A good idea is to make a subfolder in your Visual Fortran Lib folder called GL_Lib and put the four files in it; this makes it easier when you are including them in projects.

- Copy the eight .mod files from the lib folder to your Visual Fortran INCLUDE folder—for example, C:\Program Files\Microsoft Visual Studio\DF98\INCLUDE.

Whenever you start a new project in Developer Studio, you need to add f90GL.lib, f90GLU.lib, f90GLUT.lib, and glut32.lib to the project (Project. -> Add to project. -> Files).

The f90gl folder "examples" contains some example programs that demonstrate the graphics capabilities of OpenGL and serve as a good guide to using f90gl. The following are some points to note when using f90gl:

- Any program unit that uses procedures, symbolic constants, and so on from OpenGL, GLU, or GLUT must include the appropriate modules in your application with a USE statement. The modules, respectively, are OPENGL_GL, OPENGL_GLU, and OPEN-GL_GLUT.

- All OpenGL procedures and OpenGL "defined constants" are provided with the same name as in the C interface, except that names are case insensitive and names longer than 31 characters are truncated. In short, your Fortran OpenGL code should follow exactly the OpenGL code descriptions given in the *OpenGL Programmers' Guide* (i.e., the red book). This can be very useful when you want to create a Fortran version of a C program example.

To illustrate the process, let us consider the examples program named Olympic3, which is similar in function to the OpenGL program Olympic, which comes with the Visual Fortran samples:

- Create a new blank Fortran Windows Application with any name of your choice.

- Copy the file Olympic3.f90 into the blank Windows Application.

- In Developer Studio, add Olympic3.f90 to the project (Project. -> Add to project. -> Files).

- In Developer Studio, add f90GL.lib, f90GLU.lib, f90GLUT.lib, and glut32.lib to the project (Project. -> Add to project. -> Files).

In Olympic3.f90, the line at the beginning of the program:

```
program main
use olympic_mod
```

should be replaced with these lines:

```
integer(4) function WinMain (hInstance, &
              hPrevInstance, lpszCmdLine, nCmdShow)
!DEC$ ATTRIBUTES STDCALL, DECORATE, ALIAS: &
'WinMain' :: WinMain
use olympic_mod
implicit none
integer(4) hInstance,hPrevInstance, lpszCmdLine,
nCmdShow
```

Note: In the preceding code, the line beginning with !DEC$ ATTRIBUTES is a compiler directive and is shown with the Fortran continuation sign (&) at the end of the line, indicating that the code continues onto a second line. This is for typographical convenience only. If you type these lines, they must be entered as a single line.

In Olympic3.f90, the line at the end of the program:

```
end program main
```

should be replaced with these lines:

```
WinMain = 0
return
end Function WinMain
```

Compile and execute the program as normal.

Figure D.1
*Olympic rings
example using
Glut and f90gl.*

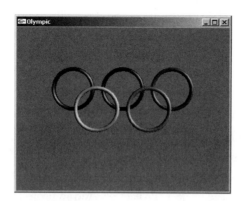

Figure D.1 shows the output from the program; the space bar can be pressed for the program to regroup the rings.

The foregoing process can be used with any of the sample programs. I have used Developer Studio to compile some of the examples that come with f90gl, and they are included with the software on the companion Web site for this book. They are a great source of inspiration for OpenGL programming ideas, whether you develop your code with GLUT or Win32. Quite a few of the programs are interactive. The right mouse button will often bring up a menu, and moving the mouse while holding the left mouse button down will often cause the object to rotate.

To run the exe files, you will need to have the glut32.dll installed in your system directory. The file glut32.dll is included with the sample programs from the book Web site. If you wish to compile the programs, you will need to download the f90gl software from the Visual Fortran Web site.

Index